T0305158

THE WORK OF REPAIR

THINKING FROM ELSEWHERE

THE WORK OF REPAIR

Capacity after Colonialism in
the Timber Plantations of South Africa

THOMAS COUSINS

FORDHAM UNIVERSITY PRESS NEW YORK 2023

Fordham University Press gratefully acknowledges financial assistance and support provided for the publication of this book by the School of Anthropology and Museum Ethnography, University of Oxford.

Cartography by Mies Irving (www.milesmap.co.uk).

Fordham University Press also publishes its books in a variety of electronic formats. Some content that appears in print may not be available in electronic books.

Visit us online at www.fordhampress.com.

Library of Congress Cataloging-in-Publication Data available online at https://catalog.loc.gov.

Printed in the United States of America

25 24 23   5 4 3 2 1

First edition

for Michelle

CONTENTS

"Prior to being a system of tools, the world is an ensemble of nourishments."

—EMMANUEL LEVINAS, *TIME AND THE OTHER*

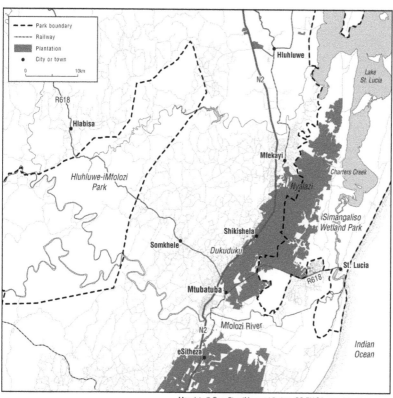

Park boundary
Railway
Plantation
City or town

0   10km

R618

Hlabisa

Hluhluwe

N2

Lake
St. Lucia

Hluhluwe-iMfolozi
Park

Mfekayi

Charters Creek

Nyalazi

iSimangaliso
Wetland Park

Shikishela

Somkhele   Dukuduku

St. Lucia

Mtubatuba

R618

N2   Mfolozi River

eSitheza

Indian
Ocean

INTRODUCTION

Repair and the Question of Capacity

The flickering of row upon row of trees shutters the light into a steady rhythm of green, break, green, break, green as the rumble-roar of the tractor pushes the highway behind it. The lonely islands of indigenous bush, imithi, staccato the plantation's lines, paced at eighty kilometers per hour as the transport rumbles up the N2 highway, one of the main transport links across KwaZulu-Natal province and the rest of South Africa.[1] The tractor-and-trailer, igandaganda, has completed its morning stops in Shikishela and Mkefayi, and in the predawn winter light I stumble out into the clearing with a group of forty women and men.[2] Ayanda, as gang boss, or umlungu, for this season's gang of silviculture contractors—hired to plant hybrid eucalypt seedlings—leads her charges in a morning prayer, giving thanks for the work and asking for safety from mechanical injury and angry elephants.

Whenever I return to my 2009 fieldwork in the timber plantations in South Africa to sift those compressed moments for a scene in which something of this regime of life is revealed, I return to this morning. There is a quiet that cloaks the group, a deep familiarity with what must be done, a strong sense of the resignation to the repetitive rhythm of the day, the urgency not to fall behind. The morning cold sits stubbornly in the limbs. The women wear woolen hats and scarves to keep off the chill dawn wind, strong boots and shin guards, skirts wrapped over workman's overalls to secure their feminine dignity, and a rucksack with water and a Tupperware container of food from home. The extra food is vital. At ten o'clock in the morning, they will break for tea and a hot cooked meal that the timber corporation began providing to workers in 2008 as a nutritional intervention meant to boost productivity—carefully calculated calories, cooked to be culturally acceptable, and intended to increase profits and reduce workplace injury. Sometimes the food provided is so bland or fatty, though, that one cannot stomach it and must therefore bring food from home, just in case.

That morning, the work was "pitting"—a row of twenty of us stood, invisibly shackled by a length of twine that marked the line, joined by the rhythm of the hoe and by work songs (izisho zokusebenza).[3] We stood two meters apart, hoe in hand, and dug a small hole at the blow of a whistle; pause; two steps forward; dig; repeat. Whistle; dig; step; repeat. Mothers, daughters, sisters, neighbors, councilors, shopkeepers, healers—kin, friends, enemies, joined by day to the line; regurgitated at dusk by igandaganda, the tractor-transport; returned to the forest factory by dawn. This was a scene of labor so repetitive as to seem timeless, immobile, even as the tractor traced and retraced its steps, eating its tail every single day, the plantations breathing and exhaling laborers with circadian regularity, the digestion and excretion of effort and value so structured as to appear law-like in their metabolism.[4] But over the course of eighteen months, I came to understand how recently this machinic organism had come to life; how its growth and development had eaten up lands, people, water; how it was making waste of bodies, lives, and wetlands.

I had come to this plantation in 2009 to make sense of a nutrition intervention, named "Food4Forests," that was being rolled out to all laborers employed by Mondi, a global paper and pulp corporation, as part of a corporate strategy for shoring up falling productivity rates. Why should labor and nutrition be conjoined in this way, fifteen years into the postapartheid compact of increasingly racialized inequality in South Africa? What I found was that those workers consumed not only the corporate calories provided by the timber company and their home-cooked pap (maize-meal) brought to supplement the nutrition program but also a cornucopia of industrialized tonics and curatives, as well as herbs, roots, and barks of indigenous flora and medicinal products derived from local wildlife. From the early 2000s, the crisis of the HIV epidemic had grown acute as the government of former president Thabo Mbeki questioned the science of HIV and suggested that nutrition and indigenous remedies offered better treatment than toxic antiretroviral drugs. As fieldwork unfolded, I tracked the circulations of nutritive substances and curative tonics through the regulated and unregulated spaces of labor and domesticity, tracing the contours of customary and constitutional orders of ordinary life. I was struck by the powerful confluence of images and substances, of histories of colonial plantations and rural resistance, of the distributions of racialized capital and labor, and of the sense of a muscular digestion of the raw fate dealt by the cruel forces of colonial, and also postcolonial, capital. Labor as a factor of production in the racialized history of the subjugation of African peoples is key to the political economy of South (and southern) Africa—but the question is how to understand the ethical, political, and imaginative stakes that make life possible, and at times impossible, in this particular postcolonial settler landscape.

By 2015, almost all of these women were rendered superfluous, displaced by machines able to perform their work more quickly and cheaply. And although the postapartheid South African government massively increased spending on social services, infrastructure, health, and direct cash transfers from the late 1990s to the late 2000s, this displacement followed a pattern of racialized displacement by the apartheid state that had been recorded by the Surplus People Project (SPP) during the 1980s. While the five-volume SPP report recorded forced removals effected by the apartheid state across South Africa, one whole volume focused on what was then the Bantustan of KwaZulu, in which hundreds of thousands of Black people were displaced over five decades to make way for conservation, military experimentation, agriculture, "villagization," "betterment planning," "black spot removals," and consolidations.[5] The "bloody miracle" of 1994, and the negotiations that saw KwaZulu and Natal joined together as the KwaZulu-Natal province and incorporated into the new Republic of South Africa, offered the hope that the state would deliver economic liberation on the heels of political emancipation.[6] Indeed, from the late 1990s to the late 2000s, South Africa massively increased spending on social services, infrastructure, health, and direct cash transfers. However, by 2005–6, ten thousand laborers, once employed by Mondi, were outsourced, "flexibilized," and "contractorized." The fourteen women with whom I worked closely over the course of eighteen months in 2009–10 provided fine-grained insight into the vagaries of that history of abstraction and displacement, a counterpoint to the narrative of liberation and equality and a variation in a minor mode on the themes of work, sustenance, and the making of the self.

This book focuses on the thick set of relations that sustain bodies and nurture distinct social and moral projects in and around the plantations, against the backdrop of national political debates, party political processes, and parliamentary politics.[7] That is, the book shows how the ability to endure the demands of life around the timber plantations has to do less with the supply and circulation of calories and micronutrients than with a concern with one's capacity to meet the demands of the day—that is, a capacity to navigate several distinct regimes, or arrangements, of life and its governance. As I show below, "capacity" is a central object of concern vital to the effort to endure, and to thrive, under conditions of extreme exploitation and fragmentation. It is the material of moral reflection, conduct, and evaluation, which Michel Foucault called "ethical substance." By this he meant a principle or point of reflection on, a question of, a subject's relation to the interconnection of truth and conduct—that which must be the object of conscious consideration; the questions a person must keep in mind in order to do what they do truthfully.[8] I argue in this book that ethical substance is better understood from the perspective of *amandla*—an isiZulu term which I gloss here as power, strength, or capacity—and that this concern with amandla is constitutive of *the work of repair*. By this I mean that the work of augmenting one's capacities is the substance of incomplete, embodied, ethical relations. Amandla does not point to a classical picture of sovereignty, in which the self is autonomous, and *power over* is the critical concern. Rather, I show how amandla, as the primary material of the work of repair, emerges from ordinary scenes around the plantations, in which mutual incompleteness, becoming with others, and a relational effort to absorb, without effacing, the wounding effects of colonial displacement, racialized exploitation, and labor, is at stake.

Glossing "amandla" as "capacity" brings into view a crucial aspect of what Jasbir Puar calls the "biopolitics of debilitation."[9] In Puar's analysis, disability is not a fixed state or attribute but "exists in relation to assemblages of capacity and debility," where the liberal state unevenly distributes the injuries of neoliberal capitalism. Drawing on Julie Livingston's distinction between disability (an identity recognized by the state) and debility (the slow wearing down of populations rather than the event of becoming disabled),[10] Puar argues that the biopolitical logic of the neoliberal state depends on modulating and distributing debility and capacity through what she calls "the right to maim." For Puar, biopolitics is a "capacitation machine"; it "seeks capacitation for some as a liberal rationale (in some cases) or foil for the debilitation of many others."[11] Attending to the ways in which some bodies are capacitated while others are debilitated reveals the form of power that constitutes the liberal state; Puar thus extends Foucault's simple binary of "make live and let die" to open out a critique of liberal investments in a laboring body whose debilitation or incapacitation is internal to the constitution of biopolitical power and is simultaneously externalized as a private concern. Puar's critique of "capacity" as a middle term that enables the "right to maim" as the grounds of the modern biopolitical state is directly relevant to the injuries sustained by laborers in the plantations; it amplifies Franco Barchiesi's argument, that welfare policy developed by the post-apartheid state, in the guise of the African National Congress (ANC), has focused on the able-bodied laborer as the worthy recipient of welfare.[12] In the chapters to follow, however, I develop the concept of capacity in a slightly different direction, while sympathetic to Puar's critique.

Through the ethnographic description of the timber plantations and their labor regime, I show how the relationship between amandla and labor power is not oppositional, and neither is it dialectical in the sense of presenting a contradiction awaiting productive resolution. For Karl Marx, a key question is what distinguishes the slave, who, "together with his labor power, is sold once and for all to his owner [and who] is himself a commodity," from the free laborer, who "sells himself, and sells himself piecemeal."[13] "Free labor" thus appears as a form of "unfreedom," of slavery even—to the wage, and to capital. In Marx's terms, labor power, the capacity to labor, consists in the appropriation of an alien power that leaves labor poorer, while also making the laborers themselves the condition of their own future, alienable, labor power. For Hannah Arendt, labor, work, and action are three fundamental aspects of the human condition and of political life.[14] Labor, for Arendt, concerns the biological processes of the human body, essential to life itself; work is that creative production of an "artificial" world of things, which yields worldliness; and action, as a counterpoint to work and labor, is what discloses the identity of the agent, affirms the reality of the world, and actualizes our capacity for freedom.

So why gloss "amandla" as "capacity" and yet retain an isiZulu word? To do so certainly runs the risk of a primitivizing ethnology. There are several motivations for such a strategy. The first concerns translation and the use of indigenous terms not as "tool" or "data" but as "key for analysis," as Paul Bohannon argued.[15] As will become clear, amandla is not some pure emic term but rather is already on the move in an intercultural space of translation.[16]

Rather than invoke a pure incommensurability or nontranslatability, I use the untranslated term to index those "invaginated" histories of invention, exchange, conquest, and resistance that precede the formalization of a Zulu polity, and an ongoing "mutuomorphomutation" of words and worlds across southern Africa, in which ideas about difference and language continue to inform debates about persons and polities.[17]

Several shades of meaning are carried in the etymology of "capacity" as an English word. (In Marx, the German is "Arbeitskraft"; in French: "force de travail.") The *Oxford English Dictionary* points to its Latinate origins: capax ("able to hold much"), from capiō ("to hold, to contain, to take, to understand"). Its ordinary senses include the ability to hold, receive, or absorb; a measure of such ability; volume; the maximum amount that can be held (the orchestra played to a capacity crowd; a factory operating at less than full capacity). Adjacent is "capability": the ability to perform some task; the maximum that can be produced; mental ability; the power to learn; a faculty; the potential for growth and development; a role, or the position in which one functions; legal authority (to make an arrest for example). Online isiZulu translations point to, and beyond, looping intercultural senses, such as "amandla okuqukatha" (the capacity to contain), "amandla okwamukela" (the capacity to receive), "amandla okwenza" (the capacity to do or act), "amandla okwazi" (the capacity to know), "amandla okukhiqiza" (the capacity to produce or make), "ukuhlakanipha" (wisdom). Flowing from the nontransparency of translation is what Dipesh Chakrabarty calls a "translucence": "what emerges from apparent 'incommensurabilities' is neither an absence of relationship between dominant and dominating forms of knowledge nor equivalents that successfully mediate between differences, but precisely the partly opaque relationship we call 'difference.'"[18] It is this "translucence—and not transparency—in the relation between non-Western histories and European thought and its analytical categories"[19] that leads to the next motivation for keeping "amandla" in tension with "capacity."

The second motivation is substantive: Marx's analysis of "abstract labor," as Chakrabarty points out, is predicated on the Enlightenment ideas of juridical equality and the abstract political rights of citizenship.[20] Labor that is juridically and politically free and yet socially unfree is central to Marx's category of "abstract labor," which combines Enlightenment ideas of juridical freedom with those of a universal and abstract human. Central to Chakrabarty's critique of Marx is the relationship between histories "posited by capital" and histories that do not belong to capital's "life process," which he calls History 1 and History 2. It is this internal relation of difference to capital (its "sublation to capital") that is partly what is at stake in insisting on amandla as orthogonal to capacity, as marking a partial difference— tethered and indexical—between the life of capital and the forms of life around the plantations.[21] Lastly, I stay with amandla to note the distance from the "capabilities" approach of Amartya Sen and Martha Nussbaum, for whom a focus on what *individuals* are able to do (i.e., are capable of) to achieve their well-being was a corrective for (then) mainstream welfare economics that depended on GNP and GDP for calculating benefits but missed finer distributional questions.[22]

Thus, what emerges from a thick description of the work of repair around the timber plantations is less a picture of alienated subjectivities or, conversely, action as an achievement that constitutes a universal human condition, and more an incomplete, mutually imbricated relationship between work, labor, and action that engages with the historically specific conditions of life around the plantations. Without adjudicating between Arendt and Marx, I show how the capacity to act, in thickly enfleshed terms that take in the plantations and their topological forms, offers a different conception of the wounding relationship between labor power and value, of political life and repair, and of the relationship between will, action, and the possibilities for "an otherwise" than has been suggested for postcolonial life.[23] What I offer is a sociography of amandla, a capacity that is not Marx's capacity to labor or Arendt's capacity to act, but that capacity to engage in the work of repair, to absorb and recirculate that wounding openness to others, including the vulnerability to alienation and the failures of action. Thus, amandla is less about arriving at what Elizabeth Povinelli calls an "ontology of potentiality" or even about "the dwelling of potentiality" and the limits of critical theory.[24] Far from being a concrete abstraction in the service of capital or critical theory, or metahistorical cure for the ills of capitalist modernity, I suggest, rather, that capacity is both situated action and metadiscursive reflection; an engagement with the multiplicity of topological forms that bear down on the question of what it means to live in one postcolonial scene of "adverse incorporation."[25] Amandla is that which is required in, and emerges from, the ordinary work of repair.

The picture of amandla that I seek to develop here, and what I am calling "the work of repair," thus resists a single definition—and the reader should expect to see several attempts to provide a conceptual outline for the term. Through the course of the book, several different formulations concatenate and point to the multiple ontologies of work, labor, and action that provide an alternative reading of the "articulation of the modes of production" debate in Marxian analyses of apartheid and migrant labor, and amplify those "invaginated" histories. What work, labor, and capacity come to mean in specific contexts thus reveals particular arrangements—of capital and labor; of machines and persons; of territories and histories—that twist, or deform, as the grammars of vulnerability and repair shift, and yet endure. Thus, where distinct ontologies of work or labor might appear in the descriptions that follow, I show how each is founded on, and emerges from, a topos—that is, a localization of forms that remain constant even as they deform. Amandla, then, emerges as that capacity to navigate and negotiate distinct topologies of life and death, and to modulate the biopolitical logic of debilitation. It is this capacity that is constitutive of repair.

This book seeks in part to describe and understand the labor undertaken by these women in and around the timber plantations—labor in the service of producing a profit for the global paper and pulp corporation—and also the conditions that make that labor possible or necessary. This book also describes the nutrition intervention and the ordinary efforts of workers to keep home, family, and body going. By providing a thick description of the materials at stake in what Povinelli calls the "effort of endurance"— wages, timber, and nutritive substances; but also ilobolo (bridewealth), kin relations, and HIV—I show how the work of repair draws on amandla as "subjugated knowledge" to capacitate modes of life that are "currently around us but without an explicit force among us."[26]

SITUATING AMANDLA

Taking amandla as its central concern, the work of repair as it emerges from the timber plantations is thus a mode of action that capacitates ethical reflection and the navigation of intersecting and overlapping topologies of life. This becomes clearer when considered in the broader, and longer, context of South Africa's centuries-long struggle for liberation from racialized minority rule and colonial oppression, the inauguration of which is popularly understood to start in 1652 with the establishment of the first Dutch settlement in Cape Town. This struggle for freedom occupies a particular place in the global imagination in the early twenty-first century, no less so after twenty-eight years of democratic governance and its successes and failures.[27] One way to read the history of that struggle is through the question over who might rightfully claim legitimate inclusion in and recognition by the state.[28] That the social compact has been underwritten by the production of surplus populations in both territorial and political economic terms is common sense in public life in South Africa. The "new" historiographies of the 1970s and '80s brought into tension the relationship between race and class as interpretive terms within which to understand the devastations of apartheid and its ongoing aftereffects.[29] Since its origins, South African political life has turned on the racialized (and ethnicized) production of difference and exclusion; the struggle (whether conceived as many or as the one, singular struggle for liberation) has been for recognition and inclusion. Often, those struggles have emerged from ordinary efforts to secure the material base of well-being, from bodily integrity to domestic reproduction and political and cosmological security. From the beginnings of South Africa's political economy, the mining industry circulated phthisis, silicosis, and tuberculosis through the racialized economy of metropole and hinterland, a circulation driven by the destruction of African families and farms, pestilence, infectious disease, and hunger.[30] The history of syndemic infectious disease, hunger, and unemployment in South Africa is long indeed.[31]

South Africa's liberation from apartheid was not only a moment of great expectations. The singular moment of 1994 is often taken as the threshold of freedom itself. It was fraught with the promise of newness and the struggle to break with a terrible past. Freedom was to be not merely a legal achievement; it was to be the grounds on which human life would flourish, and the wounds inflicted by a racist society and its state would be healed. The 1955 Freedom Charter, whose spirit infuses the 1996 Constitution, declared confidently, in section headings, that "The People Shall Share in the Country's Wealth! The Land Shall Be Shared among Those Who Work It! There Shall Be Houses, Security and Comfort!" It is a revolutionary document premised on the future anterior: when freedom has come, we will have founded a just society on these principles: "Rent and prices shall be lowered, food plentiful and no-one shall go hungry; People shall not be robbed of their cattle, and forced labor and farm prisons shall be abolished."[32] The abiding phrase that sustained several generations of liberation fighters and succored a vision of freedom and democracy was the call-and-response of "Amandla! Ngawethu!" The power is ours![33]

Why should the system of waged labor and the nutrition intervention in the timber plantations come together as they did in 2009, fifteen years after the end of apartheid? Amandla, as the central concern in the work of repair, is best understood in relation to two key themes that came into focus in that period. The first is the HIV pandemic and the second is unemployment. With regard to the first, South Africa has had one of the largest HIV epidemics in the world: it was estimated in 2009 that between 4.9 and 6.6 million of South Africa's 48 million people of all ages were infected with HIV, and about 678,550 were on treatment.[34] By 2018, 7.1 million people were living with HIV, a prevalence of 20.4 percent in the general population. The Joint United Nations Programme on HIV/AIDS (UNAIDS) reported that in South Africa, with the largest antiretroviral therapy (ART) program globally, 4.4 million people were receiving treatment in 2018, meaning that about 62 percent of HIV-positive adults were on ART (UNAIDS Data 2019). With regard to the second theme, South Africa's official unemployment rate increased from 22.5 percent in 2008 to 30.8 percent in 2020, eight months into the COVID-19 pandemic (and increased further after the attempted "insurrection" of July 2021). By the expanded definition, more than 10 million people are unemployed, or 38.5 percent of people who could be working.[35] Unemployment for young people is even higher: if the expanded definition of unemployment is used, which includes "discouraged work-seekers," the rate among people aged fifteen to twenty-four was 66 percent in 2021.[36] In 2020, over 17 million South Africans relied on social welfare grants from the state, which remain the second-most important source of income for households after salaries.[37]

When the negotiated settlement of 1994 ushered in a new era of democratic government, many of the rural and urban poor expected their lives to improve. A quarter century after the end of apartheid, many are still waiting. Inequality has worsened. Since that inaugurating moment of freedom, the notion of work as the saving grace of impoverished lives slowly evaporated as a serious proposition as it became clear that unemployment was structural and the very nature and meaning of work transformed.[38] The 92,000 people employed in the forestry sector in 2010 (in both formal and informal employment) represented a significant category of worker whose precarious inclusion within global commodity circuits has been relatively invisible. They constituted a significant category not only because the structural conditions in forestry are increasingly similar to other sectors (in that they are outsourced through labor contractors in much the same ways that mining and agricultural labor is), but also because the terms of their "adverse incorporation" are being replicated in many other parts of Africa and the global south, and now increasingly in the north too.[39] These highly structured rural labor regimes undermine "peasant" or "agrarian" economies while contracting largely unskilled rural residents into commodity production for global consumption far removed from the domestic economies in which laborers struggle to survive (Li 2011).

The shift to outsourced labor across all the industrial sectors of South Africa's economy took place as the state began to implement an unprecedented program of social spending. By 2012, the state supported sixteen million people on social grants, almost a third of the population; provided largely free services at public health facilities; supplied free education to 60 percent of learners; and paid for housing, water, and electricity in poor communities.[40] One and a half million people were on treatment for HIV, and over fifteen million had been tested. A new National Strategic Plan for HIV/AIDS was launched in 2012, and the South African National AIDS Council was restructured so that it was more representative and better governed. The death rate due to HIV/AIDS had begun to decline as a result of access to state-provided antiretroviral therapy, and a significant reduction in the rate of mother-to-child HIV transmission was achieved.[41]

The place of waged work as a key element of the techniques of government of the modern bureaucratic state has come radically into question across the world, just as new "ex-centric" locations have emerged from which to imagine collective and political life—as cogent treatises from Homi Bhabha, Jean Comaroff and John L. Comaroff, and James G. Ferguson have argued.[42] In postapartheid South Africa, a growing welfare program has shifted away from conditional payments shaped by normative visions of family and care[43] toward an expanded grant system.[44] There has also been a massive expansion of antiretroviral therapeutic regimes, including a test-and-treat program without a CD4 count eligibility criterion since September 2016, and the rollout in 2020 of an ambitious single-pill Pre-Exposure Prophylaxis (PreP) program to all at-risk population groups.[45]

Thus, because of the simultaneous growth of social spending and the increasingly technical concern with efficiency and cost, the political economy of postapartheid South Africa defies easy characterization as neoliberal or social democratic but rather combines a complex and sometimes contradictory set of political philosophies and economic policies informed by competing histories of radicalism and conservatism. While the substantial social welfare program has certainly ameliorated the suffering of many of the poorest citizens, new categories of exclusion have grown in its wake. Increased access to treatment for HIV and TB, for example, combined with massive spikes in food prices after the global financial crisis of 2008 to produce new configurations of hunger and infection, as well as indebtedness and precarity.[46] The COVID-19 pandemic since 2020 has undoubtedly worsened hunger and impoverished many more people.[47] Race remains a key modality of collective identification and rhetorical force, as well as an enduring index of material well-being. Access to treatment and employment have thus been two fundamental concerns for many millions of South Africans. While affecting particular groups of people in distinct ways, their intersecting effects ricochet across many more people's lives, profoundly shaping the economy, political institutions, and ordinary life for every citizen.

One sector in which these two concerns converge is forestry, because it has been crucially dependent on the steady and secure availability of labor power for its productivity. Labor power as an abstraction of "flesh and blood" configures the calculations of inputs and outputs, calories and costs, prices and profits.[48] At the center of this book is a group of women employed by one global paper and pulp manufacturing company in the timber plantations of northeastern South Africa. While far smaller than the mining sector in terms of investment, profits, or employment, the forestry sector, like agriculture and fisheries, is a significant contributor to the national economy despite the fact that South Africa has relatively little forest cover (in 1999, forests represented approximately 0.3 percent of South Africa).[49] Until the 1960s, the timber industry grew, like many others in South Africa, in order to service the mineral-energy complex, mainly in mining and construction.[50] The state played a direct role in the establishment of plantations to overcome the risks inherent in this type of investment, where the return takes many years to be realized. From the 1960s onward, the state supported the growth of the pulp and paper industry through a variety of subsidies and credit facilities, intended in particular for two private companies that have since become global players: Sappi and Mondi, which at that point was a subsidiary of the Anglo-American Group.[51] In 2003 the timber industry represented an added value of 1.35 billion euros (or 1 percent of South Africa's GDP) and employed more than 170,000 people, 60,000 of whom were in forestry.[52]

However, since the end of the 1980s, the sector has been experiencing a crisis to which the outsourcing of labor was both a response and a contributing factor. The contracting out of forestry operations began in the late 1980s at a time when urban protest against the apartheid regime reached rural areas and forestry workers, largely through the activism of unionized factory workers (in paper and sawmills). Until 2000, large forestry companies insisted that they relied on contractors to improve productivity, arguing that entrepreneurs would be more productive than managers. Within a few years, forestry companies had outsourced their entire labor force.[53] In 2012 the majority of the approximately 92,000 workers employed in plantation forestry in South Africa were employed by "large growers" controlling 70 percent of plantation resources.[54] The largest of these is Mondi South Africa (now a global company with operations in twenty-eight countries), which manages over 327,000 hectares of plantations and manufactures woodchips, pulp, container board, and paper.

In 2009, Mondi South Africa began implementing a nutrition intervention as part of a suite of labor reforms aimed at improving working conditions among 10,000 contracted laborers in its timber plantations. It was the culmination of many years of tinkering with the system of outsourced labor—tinkering that was not able to stop falling levels of productivity and profits. What conditions had produced such an intervention? Partly it was the convoluted history of the labor movement and its failure to organize forestry workers; partly it was the rearticulation of the South African economy with global commodity chains after the end of antiapartheid sanctions, which meant that forestry labor had to become more efficient when faced with competition from plantation labor and timber in other parts of the world; and partly it was in response to the devastating effects of HIV on the working people who sought wages in the plantations, and whose falling productivity was a problem to be managed, and intervened in. Together these conditions formed a crisis for the reproduction of labor.[55] Further, the specter of mechanization has loomed over the sector since at least the labor crises of the 1970s and provided one possible means by which to mitigate risk. Another risk mitigation strategy in the postapartheid era has been to transfer the ownership of

afforested land to claimant community trusts to place further distance between the mill and the contractors who muster that labor.

This crisis of labor thus took several forms: an increase in occupational
injuries and fatalities, productivity decline, high levels of absenteeism and
labor turnover, and a general shortage of labor. As I began to track the managed micronutrients that were delivered by catering contractors to laborers
deep in the plantations, I saw how the corporate calculations of calories and
profits drew a large array of actors into distinct points of concern. Not only
did the wages, calories, and nutrients support many others who depend on
plantation laborers for sustenance, they also embodied complex transformations of value. The conditions of labor and the means for survival, which
the nutrition intervention and other labor reforms sought to ameliorate and
augment, lie at the heart of a growing political and social anxiety around
the place of work in the distribution of rights and obligations that define
public life in South Africa and in many other places around the world. The
nutrition intervention implemented by the pulp and paper company in 2009
was thus partly a response to this conjoining of hunger and disease and its
effects on the laboring bodies in the timber plantations, an expression of
liberal concern for workers' well-being as much as for declining profits.

I started this project with an interest in understanding the logic of the
nutrition intervention, but after spending a year with timber plantation laborers it became apparent that corporate concerns with food, health, and
productivity obscured many of the elements that sustain bodies and nurture relations in contemporary South Africa. The nutrition intervention in
the timber plantations of northern KwaZulu-Natal that began in 2008 provided one point of entry for this project, but the broader story that emerged
is about how bodies *and* relations are sustained in a milieu. An account of
how these relations establish their own vital, local, norms must, as Georges
Canguilhem's history of the concept of health suggests, recognize the
particular histories and aspirations that precondition the living and its
margin.[56]

The second critical point of entry for this project was the growing controversy over the regulation of what in South Africa are commonly called
"traditional medicines"—more specifically, curatives that claimed to cure
HIV/AIDS. During 2008, the Treatment Action Campaign, a well-known
activist organization, mobilized support for amendments to be made to the
draft Medicines and Related Substances Control Act and the structure of

the Medicines Control Council in order to eliminate the circulation of "quack cures" and to speed up the approval of new, cheaper antiretroviral therapies.[57] These curative substances appealed to the signs and symbols of both "traditional medicine" and modern pharmaceuticals, and emergent concepts of immune system functioning. Beginning in May 2008, I began tracking debates at parliamentary hearings, interviewing scientists and activists, and developing a typology of the many substances available in pharmacies and on street corners around South Africa. I interviewed people who manufactured and distributed the novel curative substances that had become hugely controversial during Thabo Mbeki's presidency (during which he infamously denied the causal relationship between HIV and AIDS and refused to allow the state to distribute antiretroviral therapies), and I mapped their availability across the city of Durban and the province of KwaZulu-Natal. I began to see these substances everywhere, and to understand them better I sought out conversations at every opportunity with anyone who would talk about them.[58]

Pharmacies provide one useful way of giving an account of the emplotment of pharmaceuticals and persons, as Amanda Atwood has for four pharmacies in Harare, Zimbabwe.[59] I spent many months in the pharmacies of the small town of Mtubatuba in northeastern KwaZulu-Natal, seeking to understand the local ecologies of care and the worlds through which these curatives moved.[60] One person I came to know well was Siyanda, a security guard who worked at a pharmacy in Mtubatuba. In March 2009 Siyanda fell ill for about two weeks, and when I saw him again after his illness, he told me a story about a long translucent snake that had been making him ill and that, with careful attention to ritual, had been purged from his body in a series of purificatory gestures. It was a complex story that involved a snake sent by a malevolent junior wife of his father as well as a series of confusing visits to biomedical doctors and a contestation over the results of the rapid testing of his blood. His story is instructive because it helps frame the potential for an exoticizing view of African healing that sits in counterpoint to the everyday rituals of purification and nurturance that were important to the forest laborers with whom I worked. Siyanda's healing involved the ingestion of "purified water," bottles of which could be bought at nearby pharmacies and were used by faith healers, abathandazi, as well as blister-packs of pills discreetly supplied by his employer at the pharmacy.

A scan of the pharmacopeia available in biomedical pharmacies, cosmetics stores, and herbalists revealed a widespread practice of purging and cleansing, inside and out, that is reflected in a range of literature from nineteenth-century travel and missionary archives to twentieth-century public health concerns with diarrhea, water supply, and child malnutrition. The shifting panoply of industrial substances, products, and techniques, each attuned to the subtle efforts to heal skin rashes, to make one's face glow, to counter the enervating demands of migrant labor and the diffuse effects of racial oppression, have a complex history, delicately calibrated to the vagaries of the colonial state and its manufacture of difference.[61] As Karen Flint has shown, the pharmacopeia of colonial Natal in the late nineteenth and early twentieth centuries was a rich bricolage of African, Indian, European, and slave medicaments, and the techniques of the self that emerged through this period were profoundly shaped by colonial attempts to regulate African labor and lifeworlds.[62]

The mass consumption over the past twenty years of a set of (apparently) novel curative substances suggests an increasingly commoditized appeal to variable therapeutic interventions into health, wealth, strength, and social capacity. Many of these substances operate as purgatives and/or emetics, drawing on notions of bodily purity and social order. They suggest a continuity of symbols and practices concerning well-being and affliction, such as that described by John Janzen as "ngoma" (song, rhythm, or drum of affliction)—a term used in many Bantu languages for a set of healing practices and discourses centered on the interpretation of misfortune and the treatment of affliction.[63] It is no small irony that two of the brands of such substances I followed are named "Impilo" (life) and "Ngoma" (song/drum of affliction)—life in a bottle, the promise of health as that which is purged. However, as these nutritive-curative substances settled into particular networks of retail and consumption, their stabilization as a technique of the self entailed increasingly diverse notions of immune system functioning, bodily well-being, and social change.

The accounts of the women laboring in the timber plantations, and of many others, echoed Siyanda's explanations, and contained several common threads: snakes, blood, kin, skin, illness, HIV, ingestion, defecation, trees, herbs, liquid tonics, and texts. In tracing the circulations of the numerous and diverse materia medica and their accompanying texts, I have been confronted by the difficulty of naming these objects and their social worlds.

The colonial state sought to criminalize the sale of "traditional medicine," "quack cures," or "muthi," as Karen Flint shows.[64] At the height of the controversy over access to antiretroviral therapy, the 2008 parliamentary hearings into the restructuring of the Medicines Control Council struggled precisely to differentiate legally between cosmetic, supplement, food substance, and pharmaceutical. It is simultaneously a methodological problem of reading (that is, affording the correct status to these texts in the everyday lives of a definite group of people) and of understanding the "social lives" of these substances as they traverse scenes of codification, consumption, and recomposition.[65]

By tracking the nutrition intervention of the timber company during 2009, and the circulation of curative substances through the spaces and lives of timber plantation laborers, I began to understand something of the effort and imagination required to stay alive under numbing conditions. The people who work in the timber plantations must contend with a range of forces that splinter the effort to remain human: the fragmentation of spaces of habitation; the extraction of every ounce of labor power from the body; the wasting of the body by disease and the combined effects of many decades of impoverishment; and the erosion of trust, intimacy, and familiar modes of obligation and reciprocity.

THE WORK OF REPAIR

The central aim of this book is to show how amandla, as ethical substance, brings into alignment a disparate set of fractured, wounding materials: the timber plantations, the conditions of labor, the nutrition intervention that was piloted and implemented during 2008–10, the reactions of workers to the calculated calories, the wage, the curative substances, homesteads, kin relations, and the effort itself to maintain life and limb. The workers who build social projects in the shadows of a globalized regime of timber production contend also with the devastation of the HIV epidemic. And do so in the remnants of the Bantustan state of KwaZulu, whose fragments are sutured by the values and norms, but also contradictions and failures, of the postapartheid developmental state. Whether those materials cohere around something like a "social project" is an open question. By "social project" I mean the sense of making social worlds otherwise, well described by Povinelli.[66] Writing the social from the point of view of "social projects," specifically the project of fashioning a world in and through the space of the plantation, puts into question sociological assumptions about culture, society, and individuals, and their interrelations (see chapter 5). It attends to the projects themselves, the effort to make the world otherwise, the compositional efforts of people whose capacity to endure is critically in question.[67] Thus, amandla arises as diagnostic and technique, resource and trope, in the effort to endure a labor regime that is coterminous with, and profoundly entangled with, the colonial and apartheid, and now the postapartheid, state. The ethnography I offer here is an attempt to describe and understand the concern with amandla in social projects around the timber plantations of postapartheid South Africa. Amandla, as it directs speech and action, and subtends the labor of capital, is central to a form of ethical conduct that I call *the work of repair*.

In many southern African languages, including isiZulu, several words hover together around the English term "repair." In noun and verb forms, "lungisa" draws together repair, adjustment, correction, reform, arrangement, revision; to prepare, rectify, adjust, repair, reconstruct, ratify. There is "vuselela," meaning repair, renewal, renovation; to renew, repair, revive, rebuild. There is also "izinhlawulo," as reparations, damages, penalties, punishment, compensation, especially in the context of legitimating genealogical offspring born out of wedlock.[68] There is also "khanda," to beat, pound, hammer, or forge, but also to fix, mend, repair, doctor. All these words were in ordinary usage by the women I worked with.

In Euro-American terms, the concept of repair has been developed in several different directions across a number of fields, from Melanie Klein's reparation and Donald Winnicott's mending in psychoanalysis, to Frantz Fanon's therapeutic arguments, Ta-Nehisi Coates's call for reparations for slavery, and Steven Jackson's sociology of machines.[69] Certainly, reparation and restitution have been central to debate in South Africa on how to engage the wounding legacies of apartheid.[70] The concept of repair that animates the argument in this book is drawn from the work of Algerian-French artist Kader Attia, whose 2013 exhibition *The Repair* has inspired a range of political and philosophical responses.[71] By juxtaposing, among other things, photographs of the disfigured faces of soldiers from the First World War with severe facial injuries after having undergone plastic surgery (the "Broken Jaws") with fractured African masks, Attia reveals two pictures of repair, whose locations are suggested by the exhibition's subtitle, "From

Occident to Extra-Occidental Cultures": a modern Western conception of repair that pursues an ideal of perfection by striving for the flawless recreation of the original state. In the consumer society cycle, for example, defective objects are disposed of and replaced by new ones. The repair itself remains invisible, amounting to an obliteration of history. On the other hand, the patched artifacts of ancient cultures openly show their sutures and clamps and thus the history of the object.[72]

"Repair" for Attia points to the process of healing of a damaged state, whether in the form of bodily injuries, damages to cult or everyday objects, or the wounds of colonization that continue to make themselves felt today. Manthia Diawara draws out two levels of signification of Attia's work, both relevant to my argument concerning the work of repair. First, he says, we see that a broken body is a body that has had a weakness introduced into it, a hole that, if not repaired, becomes a sign of trauma. We need therefore to repair the hole, or the fissure, by covering it up, stitching it, or decorating it with other scars to reappropriate it and make it familiar. Secondly, we realize that the broken faces, of black and white, masks and people, utensils and human faces, are interchangeable, because their scars are relatable: "They each construct a *lieu-commun*, the myth of which can be shared with the state in which the others find themselves."[73] Attia sketches out an arc from the "practical" notion of repair—redefined as the practice through which colonized cultures appropriate the symbols of the colonizing powers into their own cultural idioms—to the juridical realm of "reparation," as in the replenishment of a previously inflicted loss.[74] By showing the scar, the wound's stitching, Klaus Görner suggests, the concept of visible repair is thus directed against amnesia.[75] By embracing these disfigurations, argues Diawara, we change the way we see the victims of trauma by familiarizing ourselves with the victims, by embracing their scars and letting them embrace ours. "By licking the Other's scars and allowing him/her/it to lick our disfiguration . . . we engage in an exchange that changes us in the process."[76] Such an understanding of repair is quite different from Arendt's reading of the Christian tradition of forgiveness as the grounds for relationships between individuals for whom "community" is an aspirational horizon and ontological premise for society.[77]

I argue in this book that the regions around the timber plantations, those specifically in KwaZulu-Natal, are a site in which repair and work come together—that is, it is a topos, or a lieu-commun—not as general figures, but as one particular, textured figuration (see chapters 1 and 5). To speak of the plantation as a topos in which repair and work come together is already to rely on a certain concept of "the plantation" as a site or system organized as an arrangement of persons, objects, commodities, and energies. But what is the relationship between the Dukuduku/Nyalazi plantations, and "the plantation" of decolonial theory? In recent years, "the plantation" has emerged as a site for tracing the genealogy of modern racism and capitalism through a history of slavery, particularly in the Americas, and for diagnosing what Achille Mbembe calls Black Reason. Mbembe has argued that the colonial system of plantation labor sought not merely to block the slave's desire to live, but to diminish their capacities to consider themselves moral agents.[78] In this space, the slave is at once object, body, and merchandise: it is "potential substance" that the planter seeks to appropriate in order to augment the planter's own power.[79] For Deborah Thomas, the plantation is a site of ecological simplification and a laboratory of terror that demarcated the limits of the human.[80] Mbembe argues that the postcolony inherits this history in its "renewed will to kill as opposed to the will to care, a will to sever all relationships as opposed to the will to engage in the exacting labor of repairing the ties that have been broken."[81] Thus, considering "political life in the wake of the plantation" requires what Deborah Thomas calls a mode of reparative "attentive recognition." Fanon's psychoanalytically inflected critique of colonialism opens out to what Mbembe calls a therapeutic reading: Fanon's "therapy" depends on recognizing the "fundamental reality according to which becoming a human being in the world means accepting one's being exposed to the other."[82] It is thus through a dimension of reciprocity and care for humanity that the asymmetry of relations might be rectified.[83] The work of repair is, I argue, precisely in this mode of attentive recognition—namely, a mode of attentive availability that is responsive to an emergent, and capacitating, vulnerability.[84]

The transformations of regimes of property, modes of production-and-reproduction, and the sex/gender/kinship systems that intermediate these colonial and postcolonial histories are not unique to this region of the world; indeed, there are powerful continuities and disjunctures with plantation economies across other regions, from the Caribbean to South America to South Asia and other settler colonies.[85] However, there is a complex economy here between the specificity of the objects and images that Attia manipulates (archival film footage, masks) and the conceptual work they do; their availability to a decolonial political philosophy; and attentive recognition that coordinates amandla and the materials at stake in the work of repair. In thinking about repair in and around the timber plantations, what emerges is not a universalizing abstraction of the figure of Black Reason, but a particular figuration of ethical, political work and capacity in the register of the ordinary. This is not "endurance" in the sense that Povinelli develops in her critique of liberalism; in the settler-colonial multiculturalism of Australia, she argues that "the-part-that-has-no-part" within liberal thought tremulously hovers just outside the door of recognition, and thus must "endure."[86] Endurance and its antonym, exhaustion, present as a social mood or tense that structures "social projects" that exist in the space between being and not-being, between potentiality and actuality. Fiona Ross suggests that while talk of ukunyamezela (as perseverance or endurance) in South Africa is certainly alive in ordinary concerns with a struggle to achieve valued goals—education, Afro-operatic performance, strike action, marriage, ideal kinship relations—it has a different relation to biopolitical life in this postcolonial context not least because people are, or might be, committed to existing institutions with and against which they struggle.[87] Thus, while an African postcolonial (and postapartheid) analytic might share some aspects of Povinelli's critique of "late liberalism," it also departs from it in crucial respects.[88] Similarly, the figuration of capacity that I suggest is at stake in amandla is not simply, or only, that of the distribution of debilitation and capacitation that Puar argues for. From the lieu-commun of the plantations, I suggest that amandla is a form of life that forcefully comes at colonial and postcolonial liberal governance as a political-ethical intervention at an oblique angle, not within the terms of liberal capitalism in general, and not in spectacular or poetic terms (although there may appear moments of the sublime), but as a resource for mundane, situated, historically reflexive action.

Complementing this picture of repair, in which the fragment and the injury are not concealed, but which enters into exchange with the Other, is an ethnographic archive that suggests an African praxis of personhood constitutively working through and with incompleteness as a key trope.[89] For Francis Nyamnjoh, incompleteness is an enduring condition, not particular to Africa in any essential way but certainly figured in its heterogeneous modes of becoming: "We are self-consciously incomplete beings, constantly in need of activation, potency, and enhancement through relationships of conviviality and ubuntu with incomplete others."[90] For Mbembe, it is the fact of "composition and of assemblage of a multiplicity of vital beings" that opens the way to an alternative conception of mutual becoming with others, however agonistic that might be, which anchors his critique of Black Reason as an internal Other to the Enlightenment.[91]

Lest we think that the turn to repair, on this reading, is merely psychic or aesthetic, or easy sophistry, it is helpful to remember the specific conditions in which these wounds appear, and to keep the material concerns of repair close to hand, between the spectacular and the mundane. The possibilities and evidence of the failure to repair are everywhere, and the conditions in which that failure appears seem overdetermining. In South Africa, on the one hand, the spectacularly violent deaths in Sharpeville in 1960, the youth uprising of 1976, the Marikana massacre of 2012, or the violent events of July 2021 in KwaZulu-Natal and Gauteng provinces, provide one chronotope of violence as event, as rupture; on the other hand, the "chronic cruddiness" of apartheid's immiserating policies, or the "unmournable" postapartheid deaths caused by HIV, TB, and SARS-CoV-2, seem to defy representation, so ordinary are they.[92] Clearly, the possibility for repair in a political register is for "actual acts of justice, of caring and repairing that which has been broken."[93] That is, justice requires repairs to "all infrastructures of life."[94] Neither is amandla a question of custom or culture in an old ethnological sense, but rather the site of an encounter between Euro-American genealogies of health and cure, body and organ, and work and labor, with its internal Other, as a question of late modernity.[95]

But if repair, as an aspect of Fanon's political thought, can be named therapeutic, then the relationship between colonizer and colonized, healing and curing, therapist and patient, healer and healed, is crucial. In relation to a history of medicine, Todd Meyers shows how Canguilhem's question concerning the possibility of a "pedagogy of healing" draws on the distinction between healing and curing: "healing is fundamentally subjective and individual, following an etymology that includes protection and security, but also to defend. Cure, on the other hand, reflects forms of internal change adhering to external validation. Cure is the success of change within, verified statistically or otherwise from without."[96] The tension between healing and cure, says Meyers, is not about nomenclature or semantics; rather, the tension is found in the lifeworlds of individuals and the moral-social world of the clinic: "It is a tension that carries with it certain conceptions of life outside the clinic walls, often with no grasp of how agency is both afforded and constrained by life elsewhere."[97] In the work of repair, I show how the composition of diverse things, persons, actions, and relations brings "healing" and "curing" closer together in a zone of "indistinction."[98] As chapter 5 argues, the radical redistribution of the clinic through the composited, conjunctural topologies of global health, wetland conservation, and plantation labor demands a capacity to navigate folded topologies of life, and thus demonstrates the interdependent, already internally, mutually, constitutive forms of life, labor, and action.[99]

The work of repair at stake in the plantations is thus not a labor of synthesis, integration, or resolution. Rather, the action at stake in repair folds healing and curing into a living politics, and a politics of the living, namely (the possibility of) shared vulnerability. To adapt Nancy Rose Hunt's formulation, the work of repair defends against the narrowing of the milieu of life.[100]

Amandla, then, points to the possibility of shared vulnerability, and its redistribution.[101] The uneven distribution of vulnerability has been well described in anthropological treatments of violence in various postcolonial contexts.[102] Rather than seek vulnerability's force in a Euro-American genealogy of political thought, we can turn instead to another archive, reflected ethnographically, for example, in Zimbabwean responses to the war of liberation, such as David Lan's ethnography of the work of healers in the liberation war in Zimbabwe; Pamela Reynolds's description of how children became healers in the reparative effort after 1980 in Zimbabwe; or Donald Moore's analysis of "suffering for territory."[103] Robert Thornton's argument that ngoma is a figuration of exposed being that must be augmented is central here.[104] Anette Wickström points to another isiZulu form of life, lungisa, putting in order, turning to the image of "weaving together" as the action of producing space and relationships over time to exert some control over a life lived under political and economic circumstances that rip and rend.[105] Further away, James Fernandez shows how in Bwiti, the "occult search for capacity" in Equatorial West Africa among the Fang is also concerned with "world reconstruction."[106] Hylton White's account of ritual action and its failures in northern KwaZulu-Natal is closer to the argument I have developed here, in that he offers a picture of the vulnerability of action to misfiring that draws the fragility and powers of the dead intimately into the political economy of postapartheid South Africa.[107] It is in this context that the centrality of amandla as both bodily capacity and ethical aspiration elicits the acts of repair occasioned by the labor regime in the braiding together of corporate and kin relations around the question of food and sustenance.

Timber plantations, conservation parks, population health surveillance, and the conjugation of customary and constitutional authority come together around the question of life in this locality: its value, maximization, operability, subjectivation, and containment. In setting the struggles and creative efforts of a group of women laborers within a history of plantations, territories, and surveillance, the book attends to the political effects on the body of the South African citizen of a mode of reasoning and form of calculation. Repair in relation to the plantations is that ordinary and yet vital concern with life across material, ethical, biological worlds as they are caught in the gears and cogs of capital(ism) and its actors in the early twenty-first century. Each of the chapters shows not only how the work of repair concerns "subtle acts of care" but also how amandla is the filament, the tissue itself, of political and ethical action that places concrete concerns with calories, capacities, and kin at the center of the operations of capital. There at the center of the timber plantation stand not only eucalypts, machines, discipline, and profit; there one finds also the political and ethical questions posed by the efforts of the workers themselves, the aesthetic and imaginative horizons that draw the world in, even as those efforts swing a wide range of materials into alignment.

The labor regime that I observed from 2008 to 2010 was already fast changing, set on a path toward increasing mechanization and disarticulation with the social conditions of the reproduction of that labor that had historically been vital to its operation. By 2020, that system of labor was unrecognizable. It had been utterly transformed by a decade of what some call the Great Recession, new modes of consumption, a slide into "state capture" under former president Jacob Zuma, accelerated flows of speculative global financial capital, and displacement by machines and flows of digital organ(ism)s and bioinformation.[108] By attending to the struggles of people living and working in the timber plantations of KwaZulu-Natal as I observed them in 2009, and recording the histories of their labor and the commodities produced by it, this book offers an alternative perspective on the relationship of capital to ordinary life—that is, it offers another perspective on life in the midst of capital, subtending capital, making capital something other than it is, rather than merely an overdetermined product of capital's operations.[109]

THE FIELDWORK

In late 2008, I began mapping the production and circulation of a set of curative substances and the public controversies and parliamentary debates about their regulation sparked by President Thabo Mbeki's notorious AIDS denialism. It was then that I learned of a nutrition intervention aimed at timber plantation laborers in KwaZulu-Natal that had been piloted during 2008 and was to be rolled out to all plantation laborers in 2009. I contacted Mondi's Transformation Office with an interest in following the rollout of this intervention and was introduced to foresters and managers of the Nyalazi and Dukuduku plantations near the town of Mtubatuba in northern KwaZulu-Natal.[110] With the assistance of Ntombifuthi, the first of two women fieldworkers with whom I worked closely, I conducted a small survey of 107 harvesting and silviculture laborers to capture some of the contours of plantation livelihoods. Ntombifuthi had previously been employed by one of the timber contractors and was looking for work when I met her in early 2009. Our questionnaire collected basic information on work history, household size, income, food consumption, illness, injuries, health seeking options, medication use, and religious activity.

I then spent several months visiting groups of laborers in different compartments of the plantations, learning about the labor regime and observing the preparation and delivery of food to the workers. During this period, I spent three months with several harvesting and silviculture work teams, observing how the work was conducted, the techniques of the body required to perform its actions, and the social relationships among the members of the teams and with their superiors. When workplace health and safety regulations permitted, I joined in the labor. These regulations specified wearing sturdy boots at all times and a hard hat and reflective vest whenever we were on private forestry land. I also worked intensively with a group of fourteen laborers over the course of a year to understand the place of the food intervention in their everyday lives.

The group with whom I worked was employed by silviculture contractors, not harvesters. While I was introduced to each of the harvesting and silviculture teams in Dukuduku and Nyalazi by the Mondi forest managers, and a general invitation was extended to all laborers to participate in my study, we were unable to recruit members of harvesting teams for the simple reason that they were too exhausted and pressed for time to participate in my research. Theirs is the most difficult labor in the plantations, the most exhausting and taxing on one's body; it leaves the least time and energy available to be spent during the working day talking to researchers. The use of the piecework system (despite its illegality) among some harvesting contractors meant that the daily quota (set by the company and agreed with the contractor) not completed on one day had to be completed on the next for the work to be compensated. Those involved in silviculture, on the other hand, were compensated at a fixed daily rate, and so were more able to spend time talking to us.

During 2009 and in early 2010, I spent time in the homes of these laborers, shared meals, and observed family life in the round. The group of fourteen women lived in two localities, Shikishela and Mfekayi, in the uMkhanyakude municipality, adjacent to the Dukuduku and Nyalazi plantations in northern KwaZulu-Natal. Each of the women was surrounded by a host of intimate relations—kin, friends, lovers, neighbors, employers, patrons, dependents, and enemies. The localities were accessible from the national highway, the N2, which connects Cape Town, Umtata, Durban, Richards Bay, Mtubatuba, Pongola, Piet Retief, and Ermelo. The N2 is a dangerous, life-giving conduit of labor, capital, and tourists. Every day the laborers were picked up along the N2, taken to the timber plantations and dropped back again, along the highway, where they took care to avoid thundering lorries loaded with sugarcane and coal, or more perilously, the overcrowded minibus taxis that frequently overturned. The truck stops and craft markets around them were clear "hot spots" of HIV, linking upwardly mobile urban life across the continent through virologically charged sexual networks.[111] The stretch of the N2 highway between Mtubatuba and Shikishela is a twenty-minute drive by car; to Mfekayi it is thirty minutes. Both localities were densifying quickly, clear examples of what was once imagined to be classically "Zulu" rurality but long since a "township in the bush."[112]

Of the fourteen women, nine lived in Mfekayi: Nomvula, Hlengiwe and her sister Gcina, Sabathile, Lindiwe and her daughter S'li, Sibongile, Nokuthula, and Thembi. Five lived in Shikishela: Ntombikhayise, Nkosingiphile, Bashingile, Apiwe, and Nkule. While these women were the pivot around which domestic livelihoods turned, and thus the people on whom we focused, we came to know their children, parents, siblings, and neighbors. Each was the only wage earner, supporting ten or more others in complex financial arrangements.[113] Some homesteads were finely adorned, with a number of additional houses and dependents; others were minimal and simple. Some lived in former barracks, rows of one-roomed hostels designed for seasonal labor.[114] All had fruit and vegetable gardens, although some were fallow during the time of our research. Only one household kept cattle, and this was because our informant's husband had retired from a lifetime of working on the mines in Gauteng and had invested his pension in livestock.[115]

Through recording life histories, kinship charts, and narratives of labor and health, it became clear that residence patterns among this group had been fluid and unstable. Each had spent considerable stretches of time living in the "forestry villages" deep in the plantations away from family; living and working in a large city (Durban or Johannesburg); and living in other localities around the plantations. Only four lived in homesteads that had an enduring patrilineal narrative; the rest were recently established or had moved from distant areas. Men were not prominent members of these households. In only two were men breadwinners, and in another two men were present as resident siblings. Two women had male partners who were resident in the yard, and for the rest, sexual partners and the children's genitors lived elsewhere, as did other male relatives. One woman was "lesbian," or in her words, "tomboy," and spoke openly of her sexuality (see chapter 4). By tracking the daily scenes of consumption in and beyond the plantations, I sought to understand how the absorption of the nutrition supplementation program into the everyday lives of this group of women articulated with *amandla* and its embodied concerns.

The fourteen women I worked with were part of a workforce that was largely feminized in the northern plantations of KwaZulu-Natal (although across the sector nationally, there are more men than women). Within contracting teams, there was a general skew in labor too: more women worked in silviculture than men, and among harvesting crews, the gendered division of labor was clear: of the teams I observed, roughly two-thirds of the teams consisted of women, although none wielded a chainsaw or measured the length of the timber. Men tended to be drivers, chainsaw operators, or stackers, while women were debarkers, weeders, and "general laborers."

From mid-2009, I worked closely with Ntombizodumo "Dumo" Mkwanazi, who was far more than a research assistant. Dumo became a coconspirator, a friend who enthusiastically threw herself into the project with the utmost poise, grace, and kindness, and yet who refused to count herself as a coauthor. Her assistance with translation and social introductions was invaluable, aided in no small part by the fact that her father was induna (local customary authority) in a nearby isigodi (customary ward/neighborhood), and that she had just returned from Norway, having completed a master's degree in public health. Her kindness and embeddedness in familiar networks of kin, clan, and local esteem meant that the women (and men) working in the plantations responded to our questions with warmth and grace. With Dumo's help, I structured household visits around interviews on particular themes such as health, residence history, livelihoods, kin relations, and religious affiliation. We accompanied members of this group on visits to town at month's end, after payday, and helped with shopping. We also attended several ceremonial and other social events.[116]

During 2009, to support the costs of fieldwork I worked part-time for a demographic and health research organization near the town of Mtubatuba and the timber plantations. I was employed by the Africa Centre for Health and Population Studies to understand why rates of participation among residents of their demographic surveillance area (DSA) in their annual HIV surveillance were low, and to contribute to strategies to improve them. During the course of that work, I interviewed demographers, biostatisticians, program managers, and field staff as well as a number of research subjects and community representatives around the DSA. While I do not discuss the findings of that work directly here, I found it to be an education in the complex institutions and social imaginaries that densely configure the terrain.[117] More specifically, I learned about some of the techniques through which demography represents social phenomena and the way their spatial characteristics are understood and represented. I also did some work for the iSimangaliso Wetland Park, which is a very large World Heritage Site conservation area that stretches up the coastline from the town of St. Lucia to the Mozambican border.

Each of these activities placed me within a matrix of particular institutional interests that shaped how I saw the world and how my interlocutors saw me. I had no access to the timber plantations without assurances to the company's management that my research would be helpful in some general, unspecified way. As an outsider with permission from corporate headquarters, I was viewed by the foresters and laborers with a great deal of suspicion at first. Similarly, while I was working for the Africa Centre, HIV surveillance participants regarded me with the same caustic eye that they cast over the center more generally. Each of these groups and their established relations of power thus shaped what I could do and ask, where I could go, and to whom I could speak. In some instances, my whiteness was at stake; in others, my maleness, class, or language. A myriad identifications shaped my interactions in a field of relations historically skewed and twisted, such that misrecognition and distrust were not merely constant challenges to understanding how social relations and lives were built in this landscape, but constituted the very terms through which I came to know something of the texture of everyday life in northern KwaZulu-Natal.

How it is that I came to stand in this relation to plantation laborers had to do not only with the broader history of colonial dislocation and the violence of apartheid; it was also shaped by my own biography. I was born in rural Swaziland (now Eswatini) to White South African exiles, fugitives from the apartheid state's security apparatus. In 1983, when I was six, our family moved to Zimbabwe, to which many South African exiles had relocated after that country's achievement of independence in 1980. In February 1990, when Nelson Mandela was released from prison and the ANC was unbanned, my parents began to make plans to return to South Africa. My brother and I arrived in Cape Town in December 1990, a month before our parents did—they took a circuitous, delayed, back-route home.

From my earliest memories, the struggle against apartheid shaped the fabric of our lives, and the violence of the security forces seemed never far away. One important story I inherited was that of one set of grandparents (my father's parents) who were antiapartheid activists and members of the Communist Party of South Africa in 1940s Johannesburg.[118] In my early sense-making, my grandfather's imprisonment in 1960, in the State of Emergency declared after the Sharpeville massacre of that year, is strongly connected to the story of my parents' detention in 1971, leading to their exile from South Africa for the next twenty years. This despite my parents' disavowal of Soviet-style communism, and their identification instead with the "new left" that emerged in many parts if the world in the late 1960s.

In retrospect, my childhood in the shadows of the struggle against apartheid, for all its anxieties and insecurities, was a form of shelter from the brutal realities of racism that I was to learn about later. Moving to Cape Town as a young adolescent, in the midst of the political negotiations leading to the first democratic election in 1994, was an education in the ugly violence of race and racism in South Africa. As Shannon Morreira has described for "liberal" Whites in southern Africa, forebears and the inheritance from them of particular forms of politics can fold together histories of both complicity and resistance, and of knowing and not knowing.[119] In truth, at the time I understood little of the significance of my family's stories and of their connection to the unfolding events of the 1980s and early 1990s. It was only much later that I came to think about these stories, as I became aware of the difficulties encountered by efforts at postapartheid redress, the messy realities of class in contemporary South Africa, and a widespread refusal to come to terms with the historical traumas of apartheid and colonialism. My own strange insertion into this new society did not align easily with existing striations of race and class. But in those febrile days of the early to mid-1990s, I could not help but be affected by an imaginary common to a certain layer of activists, including both recently returned exiles and so-called in-ziles, centered on forms of postracial solidarity that might transform this wounded society and improve the collective well-being of the formerly oppressed.

I learned anthropology during this transition, at a time when a newly reinvigorated critique of the discipline resonated powerfully with the political and social changes under way in South Africa. These helped fuel a utopian sense of emancipatory possibilities, both for society and for anthropology. Still largely White in its complement of both teachers and students, the discipline offered critical understandings of the political economy of apartheid and its migrant labor system, and of the invention and deployment of racial categories by the apartheid state—but it also made possible a critique of the ways in which old categories and forms of understanding of race, class, and gender relations and identities continued to be deployed in the nooks and crannies of postapartheid South Africa.

This was a somewhat self-congratulatory version of the discipline, which prided itself on the moral probity of its English South African ancestors, whose liberal values expressed themselves in support of the cause of the oppressed Black majority.[120] At that point, I thought I had done very well, as if somehow through my own efforts, to have such politically radical parents and grandparents, and I took no interest in that part of the family tree that did not align with these progressive sentiments.

It was only in the course of fieldwork, in the midst of the plantations (and more literally, during a visit to the provincial archives in Pietermaritzburg), that I was shocked by the uncanny discovery that the Dukuduku and Nyalazi timber plantations had first been surveyed and planted by one of my ancestors, John Spurgeon Henkel. As the first scientific forester in the Zululand region, his work in forestry extended from Cape Town to Zimbabwe, then called Rhodesia. This ancestor was my radical grandmother's uncle; his father and my great-grandfather, Carl Caesar Henkel, had been the first cartographer of the Transkeian Territories (now in the Eastern Cape province), and as chief forest officer, was stationed at Umtata, responsible for the conservation of indigenous forests and for the development of commercial forestry in the Transkei.[121] A sense of uncanny inheritance pervaded the rest of my time in the plantations, knowing that these two Henkels had played significant roles in the imperial project of dislocating African peoples in order to enable resource extraction on a massive scale. Since that moment, I have had to scrutinize critically my easy sense of self-congratulation and reexamine the long threads of racial privilege and colonial violence that brought me to that scene of labor and privileged access to the plantations in 2009. The sense in which anthropological knowledge is (unequally) co-produced with one's assistants and informants might thus include a broader swathe of interlocutors, including awkward ancestors such as these.[122]

This braided history of empire and inheritance (of privilege, education, myth, power) thus profoundly shapes my perspective and argument here, and to the extent that a disciplinary unconscious meets my own, I am caught in a web of misrecognition the answer to which is not simply an appeal to critique or rigor.[123] Certainly, spending time with each of the various groups of interlocutors in and around the plantations provided many instances in which my relative power and ignorance were highlighted, commented on, and critiqued. I became aware at some point during 2009 that those moments in which I was located as a powerful stranger were uncomfortable not merely because they activated all the coordinates of liberal compassion that so insidiously operate to maintain relations of structural violence (as Povinelli has argued for multicultural Australia); they also provided opportunities for inversion and ridicule, subtle strategies for resisting the terms of subjection that I brought into the room with me.[124] In the push and pull of thickening relationships with the group of timber plantation laborers, there were moments of deep shame in which I found myself caught in the language of liberal compassion, a language that was quickly undone and deconstructed by my interlocutors; in other moments, my informants' embarrassment or shyness signaled a more profound misalignment of anticipations and aspirations.

And yet there were many ways in which people in northern KwaZulu-Natal folded me into a standing language of intimacy or estrangement. White Afrikaans farmers, English conservationists, and Black laborers each interpolated me in particular modes of address, establishing thicker or thinner grammars of relatedness. One experience in particular sticks with me. Dumo and I were first getting to know Hlengiwe and her sister, who both worked in the Nyalazi timber plantation in mid-2009, and in one of our first conversations, in which Hlengiwe was telling us about why they had moved to Mfekayi, I found myself responding to her story of hardship with the expression, "shame!"—a particularly South African term that can be used with varying inflections to convey sympathy, criticism, cuteness, or joy, depending on the context. My response, unconsciously offered as a way of establishing grounds for rapport, was met with consternation and disgust: We don't want your sympathy! We have nothing to be ashamed of!

A deep sense of shame welled up in me that I should have uttered the word at all; the flush of shame was a moment of self-recognition, of a realization that the scene I had constructed was shot through with the struts and braces of liberal compassion and recognition to which I had tethered myself. It was a moment in which I was educated in the meanings and implications of the word "shame" as well as the coordinates of liberal care that frame its projection.[125] It was also an opportunity to observe the snarl-up of what Povinelli calls "grids": grids in which those who use the language of liberal care and those who are its objects are caught within a distribution of rights, terminologies, and materialities. Historically those terms were aligned by concepts of whiteness, privilege, and individual agency, and blackness, exclusion, and genealogical obligation. Only slowly are those grids beginning to shift. For the rest of that year, Hlengiwe never failed to remind me of that moment, and we laughed at it every time. I took it as a great kindness on her part to offer opportunities to shift those vectors of shame through laughter.

Every time I introduced myself in isiZulu, my surname became a point of contact where the grid could be shifted slightly, even if only temporarily. Apart from the general irony of an anthropologist studying kinship called Cousins, the kin term in isiZulu is used in everyday life to align intimacy and trust between people. "Umzala" (pl. abazala) means "cross cousin," in classificatory terms; that is, child of father's sister or mother's brother as well as any child of mother's siblings. In everyday speech, it is used as a term of endearment whether there is some genealogical link (through clanship for instance) or any other point of solidarity being invoked, for example umzala wam or umzala wethu (my/our cousin). Similarly, people use "ugazi lam," or "gaz'lam" for short, meaning "my blood," in the same way to invoke a shared sense of relatedness or common cause. My interlocutors loved laughing at the sense of being of shared substance across race lines, and would comment, "Hhayi uThomas akayena umlungu, ungumuntu" (No, Thomas is not a White, he's a person). While most people understand "umlungu" to be a critical (or derogatory) word for a White person, its opposite is simply person (umuntu)—someone possessing the virtues of personhood, ubuntu.

Those moments of shame and shock were occasions when the expert gave way to the fool, or when the anticipated gave way to the unanticipated, and when laughter was the mode that brought us through gridlock. If my account of fieldwork here has the look of an orderly sequence of activities and intentions, it is because, as philosopher Alphonso Lingis suggests, after the fact of discomposure, one finds ways of putting it to task.[126] There were many occasions when unexpected and unanticipated events knocked me off balance, but the only residue of those surprises I can pinpoint now are the times when shame or hilarity overtook the situation. Many of my conversations with timber plantation laborers about marriage were accompanied by wild laughter and intense hilarity. I still wonder what that laughter signified.[127] To the extent that we were able to laugh and weep together, we found(ed) a language in which to share, partially, some sense of what was at stake in daily struggles to secure life and livelihood. I remain acutely aware of the limits of such founding and sharing in the diverging trajectories of our lives since that time.[128]

THE SHAPE OF THE ARGUMENT

The book examines a labor regime in South Africa organized around the cultivation and harvesting of timber, the extraction of value and its augmentation by a nutrition intervention. By taking the privately owned timber plantations and the surrounding communal areas (under customary authority) as a space in which labor power is constructed for the production of timber and profit, I show how concepts of bodily capacity and political subjectivity are folded into late liberal projects of governmentality and productivity. Specifically, I show how the concept of *amandla points to, and draws together,* shifting conditions of possibility for forging persons as ethical actors in a particular postcolonial zone of labor and extraction.

Each of the chapters, while analytically distinct, carries forward a common set of questions regarding the imaginative and creative effort required to make it possible to live in the rural hinterlands of KwaZulu-Natal, South Africa. At the center of the book is the labor regime in the timber plantations of northern KwaZulu-Natal. My aim here is to set it in what Elaine Scarry calls the "larger representational context."[129] The difficulty is in parsing what is context from what is the labor itself, given that so much effort must be expended in many directions at once. This is what each of the chapters attempts to draw out. Scarry suggests that work is a subject that in some fundamental way is very difficult to represent partly because its essential nature is action—perpetual, repetitive, habitual. It requires a richness of elaboration, attention to the physical continuity of the worker and his or her materials. "Out of something modest," she says, "comes something immodest (survival, self-recreation, and recreation of activity and new parts of the world)."[130]

This introduction has sketched the broad concerns of the book. Chapter 1 focuses on the labor regime itself, the working day, and the substance of the nutritional intervention that sought to augment bodily capacity and improve productivity. Here I explicate the relationship between labor power and amandla as a singular index of histories of exploitation, abstraction, and repair. Chapter 2 provides an account of the history of forestry and labor in South Africa, in relation to these particular plantations, to show how labor power, as a structuring concern, emerges from within, and subtends, the social fact of amandla, that is, the work of repair, and the circulations of sustenance and substance.

Chapter 3 describes a "game of marriage," umshado wokudlala, that women in the plantations play, and which reflexively deploys a poetics of gesture, linguistic play, and contextual camouflage. Here I show how the game itself "points," in the metalinguistic sense, to the political implications of a praxiographic mode of reflection on and critique of the work of repair.[131] However, constituting kinship is not only a question of mediating and managing substance, but also about establishing, contesting, and reformulating grammars of intimacy and desire, norm and law. Chapter 4 thus turns to another set of materials that augment capacity, while also attending to the conceptual difficulty of claims about "substance" that underpin the body's capacities as well as anthropology's attempts to rethink kinship and relatedness. Here I examine a set of popular curatives that became infamous during the height of the struggle for access to antiretroviral therapy in the mid-2000s, and yet their provenance and action remain poorly understood. I show how the genealogy and operations of these substances are implicated in the ordinary work of constituting relatedness through vulnerability, and thus provide one point of articulation of a distributed work of repair.

Chapter 5 provides the final key to the work of repair, in that it shows how amandla informs both situated and situating metareflexive action— that is, the capacity to navigate distinct topologies of life. The chapter considers how folded, looping histories of spatial thinking configure health surveillance and plantation labor in postcolonial KwaZulu-Natal, the better to trace out the modalities through which people's lives are made possible, conditioned, qualified, constrained, or canceled. I show how the plantation is a topological space in which life, labor, and value become knots in a fragmented terrain whose structural forms condition the relations between life and its milieu, between people and things, and between virus and value. The plantation is one topology in which space, territory, and cartography operate to produce the context in which labor and its abstractions arise as problems to be managed, intervened in, and resolved. Another is the fluid topology of HIV surveillance that combines vicinities, persons, and virus as hot spots or intensities. The third is the work of children in composing their own maps, pointing to the layering and knotting of these events, histories, and vicinities.

In the conclusion, I reflect on the differentiated positions and perspectives that amandla, the ethical substance of the work of repair, affords or elicits; and what is capacitated or incapacitated in action and reflection on amandla.

1

LABOR POWER AND AMANDLA

This chapter examines the meanings of "power" that animate concern with "labor power" from the point of view of the laboring body and its capacity to work. Descriptively, the chapter focuses on the working day, the measurements that produce a population of laborers, the nutrition intervention, and the concern with capacity that animates the calculation of calories and profits. What emerges is not simply "power over" or the operation of governmentality in the production and extraction of value, though certainly these are key concerns; rather, I show how the various "capacities" at stake in the plantations entail particular modes of subjectivation in the disciplining of outsourced labor, the care for and by team members, the effort to sustain extended networks of dependents, and the navigation of obligations that present themselves in everyday life, each of which is required to endure the demands of the plantation. If the nutrition intervention reveals the coordinates of capital's investments in the capacity to labor, the ordinary concern with amandla shows instead how the capacity to work and the availability of the materials of sustenance are not abstract questions so much as embodied, material, grounded questions about the nature of abstraction. The chapter shows how the rhythms, coordinations, and improvisations required of bodies and relations in the plantations locate amandla deep within the folds of flesh and language. It is this folded relation between labor power and amandla that emerges as a singular index of histories of exploitation, abstraction, and repair.

For the women of Shikishela and Mfekayi who worked in the plantations, the day began at 3:00 A.M., giving them just enough time to prepare water and snacks for the day before walking for thirty minutes to an hour to a meeting point where the contractor's truck collected them. The rural paths and roads were dangerous in the dark, and they worried about falling prey to izigebhengu, thieves or criminals, along the way. Then it was an hour or more on the tractor-transport as it did the rounds picking up laborers from the communal areas adjacent to the forests. The work started at 6:00 A.M., when harvesting and silviculture contractor teams headed off to their allotted forest compartments. Every morning as the sun rose, before they set to work, the induna, or team leader, led her charges in prayer and song, followed by a "toolbox talk" by the team's safety officer.[1]

Silviculture laborers planted, sprayed, weeded, pitted, hoed, or cleared. It was less intensive work than harvesting and thus more sought after. Harvesting teams, in contrast, had a strict division of labor: operating chainsaws, measuring the timber into lengths, debarking, stacking, and loading. Each worker performed a single activity, repetitively. The most arduous of these activities was debarking, which entailed swinging an axe at the bark of the fallen tree to strip it, remaining bent at the waist for eight consecutive hours. Protective clothing was provided by the contractor and had to be worn by all forest workers, but debarkers in particular had to wear shin pads, steel-capped boots, boot covers, rubber gloves, hard hats, and visors.[2] It made for sweaty, hot, and backbreaking work, the coordination, organization, and sequencing of which depended on the embodied, syncopated rhythms of capital, kin, and local authority.[3]

The silence of hard labor was broken when cooked food was delivered at 10:00 A.M. Two small, community caterers had been contracted to supply standardized hot cooked meals to the 1,263 laborers in the two plantations in Mpukunyoni. They were mentored by ESS, a subsidiary of the Compass Group, a global food supplier that provided several million meals a day around the world, learning what it took to supply industrial quantities of food that were "culturally appropriate," "tasty," "nutritious," and profitable. Various formats were tested: where possible, the catering contractors would arrive with large steaming pots out of which they dished the food onto plates or into Tupperware boxes; in some instances the boxes were packed before heading to the plantation. The difficulty of keeping the food hot enough to prevent the growth of bacteria was a logistical challenge. In more remote plantation compartments, dry ration packs were given out—no less calculated for their caloric and nutritive value but far less popular or satisfying.

The silviculture teams I followed finished working by 2:00 P.M. on most days; harvesting teams would typically finish at 4:00 P.M. to allow laborers to complete their quota for the day. Then there was an hour's wait at the plantation gate or nearby filling station while other contractor teams completed their tasks, so that the transport trucks could efficiently return workers to their various pickup points, followed by the final walk home of up to an hour. It took fourteen hours on average from leaving home in the morning to returning in the late afternoon. Every weekday, week in and week out, the teams worked the trees, compartment after compartment.

Forest managers, contractors, and laborers all spoke of a general increase in the number of women employed in the timber sector in South Africa in the twenty years after the end of apartheid, tracking the national trend observed by Daniela Casale and Dorrit Posel of a feminization of the labor force as the mining sector shed jobs and more women found employment in cities in the service and retail sectors.[4] While men still outnumbered women in plantations around the country in 2012, there was a much higher proportion of women laborers in the plantations of northern KwaZulu-Natal (reasons given for this by managers and contractors varied, and I found no reliable statistics). Of the teams I observed, roughly two-thirds of the workforce consisted of women, although a strictly gendered division of labor was maintained and no women wielded a chainsaw or measured the lengths of the timber. Men worked as truck drivers, chainsaw operators, or stackers, while women worked as debarkers, weeders, sprayers, and so on.

As an interlocking community of small groups interacting closely through repetitive and dulling work, the women supported each other to complete tasks, to survive the physical demands of the labor, to endure the boredom of its repetitions, and to pass the time while waiting for transport home. Proxemic intimacies drew on and produced bonds of friendship, neighborliness, and kinship in enduring and surprising ways. The companies that operate the Nyalazi and Dukuduku plantations contract laborers from within a five-kilometer radius of the plantations, partly to maintain a corporate social responsibility profile framed by the Black Economic Empowerment charter (BEE),[5] and partly to address the growing political pressure to resolve land compensation and restitution claims.[6] Thus, many of the workers had relatives from the same clan (isibongo) in their teams. Indeed, most workers were mothers and daughters, fathers, brothers, lovers, municipal councilors, or chiefly subjects. In this space of industrial production, authority and intimacy within the plantation overlapped with, reinforced, and pulled against authority and intimacy outside the forest: councilors, elders, children, occupational health officers, plantation security, auditors, neighbors, izinduna (chiefs), izinyanga (healers), izintombi (girls), and izinsizwa (boys).[7] At the same time, small-scale Black contractors who employed these workers are part of an emergent labor elite that represents a broader pattern of "accumulation-from-below."[8]

One small-scale harvesting contractor I followed had three teams each delivering one thousand tons of timber per month. Most harvesting contractors employed many more teams, with contracts for many more tons of timber. Typically, a team consisted of ten "debarkers," a supervisor, a chainsaw operator, and a chainsaw conductor. For a team of ten "debarkers," all of whom were women, the workload calculation was forty debarked trees per woman per day. In winter, when it was easier to debark because the trees had a higher moisture content, about 80 percent of the team members completed their quota for the day. In summer, it was much harder to debark the trees because the bark was tightly bound to the wood, and the temperature was uncomfortably high.[9] In the heat of summer only about 50 percent of the team completed their quota for the day. What was not completed on one day had to be completed by that worker the next day to be counted as a day's work by the contractor. Thus, a woman who worked twenty-two days in a month might be paid for only fifteen days.

Most laborers were employed on a short-term contract that satisfied the existing labor law surrounding forest work. In 2006, the South African minimum wage was R834 per month (USD 122 in 2006); in 2009, the minimum wage had increased to R1,947 per month (USD 134), although I found that forestry workers went home with less than R1,000 per month (USD 69 in June 2009).[10] For a day's labor, that is, the completion of the daily quota, the wage in 2009 was around R55 (USD 7.20).[11] The day's labor was recorded in a register, along with days absent, accidents, incidents, and the maintenance of equipment, all used to calculate the forest worker's monthly wage. Workers who missed six consecutive days were dismissed for breach of contract. It was possible to underpay for days because the "incomplete" days were recorded under "absenteeism."[12] For harvesting contractors, the longer the timber sat stacked in the forest drying out, the lighter it became and the less they were paid upon delivery to the mill. The sooner the timber could be delivered, the closer it came to the contracted price. On occasion, extra teams had to be hired to avoid defaulting on the contract.

Capital costs, safety regulations, and transport costs all eroded the margins of profit for contractors. A strict auditing regime to mitigate the dangers associated with timber plantations, ensure minimum labor conditions, and maintain productivity obligated each laborer to avoid accidents, appear consistently at work, and take care of equipment. Hours worked and days absent were strictly monitored. Each contractor team had to employ a safety officer who recorded "near misses," accidents, oversights, and transgressions of any kind. Each month the paper trail was audited to make sure that all safety talks were given, all equipment maintained, all injuries reported. Any transgression was punished with a yellow or red card, forcing the closure of operations and the loss of revenue for the contractor and laborer. The self-reporting format obscured all but the most serious infractions and injuries.

Each task was defined and evaluated on the occupational health and safety risks to the worker by a team of Occupational Health Officers employed by Mondi. For example, among silviculture crews, "chemical weed control" required walking on uneven ground, the use of both arms, lifting and carrying, being in abnormal positions, and repetitive back movements. Each of these activities was evaluated according to its severity and impact on the worker's body, each in this case scoring a maximum of six, meaning "constant." A hard hat, goggles, elbow-length gloves, safety boots, breathing apparatus, reflective vest, and plastic apron must thus be worn at all times when working with herbicides, pesticides, and insecticides. For a debrancher, debarker, or denotcher working in harvesting, prolonged standing, use of both arms, eye-hand coordination, communication, near vision, far vision, and repetitive back movements all scored a maximum frequency of six. Safety equipment for these tasks included a hard hat, gloves, safety boots, metatarsal protectors, shin pads, and a reflective vest. Fitness criteria included twenty-thirty vision in both eyes, depth perception, eighty-five-degree field of vision, and controlled blood pressure and diabetes mellitus. The control of hazard exposure included noise less than 85 decibels, heat less than 30 WBGT, radiation exposure of no more than 5 millisieverts per year, and minimizing vibration on the whole body. As a result of these auditing techniques, injuries and fatalities in the plantations fell dramatically, even while absenteeism, illness, turnover, and replacement of workers intensified.[13]

FIGURE 1: Women debarking eucalyptus trees. Photograph by Jeanette Clarke.

MEASURES OF THE WORKING BODY

If the working body of the laborer and the population of plantation labor-ers constitute one axis along which life is capitalized and governed, it is because they have been extruded as calculable and governable terms within a broader matrix of racialized value. The folding together of labor power and amandla, as orthogonally posed questions of value, operates precisely through techniques of measurement and the ability to synchronize rhythms of the body, of neighborly obligations, and of domestic economies with those of the plantation system.

Three sets of data inform this argument. The first is from ergonomic re-search contracted by Mondi to inform its labor reforms; the second is from the Africa Centre's Demographic Surveillance System; and the third is my own small survey of plantation laborers. In the winter of July 2005 in Richmond, KwaZulu-Natal, and in the summer of March 2006 in Mbombela (which at the time was called Nelspruit), Mpumalanga, research teams from the Uni-versity of KwaZulu-Natal in conjunction with the Institute of Commercial

Forestry Research (ICFR) conducted studies on "rural black [*sic*] South African forestry workers" who were using manual motor methods of harvesting.[14] They noted that "South African forestry workers perform heavy physical labor which has been compared to that of endurance athletes and as such, requires large intakes of both energy and carbohydrates."[15] The nutritionists examined energy intakes per shift, carbohydrate consumption (daily and per shift), protein and fat consumption, cholesterol intake, and fiber. Little had been known empirically about workers' daily energy requirements, especially those of "female forestry workers." Earlier research had concentrated on the energy requirements of male chainsaw operators during shifts rather than on the nutrient requirements of all job categories of forestry workers of either gender over the entire day. The study sought to observe nutritional processes empirically rather than estimate energy needs using general guidelines.

Worrying about the extremely high rates of HIV among plantation laborers, the authors pointed out that "in addition, if HIV positive, [workers'] nutrient needs would be further increased."[16] The report drew on earlier research that reported average energy intakes of between 5,967 to 9,000 kJ/day for rural, Black South African adults and compared these data with those for forestry workers in developed countries whose reported energy intakes ranged between 17,832 kJ/day to 23,032 kJ/day.[17] They concluded that the energy intake of "local workers" was inadequate: "inadequate energy results in early fatigue and the inability to work effectively which in turn impacts on productivity. It also leads to the suppression of the immune system which accelerates the progression from HIV to AIDS"; this is in addition to a range of morbidities associated with highly exploitative labor and conditions of severe poverty.[18] Considering the hot, harsh environment of the plantations, the compulsory protective clothing, and the restricted access to fluids, timber plantation laborers are "predisposed" to dehydration, which leads to "reduced physical performance combined with impaired mental concentration and decreased physical coordination [which] reduces productivity and increases the potential for injury in an already hazardous occupation."[19]

The nutritional assessments of "forest workers" in Mbombela and Richmond thus produced standardized measures of nutrition and effort despite radically different social and political contexts. Richmond is infamous for being the center of the "killing fields" of the civil war of the 1980s between

ANC and IFP.[20] Nelspruit was renamed Mbombela in 2009 as part of a broader effort to Africanize public life in South Africa as a corrective to the long history of colonial oppression. It was an important stop on the trade route to the Mozambican coast and is now one of South Africa's fastest-growing cities. In Richmond, harvesting teams of ten were paid as a team, and maintained constant members; they received a large ration pack every week of beans, cake flour, salt, sugar, soy, and mealie meal; and the study was conducted just before payday. In Mbombela, they worked in large groups; did not receive ration packs but rather a bag of maize meal monthly; and the study was conducted just after payday, in the week of large civic "service-delivery" protests and two general strikes. In both sites, the vast majority of workers resided in compounds within the plantations. In Richmond, most workers (largely male) prepared their own food, while in Mbombela, half the sample had their food prepared by someone else and most women cooked for themselves. The incidence of chronic diarrhea was higher in Richmond (17 percent) than in Mbombela (9 percent). In Mbombela, chronic episodes of vomiting were reported by just 2 percent of the sample, while the question was not asked in the Richmond study. In neither site did the majority of workers use conventional medicines or "herbal or vitamin preparations."[21]

There were other differences between these two study sites. The Richmond group consisted of young migrant laborers who were mainly illiterate and had very little work experience. In comparison, the Mbombela group appeared to be an older, nonmigrant labor force who were more literate and had greater work experience. Fewer of the Mbombela workers felt that they were healthy, and yet they attended the clinic less than those working in Richmond. The average Body Mass Index (BMI) of workers in Mbombela was 22.3 kg/m2 and in Richmond was 22.2 kg/m2, in the middle of the normal range, although "the males and females BMI in both areas was significantly lower than that found in Kwambonambi [sic], just to the south of Mtubatuba] and that of the overseas forestry workers."[22] The BMI of New Zealand loggers was 28.4 kg/m2,[23] 23.64 kg/m2 for Polish fellers, and 28.1 kg/m2 for Polish assistants. By these measures, 14 percent (Mbombela) to 18 percent (Richmond) were malnourished, 65 percent (Mbombela) to 72 percent (Richmond) were normally nourished, and 10 percent (Richmond) to 19 percent (Mbombela) were either overnourished or carrying a high muscle mass. Because recommendations at the time for HIV-positive individuals was a BMI above the normal range of between 25 to 29.9 kg/m² to allow leeway for weight loss as a consequence of infections, vomiting, or diarrhea, these workers were seen not to have excess weight to buffer the effect of HIV/AIDS.[24] While the diet of Richmond workers appeared to meet their energy needs, almost half of the men and a quarter of the women in the Mbombela group were not consuming enough energy for inactive people, let alone those involved in heavy physical activity. In conclusion, the Mbombela case was considered "more representative of the general situation in forestry" despite the low number of women participating in this survey (in 2006 the Mbombela group included 38 percent women; by 2009 the Mtubatuba/St Lucia region had a far higher proportion of women, around two-thirds, although exact numbers were not available). The study was important because it formed the basis for the nutritional intervention that was piloted by Mondi in 2008 and reveals its reliance on a conception of the human body as a steam engine that transforms calories into work. Those data give no indication of the broader social context of the laborers whose energetics were so measured.

Working with two women as assistants, Ntombizodumo Mkhwanazi and Ntombifuthi Nsibande, I conducted a small survey in June 2009 of 107 laborers who worked for three contractors in the Dukuduku and Nyalazi plantations. The survey respondents were self-selected from the group of laborers present during the three weeks in which the survey was conducted. A brief summary of some of the more noteworthy results is useful, bearing in mind the relatively small size of the sample and the nonrandom nature of the selection process. We relied on a range of metrics for characterizing conditions of life for timber plantation laborers in northern KwaZulu-Natal, while remaining attentive to the complexity of residence patterns and local modes of reckoning relatedness.[25]

Of the sample, 90 percent of the respondents were women; 27 percent were between twenty and twenty-nine years old, 21 percent between thirty and thirty-four, 20 percent between thirty-five and thirty-nine, 15 percent between forty and forty-four, and 15 percent over forty-five. Of that group of respondents, the majority were involved in planting (33 percent), spraying (29 percent), or debarking (12 percent), while another 9 percent were part of other aspects of harvesting. This is likely due to the self-selecting nature of the sample, as harvesting laborers were unable to take time off from their work to participate in the survey. Thirty-six percent of the sample had been laboring in the timber plantations between four to six years, while those who had worked the longest (more than ten years) were over fifty years old. Households of laborers had on average 5.5 members, while 21 percent of households had six members. While some laborers lived alone in company barracks, most lived in adjacent rural areas; thus 22 percent lived with four children in the home, while 28 percent lived with five or six children, and some households counted many more children as dependents.

We did not ask about income amounts because the limitations on the survey would have rendered the results meaningless; rural household income and asset dynamics in South Africa are subtle and complex, requiring specific methods and tools to make credible claims.[26] However, I knew from interviews with laborers that (take-home) monthly wages ranged between R800 and R1,200 (USD 100–160); survey respondents reported that in 55 percent of households, they were the sole wage earners; and in 29 percent of households, a brother or sister also earned a wage. In 89 percent of laborers' households, at least one person received a government welfare grant, in 28 percent of cases this being the laborer herself. Others included mothers (23.6 percent), sisters (18.9 percent), or grandparents (8.5 percent). Thirty-seven percent reported not having any livestock at home, while of those who reported having livestock of some kind, most had chickens (51 percent) and very few had any cattle or goats (3.7 percent for each).[27] I conducted this survey in the middle of winter (June 2009), during which about a third of this group reported not growing any vegetables at home (living in hostels or compounds accounts for a small portion of this); very few grew either maize (3.7 percent) or cabbage (2.8 percent) at this time of year, while 49 percent grew spinach (a range of other crops were grown by a small number of workers).[28]

Households with one member involved in plantation labor tended to be better off than those with none, although livelihoods were broadly similar to those across the uMkhanyakude district.[29] These data are supported by those collected annually by the Africa Health Research Initiative (AHRI, formerly the Africa Centre for Health and Population Studies) since 2001 on approximately 90,000 people in 11,000 households in a Demographic Surveillance Area (DSA) adjacent to the plantations around Mtubatuba. The number of people laboring in the timber plantations who are residents of AHRI's DSA is not known; however, for "rural" residents of the DSA, those whose financial situation was deemed "poor or extremely poor" were estimated to be 41.7 percent in 2006; adults experiencing hunger were at 16.3 percent; children experiencing hunger at 11.5 percent; and those with employment (aged 18–65) at 26 percent. In 2006, 64.3 percent of rural residents lived below the poverty line.[30] In 2009, 37 percent of household members were eligible for an "older person's grant" or state pension, almost all of whom received it; 87 percent of households were age-eligible for a child support grant, but only 43 percent of those received one. The data from my survey accord with those of AHRI that suggest that households with at least one member working in the timber plantations were better able to access government transfers.[31]

No reliable HIV prevalence or incidence data are available for different sectors in this locality, such as forestry, sugar, mining, conservation, or industrial work. However, to give a sense of the scope of the pandemic among female timber plantation laborers in northern KwaZulu-Natal, I have combined data on HIV prevalence rates in AHRI's DSA with data from my survey of timber plantation laborers. In the uMkhanyakude district, where AHRI collects annual HIV and demographic surveillance data, HIV prevalence was estimated to be 24 percent in the general population in 2010.[32] Certain age groups, particularly among women, have extremely high prevalence rates. Peak HIV prevalence among women aged 30–34 years was observed at 59 percent while among men aged 35–39 prevalence peaked at 53 percent. I infer (figure 2) an estimated HIV prevalence for each age group of female laborers in my survey by using the age-graded population prevalences from AHRI surveillance data. Assuming that timber plantation laborers had a pattern of prevalence similar to those within the DSA, female laborers aged 25–39 (representing the majority of women laborers) could have been expected to have HIV prevalence greater than 50 percent in 2009.[33]

NUTRITION'S CALCULATIONS

Based on the nutritional studies described above, the nutrition intervention program I observed was designed to supplement workers' diets with one hot, cooked meal per working day for 12,000 workers. By 2010, the number of workers fed by the program had been reduced to 8,050. Menus that were "ethnically sensitive" were designed to deliver a varied menu of 35 percent of daily energy requirements at R23 (USD 3) per meal.[34] Three weekly menu

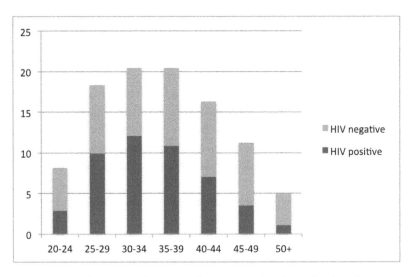

FIGURE 2: Stacked graph of HIV prevalence (percent) and age of timber plantation laborers in northern KwaZulu-Natal.

variations were designed with specific food items for catering contractors to comply with. It was important for meals to be delivered above 63°C in order to eliminate bacteria growth and because they would be tastier and thus more acceptable. "Community-based" catering contractors were "mentored" by a global meal supply corporation that taught them how to prepare large quantities of meals while generating profits (sourcing cheaper products, quantities of ingredients, the efficient chopping of vegetables, using meat with more bones, avoiding unnecessary garnishes, etc.). By drawing on regional agro-industrial supply networks for nonperishable food products, such as soy mince, beans, maize meal, and rice, and national suppliers of meat and vegetables, the contractors were able to invest profits in better transport vehicles and kitchen equipment. During 2009, Mondi planned to start several "community-based food gardens" to grow the vegetables for the kitchens, although it was unclear to what extent the food program was able to rely on these gardens. "Community" here is a slippery referent, drawing on both scalar and racial topologies. It refers indexically to the size of the catering operation established (i.e., a microenterprise), the relative distance from forestry operations (within one hundred kilometers), and the target of redress for historical injustice—Black Africans.

The question of nutrition in the timber plantations of South Africa first arose in relation to the impact of manual harvesting on the body of the worker, although in its earliest expression it was functional to the relative profitability of mechanized harvesting. Ergonomic conditions in the mines and then the plantations were important considerations in terms of time lost to injuries and fatalities through accidents. The drive to entirely mechanize the harvesting of timber, starting in the 1960s, was checked by the relative costs of machinery and labor; in the era of outsourced labor and postapartheid political pressures concerning land claims and economic empowerment, the use of manual harvesting, and the occupational health of the worker added an ethical dimension to the political economy of contractor-based timber production. As Scott et al. show, the extremely heavy demands manual harvesting placed on the worker's body are no less severe today, although its impact is more accurately gauged and Occupational Health and Safety protocols are more precisely targeted.[35] Whereas workers had been housed and fed by grower-producers until the 1990s, the return to corporate "responsibility" for the feeding of laborers after 2005 was premised on studies of nutrition, ergonomics, economics, and organizational structure. Thus, the timber corporation responded to the crisis of timber plantation labor in the 2000s by initiating a series of labor reforms of which the nutrition intervention formed one part and carried a range of moral, social, and political projects.

In late 2009, the corporation surveyed the laborers for their responses to the food program, asking questions about taste, acceptability, whether they felt stronger (84 percent said yes), happier (96 percent said yes), whether the caterers were friendly, whether the food was enough or too much, if anything was missing from the meal, if it was cooked properly, how many took their food home (38 percent did), how many brought their own food to the forest (78 percent did), how many ate anything before leaving home in the morning (35 percent did not; those who left home earlier tended not to eat), if they knew that a hot meal was more nutritious, why they weren't able to eat all their food at once, to whom they gave the food they took home (68 percent to a child), and so on.[36] In seeking to perfect the logistical coordination of a nutritious meal, the survey sought to produce a body of knowledge that would allow Mondi to advise the catering contractors, report to shareholders, and advertise its corporate social responsibility performance. The standardization of measurements (of diets and bodies) and categories ("the worker" or "the contractor," or "debarking" as an activity) have been crucial to the formulation of the nutrition intervention as an act of repair on the part of the corporation—that is, to the coordination and arrangement of the materials of sustenance that so fundamentally shape social life. In generating such a body of knowledge, various measures were brought together: taste, happiness, cultural acceptability, injury, absenteeism, bodily strength, food contamination, and all the social relations around food outside the plantations, for example, those who prepare breakfast or dinner for the laborers, the children, parents, or neighbors who receive leftovers, even the animals who pick up the scraps. Thus, multiple relations were indexed by the event of the hot, cooked meal in the plantation, and their coordination and arrangement extended beyond the limits of the plantation labor regime, bringing together kin relations, corporate management, contractors, and political authority.

FEEDING THE MOTOR

As a number of historians have shown, the development of the metaphor of the human body as motor in the mid-nineteenth century articulated a vision of society powered by universal energy and explained the astonishing productivity of the industrial revolution in Europe.[37] Anson Rabinbach's history of the "human motor" shows how the vision of the body as the site of energy conservation and conversion lent credibility to the ideals of socially responsive liberalism in the nineteenth century, which could be shown to be consistent with the universal laws of energy conservation: expanded productivity and social reform were linked by the same natural laws. Thus, various utopian social and political ideologies of the early twentieth century all viewed the worker as a machine capable of infinite productivity and, if possessed with "true consciousness," resistant to fatigue. Accompanying the nineteenth-century scientific discoveries of energy conservation and entropy was the endemic disorder of fatigue—the most evident and persistent reminder of the body's intractable resistance to unlimited progress and productivity.

The conflation of the natural and social sciences around the problem of labor power and its institutionalization in various contexts, constituted a key element in a new form of social modernity, one in which social control and enlightenment were intertwined. The concepts of energy and fatigue reflected the paradox of this social modernity: affirming the endless natural power available to human purpose while revealing an anxiety of limits—namely, the fear that the body and psyche were circumscribed by fatigue and thus could not withstand the demands of modernity. The development of a body of social knowledge concerned with work was premised on a "scientific" construction of a model of work and the working body as pure performance, as an economy of energy, and also as a pathology of work. The range of new disciplines concerned with this new modernity—social statistics, social medicine and hygiene, and a science of work—framed political arguments and influenced their outcome. It is this web of ethical, social, and political arrangements enabled by the science of the moving body, along with anxieties about the limits of fatigue, that drew together industrialized and colonial economies of value production: mines, plantations, military regiments, and garrisons all came to develop concerns with nutrition and the efficient operation of the body.[38]

In *The History of Sexuality*, Michel Foucault argues that modern biopower is constituted by two poles linked by a cluster of relations: (1) the body as a machine, "its disciplining, the optimization of its capabilities, the extortion of its forces, the parallel increase of its usefulness and its docility, its integration into systems of efficient and economic controls"; and (2) a biopolitics of the population centered on propagation, births and mortality, the level of health, life expectancy and longevity, with all the conditions that can cause these to vary.[39] In thinking through the concern with the performance of the body, its anatomy and biology, as individual and species, within and around the plantations, I am concerned with the way in which power "invest[s] life through and through" in order to produce this population of laborers.[40] As the history of labor in northern KwaZulu-Natal shows, it is not the bare life common to all that has been at stake in the racialization of territory and the extraction of profit but rather the qualifications and specifications of life in its particularities. The corporations' concern with the productivity of labor and its well-being, as the various attempts at labor reform and amelioration of the conditions of life around the plantations attest, is also an ethical project that extends beyond *zoe*, or "bare life," and seeks to establish the extent and limitations of *bios*, or "qualified life."[41]

The nutrition intervention initiated in 2009 is thus the "prime material" for diverse ethical projects; its articulation with amandla, as one ethical horizon, is fundamentally constitutive. The picture of bodily effort and techniques of administration that informed the design of the nutrition intervention have particular genealogies that animated its piloting and implementation. Indeed, the calculation of calories and the measurement of the energetics of the "human motor" that underlie the program began in nineteenth-century European science and social reform projects, at the center of the biopolitical state.

AMANDLA AS ETHICAL SUBSTANCE

While the corporation's calorific interventions invoke strength as one of the bodily capacities of a "human motor," workers in the plantations talk about amandla. The ways in which people talk about amandla in isiZulu reference a range of capacities that have to do with production, reproduction, efficacy, strength, and vitality, particularly with respect to the gut and its social meanings, but also in relation to earning a wage or being able to pay bridewealth.

Denoting strength, power, or capacity, amandla itself is a particularly potent word in South African public life. From the mythology surrounding the early nineteenth-century Zulu king Shaka kaSenzangakhona and the modes of power and virility associated with his rule; through its explicitly political deployment in the antiapartheid struggle as a rallying cry at funerals and marches; and in the late 2000s, in public critique of former President Jacob Zuma's personal life and the politics of redistribution, *amandla* remains a polyvalent concept in everyday speech. Doke et al.'s English-Zulu dictionary gives as meanings: "1. strength, power; 2. moral strength, power, authority, ability; 3. as an idiomatic expression of a man's virility and semen."[42]

As my interlocutors explained to me in the midst of the timber plantations, amandla also refers to one's social and reproductive capacities. For example, while we were talking about marriage payments of ilobolo (bridewealth), one of my informants, Bashingile, complained that the father of her children had been slow in completing his payments: "Hhawu amandla awasekho / Oh he had no power!"[43] Thus, while its expression as political power (as in the antiapartheid call-and-response of "Amandla! Ngawethu! / Power! To the people!") is most widely recognized, it carries a range of meanings in different contexts. As capacity, strength, force, or virility, amandla is a vital quality of persons (for example, in the prophet Isaiah Shembe's ability to heal), things (the nutritive substances discussed here and in the following chapter), and actions (such as ritual healing or political utterances).[44]

In the timber plantations, amandla indexes the shifting imaginative and material efforts to bring into being a form of moral personhood hinged on a set of relations to others variously conceived. I am not suggesting that the concern with amandla in the plantations is itself a salve to the wounding effects of work; rather, I am tracing the production of a set of concerns with social relations and life potentials that are tightly circumscribed within the South African experience of capital, race, and liberal forms of care. I suggest there are at least two ways to understand this. First, amandla can be understood as an integral part of the history of biopower—from the colonial margin that has always been at the center of Western projects of state making and governance. In describing the form of moral reflection cultivated in Greek and Greco-Roman antiquity, Foucault calls the way in which the individual had to constitute himself as the prime material of his moral conduct through moral reflection "the determination of ethical substance."[45] Foucault's genealogy of the use of pleasure reveals some of the commitments of ethical thought within Euro-American and Christian philosophy; at stake are the bodily and material conditions of that thought. Amandla thus constitutes the "prime material" from which bodily projects and ethical relations are constituted in the plantation. A Foucauldian genealogy of ethical practice helps retrieve one strand of thinking about techniques of the self and moral concern that informs Euro-American governmentalities. However, a more proximate critique of liberal anxieties about the animating forces of authority and power can be routed through an Africanist tradition of praxiological engagement with animism. In particular, as Harry Garuba argues, a more "relational" embrace of ways of knowing and of the ambivalences of animist possibilities within postcolonial thinking celebrates the labile exchanges between things and persons, materials and spirits, speaking and doing, and even epistemologies and ontologies.[46] Rather than revealing the mystification of value in the making of labor power, amandla points to the messy exchanges between psyche and soma, modernity and materiality.

Thus, in examining the meaning of the "power" in "labor power" from the point of view of the laboring body and its capacity to work, amandla opens up the history of the making of a rural wage labor force in its temporal and spatial specificity, and across several converging dimensions of life: political and existential, pragmatic and spiritual. The strengthening of the body at stake in the distribution of the materials of sustenance was always spoken of in terms of amandla, by management, contractors, and laborers. As an investment by the global corporation in the body of the worker, the food sits not as one type of capital alongside another—the worker has already been transformed into an economic agent, an "entrepreneur of himself" whose interest is not in the wage itself but a future earnings stream.[47] Given the concern with high absenteeism, high dropout rates, and the perception that timber plantation labor is a job of last resort, the calculated calories are thus an investment in the "skill" of the worker as a form of capital. That is, the capacity of the body of the worker is the form of capital— "that which makes a future income possible"—most at stake for the corporation.[48] However, the capacities—"capital-ability"—at stake are multiple: for the paper and pulp corporation, it is the capacity to extend the productivity of the laborer's body within a liberal ethical horizon; for the laborers, amandla indexes a thick set of local social projects in and around the plantations: marriage, reproduction, childcare, bodily integrity, and political and spiritual authority.[49]

ENDURANCE AND THE TIME OF AMANDLA

If we take "amandla" around the plantations as a thick concern with contemporary forms of structural violence and the work of navigating the relationship between endurance, ethical substance, and work in this locale, then what does it reveal about the continuities and discontinuities of social life, symbols and their forms, contexts and their disjunctures? Elizabeth A. Povinelli describes the chronotope of "late liberalism" as the shape that liberal governmentality has taken in response to a series of crises of legitimacy posed by anticolonial, new social movements and new Islamic movements since the 1960s.[50] To foreground the question of work as a critical mode of enfleshment within late liberalism is to ask not only about the distribution of employment and the precarious modes of survival in which vast populations are placed, but to ask about the character of work, its involvement in the constitution of laboring bodies, and social worlds brought into being by its coordination. This is all the more critical just as labor in its classical formulations retreats further and further out of reach, and as other forms of work and creative action come into view. In tracking the daily rhythms of the laborers over ten months, I came to understand the importance of waged work in the plantations, government welfare grants, the reliance on kin for childcare and keeping up the home, as well as the array of political, religious, and other associations in which daily life is embedded. In asking about the relationship between endurance, ethical substance, and work in the timber plantations of KwaZulu-Natal, we learn how the history of labor in the timber sector has shaped the lives of a group of women whose orientation to amandla and ethical conduct reveal the different ways in which the work of endurance is constituted, situated, and configured.

Ethnographic description of amandla, then, might proceed by tracking rhythmic structures as a descriptive method amenable to the "essential linking of material conditions, social control, and cultural value."[51] Within the various temporal rounds often assumed to structure nonindustrial modes of work, we can trace the rhythm and rhyme of work and play, the mundane and ritual, ordinary and spectacular, as a register of the specificity of these lifeworlds. Following the ingestion of carefully calculated calories and micronutrients as they confront the concern with amandla opens the gut and the substances that pass through it to the mundane work of endurance that is at stake in the plantations. Amandla indexes the work of repair required to make endurance possible within the specific temporal folds from which well-being is constructed. The continuities and discontinuities of work, labor power, and amandla thus frame the relations in the plantation precisely because of the differential orientations to ethical substance that are revealed in the hot, cooked meals of the nutrition intervention. In examining the relationship between endurance and repair, I have sought to track the ways in which work as an everyday concern of my interlocutors has been transformed over the longue durée from an object of calculation and profit into new modes of subjectivation. In this sense, relations produced by the articulation of plantations and domesticities turn on repair in minor, mundane forms.

The particularities of each of my respondents' lives, then, are located within this distribution of tenses and materials, shifting the question of endurance and exhaustion from a broader historical comparative project on the transformation of labor power to a specific examination of the mark of work on subjectivation within a late liberal regime of capital and biopolitics. In addition to the geopolitical history described in chapter 6, that specificity hangs on the particular history of labor within the South African timber sector. As I show in chapter 5, the materials from which *amandla* is figured as ethical substance are constitutive of the events of kinship in the plantation. Povinelli's rendering of ethical substance in terms of vulnerability, bodily materiality, and embodied potentiality is useful for understanding amandla as critical to the work of repair in the everyday relations of the plantation regime. Because capacity is an embodied, material, and grounded concern, amandla thus reveals the deeply folded relations between flesh and language.[52]

In early 2010, I asked Baba Njojo, a labor contractor whose story I take up in the following chapter, how much of a difference he thought the food program was making to his employees, and whether it improved productivity. "At the moment everything is great. You can see the people are healthier and have more energy. So even though the virus is in their bodies, it's not as effective as it was when they were not eating well and losing a lot of weight." However, it was difficult, he said, to compare how productive younger workers are today with his generation in their youth because they were much stronger physically then:

> Your generation doesn't want to work; they're lazy. Our meals were hardly nutritious, but somehow we were fit. Take me for instance; you can see I'm matured. Growing up we never had pap [maize meal] or rice in our diet; instead we fed on mielies [maize], which we boiled. We had wheat, spinach and sweet potatoes, food that's naturally grown and that we planted ourselves. All the vitamins and nutrients from that food went directly into our bodies and it made us strong. We never binged on junk food, which is primarily the reason we don't age quicker and are still physically well. Whenever we got sick or had flu, we didn't go to doctors but gave ourselves an enema.[53] The potions we mixed using indigenous plants, when we had an enema, actually fought off bacteria, building up our immune system. The plants were still green and fresh and worked at their optimum level in our bodies because they were boiled in pure water. So if you compare your generation with mine you would realize that young people age faster than us because of their Westernized upbringing.

Young people these days are injected with medication from the time they are in the womb, he complained. It was impossible to maintain high levels of productivity when his employees were constantly ill and too weak to work, and thus they should exercise to remain fit so that they could work faster. His technique for staying strong and fit in the plantations was to "steam" under a blanket in order to drain toxic waste from his body, leaving it purified.

"So if you and I had to stand in the sun after I've steamed, my body will be able to withstand the heat, whereas yours would not because you have not done anything to cleanse it." He also drank "herbs" that cleanse his body "via the mouth," which leaves the chest light and clear of phlegm. "The whole process tightens the chest muscles making breathing easier. It's the same as lifting weights; the heaviness builds and tightens your muscles. All these purifying and cleansing things we do help build our muscles and keep us strong. It's a great substitute for exercise." The bodily capacities to which he gestured were indexed by the practices that shaped the body and the temporal horizon in which those practices were seen to exist: "Our customs and practices helped us to grow into the men we are today. It is very different in these times we live in. People are more concerned about making money than taking care of their own health by using the herbs and roots we grew up relying on."

Baba Njojo's analysis of the strength or productivity of his workers did not register the effects of disease and hunger and the compromised freedoms of the postapartheid compact but rather reproduced the spacing of African custom and Western modernity as distinct temporalities. The work of repair to which he gestured—purifying and cleansing—is commonly understood as vital to ensuring the continuing capacities of the body, as maintaining a temporal horizon of possibility. As I show in the following chapter, the articulations of the ligaments of the body are also the ligaments of kinship, and their mattering, in the sense of how such relations are made to matter and are inseparable from the materials of everyday life, is carried in the concern with amandla. The temporal folds of body and capacity in the work of repair is not merely a contemporary concern, as Hylton White suggests in his analysis of ritual. Rather than a simple present to which cultural forms are reactive, amandla points to a more complex question of time and capacity, and is, in itself, a referential capacity that stitches the time of the body to other times, remembered and anticipated.[54] What temporality is proper to the concern with amandla and the question of work? In giving an account of the plantation system as concrete spacing of colony and custom not only through the particular relations of production, but also the refiguring of kith and kin, I have sought to outline the way in which labor power has been transformed from an abstraction and stripping away of human qualities and relations into the material from which diverse ethical aspirations are given form and taken up as capacities brought to bear on the effort to endure under conditions of late liberalism.

2

THE PLANTATION AND
THE MAKING OF A LABOR REGIME

Attending to the work of repair, with amandla as its central concern, reveals how labor power has emerged as a central node in the network of relations that structure the plantation and life on its edges. The history of how this network of relations has emerged is crucial, I argue, for understanding how amandla emerges from within, and subtends, the concern with labor power. In this chapter, I show how the work of repair at the heart of making the world, and worlds, around the plantations habitable is profoundly conditioned by histories of dislocation and extraction. The story of forestry in KwaZulu-Natal and the struggles over territory, labor, and livelihood over the longue durée is best told through the lives of the people working the lines of trees: felling, stripping, pitting, planting, driving, managing, and guarding. In this chapter I sketch out a history of the plantations and offer portraits of the lives of four individuals who were part of a larger group of people I came to know from 2008 to 2010. Their lives sketch the "grounds of all making" in the plantations.[1]

Central to my argument here is the concept of topology, on the one hand, and the way in which it frames, and is composed by, the biographies of these four people, on the other. I show how "the plantation" forms one topos from which a particular problematic comes into view—namely, how labor, and its availability, maintenance, and reproduction in postapartheid South Africa, is constituted by a history of violent conquest and forced removals, on the one hand, and the deeply entangled everyday relations between employers, contractors, kin, neighbors, lovers, on the other. In other words, structural conditions, given particular historical determinations, are taken up within, made sense of, and mediated by everyday relations.

What emerges is the way in which a relational concept of life is crucial for considering the worlds around the plantations because the work of world-making is *topological*. By this I mean two things: First, the relations between persons and things, between labor and the materials transformed by its action, and between historical conditions and biography are both structured and structuring. Second, those relations, and their webs of meaning and power, might be stretched, deformed, or inverted, while retaining some figural familiarity.[2] Thus, the plantations are constituted as one topos or problem space in which colonial conquest, racialized labor, disease, and ecology are brought together, and thereby form the grounds on which the work of repair emerges as topological. One question that arises from this account is how the biographies of particular individuals intersect with the topological force of the plantations.

In the account I offer here, I show how labor power is constructed within the problem space of the plantations as a distinctly situated concern of capital, even as it abstracts value and the relations of production. It is situated in that what counts as work, how it is marshaled, channeled, demanded, or imposed, is fundamentally a product of the delicate filagree of social relations that condition and define local worlds, as anthropology has long sought to show. It is not merely *situated* in the sense that Margaret Lock develops, drawing on vitalist histories of biology: life, or rather all living beings, shapes and is shaped by its milieu, its "environment," that which establishes the conditions of possibility for overcoming the rigors or demands of the moment.[3] Rather, it is what Kaushik Sunder Rajan calls "*multisituated.*"[4] That life is conditioned by "context" and its "relationship" to other relationships is the basis of anthropological knowledge, as Marilyn Strathern shows, and yet what constitutes "the relation"—the object, medium, technique, and telos of social and cultural thought and action, both for anthropology and its others—is an open question. Context and relation, on this reading, are not discrete or single, but always multiple and concatenating, demanding, as Kaushik Sunder Rajan suggests, a "multisituated" approach to knowledge production, ethical interlocution, and political intervention. The argument here, showing how labor power depends on the construction of the plantation as a topos, is complemented by the argument in chapter 5, in which it becomes clear how the work of navigating multiple, entangled topologies is condensed in the concern with amandla and world-making in and around the plantations.

I have interleaved biographical description and historical analysis to draw out the complex entanglements of past, present, and future in the construction of the plantation and its labor force. The four individuals I describe here include, first, J. S. Henkel, my ancestor, who was appointed conservator of forests for Natal and Zululand in 1912 and was the first scientific forester for the region. The second is Luke Mkhwanazi, who, when I met him in 2009, was employed as a security contractor by the paper corporation that owns the plantations. The third is Baba Njojo, once an employee of the corporation, who in his retirement was able to become a contractor employing plantation laborers himself. The fourth is Lindiwe Mbuyazi, a woman employed by Baba Njojo, who had labored in the plantations for many years alongside her daughter, the father of her children, and her mother. Their biographies unspool the densely compacted strata of violent removals, colonial marginalization, and precarious regimes of labor in the plantation.[5] Each figure is thus preceded by an aspect of the plantation system: colonial forestry (Henkel); securing the territory (Luke Mkhwanazi); outsourcing labor (Baba Njojo); and transformations in domesticity (Lindiwe Mbuyazi). Together, they provide a picture of how the plantations emerged as a site, or topos, in which labor power was made alienable, and thus established the conditions of possibility for amandla to emerge as a thick figuration of the work of repair.

COLONIAL FORESTRY: A GHOST AMONG THE TREES

My father's mother's father's father was Carl Caesar Henkel—a great-great-grandfather, in Euro-American kinship terms.[6] C. C. Henkel emigrated in 1856, at seventeen years old, from Hesse, Germany, to what later became known as the Transkeian Territories.[7] As a member of the British German Legion, he had just missed military action in the Crimean War because his regiment had arrived a day too late. Serving as secretary to Baron von Stutterheim,[8] a major general in the British Army and head of the British German Legion, Henkel visited South Africa for eight months and played a significant role in settling German immigrants in the King William's Town area. He then briefly served as an officer in the British East India Company in the suppression of the Indian Mutiny of 1857, during the period in South Africa that became known as the "Great Xhosa Cattle Killing," which led to the starvation and ultimate death of some 70,000 Xhosa people, and the first major military loss of an African polity to European colonizers.[9] After returning to South Africa, C. C. Henkel later became a cartographer in the office of the surveyor general for the Transkeian Territories from 1876 to 1883. It was during this period that he produced a map of the Transkei that is now considered definitive of the colonial imaginary of nineteenth-century conquest in South Africa.[10] He later became the first "chief forest officer" or conservator for the Transkei, based in Umtata, responsible for the conservation of indigenous forests and the development of commercial forestry in the Transkei.[11] His pioneering work in these fields is considered to have greatly influenced the course taken by forestry practice in South Africa.[12]

The spread of ideas and practices first implemented in the full extension of colonial governance by Carl Caesar Henkel had direct bearing on his son, Johannes E. S. Henkel, known as John Spurgeon Henkel, the eldest of his eleven sons.[13] Born in 1871 in Peddie in the Eastern Cape, J. S. Henkel joined the Cape Forest Department in 1888, working in the Eastern Cape for several years before being granted a government bursary to attend the Royal Indian Engineering College at Cooper's Hill in Surrey, where he received a College Diploma. He received the Queen's South Africa Medal for his role as a captain in the Anglo-Boer War, was appointed assistant conservator of forests in the Eastern Conservancy in 1905, and then transferred to the Western Conservancy in Cape Town in 1910 when the Union of South Africa was formed. He was appointed conservator of forests for Natal and Zululand in 1912 and was the first scientific forester for the region.[14] In 1918 he became the chief of the Rhodesian Forest Service.

Henkel's efforts at hydrological and arboreal intervention helped establish, a century later, the material arrangements of silviculture, labor, commodity, kinship, sexuality, and food that I describe here. As conservator of forests for Natal and Zululand from 1912,[15] J. S. Henkel's first order of business was to have the forests and swamps of "Zululand," that area south and north of St Lucia, including the highly contested Dukuduku forest, surveyed and assessed for the development of pine and eucalyptus timber plantations.[16] Those plantations, including Dukuduku, Nyalazi, and southward toward Durban, are now almost entirely under species of eucalyptus hybrids engineered by geneticists at Stellenbosch University to grow faster and straighter with less water;[17] they are the plots that were worked by the women with whom I conducted ethnographic work. When J. S. Henkel surveyed the forests of Dukuduku, the sugar plantations were already marching north from Durban. The timber stands developed for use in the ports and inland at the mines were a late addition to an economy already thoroughly integrated into regional and global markets. Nonetheless, his survey of the forests and the marshes of the Mfolozi Flats began a period of radical environmental and social transformation north of the Mfolozi River.

I start with these two Henkel ancestors to show how my fieldwork in these plantations a century later was tied, uncomfortably, to these arboreal underground threads of race and conquest. It was an uncanny shock to discover, in late 2009, a genealogical connection to the man responsible for establishing this particular landscape and regime of value through the surveying and draining of malarious swamplands and the planting of eucalyptus. What twist of genealogy would place me in those very plantations a century later? It was this uncanny entanglement of the arboreal and the genealogical that drew me to thinking through the traffic between techniques of inscription and description in the production of this locality. A materialist political economy would draw concrete lines between the contours of racialized privilege, histories of colonial governance, and the production of scientific knowledge in the service of a logic of improvement or betterment. A more local idiom might point to the hauntings of ancestral pasts in the present.[18]

My own biography thus loops through this uncanny history of forestry in South Africa. Forestry and the making of territory were at the heart of colonial governance in the former Transkeian Territories (now part of the Eastern Cape province) and later in Natal and Zululand. With the declaration of self-government by the Cape in 1872, the Frontier Wars and rebellions of 1877–88 and the annexations of the late 1880s, the administrative consolidation of colonial authority was finalized by the turn of the century. Chief magistracies of the various regions were amalgamated into the position of chief magistrate, one for Zululand and one for the Transkeian Territories.[19] As Richard Grove has described, forestry in the Eastern Cape and Transkei grew out of the broader development of British imperial conservationism in the Cape and beyond. As official interests in "scientific forestry," the moral "salvation" of South African landscapes, and the sustainability of settler society all merged in the Cape, the formalization of forest administration accelerated, particularly in the 1880s.[20] Following the appointment of the first superintendent of woods and forests to oversee the entire colony and the expansion of conservation efforts in the Eastern

Cape, colonial foresters began to take a greater interest in the vast expanses of forest north of the Kei River, both along the coast and in the mountainous inland areas. The dissemination of colonial authority through the Transkei was expressed through official concern with regulating popular forest use, both African and non-African, and really took off with the formal establishment of the Transkeian Conservancy in the late 1880s with Carl Caesar Henkel as its first head.[21]

The Department of Forestry in "Zululand" came into being with the appointment of G. H. Davies in 1892 to Qhudeni as forest ranger.[22] However, it was the report by the conservator of the Eastern Conservancy, J. Storr-Lister, who had visited all the forests of Natal and Zululand in 1902, that came to form the foundation for the development of forestry in what is now northern KwaZulu-Natal. Apparently, he was "greatly shocked by the manner in which the forests of the Crown Colony were being plundered and wrecked," and in describing the situation as a public scandal, he laid the groundwork for the Zululand Lands Delimitation Commission of 1902–4 to break the old focus of royal power in the east (along the coast) and move the seat of the Mpukunyoni inkosi west. Smaller groupings of Mnqobokazi, Nibele, and Gumede were left in place around the wetlands, but most of the Mpukunyoni territory became Crown Land. The control of the Crown Forests was handed over by the surveyor general to the Department of Agriculture in July 1902, and the first conservator of forests, T. R. Sim, was transferred from the Cape Forest Service and appointed in September 1902.[23]

SECURING THE TERRITORY: APARTHEID AND THE CONSTRUCTION OF THE PLANTATION LABOR SYSTEM

From the beginnings of forestry as an organized sector in South Africa in the early twentieth century, labor has been a serious concern for large capital interests—its costs, upkeep, supply, consistency, discipline, and, in short, its governability.[24] It is in this early history that we can see the making of the plantation as a particular system of relations—that is, as a topos in which labor, territory, and value were forged in the making of capital. As I show here, techniques of dispossession of land are thus inseparable from the techniques of disciplining labor. The story of Luke Mkhwanazi, a security contractor, which follows, shows how these histories of exclusion and discipline conspire to produce the plantation system as I found it in 2009.

The timber plantations and surrounding communal areas are known for their proximity to the renowned coastal wetlands (formerly the St Lucia wetlands, and now called the iSimangaliso Wetland Park) that separate the farms and homesteads from the sea. What came to be known as Zululand for much of colonial history was on the periphery of Zulu politics in the 1800s, although its incorporation into the Bantustan of KwaZulu and claimed genealogical proximity to the Zulu royal house is the story of conquest, strategic realignment, and state intervention over two centuries.[25] Pre-Shakan political formations (i.e., before the Great Disruption of 1815) have been recently revitalized, both in popular and academic registers.[26] Such reappraisals are helpful for understanding ongoing successional disputes around what is known as "traditional leadership," particularly given the fierce fights over mining rights and land claims in areas under customary authority.[27] Who should "own" or govern the plantations and their milieus is increasingly contested as the large paper and pulp corporations put more distance between sites of primary extraction, urban beneficiation, and global distribution.

Archival records show the development of a regime for the governance of forestry labor that postdates that of the mining sector and thus was able to borrow many of its techniques, despite significant differences in the locations from which that labor was sourced and then deployed. While Pondoland was an early source of mine labor in the nineteenth century, with large-scale labor migration from Zululand starting in the late 1880s, migrancy started later in the Mtubatuba/St Lucia region, and had a different trajectory because of the agricultural and plantation economy *in situ*.[28] Labor as a local concern in northern KwaZulu-Natal thus began as a function of large colonial estates experimenting with a range of export crops. After the annexation (in 1888) and incorporation (in 1897) of Zululand, the Natal government appointed a Delineation Commission for Zululand (1902–4) that surveyed and then reserved for "exclusive use" all land used by Natives (residential, agricultural, grazing) based on an assessment of the "history of the native peoples" and land use.[29] All remaining land, particularly along the coastal belt, became Crown land, intended as a potential source of revenue for the colonial economy. While the northern coastal strip had had fifty years of experimentation with various crops, including coffee, tea, arrowroot, sugar, tobacco, and cotton, it was sugar that proved to be the most successful and profitable. It was the success of sugar and the growth in the number of mills in Natal that provided the impetus and investment for extending the rail line north and establishing mills in what later became Mtubatuba in the first years after the Anglo-Boer War.[30]

During the period that the Umfolozi Co-operative Sugar Planters Company took over the St Lucia Mill in 1923 and after, labor became a critical issue for the steady supply of cane to the mills. J. S. Henkel had surveyed the forests in 1917, but it was not until the early 1920s that timber operations in the St Lucia/Dukuduku area were organized and integrated into the commodity networks that connected Mtubatuba with Durban and the rest of the country. Sugar and timber, from the 1920s, have thus been the principal agricultural commodities around which labor has been mobilized in large numbers. The building of rail lines, the planting and harvesting of crops, the maintenance of white farmers' homes, have all depended on both state investment and the disciplined organization of labor, initially Indian labor and later Black African.[31]

Although indigenous forests had been exploited, and mills established in other parts of Zululand, since the late 1880s, it was not until 1926 that afforestation began and exotic varieties of tree species were introduced (initially pine—*Pinus palustris*), initiating the deliberate shaping of the landscape for profitable purposes.[32] Thus, allotments of surveyed land were added in 1928 to the Forest Reserve to enable it to abut the newly completed Zululand railway (and in addition avoid the East Coast fever restrictions on the movement of cattle). Seven thousand acres of forestland were "surrendered" to the sugar plantations on the Umfolozi Flats and alternate land swapped in return in 1946 and again in 1949 (as returning White soldiers from the War were rewarded with land to start sugar farming on the Flats). In 1934, A. W. Bayer and J. S. Henkel, as government-appointed foresters, conducted a series of ecological studies of the Dukuduku forests to determine the stage in the succession of the veld when afforestation could be undertaken without complete cultivation of the soil, the results of which were applied to all plantations along the Zululand coast.[33] As troublesome "squatters" were partially evicted from the Dukuduku forests, and the swamps drained, making the landscape less deadly for both White settlers and Black laborers, the growing plantations (both timber and sugar) soon encountered severe "shortages" of labor, both due to malaria and "resistance to labor" amongst Black African residents.[34]

While the timber sector grew first as a service of the "mineral-energy complex," with demand for timber coming mostly from gold mining and construction until the 1960s, demand from other sectors, in particular paper and pulp for boxes and print, grew substantially in the mid-twentieth century.[35] The state's direct investments in establishing large plantations helped overcome many of the risks and costs inherent in a sector that takes many years for a return to be realized. Thus, from the 1960s onward, through a variety of subsidies and credit facilities, the state supported the growth of a paper and pulp industry, dominated in 2010 by two private companies, Sappi and Mondi, the latter a subsidiary of the Anglo-American Corporation until 2007.

The regimentation of the forestry labor regime was borrowed directly from that of the mines with regard to housing, feeding, health care, and recreation. In criticizing the exploitative system of migrant labor cemented by the policies of the National Party, the 1983 WHO report on Apartheid and Health described a "test chamber" for sorting out potential workers established by a Human Sciences Laboratory for the mining industry, deemed necessary because "not all Africans raised in the mines' periphery will be strong enough to do strenuous work in the mines."[36] "Work capability data" were important for health planning, according to the senior epidemiologist for the South African Medical Research Council, C. H. Wyndham, because they would determine

the siting of Bantu homelands or border areas, or new industries which require hard physical work. In this context, consideration should be given to the improving of the physical work capacities of rural Bantu males. This could be done by better nutrition, particularly more calories and animal proteins, and by improving their health by eradicating endemic diseases, such as malaria and bilharzia, for it is unlikely that the health and welfare of rural populations will be improved by their own efforts.[37]

The availability and stability of labor and the articulation of health as a function of profitability were thus always central features of the system of apartheid economic and spatial planning. Thus the establishment of Mondi in 1967 as a subsidiary of the Anglo-American Corporation with key support from the state deserves special attention in the context of a crisis of reproduction and impoverishment that came to a head in the late 1960s, as apartheid policies of spatial segregation took full effect.[38] Correspondence between the chief Bantu affairs commissioner and the South African Timber Growers' Association (SATGA) shows a sudden concern with recruitment and the spatial organization of labor.[39] The commissioner's instructions concerning the legalities of housing Bantu labor on farms are revealing: in terms of the Bantu Labour Act no. 67 of 1964, adequate housing would have to be given to laborers living on the farms or in the plantations; those in married quarters were not to exceed 3 percent; for those plantations near to Bantustans, growers were to "enable as many Bantu as possible to reside in their homelands under family conditions"; and the number of laborers employed full-time in bona fide agricultural activities was not to exceed the number determined by the Labour Control Board.

Following the 1960 *Report on South Africa's Timber Resources* commissioned by the minister of forestry, it became clear that there were significant problems in the collection and comparison of data from which to make accurate forecasts of demand and price.[40] By 1967, SATGA began to standardize statistics across the sector for planting, wages, measurements, and transportation in order to address decreases in productivity and profit. The key problems of labor were absenteeism, recruitment, and a "lack of discipline," and from the late 1960s, efforts were made to ensure the steady recruitment of labor in collaboration with the sugar industry (who recruited heavily from the Transkei).[41] From 1971, SATGA reasoned that improvements in accommodation and training for their plantation workforce would improve workers' "happiness" more efficiently than increases in wages,[42] and in 1972, sought to collaborate with the cane growers of Natal and Zululand in recruiting from the Transkei. The 1973 Forest Owners Association report on Bantu labor in forestry, on behalf of the Timber Industry Standing Committee on Bantu Affairs, brought to a head many of the industry's concerns with labor and its reproduction. It concluded that "for a reliable, responsible, happy and more efficient labor force, it is recommended that serious and immediate consideration be given to the formulation of a Forest and Forest Products Industry Bantu Labor Policy."[43]

It was at this point that the explicit concern with the worker less as an object of supply and demand and more as an active economic agent was initiated, and the contestations over wages began that transformed the problem of the wage into what Foucault called "capital-ability."[44] Thus, labor power was transformed from mere abstraction to ability—that is, from alienated commodity to the *capacity* to labor and to secure a future "earnings stream," as an investment in human capital.[45] This production of the worker as subject depended on the regulation of the means of sustenance, the ingestion of a dietary regime, and the physical coordination of the racialized body. The concern with the capacity of the laborer thus emerged through the restructuring of the timber regime in response to the political and economic shifts that began in the 1970s and culminated in the transition to the new constitutional order of inclusive citizenship in 1994. The assumption that labor would provide the grounds for citizenship, as a condition of freedom, has a complicated relationship to productivist totalitarianism regimes of the twentieth century, and remained a troubling centerpiece of the post-apartheid social compact, as Franco Barchiesi has made clear.[46]

With roots in the mineral-energy industrial complex, the two major paper producers established by the apartheid state were also directly implicated in the bureaucratic functioning of the system of oppression developed over the course of five decades. The volume of paper required to administer the segregation and surveillance of the population was significant, and as Jacob Dlamini has observed, rather confused and partial, not at all efficient or organized as many have assumed.[47] During the political transition in the early 1990s, state security forces tried to destroy all evidence of their activities by sending huge amounts of paper to be burned in the industrial furnaces of paper companies such as Nampak and Sappi. In 1993, former officials and agents of the apartheid state embarked on an "orgy of destruction," incinerating around 44 tons of paper and microfilm records held by the National Intelligence Service. It took eight months to feed this official archive into the furnaces of Iscor, the state-owned steelworks in Pretoria and Johannesburg, and into the paper companies' private furnaces. The Truth and Reconciliation Commission noted that this had been a conscious effort to "deliberately and systematically destroy a huge body of state records and documentation in an attempt to remove incriminating evidence and thereby sanitise the history of oppressive rule."[48]

Techniques of Dispossession

After 1994, the postapartheid government committed itself to an ambitious land reform project, focusing on three areas: restitution, land tenure reform, and land redistribution. Claims for redress were limited to land lost after 1913, the date of the infamous Natives Land Act in which 8.98 million hectares were "scheduled" as "native reserves," with provision for more land to be "released" in the future. The schedule was based on the existing reserves and locations established during the colonial period, and was intended to preserve a limited rural subsistence base for Black Africans outside of the urban-industrial centers that could then subsidize the migrant labor system by reabsorbing retired workers in old age. It was not designed to support an economically independent Black peasantry. The imposition of hut taxes and other pressures that were imposed to force men into the cash economy was an attempt to draw cheap labor into White-owned industrial and agricultural concerns while preventing Africans from obtaining a stake in cities and towns. Desire for cheap and readily available labor for White farming and industrial ventures drove government strategies to make this labor available through a range of techniques (including importing indentured labor from India and Madagascar, for example) precisely because Black Africans were so reluctant to be drawn away from the systems of reproduction that underpinned domestic economies.[49]

The 1936 Native Trust and Land Act was one of the most significant pieces of legislation in the history of twentieth-century South Africa because it touched the lives of all Black African people.[50] Drawing on the system of trust tenure developed in colonial Natal, the act created a legal body called the South African Native Trust, which later became the South African Bantu Trust, and then the South African Development Trust. In it was vested ownership of all the African reserves. According to the act, the trust was to be administered "for the settlement, support, benefit and material and moral welfare of the natives of the Union."[51] The 1936 Native Trust and Land Act marked out the geographical dimensions of the reserves and created a new category of reserve land, called "released land," designed to legalize the position of new land bought by Africans in the "recommended" areas since the 1921 recommendations of the Beaumont Commission. It allowed for land released from the prohibition placed on African acquisition of land outside the scheduled reserves to be absorbed into the reserves—thereby effectively removing more Black Africans from White South Africa.[52]

Of particular importance to the removals around the iSimangaliso Wetland Park were those conducted under the aegis of conservation, commercial forestry, and military defense. The "Mbila triangle" is one example of how contested the removals were for those areas turned into conservation and forestry projects. The excision of the triangle was approved in 1979, in terms of the 1913 Land Act, from the schedule of land allocated for African occupation, and fully excised from Natal in 1981. Sodwana, now a popular scuba-diving beach resort, was also affected in this way. The role of the Kwa-Zulu government in the excisions of these territories was controversial: while it did not approve of the excisions, it was not ignorant of them.

The oral reports of people moved in 1981 from these areas echo the themes that emerged from interviews I conducted with land claimants in 2008. People removed from the missile range zones, for example, were moved several times and received no compensation.[53] Legal maneuvering was particularly intense from the late 1970s through the 1980s. Legal contestations and concomitant ambiguities often allowed undocumented removals to continue from land around St Lucia and the Sodwana Bay area. The SPP reports were not able to document specific removals in the areas around St Lucia, Lake Bhangazi, Sodwana Bay, Nhlozi, or Nyalazi as figures did not exist and formal planning did not record them. Excisions for conservation were apparently justified in terms of compensation to KwaZulu for the loss of Hluhluwe and Umfolozi Game Reserves. However, new afforestation, dam building, and the declaration of new conservation areas all implied the removal of Black Africans from their land. Loss of access to water, grazing, gardens, and other natural resources had a severe effect on communities that were either removed wholesale or simply cut off from resources.

Today, the timber plantations of northern KwaZulu-Natal are situated in the Mpukunyoni Traditional Authority area, which includes Somkhele, the seat of power; Mtubatuba, on the N2 national highway; and St Lucia on the coast.[54] The Mpukunyoni Traditional Authority area had been governed by Inkosi (Chief) Mzondeni Mineus Mkhwanazi, who died in August 2007. After an extended succession dispute in the Durban High Court involving genealogical, archival, and expert research, Mzokhulayo Mkhwanazi was appointed in his place in 2011, settled by appeal to the provincial government and intervention by the Member of the Executive Council (MEC) for Cooperative Governance and Traditional Affairs. He in turn passed away in 2019, and an interim authority, uNdunankulu (Premier) Mkhwanazi, stands in his place until a legitimate inkosi is appointed.[55]

More proximately, these plantations are currently owned by competing forestry interests: Sappi, the South African Forestry Company (SAFCOL), Mondi, its Black-owned subsidiary SiyaQhubeka, and fragments of "outgrower" stands—attempts at "accumulation from below" on communal, customary land. The workers I got to know were all employed by small enterprises contracted by Mondi or SiyaQhubeka. Established in 1967 by the Anglo-American Corporation with a processing plant in Merebank, south of Durban, Mondi is a global packaging and paper corporation employing around 26,000 people with around 100 production sites across more than 30 countries in western and eastern Europe, Russia, and South Africa.[56] In 2010, Mondi owned or leased 380,000 hectares of land in South Africa, of which 243,000 hectares were planted with hardwoods (eucalyptus and wattle species) and softwoods (pine species). In 1997, Mondi gained certification with the Forest Stewardship Council (FSC) in order to maintain access to global pulp and paper markets. In their own words, the FSC was established in 1993 to "promote responsible management of the world's forests" so that customers would be able to "choose products from socially and environmentally responsible forestry."[57] In 2010, Mondi directly employed around 29,000 workers and an estimated average of 21,000 contractors worldwide.

The Security: Luke Mkhwanazi

While the violent histories of colonial dislocation from ancestral lands depended partly on a founding military and legal force, those territories have required constant policing for the extraction of value to continue. The plantations are no different, in that mere firepower has never been sufficient in itself to maintain racialized territorial boundaries, thus requiring complex forms of cooptation and complicity. The story of Luke Mkhwanazi, who facilitated my first entry into the plantations and whose security team guided me to the distant compartments to find the contractor teams at work, suggests a complex story of how the territory of the plantations is secured in the years since the end of apartheid in 1994. As I discovered, his role as security contractor was not merely to keep potential poachers out of the forests but to mediate a series of conflicting interests within and beyond the boundaries of the plantation. While it was in 2008 that Luke Mkhwanazi secured a contract from Mondi to provide security to the Nyalazi and Dukuduku plantations, for many years he had been active in reducing "petty crime" in Shikishela. With a team of eight employees and three off-road vehicles, he policed the perimeter of the plantations, made sure that timber and other forest resources were not "poached" by people living around the timber and conservation land, and prevented fires from being set by those looking for honey.

While he counted himself as an ordinary member of the Shikishela community, Luke himself had once been "visitor," one of those removed from conservation and plantation land in the 1950s and forced to seek the hospitality of those with autochthonous rights in Mfekayi or Shikishela. His mother and father had lived on land now under timber, although he had never returned to that place or sought out the graves of his forebears. Despite being a visitor, Luke had been appointed an induna, or local traditional authority, in 1997 by then Chief Shikishela, after whose lineage this area was named. Luke and two others had volunteered to tackle the growing problem of criminality in the area, and by working with the KwaMsane police force, had been relatively successful in reducing crime.[58] As a result, the chief asked him to take on the position of induna, with its authority inscribed in customary law, because his sons were away. When the chief died, those sons returned from urban employment and squabbled over who should rightly inherit the position. However, Luke's reputation as an evenhanded and upright person had only grown since that time because of his attempts to find income and employment for young men of the area, particularly those he had apprehended.

Two initiatives of his stand out. The first helped reduce forest fires and the massive loss of valuable timber for Mondi. By formalizing access to the plantations for young men from Mfekayi and Shikishela, supervising the extraction of honey from the hives he had set up as a side business (extracting rent from these informal honey purveyors), and limiting the numbers of young men, he was able to eliminate almost all intentional acts of arson in these plantations. A group of fifteen men extracting from thirty to forty hives can fill a twenty-five-liter bucket apiece with honey, each of which would fetch about R700, sold to passing motorists on the N2 highway. Luke calculated that in SiyaQhubeka Forests (SQF) plantations alone, honey worth R1.6 million (USD 205,000) was collected and sold in 2008 by these young men. While Mondi freely allowed honey to be collected on their property, Luke charged the young men who harvested directly from hives he had built an entry fee—a classic form of rent-seeking.

Second, he ensured that the indigenous trees being "illegally" felled in that part of Dukuduku under intense land dispute were kept for young men from Shikishela to carve wooden meat platters from, izingqoko, for sale also along the N2 highway.[59] By helping these young men establish an earnings stream, he was simultaneously helping reduce petty crime (in particular young men preying on women walking to their timber jobs in the early mornings) and bolstering his reputation as a moral figure of safety and security within and beyond the plantations. A highly qualified form of waged labor within the plantations was thus matched by these young men who, in Mondi's reports on "community benefits," stand as entrepreneurs themselves, as those who invest in their own human capital by virtue of their production of their own satisfaction.[60] Amid the bees, honey, timber, and meat trays, not to mention the meat itself, the concern with ethical conduct absorbs the various elements that constitute life around the plantations: customary law and state police; labor power and the effort to endure; forced removals and making habitable the fragments of postapartheid KwaZulu-Natal.

Property under timber is occasionally swapped between Mondi, Siya-Qhubeka, and Sappi as a fungible asset. In addition, Mondi and Sappi have sought to settle long-standing land claims with former residents by tying beneficiary claimant trusts, standing as "communities," into long-term leases. Together, these relations make arrangements between capital, territory, and property more fluid, even while the physical boundaries established by timber must be policed by Luke and his roving team of security guards. The timber corporations have understood that in order to secure the territory as a resource for global paper within a postapartheid idiom of freedom, the population must be reconceived as owners of a form of capital that can then be suitably alienated. Territory as a fungible asset emerges coterminously with the outsourcing of labor in the years immediately after the 1994 democratic transition.

OUTSOURCING LABOR

How the territory of the plantations has been secured is one important strand in this story; another is the form that labor took in the years after 1994. Baba Njojo's story of becoming a labor contractor reveals some of the complexities of these transformations in postapartheid labor power over the last three decades, during which the precariousness of workers' situations, particularly in mining, forestry, and agriculture, has become increasingly acute.[61] Despite formal labor market regulation, processes of externalization have been widespread, turning previously oppressed wage laborers into poor, casualized workers struggling to remain alive in a liberalized economy. Some have even suggested that South Africa's social and economic policies have decisively contributed to this outcome, despite copious rhetoric on the importance of "decent work," social safety nets, and a stable economy.[62] How did this happen?

While the rise of trade unions after the 1973 strikes in Durban began as an organized response to the humiliations and frustrations of the racial and technical hierarchies imposed by apartheid, the fruits of the democratic transition were dissipated in the compromises between the African National Congress (ANC) and large industrial interests in the country. The Industrial Conciliation Act of 1979 recognizing Black workers' unions radically changed the status of Black wage labor and played a decisive role in bringing about the end of apartheid. During the transitional negotiations of the early 1990s, the tripartite alliance between the ANC, the South African Communist Party (SACP), and the Congress of South African Trade Unions (COSATU) carried the hopes of many for an improvement in the living and working conditions of the Black majority. The first pieces of labor legislation after the 1994 democratic elections were critical: the Labor Relations Act of 1995 restructured the relationships between employers and employees; and the 1997 Basic Conditions of Employment Act (BCEA) provided a clear and inclusive definition of an employee, which covered all workers (except the self-employed) and strictly regulated working conditions (such as a forty-five-hour working week, twenty-one days of leave per year, sick leave entitlement, [unpaid] maternity leave, etc.). While the BCEA sought to regulate the social protection measures of all sectors, some depended on negotiated agreements—as was the case with forestry—allowing the minister of labor to intervene in defining the minimum remuneration and working conditions in a given sector if workers were insufficiently unionized to negotiate with their employers.[63]

The outsourcing of forestry operations began in the late 1980s when violent resistance against the apartheid regime reached agricultural and forestry workers through the organized activism of factory workers in the paper and sawmills.[64] However, it was not until the late 1990s that the outsourcing of labor took off in earnest. Prior to the mid-1990s, full-time employees across the forestry sector carried out all core operations in their forests. For example, in 1995 Mondi employed around 6,000 wage earners, and in 1997, after the acquisition of HL&H Timber Holdings Ltd. and a number of other smaller forestry companies, there were 11,134 wage earners. At that time, the use of contractors was limited to noncore work and operations taking place on marginal sites. Between 1997 and 2001, Mondi retrenched over 10,000 workers, that is, 93 percent of the workforce. Similar rates of retrenchment were occurring in the other forestry companies around the country, with the exception of those still owned by the state. By thus "contractorizing" their entire operations, forestry companies were able to establish their (former, White) foresters as contractors, thereby externalizing all the risks that had previously been managed internally by a vertically integrated "stump to mill" production process. By aligning with "global business trends," these companies were able to increase flexibility, save on the cost of capital equipment and fixed costs associated with full-time employees, and circumvent what was perceived as overly constraining labor legislation brought in by the new government.[65] By 2003 the timber industry represented an added value of $1.58 billion (or 1 percent of South Africa's GDP) and employed more than 170,000 people, 60,000 of whom were in forestry.[66]

As vertically integrated "grower-producers," companies like Sappi and Mondi had been able to subsidize the production of timber by that of pulp and paper, which had much higher market values. Thus, by outsourcing the most labor-intensive parts of their activities, the grower-producers were able to transfer their risks to contractors by paying them only for actual production and not providing any technical assistance.[67] The forest companies' practice of remunerating their contractors as poorly as possible contributed to the development of subcontracting, most often outside any formal rules. The new Black "entrepreneurs" providing forestry services were thus usually subcontracting to White contractors and employing unskilled workers without a contract. This is seen as part of the reason for the increase in the number of women and illegal migrants working in the plantations.

However, the situation was paradoxically seen as progressive from the point of view of the national Broad-Based Black Economic Empowerment (BBBEE) policy, which supports the creation of small Black-owned businesses as part of a development and poverty reduction strategy.[68] As a result of the total outsourcing of forestry work, many foresters-turned-contractors went bankrupt; productivity and production declined; and the number of criminal acts on plantations (arson, timber theft, etc.) rose. In response to the risk that contractors now had to carry, laborers were often paid on a piecework basis (that is, they were paid upon completion of a set task rather than of a workday), leading to intolerable exploitation: the task was indexed on the productivity necessary to achieve the production stipulated in the contract between the forestry company and the contractor, rather than on the capacity of the workers. Living conditions in forestry compounds in many plantations were reported to have also deteriorated dramatically: grower-producers no longer directly managed the compounds, isolated and overpopulated in some places, but rather outsourced their supervision along with most other forestry activities.[69]

The outsourcing of forestry operations separated plantation laborers from the better-organized factory workers in the mills, in response to which COSATU created SAAPAWU (the South African Agricultural, Plantations and Allied Workers Union) in the mid-1990s. This union organized agricultural workers, together with forestry workers, who had previously been organized by PPWAWU (the Paper, Printing, Wood and Allied Workers Union). The attempt to organize jointly two of the weakest groups of workers (in forestry and agriculture) in conditions of growing casualization turned out to be a failure, and the union soon collapsed. Membership declined and negotiations with forestry employers were difficult because the contractors were now splintered and numerous microunions appeared. As wage negotiations shifted to "sectoral determinations" and forest workers were no longer directly employed by the company but recruited, managed, and paid by labor contractors (some of them ex-forest workers), wages fell dramatically and the real incomes of many "community-based" contracted laborers dropped below the minimum wage—in some cases to lower than half of what they had been earning.[70]

Since Mondi first gained FSC certification, a number of changes to its labor practices were implemented, one crucial element of which was the "Food4Forests" program from 2008 that froms the center of this book. Jeanette Clarke has identified three phases in Mondi's labor practices between 1997 and 2012: (1) The shift from a reliance on full-time employees to the use of forestry contractors to source and manage labor during the mid- to late 1990s, and the consequent decline in working conditions for forest workers; (2) The subsequent "labor crisis" of the early to mid-2000s; and (3) The introduction of a suite of labor reforms, aimed at restoring labor productivity and providing "decent work" for forestry workers, from 2002 to 2012.[71]

According to Clarke, the impacts of outsourcing on labor conditions of individual forest workers were immediate and dramatic. In the first place, ten thousand jobs were lost and not all workers regained employment with contractors. Those who did were employed at half or less their previous wage rate on a contract basis. The lowest wage paid by Mondi in 1997 was R30 per day (USD 6.52); it was common for contractors to pay as little as R10 (USD 1.26) per day right up until 2003, when companies first began to enforce payment of the agricultural sector minimum wage among their contractors.[72] Contracted laborers lost not only job security but also a host of other benefits including pensions, access to loans, and funeral assistance. Union membership had never surpassed 30 percent on any of the Mondi estates during the years of full-time employment, and after outsourcing, union membership simply collapsed. The services and amenities provided by Mondi in the forestry villages had already begun to decline for various reasons, and outsourcing was their death knell. Meals served from kitchens in workers' villages were already being phased out, at the request of unions whose members elected to receive extra payment rather than food. After outsourcing, workers received neither the additional income nor meals. Clinics that used to provide workers and their families with primary and secondary health care were phased out, initially as a result of labor outsourcing and later because of a change in legislation that made it necessary for all persons dispensing medicines to have a license.[73] Company-supported crèches were closed too, as contractors who took over the villages for the housing of their staff were not able to maintain them and pay the salaries of the childcare workers.

Clarke identifies a second phase in the "crisis of labor" from 2002 to 2006 in which a number of "alarming trends" became evident. Productivity levels declined and absenteeism escalated.[74] It became increasingly difficult for contractors to source labor, as forestry work became "desperation work" because of the low wages, heavy labor, and lack of employment benefits. Many contractors went bankrupt, with severe consequences for both business owners and workers. While initiatives aimed at addressing problems with the "contractorizing" of the forestry industry had been suggested since the mid-1980s, it was only by the early 2000s that Mondi began to take note—that is, when the effects of the system of labor outsourcing began to be felt directly in falling profits. For example, in 1989 the South African Contractors Association was formed; in 1993 the first industry-wide workshop to address the "contractor problem" was held at Sappi's Ngodwana mill in

Mpumalanga; in 1997 the state and unions made a joint call for contractors, companies, and labor to agree to "voluntary, self regulatory agreements on minimum labor standards for forest workers"; in 1998–99 a series of Contractor Upliftment Program workshops were held; beginning in 2005 the development of a Forest Sector Charter included Codes of Conduct for forestry contracting and employment; in 2006 a "sectoral determination" came into effect that set out legally prescribed minimum wages and working conditions for forest labor.[75]

The labor reforms introduced by Mondi in 2008 were thus the culmination of many years of tinkering with the system of outsourced labor—tinkering that was not able to reverse falling levels of productivity and profits. The main impetus for these reforms came, according to Clarke, from the direct effects of the labor crisis: an increase in occupational injuries and fatalities, productivity decline, high levels of absenteeism and labor turnover, and a general labor shortage.[76] Thus, for the forestry sector to remain globally competitive amid drops in productivity and a steep decline in real wages for laborers since the political transition of the early 1990s, it constructed the timber plantation as a space in which industrial relations of force and production must rely on, and are made possible by, everyday kin relations, interdigitated constitutional and customary authority, and minor forms of solidarity.

The Contractor: Baba Njojo

The third person in this account whose life has been profoundly shaped by this history of labor power is Baba Njojo. When I met him in 2009, Baba Njojo employed ninety-five people to service the silviculture contract he held with SiyaQhubeka Forests. A tall, strong, energetic man then in his fifties, Bhekinkosi Gumede, or Baba Njojo, as his eighty-five employees knew him, was born in Shikishela and began as a "general worker" in the Dukuduku plantations in 1981, working for a state-owned company called GG Forestry. In 1986 he received training as a supervisor and was moved to St Lucia, where he worked for four years. Having married in 1987, he found the distance from St Lucia to Shikishela strenuous and asked for a transfer closer to home. Two years later he was placed in charge of the store in the Dukuduku plantation, where he worked for over a decade. After twenty years of work, having built a home for his wife and family, he no longer saw the financial gain in continuing to work. At that point it didn't seem to matter whether he was a stay-home father or working, so in November 2001 he officially resigned and went back home to live with his family. With the R50,000 pension payout he had accumulated, he bought a tractor and some seed in order to plant sugarcane in his fields and become an "outgrower" cane supplier to the Mtubatuba mill.[77] He was soon broke and had nothing to show for it. Then, by chance, a friend of his asked for a ride to a meeting on forestry tenders, where Njojo discovered his former employers awarding tenders to contractors to produce timber—harvesting, silviculture, and firefighting, all areas in which he had much experience. It was during the period of massive outsourcing and the selling off of state companies that Njojo had resigned and which now presented him with an opportunity to become a contractor himself for SQF, the new Mondi subsidiary with a "Black Economic Empowerment" (BEE) mandate. As he said later, "I had spent two decades working in the forestry business and loved what I was doing. During the briefing about what was required, something hit home. Deep down I told myself I could do this." Relying on his deep familiarity with the tasks and requirements, he decided to submit a tender himself for the work, making all his own calculations about prices for seed and equipment, the number of workers to be employed, and the distances to be driven. Very few other people who sought to be "community-based contractors" from these areas had the kind of experience Baba Njojo had.

Within a year, he was contracted to prepare and plant 500 hectares of eucalyptus with sixty employees. SQF sent him on a three-month management training course. The course gave him insight into the difficulties he would face with his workers and how to handle and overcome those challenges. Deeper experience with silviculture meant that he landed a silviculture contract, as a response to the increasing mechanization of harvesting operations. In that first year, with 500 hectares, he made a reasonable profit and was able to purchase tractors, trucks, and other necessary tools. As he had only twenty inexperienced workers at that point, he needed to hire another forty, which he did by giving jobs to those retrenched by the man who had lost the tender bid to him and whose equipment he had bought:

I basically bought his whole contract from him. So that is how my business began.

Since I had secured experienced men for planting, I was now left with the task of finding workers to do the marking.[78] The laborers I already had were going to be responsible for spraying chemical on the weeds. I also knew a lot about what was required of my workers.

It was in 2005 that I came across a problem with my male employees. Initially I had started off with just ten males and approximately thirty-five females, but later I hired five more men. The men began having relationships with their fellow female colleagues.

Baba Njojo credited the 2003 Employment Equity Act with shifting the gender balance in the timber plantations. When men began to leave employment in the plantations, he replaced them with women, although this led to problems in the plantation. The women would flirt with the men, he said, and men who felt jilted would come to the plantations with guns to mete out revenge.

If your worker has a girlfriend here at work, it's difficult to reprimand him in front of their girlfriend right there because he'll be embarrassed. They would become stubborn and aggressive. And they were courting each other a lot![79] If a male supervisor has a girlfriend in the team, she would just sit down, not working, with no productivity. So I made a rule that anyone found out with a girlfriend would be fired immediately. It stopped the problem quickly. This was around 2005 or so, and they were all doing it.

He began to notice, in his first years as a contractor, that many of the women in his teams were courting each other. "I would see them having these events and inquire about what was happening. The onlookers would tell me that this person is dating that one, and so forth. I hardly pay attention to it because I can see it's all a game to them. I enjoy seeing them getting along with each other, it helps keep the tension at bay and makes it easier for them to work as a team."

I learned in detail that umshado wokudlala, the game of marriage, is a ritualized form of play between women who work in plantations, both sugar and timber. Although Baba Njojo had heard about this game for many years, he had little idea about its origins. "It was a game they played everywhere, even in churches. It was a way of forming a friendship with someone and cementing that relationship by buying each other gifts, almost similar to a woman's club. Maybe there are those who end up in blossoming relationships with one another, although I'm not sure of it. Back then it was just a game. It is completely different to what we see now with individuals of the same sex dating and ending up getting married."

Baba Njojo was well liked, in contrast to many other contractors who did not treat their workers with as much respect, leniency, and generosity. Every year in December he threw a party for his employees to thank them for their hard work, and if his finances allowed, provided them with a small cash bonus. He used this event in 2009 to simultaneously stage a ritual to complete bridewealth payments for his mother, who had passed away in 1981. The women took the opportunity this event presented to advance their own rituals within umshado wokudlala. I take up the "play marriages" at Baba Njojo's ceremonial function directly in chapter 3, but it is the material conditions through which these relations are routed that are important here: the mustering and coordination of effort, and specifically the effort to endure, under conditions of late liberal care is what is expressed through a concern with amandla.

TRANSFORMATIONS IN DOMESTICITY AND LABOR

The fourth person whose story reveals the contours of labor and its transformations is Lindiwe Mbuyazi, a woman who worked as a silviculture laborer in one of Baba Njojo's teams. As is clear by now, the articulation of domestic economies and work regimes that I observed in 2009–10 placed the women who labor in the plantations at an impossible angle to the actual means of securing life, health, and livelihood. A substantial archive attests to the fact that there have been radical transformations of the meaning and value of work over the decades since the end of apartheid.[80] Crucially, the domestic arrangements that support that labor have themselves undergone thorough transformation.[81] In Jeff Guy's telling of it, preconquest Zulu social structure centered on the homestead, which "formed the productive communities of the kingdom and were made of the homestead-head, his wives and their children, together with their cattle, and associated arable and grazing lands."[82] These homesteads were divided into houses in the charge of the wives of the homestead, each house forming a unit of production with its own head and his cattle. On this reading of precapitalist "Zululand," the homestead was economically self-sufficient and consumed most of its own produce. There was a rigid sexual division of labor, with women working in agriculture and performing domestic labor, the men concentrating on "animal husbandry, the heavier building tasks and land preparation." The image is thus of the homestead as "not only the productive but also the reproductive community, and consequently kinship links were not only representations of reproductive, but also of productive relations."[83] For Guy, kinship is an expression of functional economic relations, subsumed as total social fact and reflexively folded into discourse.

The journey from destruction to reconstruction of Zulu society was hinged on the imposition of the "Shepstone system" in 1888, the key moment of the birth of modern governmentality in Zululand,[84] that established in law the notion of continuity with the past by retaining features of the "precapitalist" system: the maintenance of homestead production by allowing the African population access to land; the application of customary law; and the recognition of chiefly authority.[85] The folding together of "old" (traditional) and "new" ("progressive") factors in the political and administrative system of governance for Zululand is a common thread in histories of British colonial conquest that Elizabeth A. Povinelli calls "the late liberal governance of difference and the distribution of tense and eventfulness."[86] By this she means the distribution of persons whose subjectivities are imagined to inhabit the past perfect tense (of tradition and custom) and those who live in the present (of modernity and liberal democracy).

The contemporary ground for the spacing of custom and modernity in the birth of Zululand and its "anthropological justifications and rationalizations" can be seen, as Guy suggests, in a triad of social forces around which the reconstructed Zulu society was built: the hut-tax, wage labor outside Zululand, and the retention of homestead production within the colony.[87] The growth of a waged labor economy in the very sites of expulsion and expropriation of splintered Zululand is not an exception to the general pattern of forced migrant labor that was established across southern Africa but rather is a core feature of the colonial extraction of value. In this context, the interdigitation and differentiation of African, Afrikaner, and English identities and their associated modes of production and residence in the Mtubatuba region made it impossible for the logic of separate development to be implemented in its pure form. Similarly, the differentiation of class interests over the same period cuts across the production of categories of race and ethnicity, making neat claims about bosses and workers, citizens and subjects, peasants and proletarians very difficult.

The Laborer: Lindiwe Mbuyazi

When I met her in 2008, Lindiwe Mbuyazi had spent two decades in the plantations. Lindiwe was induna to her team of silviculture workers, and she claimed membership of the Mbuyazi clan that had successfully resolved a land-claim with the iSimangaliso Wetland Park in 1999.[88] Lindiwe's stature as a responsible and fair figure of authority within the plantations was strengthened by her reputation in Mfekayi as an industrious person from a hard-working family. Her daughter S'li, who began in the plantations four years before, when she was twenty years old, worked in the same team. Lindiwe's mother, Elizabeth, ugogo, that is, grandmother or elderly woman of the home, had worked for many years in the nearby sugar plantations on the Mfolozi Flats after her husband died. Lindiwe's son Shakes worked as a stacker for a contractor near St Lucia, who had a silviculture contract from SiyaQhubeka, the Black Economic Empowerment subsidiary of Mondi.

Lindiwe's homestead (umuzi), named Mbuyazi after her father's clan, was home to eighteen people, not all of whom were counted as resident: Lindiwe; her sister Meyi and her four children (Bongani, Rose, Bheki, and Kevin); a second sister, Jabu, and her daughter Nonkululeko; a third sister, Zanele; Lindiwe's son Nkosinathi; and her mother, Elizabeth. Nonresident members of the household included two other sons, Sandile and S'qiniseko, a daughter, Siphe, and twins, Sipho and Nosipho. S'li's three children also resided in this household (but not S'li herself); a fourth did not survive birth. Lindiwe's son Sandile was in his final year of high school and studying for his matriculation examinations. Her older sister Meyi sold secondhand and knockoff-brand clothing and lived here with her three sons and a daughter. One of her sons, Bongani, worked as a security guard on a large, White-owned agricultural farm to the north, near Hluhluwe, while his girlfriend worked in a hotel in the coastal holiday resort of St Lucia. The home had a garden that had not grown much since the regional drought began in 1998. In late 2009, they were growing maize and squash, and it fell to Lindiwe's aged mother to tend and weed the field while she cared for the infants whose mothers were working in the plantations. Despite her failing eyesight, she also took care of five head of cattle, five goats, and many chickens.

Four adults in Lindiwe's homestead received government welfare grants.[89] Lindiwe received a Child Support Grant (CSG) for four of her children; S'li received a CSG for her three children; Meyi received one for her child; and ugogo received a pension. The two women earning wages were responsible for buying all the groceries for the household, which meant that Bongani, the oldest man in the household at age twenty-eight, could use all his earnings to save up to pay off his mother's bridewealth and for the cattle that would allow him to start his own home with his future wife under his father's name, Nxumalo.[90] The capacity to provide cattle and the cattle themselves together constitute the "ethical substance" of Bongani's efforts—the substrate of what others around him refer to as his *amandla*.[91]

The father of Lindiwe's children, Shongwe, had not completed his payment of bridewealth, and he was an intermittent member of the household. He had worked for many years in the gold mines near Johannesburg, and when he was laid off in the late 1990s Lindiwe found him a job in the timber plantations as an induna to a harvesting team. He had tired of this work and, according to Lindiwe, preferred to idle at home. After a period of unemployment, he heard about a job as a driver in Umtata, in the Eastern Cape (about a day's drive from Mtubatuba), where he went to live for a time, during which he found a girlfriend, a "Xhosa girl." When Lindiwe found out about this woman, she visited Shongwe and his young partner for a month in Umtata to see what had happened and to claim him back. After an awkward month learning to speak isiXhosa, she returned to her job with Baba Njojo, living in Mfekayi. Shortly after, Lindiwe was surprised to receive a phone call from the young woman in Umtata asking for her help in leaving Shongwe and finding work in KwaZulu-Natal. Lindiwe secured her a job working for Khula, a harvesting contractor, and she came to live with her briefly. Shongwe decided he had no reason to stay in the Eastern Cape and returned to KwaZulu-Natal, not to Lindiwe but to his patrilineal home. Lindiwe was able to secure a job for him with Khula too, as a driver of a fire truck. When he found the young woman from Umtata there, he fought with her, and was fired as a result. Again, he didn't work for a while, until another large BEE contractor heard that he was unemployed and hired him as a driver for a harvesting crew.

Lindiwe also had three izintombi, or girlfriends, in the timber plantation, relations forged in the game of marriage, or umshado wokudlala, described above. One of these women worked for Khula, one was in her own team, and another also worked for Baba Njojo but in a different team. She had not accepted proposals from other insizwa, or young men, she said, because she was already married with wives of her own. All the members of Lindiwe's team were taken up in umshado wokudlala, some within the team, or within the same contractor group, or with women in other contractor groups. One of her team members, Fikile, was married, in umshado wokudlala, to a woman who worked in the contractor's office, Nobuhle. It was in her home that another team member, Nomvula, stayed to avoid the dangerous walk in the early mornings from the yard to the tractor-trailer pickup, and who had recently married Zifikile, a woman in another timber contractor team, at the crossroads.

In sum, relationships within and beyond the plantations are thickly configured by tasks and economies that crisscross domestic and industrial spaces.

STEPS TOWARD A TOPOLOGY OF PLANTATION LABOR POWER

Plantations have long been a key site for understanding the history of slavery, colonialism, and racialized capitalism, from Sidney Mintz's suggestion that "the plantation" constituted a sociocultural type or an institution that hinged the Old and New World economies and political systems (and thus linking "slaves" to "proletarians" in complex ways), forging the modern world food system, to the "essential machinery within a new form of calculation and planetary consciousness."[92] Plantations have been fertile ethnographic subjects in themselves, as key sites of colonial subjugation, mercantile profit, and the formation of colonial as well as postcolonial subjectivities, from Mintz's historical anthropology to Valentine Daniel's history of the coolie.[93] It has also come back into focus, particularly in the US context, as a framework for understanding the history of racial capitalism in the Americas, as well as contemporary debates on citizenship, sovereignty, and the terms of the social compact in twenty-first-century liberal democracies. As Adom Getachew and Christopher Taylor noted in their 2019 course at the University of Chicago on the "global plantation," "From its emergence in the late-medieval Mediterranean, to the slave societies of the New World, through its late colonial heritage in Africa, Asia, and the Pacific, the plantation has been a paradigmatic institution of racial-capitalist modernity."[94]

Two strands of the recent scholarship on plantations, not opposed to each other but distinct, both place into question what it means to be human in strong philosophical and political terms: a thoroughly global organizational logic premised on the dehumanization of Africans and other colonized peoples; and, equally foundational to the history of modern capital, the production of a split "nature/culture" binary premised on the distinction between human (Euro-American) reason and natural capital, leading to the ecological crisis that imperils life.[95] Particularly resonant here is Deborah Thomas's framing of the plantation in terms that Sylvia Wynter identified as a constitutive tension between the "logic of the plantation" and its internal threat—namely, "the spaces within which enslaved people maintained a conception of themselves as human rather than as property."[96] And finally, as Ryan Cecil Jobson argues, anthropology has an uncomfortable relationship with plantations in that it has struggled to acknowledge its "complicity in the structures of dispossession taken up as topics of research."[97] In Savannah Shange's powerful words, "Fieldwork is never completely out of sight of another set of fields—cotton, cane, tobacco, rice."[98]

The development of the plantations as a racialized regime of extraction is embedded within the workings of the apartheid state; for the postapartheid state, the reproduction of a semiskilled labor force became an increasingly acute problem as the political context changed during the 1990s. The timber plantation is a topological space in which several distinct questions of life, labor, and value intersect and are worked out. I have sought to situate those materials within the topos of the plantations as a particular node in a much more distributed assemblage of (post)colonial extractive economies. The question of labor, its availability, maintenance and reproduction in postapartheid South Africa, can only be understood in relation to the history of violent conquest and forced removals, on the one hand, and the deeply entangled everyday relations between employers, contractors, kin, neighbors, and lovers, on the other. For example, Baba Njojo's journey to becoming a key mediating figure of production and reproduction needs to be placed within a longer arc of the construction of forestry and timber as key sectors of the colonial economy a century earlier. Lindiwe's role as "team leader" was spoken of in terms of "induna" and "umlungu," "chief," and "white man" or "boss" respectively, neither of which reflects the fact of her mother and daughter both working in the plantations. Luke Mkhwanazi and J. S. Henkel, a hundred years apart, are tied to each other through the effort to produce and secure the territory.

In giving an account of the history of plantation labor in northern KwaZulu-Natal and the way it shaped efforts to endure, the difficulty is how to understand the relationship between labor power as a key concern of the colonial and apartheid state, and vital element in the logic of capital, along-side popular and vernacular terms for the capacities of persons and institutions. Amandla sits within and beyond the terms of labor power, and it is this concern with effort and work on the self, as an intersubjective, collective, ethical, and political subject, that frames the history of the timber plantations and their labor. Amandla as both bodily capacity and ethical aspiration thus indexes this braiding together of corporate and kin relations through the work of repair brought into relief by concerns with food and sustenance, hunger and ingestion, curative and healing. The effects of such histories of colonial dislocation and capitalist plantation economies have had a devastating impact on the health of people living around the plantations. In other words, everyday relations are taken up within, are made sense of, and mediate structural conditions and their historical material determinations. But what are the materials that make for "material conditions"? And how are they mediated? The previous chapter described the calories distributed by Mondi's nutrition intervention in 2009. The following chapters show how a range of materials are assembled in the actions and imaginative responses of laborers around the plantations in mustering, containing, augmenting, and reproducing amandla, or capacity.[99] The next chapter describes umshado wokudlala, the game of marriage, that women in the plantations play. The "game" is significant, I argue, because it performs a praxiographic critique of labor power and efforts to ameliorate its wounding effects, with implications for how we think about endurance, work, and repair.

3

THE GAME OF MARRIAGE

Amid the eucalypts or along the side of the road on the way home, women who labor in the timber plantations play a game they call umshado wokud-lala. I was told the game was also played in other plantations and agricultural settings in northern KwaZulu-Natal, and beyond. A possible gloss in English might be "game of marriage," "play marriage," or "playing-at-marrying." An anthropological rendering of the term would suggest that it is a practice that celebrates affectionate relations among women by riffing on customary marriage practices. While carefully ritualized and heavily invested in, the "game" finds safety from homophobic violence by operating in the register of "play" and frivolity. I bracket "play" and "game" here in an attempt to keep alive the drifts of meaning between my English glosses and the isiZulu terms used for a social form that actively provides "camouflage" for its participants while also more receptively allowing the play of signs between times, places, and events.

Attending to words and lives brought together by the umshado wokud-lala on the edge of the timber plantations, I was struck by the tones and textures of participants' utterances, as well as the registers of feeling through which the flow of communicational interaction was achieved or abandoned. In the transcriptions of my informants' explanations, I have tried to capture some sense of the laughter that frequently accompanied our discussions about umshado wokudlala because it seemed that laughter revealed something of the ways in which jealousy, love, and sexuality were given life (and cover). The combination of outward mirth, embarrassment, and shyness mixed with a sense of seriousness and real personal investment within the group points to its ambiguous, imaginative, and forceful vitality in the forms of living rendered from the available materials of plantation life.

In this chapter I offer a description of the game and its various presuppositional texts in order to trace the political and ethical implications of how
umshado wokudlala conditions the work of repair.[1] By naming and describing the elements of what my interlocutors called a "game," I parse some of
the "presuppositions" of the ritual moment—that is, the various texts, traditions, and trials that are indexed by the gestures and utterances of the participants as they bring kin terms and affections into new relation.[2] In
drawing on linguistic analyses of kinship which show how sign vehicles are
stitched to their contexts of use, I seek to amplify the interpretive and political possibilities for thinking about how care, intimacy, and relatedness
are constituted.[3] In order to make sense of the efforts, investments, and
actions entailed in the game of umshado wokudlala, I give a history of
anthropology's invention of kinship and customary marriage in southern
Africa. Then follows an account of two ritual events, and a set of reflections
by three participants. The chapter ends with an analysis of the implications
of the forms of praxiographic critique that the game itself stages for how
we think about endurance, work, and repair.[4]

SEX, GENDER, AND KINSHIP:
PERFORMANCE IN SEARCH OF CRITERIA

Since the earliest anthropological and missionary reports on the processual
nature of "African marriage," colonial administrations in South Africa
struggled to specify criteria for what constituted a "customary union." The
recognition of Native Law in 1848, followed by the Native Affairs Commission of 1852–53, which sought to outlaw polygamy and ilobolo in pursuit of
a more "civil" approach to the administration of native affairs, and the formalization of customary union under the Shepstone system with the promulgation of the "New Marriage Regulations and Fees of 1869," were critical
moments in the stabilization of an object of colonial scandal.[5] In their concern with grasping the minimal criteria of marriage and the adjudication
of property, early twentieth-century colonial legal and administrative texts
produced a naturalized assemblage of terms such as "bride," "wedding," "ritual,"
"ancestors," and "religion." Through the exercise of law, the customary—
and in particular, "customary union"—took shape alongside a picture of
who was party to the exchanges, the nature of their consent, the "attitudes"
appropriate to the event, and the property that was exchanged.[6] Julius

Lewin, advocate of the Supreme Court of South Africa and professor in Native Law and Administration in the Department of Social Anthropology and African Government at the University of the Witwatersrand during the 1930s and 1940s, complained that "Native law [has not] received adequate attention from social anthropologists, who are seldom interested in the issues raised by its legal recognition," by which he meant formal recognition by the state since 1929, despite a growing ethnological literature.[7] By that time, customary law had long been an object of codification and an instrument for extracting labor and revenue from Africans. Lewin summarized the status of native "marriage" in "law" in 1947, just prior to the beginning of National Party rule and the legislation of apartheid:

> The Native Administration Act of 1927 draws a clear distinction between a marriage and a customary union entered into by Natives. A marriage is defined as meaning the union of one man with one woman according to law, but does not include any union contracted under Native law. A customary union is defined as meaning the association of a man and a woman in a conjugal relationship according to Native law and custom, where neither the man nor the woman is party to a subsisting marriage.[8]

Lewin continued, "The President pointed out that ethnologists have described very fully the various steps in the gradual process of Bantu marriage," which he summarized for the purposes of jurisprudence as a three-step process:

1. The first stage affecting the attitude of the parties involves visits, pourparlers, and the exchange of social courtesies all designed to establish concord between the *groups*, culminating in the consent of the groups to the proposed "marriage."
2. Then follows stage two when the extent of the *lobolo* is arranged and the cattle and the woman are exchanged. This is the important moment in so far as the legal aspect is concerned and is the contract proper of the "marriage." It is frequently accompanied by other social and religious ceremonies, but as between the *groups*, i.e. the contracting parties, this stage completes the transaction.
3. The third stage involves the bride personally and not the groups as contractors. It is necessary for her to leave the ancestral kraal formally, to which end a sacrifice is offered and a feast is held, the an-

cestors being involved and the gall of the sacrifice being sprinkled over the bride who is adorned with the bladder symbolically. Her severance from her own group thus accomplished, it remains to aggregate her to her husband's group. Here also a sacrifice serves as the medium to inform the ancestors of her presence and again the culminating act is the anointment of the bride with the gall of the sacrifice. Other ceremonies are incidental.

But these acts are mere ceremonial and ritual which affect the bride personally. They form the religious element of the proceedings, and their absence no more invalidates the completed contract than does the absence of prayer, music, singing or a wedding reception in a European marriage.[9]

In the legal concern with grasping the minimal criteria of marriage and the adjudication of property, terms such as bride, wedding, ritual, ancestors, and religion appear already naturalized—that is, assimilated to the *spacing* of the genealogical society of constraint supposedly indexed by these "stages" and the civilizational weight of law.[10] It was through the exercise of law that the customary—and in particular, "customary union"—took shape alongside a picture of who was party to the exchanges, the nature of their consent, the "attitudes" appropriate to the event, and the property that was exchanged. Lewin then summarized the key judgments across South Africa on what constitutes a customary union—the minimal performative difference: "The essentials of a Native marriage are: (i) consent of the contracting parties; (ii) payment of the dowry; (iii) delivery of the bride. Anything more than this is purely optional."[11] The performative essentials were thus taken to be the evidentiary basis of adjudication. I note here how terms like "marriage," "husband," and "bride" operate indexically within the space of colonial law, drawing together different orders of meaning—specifically British colonial ideas of marriage and ethnographic representations of African custom—and authority in the execution of colonial administration. Even postapartheid legislation seeking to "harmonize" the relationship between common law and customary law on the question of marriage has been premised on the possibility of arriving at a set of minimal performative conditions for the satisfaction of legal recognition of "customary marriage."[12]

However, recent literature on language, sex, and gender in South Africa addresses a range of questions about how sexuality and marriage might be rethought in more explicitly queer terms in postapartheid South Africa.[13]

As Kirk Fiereck, Neville Hoad, and Danai F. Mupotsa suggest in raising the "queer customary" to view, a more critical return to the archive would suggest that the "natural history" of customary marriage in South Africa contains within it a queer possibility that is also amplified in contemporary social projects such as umshado wokudlala.[14]

One example of that queer possibility is Gluckman's 1950 comparative analysis of Lozi and Zulu marriage, which is significant because it was the first to produce a typology of marriage that could be applied comparatively across African contexts.[15] By that time, the ethnographic and missionary record clearly articulated the range of symbols, gestures, and words that marked out a domain of action called "Zulu marriage."[16] One of the critical features understood to underwrite the practice was ilobolo, or bridewealth, a form of payment that scandalized the colonial gaze because it offended "civilized" sensibilities regarding the sanctity of marriage and its abasement by an economic transaction. Despite a shifting moral horizon of concern, the exchange of cattle for women has been central to anthropology's model of indigenous African life as a normative baseline prior to the disruptions of colonialism, rather than as an imaginative response to early nineteenth-century conditions with a genealogy first within colonial administrations' attempt to generate a labor supply, and then within a disciplinary interest in making sensible apparently irrational customs.[17] Gluckman's analysis took features such as payment, the ceremony, and the delivery of the bride as indications of the degree to which colonialism had affected Zulu and Lozi societies: "But modern conditions have borne more severely on the Zulu [than on the Lozi]. Nevertheless, despite the abolition of their kingship, and the effects of labor migration, Zulu marriage is firm and enduring. However long a migrant is away, his wife should not be divorced. She can bear children for him by his kinsman or a lover."[18] By developing a typology of families formed by Zulu marriage, Gluckman relied on the difference between descriptive and classificatory kin terms to render the distinction between pater and genitor as a structural figuration of attitudes and norms concerning legitimate reproduction. The grid of descriptive-vs-classificatory terms and the norms of affection resulting from their structural functional relations was thus foundational, in the sense of grounding a picture of social relations, to the analysis of kinship and marriage as naturalized expressions of social structure.[19]

Borrowing Evans-Pritchard's terms for Nuer marriage, Gluckman described seven "types" of families formed by marriage:[20]

1. The natural family ("a man living with his concubine and her children").
2. A simple legal family ("a man and a woman for whom he has given marriage-cattle, and her children").[21]
3. Leviratic family ("Where the husband dies and an approved relative of his lives with the widow and the children, he begets more children for the dead man").[22]
4. Ghost marriage (marrying a kinsman of a deceased man to raise children in the dead man's name);[23]
5. A form of marriage in which a woman gives marriage-cattle to another woman in order to produce sons for her father's lineage. Gluckman does not provide a "name" for this type as he does for the others. Of significance here is the centrality of custom ("enforced by ancestral wrath") and the continuation of the agnatic line.[24]
6. A "simple marriage," in which an impotent Zulu man can marry wives with whom he asks a kinsman to have intercourse, so that he can get children.
7. The family of those who contribute cattle: a child of the chief's head wife belongs to the groups who each contributed cattle for his marriage, constituting the basis of his rightful claim to the heirship.

These seven forms of marriage, says Gluckman, all depend on the legal consequences which flow from the cattle a Zulu man gives for his bride.[25] "The cattle make him pater of all her children, whether or not he is their genitor."[26] Thus, because "classificatory kinship" diverges from the facts of biology, the institutionalized figure of the pater, who can be male or female, dead or alive, singular or plural,[27] allows for the structural reproduction of the lineage to be disconnected from biologized or fixed relations of gender.[28] Although Gluckman does not take forward the performative implications of such a gesture, merely noting the structural movement of kin terms, the analytics thus rest on the action of the transfer of cattle—a gesture conditioned by "custom" and colonial law.[29] Gluckman's typology establishes an early ethnographic record of the disarticulation between sex, gender, and kinship.

At stake is the importance of gestures, words, and situational contexts to questions of who is doing the marrying (where "doing" might be understood to involve particular utterances, gestures, and settings), what is consented to, and the possibility of (partially) successful performance.[30] Thus, the ethnographic archive appears to contain within it a suggestion that questions of paternity, maternity, and lineal reproduction hinge on a set of performative criteria.[31] A substantial archive on "woman-woman marriage" in Africa confirms this notion, the critical feature of such marriages being the payment of "bride-price" to acquire a husband's rights to another woman in juridically sensible terms. As Joseph Carrier and Stephen Murray, and Denise O'Brien, note, more than thirty groups around Africa, and at least nine Bantu-speaking groups in southern Africa, are described as having some type of female husband. Many of the examples cited are taken as evidence of how African patrilineal descent accommodated alternative figurations of the relationship between sex, gender, and kinship.[32]

While these examples extend patrilineal descent, the cases described by John Blacking and Judith Gay suggest a different direction altogether.[33] Both cases involve young women in boarding schools. The first, John Blacking's description of Venda girls' "play" at high schools in the 1950s, sits in contrast to the "traditional initiation schools" for young girls. The two institutional modes mirror each other as much as they mark off two domains: the "modern" school with its "European" sensibility, replete with "sophisticated" love-letters in English, passionate jealousies, and scope for individual choice and taste, and its "traditional" counterpart that readies young women for customary marriage. The second case describes "mummy-baby" relationships at rural high schools in Lesotho in the late 1970s. Gay's analysis points to the possibility that the game served as an education into the roles available for women during the period of high apartheid: "Western" high schools were a space in which desire and choice were mapped out in new ways for women, opening on the one hand the possibility of love and romance for modern subjects about to enter urbane South Africa; and on the other, preparation for the imminent feminization of the labor force across southern Africa, reshaping the contours of (heterosexual) love and companionship.

The women in the timber plantations who performed umshado wokudlala labored in a regime that had been feminized and redomesticated since the early 1990s: that is, where workers once lived in barracks within the plantations and were cared for by the timber companies that employed them directly, in the 1990s and 2000s they lived "at home" on the edges of the plantations and were employed by contractors.[34] The relationships between plantation workers were layered not only by the many hours spent toiling together but also by locally woven threads of solidarity consisting, most directly and frequently, of mother-daughter dyads, clan affiliation, neighborly familiarity, generational codes of respect, and customary authority. Below I describe two ritual events, punctuations in the longer game of umshado wokudlala, and then attend to reflections on the game offered by the women who labor in the plantations.

FIRST EVENT: UKUQOMA

In late October 2009, after a day of backbreaking labor, two women from the plantations staged a ceremony, which they called ukuqoma.[35] They stopped the transport trucks in the middle of a four-way intersection on the way home to Mfekayi, in order to avoid the sanctioned terrain of the homestead. They constituted the ritual moment through words, steps, gestures, songs, and gifts, each repurposing the elements of heteronormative customary Zulu marriage. By tracking the various role inhabitations and their gestures, utterances, and physical positions within the ritual space constructed on the side of the road, it is possible to trace the referents, signs, and texts aligned against the grain of conventions of Zulu customary marriage.

Nomvula and Zifikile, the couple in question, worked in different teams within the Nyalazi timber plantation. The women were all wearing their work clothes: heavy gumboots; standard-issue blue overalls printed with the name of the contractor; a skirt, either long or short, over the pants; and a head cloth, cap, or woolie hat.[36] Faces were painted with red ochre as protection from sunburn, and everyone carried a grass basket with a few things for the day—water, food, or an extra jersey. The laborers formed two groups: those who now stood as family of the insizwa, "young man," or "groom" (Nomvula), and those of the intombi, "young girl," or "bride" (Zifikile). The "bride" and her family retreated up the road, to reappear fifteen minutes later. The "young man," insizwa, and her "family" gathered on the ground, sitting in the appropriate way that men sit, some with their legs drawn up and splayed as men do, others on their haunches. As joy and humor set in, the cry of "insizwa!" went up, collecting all the family of the insizwa who already had girlfriends, or izintombi. One woman ran out with a knobkerrie, waving and dancing with it, beating up the dust with full masculine force.[37] Men from the immediate neighborhood stood to one side, amused, knowing what was to come, and laughed at the sight of such gendered performances so flawlessly executed by these "young men."[38] But they also knew that this was not their business.[39] Men may have gestured toward such alliances, but this was seen as "fooling around," "not really doing it," and was not accepted. Umshado wokudlala was a game that only women working in the forests played.

Izinsizwa each took a turn to dart out off the ground to perform an impressive turn on the road, a particularly high leg throw or sexy hip thrust, as men are supposed to do, singing the songs that would normally be sung for ukuqoma, accompanied by strenuous dancing. The approaching party of intombi and her family was announced with ululations and a dizzy distribution of cheap sweets for which the crowd playfully jostled, until the bridal party arrived and gathered in a half-circle in front of the seated izinsizwa to present their gifts. These were all gifts that Zifikile as intombi had bought for this event, and her friends, standing as family, each came forward to present them to Nomvula, insizwa, who was sitting in the center of the round. Tea trays, plates, bowls, glasses, teapots, spoons, washbasins, and toiletries were all opened and appreciated. Nomvula herself had to be instructed how to sit like a man, with knees drawn up, crotch open, and arms resting on knees. As Nomvula's age-cohort corrected each other on the appropriate way to display the gifts, they addressed each other as "bhuti" (brother).

FIGURE 3: The gifts of wayemgaxa, including grass mat (icansi) and dishes.

FIGURE 4: Gifted blankets covering the shoulders of intombi and insizwa.

FIGURE 5: Sun umbrella with banknotes and sweets.

Next came a plastic washbasin and a green towel with the words "I love you" (in English) stitched into it, which was thrown around Nomvula's back; a pink facecloth draped over her shoulder; and a mirror for putting on makeup.[40] Nomvula untied an orange scarf from her neck and tossed it aside aggressively. A member of intombi's party took from the washbasin a series of toiletries, showing them to the groom before replacing them: a comb, toothpaste, deodorant spray, and camphor cream, which she rubbed onto the groom's face to demonstrate its use. At each step, there was increasing mirth, laughter, and hilarity, as the pantomime of heterosexual marriage unfolded in playful accuracy. Next a brightly painted umbrella was unfurled and placed over the groom. Pinned to its top was a profusion of banknotes and sweets. The money constituted a significant portion of the expenses of the event, and was referred to as ilobolo, bridewealth.[41] The event concluded with the display of a large warm blanket (made in China), the essential currency of any rural ceremony in South Africa, and the sharing of fizzy drinks substituting for home-brewed alcohol, umqombothi, a key symbol of domestic reproduction and ancestral authority. Within a few minutes, the plantation laborers were back on the trucks heading home. They called this event ukuqoma, "to accept," rendered in ordinary speech as intombi uyaqoma insizwa, "a girl accepts a young man."[42] When I talked to Nomvula a few weeks later, she described this event as wayemgaxa: "the stage of covering the girlfriend with a blanket."[43] Her description two days later was instructive:

> Well, I saw this (practice) and I wanted to tell the girl that I love her. It is just a game. It's like we are friends, in actual fact. Very close friends. If I have a problem I can tell her, and she can solve it for me; she also tells me if she has a problem. In order to show how close friends we are, she has even been to this house. They even know her in this house. The day she accepted my love proposal she gave me a plate and a tray to show that now I can say that I now have a very close friend. Then afterwards I have to produce a ceremony [umsebenzi] like the one that we did. In actual fact if you like, you can do it at home. Seeing that at home it wastes a lot of money because you have to cook for everyone, I thought it was better to do it there [in the crossroads]. That wasn't the end. We also have to get married [to each other] in the end.

When Nomvula first started working in the forests, in 2004, she was approached by some of the women asking if she would accept to be engaged to them. She refused, not wanting to be intombi (young woman), and waited to see how the game worked. A year later she decided to approach another woman, as insizwa (young man) herself. The burdens of intombi are too many (paying visits, doing laundry, cleaning, and other chores), although Nomvula had not made Zifikile do these things. For his part, an insizwa should treat his intombi with small gifts, perhaps food, clothing, accessories, or roses.

Initiating a relationship is difficult because it takes time to save up enough money to pay for all the necessary elements of the ritual, and to continue with the requisite gifts and mutual support. When pressed about the costs, Nomvula admitted that it was not really about the money as such, but the significance of the ritual event for their relationship and for their families: "It's just a good old wedding, but it's not the kind of thing you do at home, because, well, at home, there are the 'people under the earth,' you see? We believe in the ancestors.[44] What would they think we are doing? So we usually do it at a school or in the road."

To proceed through the various stages of the marriage process, Nomvula had to be very careful: on the one hand, not to anger amadlozi (ancestors) by holding the ritual inside the yard; on the other hand, to ask permission from the elders in her home in a respectful manner because it would have quite an impact on their finances. It took a long time to get all these affairs in order, not only because of the permission she sought from her family, but also because of the expense involved in holding the event. For example, at the crossroads that day, in the event named wayemgaxa, it was the critical gesture of placing a necklace (ucu) around her neck that needed to be performed (emgaxa)—requiring thereby the purchase of the necklace itself, drinks, sweets, gifts, blankets—and arranging for the teams to take time out on their way home. If they were to get "properly" married, she would have to ask permission all over again.

For Valentine's Day, Nomvula bought her intombi a Valentine's cup with flowers on it, but had not yet received anything herself. She took care of the plastic rose in a clear packet that Zifikile had bought her the previous year, on a dresser by her bed. The exchange of these romantic gifts was accompanied by expressions of love, and they had kissed. Nomvula's family had enjoyed the expression of love they saw in the gift she was giving to Zifikile, and remarked on it to her. While her umam'omncane[45] was delighted by the whole idea of umshado wokudlala, her girlfriend's parents were not, and they refused to allow Nomvula to visit the yard.

The next step for the two women as a couple was umshado (marriage). Doke et al. suggest that in early colonial translations, -shada (v.t.) was reserved for civil or Christian marriage, as distinct from "native custom." The stitching together of custom and civil rites in umshado wokudlala creatively shifts the alignments of jural, legal, and affective domains underlying the supposed unity of gender and kinship. In that event, the couple would combine umbongo and umshado, but it was unlikely to happen soon, she said, because it was expensive (the total cost of ukugaxa, the ceremony of covering the shoulders with a blanket, was around R800; in 2009 around USD 100, USD 47 in 2020). One can communicate to one's partner the upper limit on how much should be spent on the occasion. Zifikile was spotted by her family members leaving home with all the dishes, washbasins, and other small things for the ceremony, so they told her that they were expecting her to come back with at least as much value in return gifts. It took her two months to save for the event (R400 each month). In addition to these gifts, the young man, now referred to as umkhwenyana, is responsible for buying a case of drinks and cake. He should buy a suitcase filled with clothes, shoes, and so on, but as it turned out, Nomvula was afraid that she would buy the wrong things, and thus gave Zifikile the money to get whatever she liked. She was also supposed to buy a pillow and icansi (the ubiquitous traditional reed mat), which she promised she would get soon.[46] She had written out a list of people in Zifikile's family and the gifts required for them; Nomvula, in turn, received enough dishes (and other gifts) for each of the members of her family, even for her little boy, "just like in an actual wedding." The relationship was founded on her admiration for Zifikile. The fact that they were jealous of each other's male partners and feared the seductions of other women gave the game a serious quality for Nomvula: "What can I say? I really love her. I'd be so offended if I found out that there is someone else and they love each other, and if she has chosen them I'd be so upset" (laughter).

Over the course of fieldwork in the plantations, I became friendly with Shumi, a transport driver for Njojo contractors. He was the boyfriend of S'mangele, Nomvula's sister, and he had begun ilobolo bride-wealth payments to her family. They had one child together. Toward the end of the fieldwork, in response to my interest in the marriages between women, he "proposed" to me. We would joke about it whenever we saw each other and he would dance in front of me to make the women laugh. We began to make plans to hold some kind of event before I left Mtubatuba, but I left without having done anything about it. We were both serious about this play, in some sense, perhaps for different reasons; for whatever reason, I did not take the next step in staging an event for us. I was unsure if it was my place to suggest it, and if I did, with what implications.

One day, while chatting to Nomvula about the bridewealth and various family relations, she told us about the cattle that Shumi had paid for S'mangele, and that they were in Manguzi, up in the north, with her mother's brother. I jokingly asked her, "What if he paid that to me instead because he asked me to marry him? What do you think about men in the forest marrying each other?" Nomvula replied, "They're just fooling around, they are not really doing it. Anyway the others don't accept it. Shumi says that Nxumalo guy [a fellow plantation laborer] is his girlfriend, but Nxumalo scolds him (when he says that)." I did not follow up the queer possibilities of umshado wokudlala among men in the plantations, but such a comment points to a mutual dissimulation within which same-sex desires operate around the plantations.

Shumi regards Nomvula's "girl" (intombi) as a friend; when I asked Nomvula what Shumi says to Zifikile, she took this to mean "what does he call her"—as in, what term of address does he use with respect to her. "He says, 'umnakwa'"—here she used the stem, which Zulu-English dictionaries give as "sister or brother-in-law." In practice, it is always used possessively, deictically locating the speaker and listener, for example, my brother-in-law, umnakwethu, or his/her brother-in-law, umnakwabo.[47] Nomvula's comments revealed the sensitivity of kin terms to contextual arrangements of speakers and addressees, and the range of kin implicated in the "game." I take up these implications below following the accounts of Thembisile and Thabisa that complicated the "nonserious" aspects of the game. In following the registers of feeling and play in which the making of meaning of kinship is performed, a different kind of grammar began to emerge.

In December 2009, Baba Njojo hosted an end-of-year function for his 120 employees. On this occasion, three couples were performing different stages of the marriage process of umshado wokudlala, using the opportunity presented by their employer's function to stage the event. Njojo himself was using the occasion as both a ritual for his mother and a party for his employees to thank them for the year's work. Unlike other contractors, especially in harvesting operations, he had built a reputation for treating his employees well. Njojo's mother had passed away in 1981, but the family needed to have her marriage completed for the patrilineal ancestors to accept the next generation of wives marrying into the lineage. Njojo described the event for his mother as ukukhunga: meaning to tie up, tether, or hang, specifically in reference to the gallbladder of a beast sacrificed in intercession with the ancestors. The semiotic mediations of ukukhunga bring bile (inyongo from the gallbladder), communication with the shades, and gift exchange into close relation. The giving of a gift, in this case a cow from Njojo's matriline in oPondweni to the deceased mother's sons for ritual slaughter, was part of the occasion, and its importance to ideas of vitality, health, and kinship cannot be overstated.[48] The weave of the events thus entailed a complex braiding of generations, gestures, utterances, and relations that together constituted a dense series of laminations and metadiscursive signs, pointing to shifting conditions and conceptions of marriage and lineage as well as to the materials available for nurturing employees and kin.

This concatenation of events, each with its associated set of recognizable gestures, utterances, and sequences, is a vital quality of Zulu ritual, and the constitutive elements of the context that day resonated between several different registers of "ritual."[49] The ukukhunga ritual had started the day before as per custom: the brewing of traditional beer, umqombothi, and slaughter of a beast, which had been left to hang overnight. The women's marriages were concluded before the party itself began for the forest laborers, whose general presence and participation in the meal and festivities constituted the conclusion of the ritual event for Baba Njojo's mother. While the slaughtered meat was being prepared, the three couples made their own preparations in the open grass beyond the yard. They arranged their piles of gifts and drinks with enough space between them. The brides' parties established themselves to the left of the main entrance of Njojo's yard, the grooms' to the right, mirroring the arrangement of men and women waiting for the feast in the two linked garages adjoined to the main house.[50] The ceremony for the first couple, Nosipho and Nolwazi, proceeded similarly to that of Nomvula and Zikifile, already described: dancing, presentation and display of gifts to insizwa, including kitchen utensils, icansi (reed mat), blanket, and towel for wayemgaxa—the crucial gesture of covering the shoulders.

The next couple, Senzeni and Nana, began similarly. After the gift giving, Senzeni, as insizwa, lay down on the mat (icansi) for her bride to cover her with new pink bath towels, as large, beautiful printed yellow fabrics were spread around them as a screen, marking off a symbolic bedroom in which the couple lay together and kissed. The third couple, Fundiswa and Sibongile, had arranged for the gifts to be distributed, this time from the groom to the bride in an act of giving thanks (ukubonga, v.t.; umbongo, n.).[51] The groom's party approached in a line from the right carrying crates of fizzy drinks and bags of clothes and linen, this time singing to the bride and her family, with the young men who had recently married leading the party. Fundiswa was seated, ladylike as izintombi should be, under a bright red sun-umbrella, on the top of which sweets, money (several hundred rand in large denominations), and a facecloth were pinned. The various young men of the groom's party unpacked the bags of gifts and displayed each item; this time, cloth and clothing including underwear, towels, blouses, headscarves, and pinafores (vital attire for proper, respectable women), skirts, jackets, shoes, umbrellas, and several large soft blankets, in addition to curtains, doilies, washcloths, grass mats and cosmetics.[52] All of this was accompanied by the continuous singing and dancing characteristic of heterosexual customary marriage events.

The group then retreated from the midday sun to the shade of the twin garages adjacent to Njojo's house, wherein the categories "men" and "women" assumed their conventional hetero-designations and any questions about who were izinsizwa or izintombi were left aside.

SERIOUS AND PLAY GIFTS

I turn next to Thembisile, another member of the group with whom I worked, who had initially felt differently about umshado wokudlala. She explained that she had previously been unable to take the stages of umshado wokudlala any further than the initial "acceptance" (ukuqoma) because she had not yet completed the customary marriage process with Gazu, her children's genitor. It was only under duress, and with money borrowed from Thembisile, that Gazu had finally been able to settle the gifts to her family that constituted the finalization of their marriage. Since he had presented several cattle over the years, and two head were outstanding, they agreed that the final gifts would be those of izibizo.[53] The izibizo refers both to the institutional moment in which counter-gifts are specified and presented, and to the objects themselves, including the iconic three-legged pot that the mother of the departing bride uses to cook with on the day her daughter leaves for her husband's house. What remained were domestic goods[54] for Gazu to give to Thembisile's family, and hers to give to his.[55]

This circulation of gifts and the events named after them provide the material substrate for umshado wokudlala among the women in the plantations. But until Thembisile had completed the "serious" wedding process, she could not be seen to be trifling with a game: wasting precious income and savings, when the more serious business of securing her children's inclusion in their father's lineage was at stake. The laughter that accompanied our conversations, and Thembisile's insistence that to play umshado wokudlala was to suffer a form of madness, were echoed in all my conversations with women laborers on the topic: to play this game is a wasteful, useless, nonproductive expenditure. As Thembisile explained, "I should be making things right for my children so that when they want to get married it will not be said that their mother is not yet married. Yeyi! It is like the money that you have taken and thrown up in the air, you see? You will see this if you really think about it carefully." Thembisile was scathing about those women who do spend large amounts of money in the game: a frivolous waste of money, a neglect of more serious domestic obligations, and a fruitless investment when one should be building one's own house. Not having secured one's serious marriage, she said, left one vulnerable in the event of the death of the father of one's children.

As scathing as she was about the irrationality of the expenditure, Thembisile was also enthusiastic about the competitive aspect of showing off how well one could display one's generosity. The basic sense of the performance is captured well in her description:

On the day when the gifts of thanks[56] are handed out—that's when real stuff happens, my child. That's when I would take a suitcase and buy my girlfriend things from head to toe. I would also buy her mother a blanket, a scarf and a pinafore. Then I would buy a cake and some drink, and have a performance there at work.[57] We would ask everyone, "please stop and watch, today we're having umbongo." We do it right there in the middle of the road. They turn off the trucks and then we come out with all the things; everything is there for ukwembesa.[58] It's just like we do it normally at home. We put the gifts down in the middle. The older sister of the bride then distributes the gifts-that-cover.[59]

In the extension of gifts from the pair to other (genealogically recognized) kin, the splendor of the generosity of each of the events is transformed, introducing a slippage between pure gift and self-interested investment.[60] Thembisile described umshado wokudlala as both a game and a stokvel or informal savings group.[61] The slippage is marked by anxiety about its performance and the sense of trust between the participants. The investments of money and time are, after all, substantial. For example, according to custom, insizwa's sons should reciprocate with gifts to their father's wife—in this case, their mother's intombi. Thembisile did so on their behalf by slowly accumulating gifts bought with the help of their government Child Support Grant (CSG), so that she could give them to her various izintombi over alternating months. Here, the state's obligation to its citizens is intercalated with the performatives of kinship and desire.

The scarves and blankets that Thembisile bought are worth more than what izintombi have given for her, constituting a generosity explicitly countering the cheapened reciprocity currently at work in the game. A range of feelings and intimacies are engendered by these gifts: Thembisile spoke of "making it very beautiful" when partners help each other complete work tasks in the plantation and of disclosing one's problems and anxieties, sharing secrets and advice. There was also a great deal of jealousy between women when their partners appeared to be flirting (ukushela) with others, sometimes causing relationships to break up.

Apart from the straightforward use of intombi and insizwa for the principals, other kin terms were used to index the mobility of other relations. Thembisile, for example, would sometimes call her intombi "the mother of my children" or just her first name, Zodwa. On other occasions they might call each other by their clan name/isibongo.[62] Zodwa often responded to

Thembisile's terms of address with "father," baba. Her son's girlfriends called her mamezala (mother-in-law) out of respect,[63] and she in turn addressed them as omakoti or with their isibongo, such as Ma Mkhwanazi. Gazu was amused by these terms, and addressed Thembisile's women as umnakwethu/ our sister-in-law,[64] indicating a relation of respect and intimacy. He helped her when she was buying the various gifts, cakes, and drinks for the um-bongo event described above. Gazu supported the game in the plantations where he worked and encouraged his wife as insizwa.

The words, objects, gestures, and feelings in circulation in umshado wokudlala suggest that property and value are co-implicated in the bend-ing of the meanings of marriage, sex, and kinship.[65] The investments of time, energy, and money in the game show that the relations at stake were not inconsequential, despite the women's protestations that they were not "seri-ous." The set of everyday material objects that circulated through the ritual point to other scenes of significance: the gifted "dowry," as elements of the processual events, included domestic items such as plates, washbasins, and mats; a "trousseau" of facecloths, blankets, fabrics, towels, and clothes; toothbrush, paste, earrings, deodorant; and umbrellas on which were pinned the cash that has long been central to the great transformations of southern African life.[66] As these objects circulated through the performances of the marriage events, they destabilized notions of dowry and bridewealth as they formed surprising alliances between umbrellas and blankets, gumboots and protective gear, lunchtime sweets, transport trucks and crossroads. The net-works of value they enlivened, and the very bodies they were attached to, point to a series of exchanges and substitutions between the "game" and its serious counterpart.

AMATOMBOYS

Thabisa was the only person in the plantations I knew to be open about her same-sex orientation. Her comments on the game are instructive in light of her identification as a "tomboy." For Thabisa, there was nothing playful about umshado wokudlala: "At work, they think of this thing as a game. But as for me, I'm serious. I'm a tomboy. When I say I love a person, it's not a joke, I'm serious. A problem arises when you have to visit a person (at home). Obviously when you visit a person, things get messed up."[67] There were other "tomboys" in the plantations, but none were as open about their sexuality.

She was tough on her girlfriends about being exclusive, while maintaining her right to have other girlfriends. In describing the woman she was most serious about, Thabisa said that her girlfriend, "TK," was "playing" when in the plantation (for the benefit of the other laborers), but "serious" when alone with Thabisa. TK's hetero-boyfriend, a man named Zeb, was not aware that she was in a sexual relationship with Thabisa. The game in the plantations provided a cover for their more "serious" relationship. Over the Christmas break that year, he had begun to suspect their sexual involvement, leading to a confrontation in which Zeb had accused Thabisa of being nkonkoni—a local slur for homosexuals.[68]

While Thabisa was openly "out" as a tomboy in the plantations and at home, TK did not identify as a tomboy, but as a "female" (owesifazane).[69] Thabisa presented herself as an accomplished lover, bragging about how much sexual pleasure she gave women, how many girlfriends she had, and how physically violent she could be, as a mirror of local Zulu masculinities. When I asked what a "tomboy" was, her response was to show us a small photo album in which she was posing in men's clothes in various urban holiday locations on the KwaZulu-Natal coast, with her arms wrapped around women in short skirts. To be a tomboy, she explained, is the same as nkonkoni, a term with similar valence as the more widely circulating insult isitabane.[70] These are heavily pejorative terms, to which tomboy (pl.: ama-tomboys) is a counter.

Despite a strong taboo on open homosexuality in this region, Thabisa thought that most people in her area were aware of gay and lesbian identities.[71] Thabisa talked about "really getting married," but she didn't see the need for registering the marriage with the Department of Home Affairs. She would rather do a "normal wedding" in which a priest from the locality officiated, because she had no interest in any of the events or stages of umshado wokudlala in the plantations. If she and TK were to marry (ukushadisa), they would each be doing different types of things: "What can I say? We'd be doing the real thing [laughter]. What else? She would be doing the work thing and also doing what she has to do for me." While Thabisa had not contributed to umshado wokudlala, TK, on the other hand, had given her ukubambisa gifts. Next would follow the stages of ukugaxa (to cover the shoulders with a blanket) and ukubonga (to thank). "We haven't planned that yet. We'll have to wait and see because we have had a few break-ups recently but maybe [that will happen]."

Thabisa pointed out that not everyone who participated in umshado wokudlala wanted physical intimacy. In a revealing reference to the terms of the game described by Judith Gay among high school girls in Lesotho, Thabisa suggested that,

> I suppose some people just like to say, "Oh I have a mother." For instance, maybe one of them likes to come to work in the morning and greet their partner, "Hi mamo." You see? And the other one is ubaba [father]. Then they would phone each other, just to say "How are you mama," or "You know mamo bought me a surprise, babo bought me a surprise." They just like playing such games. It's like a stokvel. They're just showing off. "Oh my friend you see, babo did this for me. Please come and see. Oh they're so nice!" They just say these things. Even though you didn't ask, you'd hear from them all about it. Maybe one of them has a girlfriend but she doesn't buy anything for her, and you as a girl you also don't buy anything, so you're both the same, you're just mud. You have no story, you're just wasting time.[72]

CONTEXT(S) AS SIGN(S)

The events of umshado wokudlala, and the investments, jealousies, and laughter that they elicited, raise a number of questions about how proxemics, vicinality, mutual aid, intimacy, and care are coordinated in everyday struggles of making do. The capacity to locate these relations both spatially and temporally is as much a problem of naming, and of coming into knowledge of, the conventions, forces, attractions, and possibilities of marriage and desire.[73] The material here suggests that the relations articulated around and through the game cohere not because of the repetition of idealized structures, taken-for-granted terms of address, or role inhabitations. Rather, it is that the tender and careful arrangements of kin terms, desires, and material objects help bend the meanings of sex, gender, and kinship toward a minor form of "the otherwise."[74]

Reflecting on the various elements in the recomposition of the game, particular features stand out: shaping the body to indicate (a play with) gender (sitting, lying, dancing); the in-between spaces of performance; gestures such as tying the necklace, presenting the gifts, sitting together on a grass mat; singing wedding songs from wife-givers to those receiving wives; and the use of material objects such as blankets, plates, and money pinned to the umbrella. Interpreting these referents is not a straightforward question of placing signs within a context, for example the history of the state, its antecedents in precolonial modes of authority, and its concern for the family (as might be seen in, for example, Jeff Guy's account of Zulu social structure).[75] A critical rendering of such a history would note the presence of a certain ethnographic tradition that busied itself with a "collection of lists of words and phrases" alongside naturalized accounts of landscape and social relations, as if they were so many data points, providing a functionality of comparison and persuasion that might stabilize claims about the proper ordering of languages and people.[76] To some extent, the genre cannot avoid it. To situate the women's accounts within a "context" is thus to invoke, involuntarily, the genres and fields of relations in which ethnographic accounts of "Zulu marriage" have been produced.

If the contemporary terrain of labor, desire, and social reproduction is merely the "product" of history, how then to locate the force, inventiveness, and improvisational qualities of the game, and of kinship more generally? Distinguishing clearly between text and context, or figure and ground, becomes, as Michael Silverstein suggests, a matter of tracking both the presuppositions indexed in communicative events and their entailments, or uptake.[77] The game of marriage suggests that it is not a given which elements or terms of a "context" might constitute a "system of terminology" and which a "system of affection" in some structurally determinative sense.[78] It also cannot be assumed how they come to be available for use in language-in-action. Rather, umshado wokudlala shows that terms have to be learned in *particular* contexts, the appropriateness of which is betrayed after the fact of their usage, in the forms of life that emerge *with* such grammars.[79]

Between the constraints of a system of signs (tethered in some necessary fashion to their objects) and the circulation of diffuse, noninstitutionalized attitudes, how are we to consider the creativity of umshado wokudlala and its social or political effects?[80] Understanding "kinship" as a system of signs shaped by a grammar, as Claude Lévi-Strauss suggests, is an invitation to consider how kin terms and the affections they accompany shift and transform within such a ritualized, playful form.[81] The ritual performances of umshado wokudlala demonstrate how the pragmatics of constituting care, intimacy, and relatedness around the timber plantations both shaped and were shaped by the metapragmatic function of kin terms—that is, the uses to which kin terms were put, to index shifting material conditions and fluid webs of meaning. The rituals, gestures and utterances of the women who caught on to the game in the timber plantations thus reveal how relations are constituted and gain expression in ways that embrace the contingent, dynamic, and flexible terms engendered or demanded by late liberalism and racial capitalism. The distinction itself between "playful" and "serious," as it emerges from the utterances and performances of the actors, is destabilized and becomes a matter of fluidity and invention in its practice.[82] Indeed, the claim that gender and kinship constitute a unified field comes under strain when their respective systems produce alternative arrangements of gender, sex, and relatedness. Instead, the game suggests an openness and fluidity between kin terms and scenes of deployment, requiring a "reading" of text-and-context.

QUEER CAPACITIES

Umshado wokudlala shows that the relations between kinship, gender, and sex do not follow on from each other in any necessary fashion. Rather, the game indexes shifting conditions of possibility for using kin terms and constituting care, intimacy, and relatedness. While the ethnographic archive contains within it a long record of normative assumptions about the relationship between gender and kinship, it also shows how kin terms do not necessarily correspond with sex-gender systems.[83] In their essay on gender and kinship, Sylvia Yanagisako and Jane Collier suggested that feminist critiques of the social construction of gender left the supposedly biological fact of sex unexamined. Similar to the way in which David Schneider showed how anthropology took for granted the supposed difference between classificatory and descriptive kinship, thereby assuming a biological basis for descriptive kin, Yanagisako and Collier suggested that anthropology had dragged the residue of a Euro-American folk system into feminist critiques of gender and that concepts like "man" or "woman" are themselves premised on a folk-cultural matrix of ideas about biology and reproduction.[84] They argued instead for a unified approach to the study of gender and kinship that would show that they arise together through practices of meaning making and the historical dynamism of "social wholes" within particular matrices of power. Such an analysis, they argued, would account for the ways in which systems of gender, kinship, and sex arise together in ways that produce inequality or violence. In this sense, to talk about "women" in the plantations as if this term were a stable or self-evident referent is nonsense—the word itself drags with it and imposes a huge array of relations, terms, affections, policies, forms of violence. To know anything about the meaning of "gender" or, for that matter, "sex" in this place is to learn the history of the colonial encounter, the reinvention of misogyny in the production of capitalist value, and the new distributions of violence that pervade urban and rural life in South Africa. And yet I have also taken issue here with the notion that gender, kinship, and sex conform to a consistent grammar, or produce predictable meanings or practices. Between a system of terminology (of kin terms) and a system of institutionalized attitudes (such as respect or familiarity) we can see how feelings, expressions, objects, and places can be rearranged and realigned to bend the meanings and possibilities of kinship to other ends.

The words and worlds of the women laboring in the timber plantations are weighted by the histories and possibilities for constituting relations and relatedness in this particular terrain.[85] However, tracing the contours of those histories and possibilities reveals some sense of the risks and provisionalities entered into and sustained by umshado wokudlala. As the events of, and commentaries on, umshado wokudlala show, language-in-action puts at risk the meanings of terms like boyfriend/girlfriend, or insizwa/intombi, that are often assumed to be stable and consistent. Not only are kin terms destabilized, but concepts of "man" or "woman" that supposedly secure their meaning in one way or another also come into question. It is not simply that sex, gender, and kinship do not arise together in any necessary way, but also that words may be grafted onto various configurations of intimacy so that participants may "relax" into existing orders of meaning.[86] For example, when Thabisa says that her girlfriend tells others in the plantation that they are together, the meanings of "insizwa" and "intombi" are braced by the terms of "umshado wokudlala"—which offers shelter from homophobic violence.[87] In addition, the game provides a shelter for whatever meanings and sexualities they bring to their private lives so that Thabisa can say, "When she is with me, it's serious." Thus, the system "serious/play" provides a structure that braces the meanings of kinship, gender, and sex against the radical shifts in material conditions in which domestic economies, production, and reproduction are arranged, providing openings for the otherwise as well as the reinscription of more normative heterosexual sex-gender-kinship sign systems. Thomas Hendriks, in describing male intimacy in urban Kinshasa, suggests that "the actual relationship between queerness and normativity was . . . more complicated than any simple opposition might suggest."[88] Umshado wokudlala, I suggest, operates in this space that Hendriks calls "beyond anti-normativity."

Finding a language for the risks, provisionalities, and political implications expressed in umshado wokudlala and its articulation with the material substrate of life around the plantations is a challenge. As Kirk Fiereck argues, the extent to which such gestures and utterances might not merely "cite" heteronormative action but performatively conjure queer possibilities of the otherwise for a range of audiences is critically in question.[89] If anthropology understands kin terms through the systems of gender, kinship, and sex, it is because kinship is the dominant mode through which anthropology understands life. The modalities of comprehending obligation, relatedness, and reproduction undergo a degree of what Lévi-Strauss called "torsion" in the practices and utterances of the game's participants, suggesting that securing their meanings and referents is a much trickier affair than many accounts of marriage would have us believe.[90] The materials coordinated by and through the game thus point to and demand what Hendriks calls "a more capacious understanding of both queerness and normativity," one that circles around the political "limits and possibilities of actual lives within and beyond multiple norms, queer or otherwise."[91] Drawing together African(ist) critiques of queer theory, Eve Sedgwick's notion of "reparative reading," and Francis Nyamnjoh's appeal to incompleteness, Hendriks's argument for an openness to queer futures within and beyond games of normativity and transgression is helpful for making sense of the efforts, investments, and actions entailed in the game of umshado wokudlala.

What relation does this "game" have to the labor within the plantations and to the conditions of possibility for life outside the plantations? At one level, we might say that the game of umshado wokudlala is "about" forming relations of mutual aid between very poor women, facilitating loans, gifts, or offering moral or emotional support in difficult times. Or at another level, that it is "about" establishing relationships between families such that heterosexual introductions can be made between relatives, in support of heterosexual, lineal reproduction in an imaginative effort to reconstitute a world fractured by the devastations of apartheid and the havoc of HIV/AIDS.[92] Or in a Marxian mode, we might say that the game is elicited by the relations of production and reproduction that articulate global capital and rural proletarianized ex-peasants, a vital complement in a minor mode to the instituted, recognized hetero-kin relations that underpin the labor regime, including relations both dead and alive.[93] Putting into question the purchase that functionalist, structuralist, Marxian, performative, or queer readings offer such material is to resist foreclosing on the effectiveness or capacities so vitally at stake in the game.

Amid the plantations, the labor regime, the curative substances, I have suggested that force, power, strength, invention, and incompleteness emerge as tropes that move between the logic of plantation labor, the game itself, and the interpretive, hermeneutic effect of the work of culture.[94] To say what the game is "about" is already to have engaged in a form of explanation or sense-making that necessarily abstracts elements and principles and connects them to others—a peculiar form of reasoning familiar to anthropology, tinged not a little bit with the elements of a "hermeneutics of suspicion."[95] A so-called paranoid quality of such a hermeneutics derives not only from such ordinary concerns as those that surround the stakes of sex and sexuality in the time of the virus—in this case HIV—but also from a broader anxiety around reproduction as an ambivalent investment by the state.[96] But what if such explanations, and in particular the force of critique, which Ricoeur names the hermeneutics of suspicion, are resisted, or at least delayed—what else comes into view?

Umshado wokudlala reveals the work of repair to be creative and imaginative, contingent but not arbitrary, necessary but not overdetermined. Its crucial, marginal quality is capacity—capacity to forcefully open up material conditions and relations to becoming otherwise. The people who work in the timber plantations must contend with a range of forces that splinter the effort to remain human: the fragmentation of spaces of habitation; the extraction of every ounce of labor power from the body; the wasting of the body by disease; the combined effects of many decades of impoverishment; and the erosion of trust, intimacy, and familiar modes of obligation and reciprocity. But there is also the force and unpredictability of joy, play, and the remaking of received materials. The imaginative possibilities indexed by amandla, force, or capacity, are significant for their political, ethical, and aesthetic implications.[97] The game offers a partial reprieve from the harsh conditions of labor and establishes a site and mode of creative action in which the fruits of such creativity are relatively underdetermined—unmotivated, as Michael Silverstein might say. Fluidity, openness, plasticity, and the play of the frontier thus elicit form, structure, and determination.[98] What is at stake is amandla itself, as both force and capacity, and a politics of structuration in a minor key.

4

REPAIR AND THE SUBSTANCE
OF OTHERS

In the timber plantations, nutrition and productivity contain, and emerge from, the logic of labor power and a history of colonial dislocation. That labor system also depends on a thick set of social relations for its internal coherence and operations, as the previous chapters have shown. Orthogonal to labor power is the work of repair, which takes as its central concern amandla. Amandla, I argue, is that capacity to contend with, navigate, and establish a relationship to the demands of the day. While the timber corporation understands its calculated calories as augmenting the "human motors" in the plantation-factory system, I have suggested that a range of ordinary materials, including food, medicines, and kin, are taken up within everyday efforts to constitute ethical action, which is coordinated by (the concern with) amandla.

In this chapter, I examine another set of substances which reveal a genealogy of amandla situated firmly within the history of the laboring body and the regulation by the colonial and apartheid state of who and what can heal—namely, the curative substances that circulated through the homes and conversations of plantation laborers alongside other food and medicines. The substances I address here elude easy naming and description as either pharmaceutical, traditional medicine, or supplement. I argue that (what we call) "the gut" is a key site of bodily mediation that situates, enables, and transforms everyday relations. I show how the large circulation of substances that augment the exposed person of the laborer articulates with the production of value in and around the plantations. If the gut is one key locus of the work of repair, its action is to transform that which enters or impinges on it, twisting inside out the tropes of custom, calorie, and kinship as they condition life around the plantations. Further, if health, as Georges Canguilhem suggested, is less an absolute threshold than the way in which each form of life establishes a norm in its relationship to its milieu, then the curative substances, and the gut through which they pass, raise a question regarding how the body bears the traces of assaults on its capacity to endure the conditions of plantation labor.[1] By attending to the circulations of substance, and the utterances and gestures that accompany them, we can see how the effort to augment one's capacity entailed in the work of repair draws together the materials of world-making. What emerges, then, is the way in which the work of repair is conditioned by a necessary and constitutive vulnerability to others, and to the world.

The chapter focuses on Siyanda, a security guard I came to know in the town of Mtubatuba, whom the plantation laborers all knew well, and situates the controversies around curative substances in the fight for the state provision of free antiretroviral therapies (ART) during the 2000s. I explore structuralist and symbolic accounts of "Zulu" ideas about health, the body, and the gut and put them in conversation with emerging scientific knowledge of the role of the gut in mediating nutrition and HIV. I argue here that ingestion, absorption, and ejection should be understood as crucial gestures that situate persons and working bodies in particular histories of violent displacement and exploitation; and enable a metareflexive, embodied effort that constitutes ethico-political, embodied action. The actions on, with, and through (what we call) "the gut" draw together a complex of gestures, tropes, dispositions, and materials that the work of repair directs toward world-making. Thus, the enteric mediations involved in augmenting amandla—that is, of past and present, inner and outer, abstraction and concretization—are what is at stake in the effort of cultivating a relation, and therefore an ethic, that recognizes our capacities for wounding and being wounded. What concerns the work of repair is thus an enfleshment of ethical conduct—that is, "ethical substance" conditioned by a necessary and constitutive vulnerability to others.

I first met Siyanda in January 2009 when I began spending time in the pharmacies, clinics, markets, and healers' consulting rooms of Mtubatuba. We got to know each other slowly over several months at the pharmacy, where he worked as a security guard, and it was a slight shock when I realized I hadn't seen him in a while: in February he had fallen ill and for a month he was absent from his watch. When I saw him a month later, he told me that he was feeling better in his body but now his eyes were suffering and he could not see clearly. The generic spectacles on sale in the pharmacy were not helping and the only salve was snake fat. Conventional eyedrops were useless, but the snake fat (umuthi wenhlwati) for sale in the pharmacy (alongside a plethora of "wild" animal fats commercially available) was beginning to restore his vision.[2] We began, thereafter, to discuss our health each time we saw each other, with Siyanda always mentioning how effective the various "traditional" curatives he was using were (imithi, and, pointedly, not the biomedical pharmaceuticals), and with me finding new ways to describe my health in isiZulu. He mentioned that his affliction was caused by a long snake in his belly, an image that permeates southern African mythology.[3]

By Siyanda's account, in March 2009, his affliction had been caused by abathakathi, "witches," who had been trying to kill him. The causal agent was muthi that had been placed surreptitiously in his path so that, unknowingly, he had stepped over a lintel at home, allowing the snake to enter his body through the legs.[4] This had been revealed to him by umthandazi, a faith healer, whose diagnosis had detected the presence of witchcraft.

S: The faith healer told me that a certain air (umoya) had entered my body, moving up and down, even in the spinal cord, and she found out that it was actually a snake here in my body.[5]

TC: Did they say how the snake entered into you, entered into your stomach?

S: They put it in you while you're dreaming by blowing the medicine in your dream and calling out your name; that's how it gets into you while you're sleeping.[6]

To treat this affliction, Siyanda was instructed to pray as per the healer's directions and to drink a quantity of "purified water" (on sale in the same pharmacy for R15.99 [USD 1.96]) that had been prepared by the faith healer with the appropriate accoutrements—two matchsticks and ash from the fire in the hearth of Siyanda's home. He was to do this in the yard of his homestead, and before crossing the threshold, he was to address his father's shade directly, imploring him to speak on his behalf to those responsible; to ask that they should stop harassing him; that they should know their attempts to harm him would be useless; and that they should remain in their own homes. It was important, Siyanda told me, to remember to place a one-rand coin in the purified water before he drank it and to address one's fathers respectfully.

Within half an hour, the snake was purged—"head first, just dead, just like that"—and he immediately felt better. It was a thick, translucent, colorless snake, "this long," he said, holding his arms out. The people who sent this snake had done so by collecting soil from the graves of his family members and had blown it into the air with a mixture of plant materials, umuthi, and calling out the names of various kin. Indeed, in recent months, several family members had died and others had taken seriously ill. While Siyanda was excited to tell me about the snake and the successful outcome to his ordeal, he was more hesitant to reveal the snake's origins—who had sent it and why. For a while, he would only say distant relatives were implicated.[7]

In Siyanda's articulation of the source of his affliction, he identified the people of his natal home, owasekhaya, his kin, as far-but-near, without naming the individuals. In all our discussions about health, the snake featured as a means by which to locate each other as witness and informant, the afflicted and the concerned, traditional and not biomedical. In these conversations, he would assert the jealousy of these close-but-distant kin, their attempts to harm him, and the power of the substances to strengthen him. Later in the year, as his muscle-bound body diminished visibly, he let slip to me that he was in fact on ART. He was quick to reassure me that the "immune boosters" he was consuming were effective, and that the nurses at the local clinic were wrong when they told him the results of a certain, unnamed test. His story was surely a common one, offered in the vocabulary thickly grown between public and private worlds, and between registers of bravado and fear, custom and biomedicine. The articulation of witchcraft, ingestion, disease, and kin relations was hinged for Siyanda on a question of skepticism regarding the criteria for knowing kinship and ill-being.[8] His health thus became a chronic concern, the events of kinship knotted by ongoing, unresolved doubts about the sources of his afflictions.

Siyanda's experience with the snake in his gut was a clear expression of a widespread trope of illness and kinship across southern Africa. The women working in the timber plantations were deeply familiar with this image of the snake, and indeed helminths are common in this region, particularly schistosomiasis, and discussed in these terms.[9] But while the women working in the timber plantations spoke of their own afflictions in terms of other figures of distress, they spoke in similar terms about the importance of treating the gut to heal broken kinship relations and attend to minor everyday health concerns. The importance of purifying blood, cleansing the body, and strengthening the immune system (referred to in isiZulu as amasosha omzimba, the soldiers of the body), as concerns of both kinship and lineage, were key tropes in the plantations, as were the various substances: water, snake fat, purgatives, painkillers, and, later, antiretrovirals. In Siyanda's working life as a security guard, physical and social concerns with his capacity to provide security were brought together in this illness and through his response to it.[10]

For laborers in the timber plantations, popular curative substances that were vitally important to their well-being and capacity to labor included muthi in its most elemental form, as raw plant material, and amakhambi,[11] composed and prescribed directly by healers such as izinyanga or izangoma. More mundane and less obvious as signifiers of custom were the impure industrial hybrids circulating through cosmetics stores, pharmacies, and street stalls.[12] The origins of those hybrids can be traced to the industrializing centers in the late nineteenth century, such as Durban and Johannesburg and smaller, regional towns, to which migrant laborers were drawn and pushed by the colonial system; their archival traces suggest an enduring concern with capacity—specifically the capacity to labor for capital, in the sense of the alienation and embodiment of one's effort in commodities, but also to provide, to take care of, or to secure lineal reproduction and kinship relations—that is, the total life-giving effort toward which hunger directs the will.[13]

In the timber plantations, bodily capacity to labor for a wage was only partially about calculating calories and maximizing productivity— after all, the nutrition intervention on the part of the corporation was squarely about shoring up falling productivity and profitability. It was more than simply profit maximization in the limited sense; it was also framed as "corporate social responsibility"—that is, as an ethical response to a humanitarian crisis. As for laborers, the cooked meal was also an object of moral and ethical concern. It enabled one to earn a wage, or to feed children or even domestic animals. And alongside the calculated calories were home-cooked food, curatives, and biomedical pharmaceuticals. Following the trajectories of cooked corporate food and popular curatives as they entered into laborers' lifeworlds thus revealed a concern with "capacity" as a central trope through which persons and relations are constituted, and around which worlds are stitched in the ordinary work of repair. Capacity, or amandla, here was not a simple abstraction or calculation (viz., "labor power") nor some ethno-artifact of custom. Rather, it was a source of value in itself with generative force emerging from its historically contingent fabrications. As Baba Njojo's comments at the end of the first chapter suggest, the embodied techniques of augmenting one's capacities are indexicalizing gestures that point to complex folds of history and structuring possibility.

In tracking the numerous substances available in pharmacies and cosmetics stores, on street corners, and in industrial warehouses, specifically those for cleansing the body and "boosting" the immune system, it became clear that what was at stake was not simply "social reproduction" in its neo-Marxian sense, and the circulation of alienated and materialized labor, but the ways in which the natural and social might be mutually absorbed within the folds of the gut. By thinking *with* lineage and kinship, a network of alliances begins to emerge that reveals the intimacies between self and gut, psyche and soma, and substance and kinship. Siyanda's experience of the snake and the plantation laborers' concerns with medicinal substances and kin relations bring into focus the gut as the site of the "enfleshment" of the social.[14]

GUT POLITICS

During the first decade of this century, the gut was a site of intense political contestation in South Africa, as debates raged about the role of nutrition and supplementation for the treatment of HIV/AIDS. The fight for access to antiretroviral treatment for HIV in South Africa was at its crescendo, and then President Thabo Mbeki's infamous "AIDS denialism" made space for the figure of the "quack cure" and the snake-oil salesman to reenter public life.[15] The Treatment Action Campaign's tireless activism for a coherent state strategy for antiretroviral distribution included litigating against "quacks" and their cures, in particular the German vitamin proselytizer Mattias Rath and the "Zulu traditional medicine" entrepreneur Zeblon Gwala and his "miracle cure," Ubhejane (Rhinoceros).[16]

Through heated public disputes, nutrition as a scientific object with an as yet uncertain relationship to HIV and TB began to separate from the ordinary materials of sustenance.[17] In 2007, the Academy of Science of South

Africa (ASSAf) launched a study of the relationship between nutrition, HIV, and TB. Initiated at the height of the struggle for access to treatment, the ASSAf study was one of the first reviews to summarize then novel scientific understandings of the gut, and it seemed poised to provide a crucial intervention into the uncertainty surrounding HIV treatment and nutrition. The ASSAf report affirmed the importance of nutrition and showed how crucial the gut is to immune system functioning. In particular, the gastrointestinal mucosa and other mucous membranes were recognized as having a special role in the production of CD4 T cells. The special characteristic of these membranes was their bipolarity: "There is a polarity in epithelia that is different from all other tissues, in which one side of the epithelial cell faces 'self,' whereas the other side faces 'non-self.'"[18] The ASSAf report summarized these findings by describing

> the exciting novel conceptual understanding that the gastrointestinal tract is a major anatomical front line of the disease, and that lymphocyte activation is a key step in the CD4 T cell depletion that defines AIDS. Together, these insights have major implications for our dawning understanding of the intersection between nutrition and HIV/AIDS, both in terms of the potential impact of HIV infection on nutritional status, and in redefining our conceptions of how nutrition intervention might impact on HIV/AIDS pathogenesis.[19]

With a long history of syncretic healing and pharmaceutical forms, the late 2000s saw an expansion of commoditized curatives that slip and slide in and out of loose definitions of "traditional medicine," "muti," "vitamin supplement," or "Traditional, Complementary, and Alternative Medicine" (TCAM).[20] However, the popular substances that circulated through factories, pharmacies, and homes did not always conform to the image of the quack cure. Many of them fed an ordinary set of techniques of self-care and sustenance, strengthening and augmenting the person in a time of epidemic death, and they were vital to the everyday efforts and horizons of timber plantation laborers in 2009. On the one hand, "the vitamin," as sign vehicle, operates by means of the scientific authority of the randomized trial and peer-reviewed publication.[21] On the other, Ubhejane provided a powerful symbol, the rhinoceros, which mobilizes the totemic force and signifying power of the whole animal and its occulted horn in healing cosmologies across southern Africa.

I began tracking the proliferation and circulation of what I first thought of as "nutritive substances" at the 2008 parliamentary hearings into the restructuring of the Medicines Control Council (MCC) in Cape Town, South Africa. Those hearings had been prompted by a crisis in the administration and regulation of pharmaceuticals that had begun to flood South Africa in the wake of the large-scale tuberculosis programs of the 1990s and 2000s and, after 2005, new government policies to provide lifesaving ART. Part of the friction in the hearings was generated by a concern with how to define various substances: What should constitute a pharmaceutical substance, and what kinds of medicinal claims could it legitimately make? What should constitute the legal difference between cosmetic, supplement, food substance, and pharmaceutical? Should complementary medicines be regulated by the MCC, and do they include "traditional medicine"?[22] I interviewed scientists and authors of the 2007 ASSAf report on the relationship between nutrition, HIV, and TB; I searched national and provincial archives for material on the advertising and regulation of curatives that have long troubled government regulators; and I conducted in-depth interviews with dozens of business owners, small-time entrepreneurs, and street sellers, as well as the pharmacists and distributors involved in selling these curatives.

In early March 2009, the Zulu-language radio station Ugagazi FM hosted a debate on a Sunday morning, in the prime sermonizing slot of 10:00 A.M. to 12:00 noon, between traditional healers, doctors, and government officials about these substances and HIV. The debate grew heated around the question of why medical doctors did not refer patients to "traditional healers," izinyanga and izangoma, when there was nothing else they could do—why couldn't they refer to each other? I heard about this vociferous debate for months from friends around Mtubatuba.

Debates over what counted as a healing substance, who was empowered to heal, and the precise nature of the affliction were thick in the air. In 2009, HIV specialist doctors in Mtubatuba complained that so many of their patients were still dying because they presented so late, when their CD4 counts were already low, having tried all other healing modalities and therapeutics.[23] I conducted interviews with dozens of street sellers, pharmacists, cosmetics reps, and "alternative medicine" vendors around KwaZulu-Natal and learned that the market in curative substances had indeed exploded since 2000—precisely during the height of the controversy surrounding former president Thabo Mbeki and minister of health Manto Tshabalala-Msimang's policies regarding the state provision of antiretroviral therapy.[24]

Although some of these substances explicitly claimed to cure HIV/AIDS in the years after 2000, very few do so anymore after the success of the Treatment Action Campaign (TAC) in prosecuting one such claim with the Advertising Standards Authority in 2008. That case established that no product might claim publicly to cure a disease for which no biomedical cure has been found. Since the court found in favor of the TAC, most substances simply stated the acronym "HIV" on the long list of ailments on the side of the bottle, or showed the most compact symbol of its relationship to HIV, the red AIDS ribbon.[25] Since 2008, HIV activists have made many attempts to regulate these and other "complementary medicines," with very little success.[26] From February 2002, when the call-up notice for complementary medicines was published, to 2010, approximately 155,000 submissions were received. Their interlaced industrial production, commercial circulation, and private consumption point to a complex of concepts and practices concerning the sustenance and maintenance of social relations. As an inexact instance of a type of substance within an "ecology of pharmaceuticals" tracking urban and rural interdigitations, the substances in their contemporary configuration index new social forms and their attendant conditions of life in contemporary South Africa.[27]

DURBAN AS PHARMACEUTICAL ECOLOGY

Every pharmacy I visited in KwaZulu-Natal sold a cornucopia of curative substances, and every month several new bottles and brands arrived courtesy of a traveling salesman or an order placed with Alpha-Pharm, the principal supplier of most regional pharmacies in the province.[28] To understand the rural-urban circulations, and the production and consumption of what I came to call "curative substances," I mapped their sales across the bustling center of downtown Durban, the provincial capital of KwaZulu-Natal. The city is a complex pharmaceutical ecology bursting with therapeutic substances of all kinds. Sold on the streets and in the arcades around the Warwick Junction market, the beating heart of what Hart et al. call the "human economy" of the old city of Durban, they found a home among the banal objects of everyday domesticity: next to tables stacked with pots and plastic kitchenware was a pile of enema bottles, or rectal bulb syringes, in five different sizes; on the street corner next to fluorescent sweets and crisps sat household disinfectant in old whiskey bottles; on another corner, seawater and bath salts in bright pinks and blues, all to be ingested, were displayed; in cosmetics stores sat row upon row of bottles of curative substances such as Ngoma, Vuka Hlale, or Uqedizikinga.[29] In the pharmacies and herbalist shops that crowd downtown Durban, common painkillers found a home alongside snuff, animal fats, prescription drugs, and rat poison.[30] I interviewed traders, producers of the substances, and pharmacists to understand the various economies through which the products traveled. The substances are advertised by the labels on the bottles, adverts in newspapers, flyers handed out on street corners, and signs on shopwindows, competing with a cacophony of other texts that crowd the urban fabric. Corporate billboards for cell phones and funeral plans sat alongside colonial-era street signs superimposed by the names of postapartheid struggle heroes; electioneering faces stared down from lampposts promising better futures; and shopwindows announced cheap furniture sales, free abortions, cures for HIV, or consultations with East African Healers.

Behind each of the substances stood an entrepreneur hoping to strike gold. Some of them did. As some brands have waxed, others have waned. Each new generation is more stylized, packaged, and medicalized. For example, Vuka Hlale, translated roughly as Wake Up and Go, was one of the older products still on the market (since 2001). When I interviewed the rich (White) businessman who owns the brand, in November 2008, he was composing advertisements for a new, extended range of products, including a general tonic ("African roots for all diseases"), a natural sex enhancer for men (Vukahlale Isikhokho), a *power powder* (vitamin C), an aloe gel, spirulina capsules, and soap. Two of the most successful products on the market, Ugazi and Uqedizikinga, are made by the same company but for different markets: one working class and the other more affluent.[31] They each contained the same range of products. A "family resemblance" existed between these substances. For example, Imbiza Nos. 1 to 6 were: (1) Hlanza ingaphakthi—Body Cleanser; (2) Umanqoba—Immune Booster; (3) Imfihlakalo—Women's Corrective; (4) Impumelelo Yabesilisa—Men's Libido; (5) philisa tablets—Spirulina; (6) Women Lovers Powder [sic]. They also sold body splash, body wash, body lotion, bath salts, massage oil, and six types of soap (for luck, for beauty, for love, for clear skin, and so on). The family resemblance connecting these products is a set of bodily concerns—blood, skin, stomach,

UVUKAHLALE

P.O. BOX 37219 • OVERPORT • 4057 • KWAZULU NATAL
TEL: 031 202 1082 • FAX: 031 202 2147

AFRICAN ROOTS FOR ALL DISEASES

- Relieves bile
- Painful joints, arthritis
- Abscess relief
- Improves blood circulation
- Encourages activity in women
- Relieves muscle cramps
- Relieves backache
- Maintains a healthy uterus
- Burning urine
- Excessive perspiration
- Relieves colic
- Sexually transmitted infections (STD)
- Helps with dizziness

- Helps with menstrual pain
- Improves condition of blood
- Cleanses the kidneys
- Guards against witchcraft
- Increases appetite
- Treats flu
- Improves male erection
- Relieves muscle spasms
- Removes body lice
- Relieves constipation
- Helps with normal breathing patterns
- Improves body odour
- Maintains a clear, healthy skin

- O ntsha nyoko le seso
- Masapo le serame
- O fedisa mathopa
- E O neha madi a matjha
- Madi a mangata
- O etsa bomme ba kgothale
- Ho finyela ha misifa
- Letheka le bohloko
- O hlatswa senya
- Moroto o tjhesang
- Ho fufulelwa
- O ntsha sejeso
- Hat o sa fumane bana
- Mahlaba
- Dropo

- Modikwadikwane
- Methapo le madi
- O fedisa silumi
- Mahetla a bohloko
- O hlatswa diphiyo
- Ho ruruwa ha mmele maoto
- O ratisa dijo
- Mokgohlane
- Motsosa Pooho
- O fodisa manonyeletso le
- O fedisa dinta tsa senana
- O fedisa ho pipitlelwa
- Letshweya
- O fedisa phika le lebe
- Phekola letlalo le lebe

UVUKAHLALE ISIKHOKHO
Is a natural sex enhancer for men. The natural herbs contained in this mixture have long been used as a tonic and aphrodisiac. It is a natural testosterone booster and increases sex drive and red blood cell production. When used continuously it will help to maintain a more powerful erection.

NATURAL HERBS
The natural herbs in this mixture assist the body's innate capacity to recover and repair itself. The emphasis is holistic, this means treating the entire body. By using this mixture on a regular basis it will go beyond treating the immediate symptons and treat the entire person's well being.

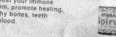

POWER POWDER
Take half a teaspoon daily to boost your immune system, promote healing, healthy bones, teeth and blood.

SPIRULINA CAPSULE
When 2 tablets are taken twice per day assists in boosting your immune system.

ALOE GEL
When used 3 times a day is the ideal remedy for minor burns, sun damage, cuts, abrasions, and wounds and assists in healing, protecting, soothing and moisturising the skin.

UVUKAHLALE SOAP
When used 2-3 times per day is the ideal solution for mild skin infections.

FIGURE 6: Poster for Uvukahlale.

strength, reproduction—as well as reference to "natural herbs" and the promise of boosting the immune system.[32]

On a day in late January 2009, having explained my interest in immune boosters and izifo zonke, I fell into conversation with a nurse behind the counter of a particularly busy pharmacy adjacent to Warwick Junction as she attended to customers. She explained to me that when clients described their ailments, she knew immediately what kinds of medications they would need: a blood cleanser, an immune booster, men's or women's corrective, Power Powder™, or an allopathic pharmaceutical. She cautioned me against the curatives that lacked proper packaging or a barcode; one should use the better-known or established brands. The labels of each bottle, whether *immune-booster* or *izifo zonke*, made careful use of texts and images. To take one example, on a white plastic bottle containing one liter of a dark brown liquid was written "Vuka Uphile (Herbal Remedy). Immune booster. R45 in RSA. Natural Herbs—Amakhambi. Newly Improved." Around an AIDS ribbon ran the words "Wandisa Amasosha—Wehlise iHIV" ("It increases soldiers of the body and decreases HIV") followed by a barcode. On the back of the bottle, two columns listed the ailments it treated under the title "Natural Herbs—Amakhambi"; on the left the isiZulu terms, on the right the English. As with all these texts, there was a doubling and slipping of language, sometimes between isiZulu and English, or seSotho, isiZulu, and English; sometimes only in isiZulu (see table 1).

Tracing the "social life" of these substances reveals something of the regimes of truth and value through which they were produced.[33] The cornucopia of meanings and forms of these substances has long been of state concern. As Karen Flint's work has shown, the colonial state in southern Africa struggled to name and police a plethora of materia medica, techniques, roles, offices, and claims, from the late nineteenth to the mid-twentieth century. State and provincial archives are filled with petitions, advertisements, legal cases, regulations, seeking to stabilize distinctions between "witchdoctors," "sangomas," "inyangas," "sanusi," "African doctors," "muthi," "medicines," and "health."[34] A huge cast of actors fills these archives in a century-long struggle to stabilize the meanings of and distinctions between "biomedicine" and "traditional medicine."

One such actor was Paul, the sales manager of a large distribution company that sold Ugazi and Uqedizikinga using a "direct selling," "network marketing" strategy in which buyers, all of whom were women, mostly

TABLE 1: Ailments and cures of "Vuka Uphile (Herbal Remedy)"

Natural Herbs—Amakhambi

Ushukela	diabetes
Isifuba—TB	TB
Izinso	Kidneys
Amathambo	Arthritis
Iqolo	Lower back
Umvusankunzi	Wake the bull up
Umkhuhlane	Flu
Isilumo	Menstrual pain
Esenhliziyo	Of the heart
Ukuqunjelwa	To be constipated
Ukukhabula Kwezingane	Inhalation
i-Drop	STI [unspecified]
Inyongo Nesiyezi	Bile and Dizziness
Isifo Samehlo	Eye disease
Izindlebe	Ears
Uvula Inhliziyo	Opens appetite
Uqede Izikelemu	Destroys worms
Amalumbo	Bewitched
Izinyawo Ezivuvukele	Swollen feet

Instructions: Drink a ¼ of glass after a meal. One in the morning and one at night. No side effects—just herbs. Safe to use after 3 months of pregnancy

bought directly from a warehouse in Durban for resale in cosmetics stores and street stalls around the city and province. While containing the same substances and range of products, Ugazi was targeted at a working-class market, Uqedizikinga to a more affluent market, which was reflected in the stylized packaging. Paul was anxious to reassure me, lest I report his business to authorities, that the most important treatment for HIV was antiretroviral therapy, and that Ugazi was not a cure for HIV (given the ongoing press coverage of the Treatment Action Campaign's fight to have "quack cures" banned). "It's about basic health," Paul told me, "This product is a mix of the two. It's the only product on the market made in a lab and it's carefully formulated.[35] It's not from a sangoma—these herbs are not muthi. Like Sutherlandia, it's well known in the scientific world and in the Zulu world." When I asked what ugazi meant as a "Zulu" concept, he quickly referred me to his assistant, Pretty, a woman who staffed the sales office and whose task it was to explain the efficacy of the substances to clients. In a small showroom to the side of the warehouse, stocked with bottles of the various substances and decorated with the glossy advertising posters for both low- and high-end products, she explained that while ugazi meant attractiveness or good luck in the context of the substances, the word was also used to denote blood; to describe a relative, or as a familiar term of address for "cousin,"[36] among many other inflections. Each of the products had a specific formulation, she explained:

> Number One is the Body Cleanser—for cleansing the system, for clearing the skin of pimples. If your stomach is dirty, if your blood is dirty, it causes pimples—the dirt comes out of the pores. To finish the pimples, use the cleanser. It's the inside and the outside. It's a bit like a laxative—like Laxa. Like when you have that yellow stuff that comes up the throat—that you must spew.[37] It is good for ulcers, piles, stomach, itching, paining, for dirty water in the womb, for discharge, for burning urine. And for that yellow liquid stuff. For constipation too, for those who don't like to use the syringe, to go to the toilet like normal. But you must use it for one week only. If you use it for longer, then the body loses too much water. You must not use it for HIV and TB, it will make you weak, and you already don't have enough water in the body.

When I asked Pretty to elaborate, she explained that the sellers (of these products) are like doctors in that they have to explain what the products are good for, inquire into their clients' problems, tell them that they should only take these medicines if they are strong, or, for example, if they're constipated. Everybody who buys the product gets a training session so the seller can explain how it works and let the client ask any questions. Cleansing the stomach is important for cleaning the skin because one's blood is "dirty." If one's blood is dirty, it is because one is dirty on the inside: "for example, those people who like to eat sugar—it causes them to vomit yellow stuff—what they call inyongo. If you have too much inyongo, it causes dizziness and fainting. It's from eating too many sweet things. Juice, sweets, sugar—of buying all these nice things—cakes, sweets, chocolates. That's why you should cleanse at least three times a year."

Inyongo, Pretty told me, was basic to life: "If I am alive, I must have it in my body, but not too much of it. If you have too much, you spew—it overflows.

So therefore you must use Number One." Number Two is the Immune Booster, which one uses if one is weak, has HIV, TB, cancer, or arthritis. One cannot take the cleanser, because one is already losing water, but one must "boost the system" or "boost the immune."[38] The traders I spoke with in Durban, Pietermaritzburg, and Mtubatuba would explain that customers asked for a curative that would "cleanse the body" (ukuhlanza umzimba) or "cleanse the blood" (ukuhlanza igazi), because of "witchcraft" that was afflicting them, and it was the type of affliction that would be cured by an enema or by "spewing."[39] The range of Ugazi and Uqedizikinga products also included bottles of Women's Corrective (No. 3) Men's Libido (No. 4), Spirulina (No. 5), and Women's Lovers Powder (No. 6).

Key to the production of pharmaceutical value for this class of products is their relationship to circulating workers who have moved between rural and urban sites of production and reproduction for 120 years, and the complex economies of healing techniques, competition regulation, and racial governance.[40] Johannesburg and Durban have been the two major cities in this region drawing African labor into global economies, but they are merely nodes in broader, more sprawling networks of commodities, labor power, and therapeutic economies across rural and urban locations.

A REGIONAL PHARMACY

In the Alpha Pharmacy of the small market town of Mtubatuba, two hours north of Durban, biomedical pharmaceuticals, "White" complementary medicines, and supplements occupied the bulk of the store, while "African medicines" lined the shelves on one wall.[41] At the back was a dispensary with two windows: one side for biomedical pharmaceuticals dispensed by White, qualified pharmacists, speaking English; the other for supplements and complementary medicines, staffed by Black nurses, speaking isiZulu. On the far side was a photography station where customers had pictures taken for identity documents.

Peter, the chemist who owned the pharmacy, was happy for me to spend time with his assistant Dumisani, who was in charge of keeping the muthi shelves stocked and fielding the traveling salesmen who would drop off samples of their latest cure-all every week. Peter explained to me that all small independent pharmacies were struggling in South Africa because of various legislative shifts in recent years. This had partly to do with the government's regulation of "single exit prices" on major pharmaceuticals; and partly it was because an increasing number of customers used mail-orders for their pharmaceutical needs so that they could avoid collecting their orders in person (and thus avoid being seen). It was also partly a result of the consolidation of pharmaceutical retailers into a few large networks (Alpha-Pharm being the largest in KwaZulu-Natal). As a result, like others, Peter had to rely on the sale of "complementary and alternative medicines" to make up for the loss of business. By "complementary," he meant all those substances not registered as pharmaceuticals with the Medicines Control Council, and not making direct medicinal claims—for example, vitamins, food supplements, sex enhancers, animal fats, and cosmetics. While he was critical of cure-alls making wild medicinal claims, he was not in a position *not* to sell them. By placing Dumisani in charge of "African medicine," he was able to turn a blind eye for the most part. Each of the four pharmacies in Mtubatuba did the same thing, as did pharmacies around the province.

As I observed Dumisani's interactions with customers during long summer afternoons in the pharmacy, I learned about the categories of nutritive substances: those curatives called *izifo zonke*, "all diseases," that operate by "cleansing the body" through purgative and emetic properties; immune boosters (in English and in vernacular usage); and more "traditionally" themed muthi usually bought by healers, such as the fat of a snake, a hyena, or a dolphin. "Dutch medicine" had its own shelf, as did paraphernalia for use by faith healers, such as purified water, incense, and candles.[42] Soaps, creams, bath salts, and sexual performance supplements rounded out the nonbiomedical offerings. All these folk remedies were highly commoditized and standardized, manufactured synthetically in Johannesburg or Durban. Izifo zonke and immune boosters were the most sought-out commodities by both men and women. Customers would approach Dumisani first to ask his advice, and he would ask them discreetly what was ailing them. If they indicated a problem in the stomach or a general enervation, he would suggest a cleanser; if they hinted that they had a more serious problem that required treating their immune system, he would suggest a product he thought most efficacious.[43]

A tall, slight man his midthirties, Dumisani took care to look presentable and respectable at all times. His stable job in the pharmacy was allowing him to pay off the cattle of bridewealth to his wife's family in the far north of KwaZulu-Natal, and he took pride in his ability to advise clients which products to use. As he explained to me quietly, one had to be very sensitive to what the customers said because often they didn't want anyone to know why they were buying a particular pharmaceutical or substance. One understood, he said, that customers asking for an immune booster were most likely HIV positive, while those buying izifo zonke often hinted that there were family troubles afflicting them about which they were not at liberty to say much. Dumisani carefully mediated the pharmaceutical landscape for customers, deciding when to refer them to his boss for biomedical treatment and when to direct them to vernacular curatives.

As Siyanda put it to me outside the pharmacy one day, "If you're sick, your strength is finished, your blood is weak because you do not eat properly [Igazi vele mawugula ayaphela amandla igazi alibibikho ukungadli]. It's because the blood is weak, that's why. It doesn't mean that I'm positive."[44] Dumisani was convinced of the power and force of the various immune boosters, supplements, and cleansers he oversaw, as much as he was of the biomedical pharma. Each had its place and each was used according to the nature of the affliction. He advised those whom he knew to be HIV positive to seek treatment at the dispensary from the pharmacists, and recommended that they also take an immune booster to supplement those drugs. Dumisani took care in advising customers how much, how often, and for how long to take them, reading and interpolating the labels on the bottles.

From these brief portraits of intermediating actors such as Pretty and Dumisani, the pharmacists and businessmen they work for, the factories in which such substances are manufactured, and the diverse scenes of retail and consumption across which the social life of pharmaceuticals come to life, what emerges in faint outline is a complex picture of situated pharmaceutical value: a situated history of fatigue, intimate narratives of affliction, shifting techniques of the body, and bricolaged therapeutics that point to the folding together of ethical, social, political, and physiological process.

ZULU KINSHIP AND THE GUT

As Siyanda's story and Dumisani's advice to his clients suggest, the events of the gut have to do with the events of kinship, and of social and political power more widely.[45] The archive on preconquest Zululand suggests that fluids, substances, bodily processes and powers, and the varied materials of reproduction were all central to the constitution of self and society, and of politics and power. The secret knowledge of healing, the manipulation of nature, and the mediation of the spirits in the interests of the clan were organized around lines of political authority and embodied in the chieftainship through a shared paternal ancestor. Thus, the well-being of the nation was embodied in the well-being of the sovereign (at least during the consolidation of Zulu power during the late eighteenth and early nineteenth centuries). The coterminous nature of political power (including kinship) and spiritual/medical power was transfigured through colonial conquest into state concerns with persons and families.[46] While the place of customary authority within constitutional law remains contested in postapartheid South Africa, the Zulu king remains symbolically tied to fertility and reproduction through ritual and performance.[47] However, despite the "merely cultural" character of these performances, there remains a question about the material exchanges underlying political and social life (e.g., the ritual sacrifice of a bull and the annual reed dance festival). In Paul Bjerk's reading of the James Stuart Archives, political authority under the Zulu king Shaka (1816–28) was organized by the king's control of the flow of milk in society.[48] Metaphors and practices surrounding human and bovine milk and semen appearing in the James Stuart Archive of Zulu oral history suggest a "milk complex" rather than a "cattle complex." While arguments such as Bjerk's raise tricky questions about the conceptual and historiographical status of belief and religion in southern Africa, others, such as Paul Landau's and David Maxwell's, evoke more clearly the splintering and remaking of political, ritual, and domestic economies in the colonial encounter.[49]

The concern with bodily fluids is captured in one of the earliest ethnographic accounts of Zulu life. A. T. Bryant describes how:

> The clyster and the emetic are special favorites with all natives. I suppose they resort to this means of treatment more than to any other, even than to actual dosing. Practically all those common attacks of passing indisposition to which one is periodically liable, as well as most of the more important febrile complaints, are ascribed by them to the bile (iNyongo), and their first step is to clear the excess of this fluid out of the system by one or other, or both, of the above methods.[50]

The importance of inyongo—bile—remains vital today in my own informants' descriptions of why they consumed particular substances. An extensive literature on "Zulu thought" has sought to locate such concepts of "bile" in structuralist terms or as analogues to Western definitions of disease.[51] Ngubane, for instance, describes the Zulu concept of pollution in terms of umnyama, literally "darkness of the night." The darkness is symbolically seen as representing death while the daylight represents life. Umnyama, Ngubane argues, as a term used to represent death or "near death" can be translated as pollution, for lack of a better English word to convey this complex Zulu concept. Pollution for the Zulu, she suggests, can be seen as a marginal state believed to exist between life and death. It is conceptualized as a mystical force that diminishes resistance to disease and creates conditions of misfortune, disagreeableness, and repulsiveness.[52]

These structuralist accounts of "Zulu thought" posited that all situations that are a manifestation of reproductivity or cessation of life are polluting in differing degrees of intensity, this being measured by the extent of the contagious nature of each state of pollution. Reproductive emissions such as seminal fluids, or menstrual blood, are therefore polluting and so are gestation, lactation, parturition, death, bereavement, or treatment with black medicines that symbolize death. Ngubane focuses on the moments of birth and death because they are the most intensive with regard to pollution, as well as on the figure of the married woman because of the marginal position she occupies: "Not only because as a wife she is a link between two corporate groups in a lineage structure, but also because as a mother her marginality is manifested in situations which give rise to pollution."[53] Controlling the flow of vital fluids is continuous with political power and social well-being generally, but particular significance is given to "reproductive emissions."

"Zulu thought," according to Ngubane, is based on the notion that as long as one lives, one defecates, urinates, produces saliva, tears, and mucus as part of the body's functions; however, while the flow of menstrual blood and seminal fluids can dry up and stop, a person continues to live. The cessation of such emissions, however, would arrest the continuity of the society. The concern over the reproductive emissions is not only over the good health of the living but over the replacement of the generations. If society is to be perpetuated, it must have the means of maintaining life, that is, food. Hence pollution affects not only the people but also their main means of livelihood, namely, cattle and crops.[54] Pollution, then, we might say, is not merely a "symbol" of "matter out of place," as Mary Douglas famously put it,[55] but rather an indexical sign vehicle, a situated concern that strings together actors, roles, conditions, and substances—and its key attribute is its power to mediate the confrontation between life and death.

Thus, we return to the difficulty of naming this particular force or quality, a certain capacity to mediate the relationship between life and death. Here then is a genealogy of amandla, threading together the body, the lineage, the nation, the cosmos, situated in the particulars of South Africa's liberation struggle and the contradictions of postapartheid capital and labor. As capacity, strength, force, or virility, amandla is a vital quality in question in the nutritive substances as they work through the gut. Axel-Ivar Berglund describes Zulu concepts of the power of fertility in a clan and lineage in terms of heat, ukushisa, work, or desire (ukufisa).[56] All are enveloped in the general term "amandla." Anger is also termed "ukushisa," the subject discussed determining which aspect of the power is being referred to. Thus, anger and fertility are intimately linked. The lineage shades, or ancestors, are also intimately associated with the concepts of fertility and particularly the sexual act. As Berglund recounts, "While the male lineage shades are identified with the male fluid, those of the female are said to be associated with menstrual blood, both parties playing important roles in procreation. The female's shades continue to feed the fetus with blood while growing in the womb, the continued deposition of male fluid in the woman during pregnancy being accepted as the male shades strengthening of the unborn child."[57] After birth, the shades continue to form the food of the child by transforming the mother's blood into milk by "working on the breasts." "As they were putting the food of the child into the womb before birth, so now they are putting it into the breasts after the delivery."[58]

Drawing on Hylton White's analysis of affliction and the remaking of difference through the architectonic grammar of ritual, domestic space, and livestock, Jason Hickel repeats a structuralist reading of Zulu thought in his description of bile and stomach between human and bovine forms:

> For rural Zulus, the process of building up a homestead through marriage, bridewealth transactions, legitimate reproduction, life-stage ritual, and socially productive exchanges stands in for a broader process of creating kinship from individuals, culture from nature, cooked from raw, domestic from wild. Indeed, the crucial metaphor is one of domestication, analogous—during sacrificial ritual—to the passage of mulch through the digestive system of the cow: each of the cow's four stomachs

represents, in order from first to last, increasing association with the umndeni [the house] and its ancestors. In addition, the gallbladder (inyongo), the bile of which is understood to make digestion possible, is regarded as the most sacrosanct of all ritually significant organs.[59]

In classic Lévi-Straussian style, Hickel describes Zulu ritual slaughter of a sacrificial cow and the distribution of its parts in terms of a "textbook of normative social order, a mnemonic of morality that reminds the community about the roles, statuses, and rights of properly social persons,"[60] a guide to social action that performatively reinstantiates the homestead and society itself, "as if recuperating the inscription of an older social order from beneath the worn parchment of the real (cf. White 2001)."[61] The act of disaggregating the beast and distributing its pieces is known as ukuhlukanisa (lit., "differentiation"), "for it produces differences that rural Zulus take to be so crucial to social being."[62] Hickel gives a partial list of fifty-nine anatomical parts, their English translation, and the related gender, status, and mode of preparation. Table 2 presents a selection from Hickel's list, focused on digestion.[63]

Hickel's structuralist analysis shows how the meat of the head metaphorically extends outward while the meat of the stomach centers inward, reinforcing the symbolic dichotomy between the head as the principle of male hierarch and political extension, and the stomach as the principle of female reproduction and domestic centeredness. The differentiation of male cuts that extend beyond homestead kinship to people throughout the community who occupy the generalized category that each cut represents sits in contradistinction to female cuts that are limited and sold to persons related to the homestead.[64]

A more materialist reading would take Hickel's analysis to point to a digestive trope in "Zulu ritual" in which umswane, or undigested cud in a cow's stomach, is vital, vibrant matter in ordinary efforts to constitute personhood. Put together with Bjerk's rereading of the James Stuart archive in making an argument about the centrality of milk and control over its circulation as the central political and social fact of precolonial Zulu society, a continuity of concern emerges with sustenance, ingestion, absorption, incorporation, and relation, by means of milk, meat, maize, gut, stomach, bile, and their associated mundane and ritual entailments. Such a materialist approach resonates with Joost Fontein and John Harries's argument

TABLE 2: Partial list of bovine anatomical classifications typically used in rural Zululand

Anatomical part	Translation	Gender	Status	Preparation
Inyongo	gallbladder	none	ancestors	none
Usu	first stomach	female	agnates' wives	boiled
Itwane	second stomach	female	agnates' wives	boiled
Inanzi/incekwa	third stomach	female	senior wife	boiled
Umswane	cud	female	females	none
Amathumbu	intestines	female	—	—
Amathumbu omhlope	"white" (large) intestine	male	headman, men	roasted
Amathumbu omnyama	"black" (small) intestine	female	agnates' wives	boiled

Source: Jason Hickel, *Democracy as Death: The Moral Order of Anti-liberal Politics in South Africa* (Berkeley: University of California Press, 2015), 160–61.

about the vitality and efficacy of human substances in Africa. They draw out a conceptual problem, as they see it, in the way that material, corporeal substances have been understood in histories and ethnographies of Africa, in an effort to reread the entanglement of things and lives, for a "symmetrical" anthropology of blood, bone, flesh, and skin."[65] While they ask after "human remains," we can take their question about the meaning of corporeal substances and the things themselves as a useful one for thinking "the gut" and what passes through it; substances' agency and affordances, efficacy, and vitality cannot simply be reduced to the meanings bestowed upon them. Fontein and Harries thus seek to articulate the "excessive potentiality of matter" as that which exceeds the work that people do of "constituting things as social objects," what Christopher Pinney, cited by Fontein and Harries, calls the "torque of materiality"—that which resists interpretive closure, or "def[ies] the temporary stabilization of the 'thing' into a social object or subject."[66]

Harris Solomon suggests that "metabolic living" is a grounded, materialist approach to understanding the transformations of calories and laboring bodies as they engage their environment. In describing how people in Mumbai, India, make sense of the relational capacities of elements like pollutants, adulterants, sugars, and trans fats, Solomon suggests that "those who feed, eat, breathe, and labor do so often in nonindividuated arrangements with immediate and extended families, friends, and communities."[67] Ethnographic attention to the situated trope of "absorption" is compelling, but less clear are the particularities of meaning that distinguish such modes of living from other situated practices. At stake is how particular utterances thread the body and its milieu. How do words and fluids come together in the vital concern with life in KwaZulu-Natal?

FLUID SUBSTANCES AND ANGRY WORDS

Siyanda's illness and his oft-repeated concern with amandla centered on a number of fluids, some consumed, others expelled, as he sought to soothe the witchcraft directed at him by the evil words of his kin. The close relationship between various modes of confession, that is, the expelling of hot, heavy words and the expulsion of fluids, threads through many accounts of African modes of healing. As Berglund suggests, expelling liquid is an engagement in the interests of fertility and hence the opposite of witchcraft and sorcery, which aim at killing and annihilation. Instructions given to Siyanda to dispose of bodily excess outside the domestic space are common to healing practices around southern Africa, and that which is not (or cannot be) expelled normally, which is thus evil, must be cast out through aids such as enemas and vomiting. Timber plantation laborers and pharmacy customers I spoke to attested to the huge range of substances, both botanical and synthetic, consumed to achieve this. Ukuhlanza, which Berglund gives as "[a] Zulu idiom refer[ing] to vomiting and an expulsion of feces after an emetic or purge," is key here, although the Doke et al. dictionary term Berglund references gives a wider range of meanings, many of which were given to me in translation in my inquiries into the commoditized curatives: to purify, cleanse ceremonially (as at a death, burial, when the slaughter of a beast or the use of ashes is carried out—to purify the hands, to purify a girl after the puberty ceremonies, to cleanse a widow from death stigma); to confess, make amends by apologizing, soothe; exculpate, excuse, clear of fault.[68]

As mentioned, water and bile have vital force, as all the ethnographers of this region attest, including Bryant, Krige, Ngubane, Berglund, and Hammond-Tooke. In brief: people who have been exposed to sorcery cause vomiting by drinking quantities of water and bringing it up by either inserting their fingers as far into the mouth as possible or using a feather. Those who do not vomit are suspected of evil, ubuthakathi, of being a witch (umthakathi), because abathakathi (pl) are unable to vomit and have no fluids to pass. If anger is not expelled, it has the potential to build up in the form of ubuthakathi, so apart from purgatives and emetics, spitting is another form of purification that relies on the expulsion of fluids, and there are many occasions when spitting in connection with the purification of anger and evil takes place. "First the man speaks out his anger with words. That is the first thing, the matter of words. Then he spits. That is the next thing. That is the sign that he has spoken to the end and that the evil has come out. When he spits, the evil comes out. There is nothing left in his heart. He washes his speaking with the spittle."[69] "Male emission," or ejaculate, is another form of fluid whose expulsion is an important symbol of purification, and which thus necessitated men "cleansing" outside the homestead before sexual intercourse with wives after having any association with angry competitors, court cases, returning from prison, labor in towns, or any other dangerous enterprise. These kinds of association carry the risk of contamination with isifo sesisu (sterility in the wife, i.e., ubuthakathi directed toward destruction of the homestead's fertility). Thus, the expulsion of water in vomiting and enemas, spitting, and ridding oneself of evil medicines in male emissions, references both anger and vulnerability to other's ill-wishes, both of which entail activated ubuthakathi and require active steps to rid oneself of evil, as a cultivation of one's well-being. These concerns shimmered throughout the many conversations I had in street stalls, pharmacies, and markets between Durban and Mtubatuba, as well as the discussions about food and pharmaceuticals that I had with the timber plantation laborers.

GUT RELATION

Around the plantations of KwaZulu-Natal, the various ways in which human relations come into question, as necessary vulnerability and vital force, become clearer when understood as a series of exchanges between fluid and bodily substance, between words and affects, and between capacity and well-being. Thus, the ingestion of nutritive substances exceeds the pharmacological questions of efficacy (whether in the register of biomedicine or traditional curative) and draws into the body the moral and relational aspects at stake. As Siyanda's attempts to secure his well-being suggest, two moral issues arise in the context of medical treatment. First, it is important to trace the cause of the suffering; and second, the effective capacity of medicines is contingent on good moral standing and correct action, broadly conceived.[70] As Siyanda's and others' stories suggest, we can see how the consumption of nutritive substances indexes the enfolding of bodily and social concerns in the management of well-being, centrally mediated by "the gut." In the context of the massive effects of HIV on the social body in contemporary South Africa, cultivating the capacity to *endure* becomes a question of how the body bears the traces of assaults on its attempts to establish a successful relationship to its milieu. Following Canguilhem's insights into biomedicine's knowledge of health, I suggest that "the gut," as an object of scientific knowledge production, public health policy, and everyday action, emerges as a site from which ordinary and institutional norms and normativities are produced.[71]

The large circulation of substances that augment the exposed person of the laborer reveals how the production of value in and around the plantations articulates with, elicits, and reproduces forms of life not accounted for in standard sociological narratives of life or labor. Where some accounts offer "the rural poor," ignorant or exploited victims, or deracinated and alienated urban lumpen as relatively undifferentiated categories of person, these substances point rather to ordinary modes of self-care and an imaginative remaking of symbolic materials and structural conditions. More specifically, they pose a question about pharmaceutical value: how it generates and is generated by unstable grammars of relatedness. Unstable in that they are sometimes nourishing, sometimes poisoning; feeding, diminishing, disrupting, or augmenting value across arrangements of rights and rituals, bodies and capacities, care and violence.

The gastrointestinal tract has become central to the claims of medical science in searching for a breakthrough in HIV pathology, to the political battles of those making use of science as the basis for making rational health policy decisions, and at the same time articulating for many people the symbolic importance of the belly in the development of a biosociality concerning what is ingested, absorbed, found to be nutritive or threatening, and expelled.[72] Recent advances in enterology suggest that the enteric nervous system (ENS) is not only an anatomically heterogeneous and functionally specialized nervous system that bears a stronger resemblance to the central nervous system (CNS) than to other peripheral systems, but that, as a "second brain," the neurons in the gut are functionally and morphologically similar to the neurons in the brain.[73]

Elizabeth Wilson's rereading of Freud's early writings on the nervous system suggests that biology—"the muscular capacities of the body, the function of the internal organs, the biophysics of cellular metabolism, the microphysiology of circulation, respiration, digestion, and excretion"—should be understood differently in its relationship to the social/psychic.[74] Rather than an inert body that merely expresses psychic processes, as conventional psychosomatic theory has it, Wilson suggests we think in terms of neuronal relations formulated on the basis of an "obligation" to the psyche to give up their excitation. Rather than a metaphor (bringing the meaning of obligation to bear on psychosomatic action when it is properly applicable to another domain, that of social relations), Wilson takes Freud to mean that "neurological obligation" is one way of understanding a relation between psyche and soma in which there is "a mutuality of influence, a mutuality that is interminable and constitutive."[75] Rather than a structure in which neurology is affectless matter and nervousness and melancholia are immaterial psychical states, Wilson sees a "kinship among the psychic, nervous, digestive, circulatory, and excretory systems."[76] If biology is only now beginning to understand that the gut forms an absorptive skin between the self and world, "allowing the outside world to pass through us,"[77] the curative, "nutritive" substances speak to an understanding of the internalization of relations that extends far beyond a notion of psychic action embodied in the central nervous system. They present us with a picture of the gut, attuned to the world as it passes through it, as a vital organ in the maintenance of relations to others. In Wilson's terms, ingestion and digestion are not metaphors for internalization, as some anthropologists have suggested (e.g., David B. Coplan; Sidney W. Mintz and Christine M. du Bois; Nicolas Argenti),[78] but "actual" mechanisms for relating to others. Gut pathology does not so much "represent" a breakdown in relations as enact it enterologically,[79] as a direct interruption to the process of remaining connected to others. Gastrointestinal difficulties such as bloatedness, nausea, vomiting, constipation, and diarrhea are thus modes of distress, enacted enterologically. Interventions into the gut are thus modes of distress distributed in and across the social/political as moments of enfleshment.[80] As we see in Siyanda's illness through which his distress was enacted, the boundaries of his body were exceeded as his illness absorbed the relationships between kin relations on the one hand and curative substances on the other, showing how the natural and social, the nonhuman and the human, mutually constitute each other.

On the one hand, such an approach stands firmly opposed to the transcultural psychiatry of "culture-bound syndromes" that reifies culture and relies on diagnostic terms such as "schizophrenia" and other classifications from the Diagnostic and Statistical Manual of Mental Disorders (DSM).[81] Instead, I draw sympathetically on Karen Ensink and Brian Robertson's approach to "indigenous categories of distress" to make sense of embodied, situated, and relational experiences of affliction.[82] On the other hand, even such a strongly emic approach to "indigenous" forms of affliction struggles to make sense of the material articulations that hinge life, livelihood, and historical context in this region. Indeed, anthropology's own struggle with its attachments to stubbornly Euro-American concepts of relatedness rely on unstable notions of substance to underpin claims to a "theory of kinship." Here, I am informed by Janet Carsten's approach to the study of kinship, and in particular her analysis of the unstable concepts of substance that have buttressed various critiques of "kinship studies."[83]

As Carsten has shown, the concept of substance has become a critical element of the post-Schneiderian critique of kinship studies, helping unlock the ways in which Euro-American tropes of blood informed classical anthropological theories of kinship. Subsequent uptake of this critique thus sought to show how "substance" could be understood in more processual terms, to show how persons were constituted through their relations with others. Thus, as a catchall term, it has been used to trace the transformation of food into blood, sexual fluids, sweat, and saliva, and how they passed between people through eating together, living in houses, having sexual relations, and performing ritual exchanges. The contrast between an image of bodily substance as fluid and mutable and one in which it is permanent and fixed is linked, Carsten shows, to the ways in which anthropologists have contrasted ideas of the person in the West and the non-West (specifically India and Melanesia). She demonstrates how the availability of "substance" as a polysemic concept has allowed its meaning to shift radically from "essence" or material to fluid or transformable permutation as it traveled from its initial American context of use to India and Melanesia. Such is the basis on which Marshall Sahlins, in his attempt to integrate this critique of kinship and substance, seeks to arrive at a more materialist metaphysics of "mutuality" in a firmly humanist mode.[84]

What does this mean for how we think about the gut, relatedness, and nutritive substance in and around the timber plantations? By tracing the circulations of commoditized curatives as they traveled through modes of industrial production, regional markets, and a domestic poetics of bodily care, a clearer picture of enteric mediation comes into view. The gut, as an unstable collection of organs, beginnings, and endings, is thus both a medium through which signs are communicated and an active agent in the shaping of meaning, as both Elizabeth Wilson and James Wilce suggest.[85] As a key site of bodily mediation and of "exposure,"[86] "the gut" thus enables and invites both discursive commentary about, and reflexive action on, one's body and its relation to others and its context(s), thereby situating, enabling, and transforming, relations. This is what Michael Silverstein might call its "metapragmatic function," in the register of embodied action.[87] Thus, we can see how the manipulation of flows of substance in everyday life sets in motion presuppositional signs indexing a folded world of custom and righted relations with forebears and current kin.[88] The varied presuppositional material indexed by the production, circulation, consumption, and excretion of industrial curatives thus points to the retrospective folds of ritual thought; however, such a claim presents a challenge to how we understand historical consciousness to be free of, or constrained by, the structural contradictions of capital in postapartheid South Africa. I argue here that such ingestions, absorptions, and ejections should rather be understood as indexically calibrated, (meta-)pragmatic gestures that bring together histories of violent displacement with contemporary struggles to engage the political economy of postapartheid life in the register of the ordinary.

As such, these gestures are ethico-political, embodied actions that mediate past and present, inner and outer, abstraction and concretization. We can thus speak of a complex of gestures, tropes, dispositions, and materials that the work of repair reaches out, in widening arcs of concern, to draw together as world-making. This is what Francis Nyamnjoh calls the incomplete work of eating-and-being-eaten, that is, the ouroboric, cannibalistic precondition of agonistic conviviality, and of becoming.[89]

Thus, beyond the importance of tracing the particular forms of "metabolic living" that sustain the transformations of calories and laboring bodies as they engage their environment, the work of repair draws in, twists inside out, the particular tropes of tradition, healing, or kinship that are often invoked in descriptions of southern African life beyond metropolitan edges, and points up the impure commingling of signs, gestures, politics, and histories of living on after violence, and after the end of labor. The work of repair is conditioned by a necessary and constitutive vulnerability to others, or more particularly the Other, that is, to the world. The substances that pass through the body are phenomenologically rich or powerful actants that drag world and body into relation by means of a reciprocity of exchange between situated, vulnerable persons and their contingent milieux. Rather than resort to an argument about symbol or culture as a discrete domain untouched by overdetermining (and dangerous) bodily matter, or a claim to "traditional" or indigenous cosmologies of healing (for example, Robert Thornton),[90] we can instead draw on recent understandings of the brain (Catherine Malabou)[91] and gut (Wilson)[92] that point to a psycho-neuro-enterology that historicizes and renders plastic the gut and its contents as interinvolved agents in the always-partial and incomplete (and possibly failed) work of repair. At stake is not so much the porosity of the body (Solomon)[93] or the end of a Euro-American concept of the autonomous individual who is now made-multiple-through-microbes (Tobias Rees et al.),[94] but the effort of cultivating a relation, and therefore an ethic, that recognizes our capacities for wounding and being wounded (Stephen Mulhall)[95] and elaborates the means by which we make the world habitable, survivable.

5

IN THE VICINITY OF THE SOCIAL

When I met Nobuhle Zikhali in 2009, she lived in a homestead nestled in the bend of the Nyalazi River as it curves along the perimeter of the plantations. The home was surrounded by newly planted stands of sugarcane and eucalyptus, the private investments by those who had gained permission from the induna (chief or customary authority) to use communal land for commercial agriculture. After the labor reforms of the 1990s, when laborers no longer lived in the plantations in company accommodation and instead received the benefit as cash, Mondi preferentially employed "local" workers from within a five-kilometer radius of the plantations. This is how Nobuhle found work in the plantations in 2003, initially for a silviculture contractor named PEPS for the first year. After that contract ended, she transferred with a group of others to Njojo Contractors, named after Baba Njojo, the paternal figure who was contracted for silviculture services by Mondi's subsidiary SiyaQhubeka. Three senior men in Nobuhle's family also worked in the plantations but had passed away many years before.[1] The great house of her father's lineage, Zikhali, sat in Ntondweni, and when her father's mother passed away (and after the Zikhali patriarch had died also), the house, meaning the patriline and its associated members, relocated to Mfekayi, to this yard where she currently lived.[2] Nobuhle had heard that her paternal forebears had come from the south, near Durban, from a locality called Palestine, although they had moved north early in the twentieth century to Mbila, on the northern edge of the iSimangaliso Wetland Park, near Mbazwana, before moving to Mfekayi during the upheavals of the forced removals in the 1970s.

In 1997, the people of Mbila, under the chieftainship of Moses Zikhali, were party to the first wave of settlements of land claims made on the iSimangaliso Wetland Park.[3] While Nobuhle's paternal elders share clanship with the Zikhali customary authority in the Mbila area, her claims on those paternal relatives were precarious. Her gogo's status as a visitor or stranger to the Zikhali house (having married in) was only ameliorated by her seniority: "When ukhamba [an herbal medicinal drink] is brewed for 'those-under-the-ground,' it is then drunk by the owners of the house; we the outsiders do not drink it," Nobuhle told me.[4] Nobuhle's gogo's maternal family hailed from KwaMsane, the center of which was now a "township" on the edge of Mtubatuba.[5]

In 2009, Nobuhle lived in a small, square room, ifleti, made of mud bricks and branches, that stood apart from the other rondavels in the Zikhali homestead in Mfekayi, its roughness a function partly of the state of the household and partly of her own precarious place within it.[6] There was room enough only for a stool and a bed for her and her three-year-old daughter, Bridget, the light of her life. When Nobuhle was in the plantations, Bridget was cared for by ugogo, the matriarch of the household. The homestead was arranged like many in the region: a central rondavel with several outlying rooms arranged in a semicircle so that the yard's entrance faced the road. The twelve members of the family were arranged across three adjoining homesteads, surrounded by stands of sugarcane and eucalyptus planted by "out-growers" and contracted to the mills in Mtubatuba.[7] Nobuhle's place in her father's homestead was uncertain, even though she shared his clan name, Zikhali. Nobuhle and Bridget cooked and shopped for themselves. Her two older children, Ntombi and Sizwe, moved between paternal and maternal homesteads over the course of 2009, between Esikhawini and Mfekayi. Bridget's father had been hit and crippled by a car the year before, and he was living with his wife in a distant area to the south.

As I asked Nobuhle and other laborers about their life histories, I began to piece together the various ways in which clanship, dislocation, and livelihoods were interwoven in the violent history of what is today called "KwaZulu-Natal." Rather than reach for a genealogical chart to map these threads, as anthropology's key trope, such events can be thought of as knots in a narrative that tie together a life.[8] The texture of these experiences as they knot together routes and worlds, as ordinary, unspectacular, and ongoing, give the lie to the alienating flatness of labor's repetitions and situate Nobuhle's efforts in and adjacent to the plantations.[9]

This chapter is about the timber plantation as a topological space in which several distinct regimes of life, labor, and value intersected and were worked out, and in which specific social projects were enacted and acted upon. Departing from Annemarie Mol and John Law's well-known elaboration of the concept of "social topology," I draw together here knots, fragments, layers, and sedimentations in order to pose a question regarding the nature of "the social" in contemporary South Africa.[10] To understand its wounds and the various reparative efforts to forge a new relation between citizen, society, and the state, we need to ask on what grounds those reparative gestures operate. Specifically, in this chapter I aim to situate the efforts of the people who labored in the plantations within three distinct topological forms. "Situating" these topological forms does more than give a "local habitation" to labor; rather, describing these three topological forms reveals the particular work entailed in navigating distinct histories of power, territory, violence, and profit.

The first topological form is the cartographic construction of the colonial territory, with its invention of tribes, peripheries, and national borders. The second is the fluid topology of HIV surveillance that combines vicinities, persons, and virus as hotspots or intensities. The third is the work of children (Nobuhle's children) in composing their own maps, pointing to the layering and knotting of these events, histories, and vicinities. It is here that the incomplete work of amandla, which is the concern with capacity and the possibility of repair, points as much to reassembling and recirculating as it does to the possibility of the misfiring of meaning and limitation of action. At stake is the capacity to navigate these topologies and the forces they bring to bear on ordinary life.

The spatial form of the plantation is shaped by the calculative history of forestry science, by the production process, and by the botanical requirements of the tree species. In turn, this spatial form shaped movements of people, calories, trucks, and timber. "Compartments" of eucalyptus were about a kilometer long and half a kilometer wide, and the fifty-hectare plots were worked for several weeks at a time.[11] While older eucalyptus hybrids took about eight to nine years to grow before being ready to harvest, the newer hybrids have much quicker harvesting times of about four to six years. The laborers' daily rhythms were coordinated by long, straight rows of eucalyptus trees, by the spacing of trees and laborers, and by the calendrics of harvesting, clearing, and planting. Deep in the plantations, those straight lines were occasionally interrupted by islands of indigenous trees that provided the materials of imithi, traditional medicine that can only be harvested from indigenous flora and fauna.[12] The lines of timber that grew over the former homesteads and graves of those who lived on this land before their displacement and forced removal during the twentieth century obscured those histories and even memory itself.[13]

The patchwork landscape of communal areas with dispersed homesteads, timber plantations, conservation parks, towns, densifying informal settlements, and commercial farms had been produced by a violent history of conquest and dislocation. As a palimpsest of spatial catastrophes, it could be read as a series of cartographic nightmares, each seeking to separate out territories of Whiteness and Blackness, colony and custom, a civilizational telos in which African political and spatial forms were torn asunder in the service of improvement and (racialized) capital.[14] On this reading, the tricks and tropes of mapmaking and territorial sovereignty were the materials of racialized exploitation, onto which was layered, like geological strata, the networks of global capital and state welfare in the postapartheid period. However, a sharp progressivist periodization such as this is inadequate for understanding the operations of multiple forms of spatialization at work here, because the relations at stake in each of the varied spatial forms operated differently—and differentially—leading to overlapping and yet quite different political and social concerns.

The plantation is not simply row upon endless row of genetically modified gum tree; it is a complex assemblage of people, machines, plants, and animals. It also comprises layers, knots and sets of relationships, modes of composing labor, calories, policies, markets, and calculations and rationalizations. The plantation is both a type and a token, a logic and a set of historical specificities, each a form of life, premised on and operationalizing very different concepts of "life."[15] Each form of life anticipates and entails distinct relations and rationalities, producing a series of varied problematizations or *plantation-analytics*.

Amid the timber plantations, first planted in the 1910s in drained swamplands, are remaindered spaces now under conservation in the iSimangaliso Wetland Park, or fragmented "customary lands" surveilled by global health and since 2008 cannibalized by coal mining. People forcibly removed from the wetlands by colonial and then apartheid governments now lived around the plantations and wetlands, folded into the Demographic Surveillance Area (DSA) of the Africa Centre for Health and Population Studies (AC), and navigated overlapping systems of municipal and customary law. The plantations, the wetland park, and the DSA were three spatial forms that employed the techniques of classical biopolitical power in constructing and circulating their concerns by means of municipal boundaries, satellite-based geographic information systems, remote sensing, and statistical techniques. However, they also depended on variously codified versions of "customary" or "tribal" law, kinship, and domestic reproduction. Each of these authorities set in motion particular distributional regimes that shaped life here in important ways: one was concerned with trees and timber, labor and profit; another with species diversity, hydrology, and claimant communities; the last, with blood, data, and population. Each of these regimes translated locality into spatial forms available to calculation by means of specific concepts, relations, and actants, each with social and political implications. In classical sociology, these are the means by which "the social" is constructed, managed, intervened into, and "capitalized." It is not clear, though, to what extent the actual relations between people, collectives, political forces, and nonhuman forms of life around the plantations constitute "society" in the conventional sense, or whether the histories of these localities conform to these terms.

A standard dictionary definition of topology points to mathematics: topology (place, location, study of) is concerned with the properties of a geometric object that are preserved under continuous deformations, such as stretching, twisting, crumpling, and bending but not tearing or gluing. A topological space is a set endowed with a structure, called a topology, which allows defining continuous deformation of subspaces and, more generally, all kinds of continuity.[16] By considering the various deformations of the relationships between laborers, corporations, state, chiefs, citizens, and subjects, one can track the continuities of the structural relations, even while conditions and individuals changed. Framing the plantations, wetlands, and DSA in topological terms puts into question any simple rendering of either a history or a spatial form that inserts labor in this context into a neat telos of globalization or, for that matter, alienation.

In this chapter, I develop an account of how "the living" establishes a politics of topology. "The living" is a term Georges Canguilhem develops as a way to name diverse forms of life in dynamic relation, as a vitalist tradition in biology suggests—that is, "life" as that which exceeds rational decomposition and calculation.[17] Which concept of life animates anthropology is less clear, but as scholars of science and technology have shown, ideas about biological life forms and their relations with humans and infrastructures are one means by which the social, the biological, and the ecological have been construed as "related."[18] What emerges is a picture of how the forms of living constituted in response to the devastating dislocations from lands and recruitment into the exploitative labor relation in the timber plantations must mount a creative effort that reorganizes coordinates of living and dying, making and unmaking.

What I call the work of repair is the key mode through which living is made possible in the context of the history of plantation labor in northern KwaZulu-Natal. Such a claim demands a clearer conception of the milieu, both in its historical formation and as a set of spatial referents.[19] By working through several histories of spatialization in and of this region, what emerges is less the domination of one particular spatial logic that renders labor alienable and society alienated, but rather the interplay and slippage between several different regimes of spatialization, localization, and dislocation or displacement. Thus we can ask: What does this (or that) particular topology capacitate? Colonial maps that tie tribes to territories enable the displacement of people from their lands; health surveillance produces a relationship between a pathogen and an individual; children's drawings hold open the possibility of "imaginal caring." At stake is what picture of the social is available for understanding the work of repair and its place, and emplacement, in postapartheid South Africa.

Reviewing several cartographic efforts to map and organize the territories that constitute the plantations, the conservation wetlands, the demographic surveillance area, and the so-called communal areas under customary authority that abut the plantations helps clarify the different "social projects" at work that intersect in the problem-space of the plantation. Population health surveillance, wetland conservation, and timber production each deploy a set of technologies and techniques, actors and objects, models and projects. They all work toward distinct horizons, but by different means. By asking about the divergent concepts of "the social" that were deployed in and around the plantations, the wetlands, and the demographic surveillance area, what comes into view are the political ends that each of these topologies capacitated, and the relationships between them. It is this play and slippage between topologies that is vital to understanding amandla as a logic for navigating particular histories of cartographic violence. What this play of topologies looks like is hinted at in the figural expressions of the children whose "maps" I describe below. The hinge around which topologies operate here is the notion of "vicinity" as it comes to enliven the distinct projects at work around the plantations.[20] How "vicinality" articulates with amandla, then, as a "politics of life" becomes clear by the end of the chapter.

FIRST TOPOLOGY:
COLONIAL CARTOGRAPHIES AND ORIGIN MYTHS

The first topology is that of the colonial cartography, whose constitutive violence has reorganized ordinary life in the service of colonial profit, and whose techniques remain at the core of postcolonial governance. A history of cartography in this place rests on several founding myths which come into view as one reads this archive against the grain, in an effort that Carolyn Hamilton and Nessa Leibhammer call "untribing the archive."[21] As Mbongiseni Buthelezi argues, "we need new names too" for drawing out the lives and histories of those occluded by colonialism's techniques of recognition.[22] If "untribing" and finding new names constitute one type of reparative effort, it has been preceded by the postapartheid project of state-led land reform, which took as its horizon of concern the alienation of people from their lands by the 1913 Natives Land Act. I show here how a longer history of cartographic capture underlay the forced removals after 1913 and established the (spatialized) conditions of possibility for postapartheid redress. Crucially, this cartographic capture is sedimented into the operations of HIV surveillance, as I show in the following section.

The Standard Encyclopedia of Southern Africa and the Dictionary of South African Place Names, both published during the height of "grand apartheid," claim that Lake St Lucia and the cape associated with it were named by Portuguese navigators in 1507.[23] Dominy, following Cortesão, suggests that Cape St Lucia is accurately represented on three Portuguese maps that predate 1507—namely, the anonymously produced planisphere called the "Cantino" map of 1502; the slightly later "Hamy-King" chart of 1504; and Nicolo de Caverio's planisphere of 1505–6.[24] The Cantino planisphere is the earliest surviving map showing Portuguese discoveries in "the East" and "West" and is credited with being an early and accurate presentation of the world known to Europe at the start of its age of empire. It labors under the sign of a secret and a betrayal: as a copy of the official prototype that was held in secret, it is thought to have been acquired by the Italian Alberto Cantina when he was sent by the Duke of Ferrara to gather exploration intelligence from the Portuguese in 1501 and bribed a Portuguese government mapmaker to make a copy for him. It is also suggested that this cartographic work may well have been the result of a secret voyage of exploration that predated Vasco da Gama's voyage of 1497.[25] The Portuguese explorers who first identified what would later be called Santa Lucia (perhaps on da Gama's secret voyage before 1497, but certainly by 1507) are not recorded as having ventured ashore, but the accounts of Portuguese shipwreck survivors later in the sixteenth century provide the first written information on the iSimangaliso region. The survivors of the 1552 shipwreck of the Portuguese galleon Sao João walked from what would later become Port Edward to the mouth of the Maputo River, but little is known of their journey. It is the 1554 survivors of the wrecked galleon Sao Bento, making their way north by foot along the coast to Delagoa Bay and finding it impossible to cross the estuary they called Rio de la Medãos do Ouro (River of the Sands of Gold), who gave the first detailed written account of European presence there.[26] However, it was on December 13, 1575, on the feast of Saint Lucy, that Manuel Perestrello renamed the Rio de la Medãos do Oura as Santa Lucia.[27] Each of these stories of "discovery" involved wreckage, naming, the recording of European deaths, and contact with "savages."[28] Each of the many European expeditions then journeying up the east coast of Africa during the sixteenth century developed more detailed charts of the coast and its interior, replete with geographical terminologies, tribal taxonomies, and conventions of map reading.

Archaeological evidence suggests continuous occupation of the area between Maputo and Lake St Lucia from at least the thirteenth century, probably 1250, and accounts of numerous shipwrecked sailors provide a patchy but continuous record from 1589.[29] Hedges reports that in the mid-sixteenth century two Ronga ("Southern Thonga") chiefdoms were in control of the region and in contact with the Portuguese, who were still paying tribute to "Tembe" chiefs in 1823.[30] Webster argues that while an autochthonous population in the region north of Lake St Lucia, augmented by immigrants and refugees over a long period, may not have had much political cohesion before the upheavals of the early 1800s, emergent allegiances and polities ebbed and flowed as successive waves of political control washed over them. Thus, just before the huge social and political transformations of the early 1800s, the Thonga were probably the preeminent political force in the subcontinent as neither the Swazi nor the Zulu states had yet been constituted. Thonga power and influence reached its height during the rule of Mabhudu of the Tembe clan (ca. 1740–98), with trade and military power growing under Mabhudu's pioneering organization and centralization of young men into age regiments (amabutho).[31]

In the late eighteenth century, the Swazi and Zulu states began to coalesce into powerful political units, eclipsing Thonga formations. This power shift led to the huge upheavals of the early 1800s that worked their way through southeastern African polities along complex networks of trade, patronage, and obligation across much of southern Africa.[32] Accounts of the incorporation under Zulu authority of areas in what today is northern KwaZulu-Natal tend to focus on Shaka's use of the age regiment as a school and military unit that allowed the expansion of political control.[33] When Dingiswayo kaJobe instructed Shaka kaSenzangakhona to take over the Zulu "chieftainship," with the fealty of a small group of about two thousand people in the early 1810s, the strict training, strategy, and discipline that would later capture the imagination of European historians became terrifyingly effective.[34] Taking over command from Dingiswayo in 1818, after Dingiswayo's murder by Zwide of the Ndwandwe, Shaka became the strongest ruler north of the Thukela River.

Under Dingiswayo's leadership, the Mthethwa people had expanded into the ivory-rich coastal region, forcing Tsonga/Ronga-speaking people to move away from the Mfolozi valley into the area around the estuary and lakes of St Lucia. The aggression of the Thembe inkosi to the north at the same time further concentrated Tsonga/Ronga-speaking people around Lake St Lucia.[35] The internal political rivalry among the Mabhudu amakhosi and their relatives to the north of Lake St Lucia meant that by 1824 Shaka was able to take advantage of those divisions and extend Zulu authority over the Tsonga/Ronga-speaking people to the north.[36] The area was never formally incorporated into the Zulu state, but the Mabhudu *inkosi* Makasana paid tribute to the Zulu kings. When Makasana died in 1853, Mpande, Shaka's successor, was able to tighten control over the Tsonga/Ronga-speaking people of the coast.

Boer (nascent Afrikaner) trekkers asserting bootstrap claims to territorial sovereignty forged the Republic of Natalia with St Lucia Bay as their northeastern boundary, establishing the terms of race, nation, and territory that would shape the twentieth century so powerfully.[37] After their defeat by the British in 1842, the Voortrekker claims to Zululand lapsed and the northern border of the new Colony of Natal was established along the Thukela River. Britain, however, established an early "preemptive" claim to St Lucia Bay which was intended to forestall any other European power from acquiring the bay and lake as a possible port. The British commissioner to Natal in 1843, Henry Cloete, "persuaded" King Mpande to cede the bay to Queen Victoria.[38] This claim remained dormant and the area remained part of the Zulu kingdom until the Anglo-Zulu War of 1879, although it was always on the fringes of political developments.

The political tumult of the early nineteenth century also pushed newly formed groups of refugees southward toward the Cape Colony, forcing a series of negotiations and accommodations around land acquisition and livelihood between African groups. Those living closest to the Cape, such as those who became known as Mfengu and Xhosa, experienced the forces of British colonial expansion earliest and most directly, culminating in the tragic Cattle Killing episode of the late 1850s.[39] In the midst of the famines and upheavals of this period, the Lake St Lucia area was being stitched into Zulu "royal" authority through the installation of a new young inkosi, fourteen-year-old Nozingile, who was genealogically tied into Mpande's royal line through marriage, and thus an ally of the Zulu state.[40] Following what has been called the "Zulu Civil War of 1856," Cetshwayo kaMpande settled some of his followers around Phongolo. The border amakhosi south of Kosi Bay became increasingly independent of the Mabhudu inkosi as Zulu power and influence over the Mabhudu amakhosi increased both north and south of Lake St Lucia. As the nineteenth century progressed, the lower Mfolozi valley fell under the control of the Mphukunyoni amakhosi (the name has changed to Mkhwanazi in the course of the twentieth century). The most significant of these, Somkhele kaMalanda, ruled in the second half of the nineteenth century. An inkosi of considerable power, he came from a family that had first risen to authority when his grandfather Velane was an induna of Dingiswayo kaJobe. During the reign of Shaka, Somkhele's father Malanda kaVelane was "raised" to become an inkosi and was given the important role of guarding the eastern coastal region and keeping any southward Mabhudu harassment in check. Although beholden to the Zulu state for the power they held, the Mphukunyoni amakhosi were far from the seat of royal power and acted as a powerful regional force, particularly once Malanda kaVelane married into the royal household. (Somkhele in the twenty-first century is the locality in which the seat of Mkhwanazi customary power, the lavish offices of the Africa Centre for Health and Population Studies—and the center of their Demographic Surveillance Area—and the new Somkhele coal mine all overlap.)[41]

In the early 1870s Britain and Portugal came into conflict over the crucial question of trade rights on the southeast coast. They turned to the French president MacMahon for arbitration, who carved the territory of the Mabhudu inkosi in two with no interest in local conditions or polities. All the land from Delagoa Bay (modern Maputo) to 26′30″ (just north of Lake St Lucia) was granted to the Portuguese, while everything south of that, and as far west as the Mkhuze River, became part of the Zulu kingdom, and therefore in the general sphere of British interest. In 1876, the year after the MacMahon arbitration, the Mabhudu inkosi Nozingile died and his brother Muhena became regent with the support of Cetshwayo kaMpande, the Zulu king. After the Zulu defeat at the hands of the British in 1879, Nozingile's Swazi widow Zambili managed to secure the throne for her juvenile son, declared herself queen-regent, and forced all other claimants into exile. While the iSimangaliso/Somkhele region was not directly affected by the Anglo-Zulu War of 1879, at its end the English Crown divided the defeated Zulu kingdom into thirteen separate territories under various "kinglets," mutually antagonistic local potentates, many of whom had been hostile to the Zulu royal house. The eastern shores of Lake St Lucia were allocated as territory to Somkhele, chief of the Mphukunyoni clan and an Usuthu supporter, that is, one loyal to Cetshwayo's cause, whose heartland lay inland, to the west of the lake.[42] After another period of civil war in 1883, intruding Boer farmers proclaimed a "New Republic" in Zululand on land extorted from their support for Dinizulu, successor to the late king Cetshwayo. In defeating challenges to their choice of Zulu leader, the Boers laid out farms across the breadth of Zululand, right up to the Indian Ocean coast, and planned a town port to be called Eugenie on the St Lucia estuary.[43] The British responded the following year by activating their dormant claim to the bay of St Lucia and on May 14, 1887, annexed it to the Crown, along with the rest of the Zululand coast, to forestall Boer plans and deter European infringement on British interests.[44]

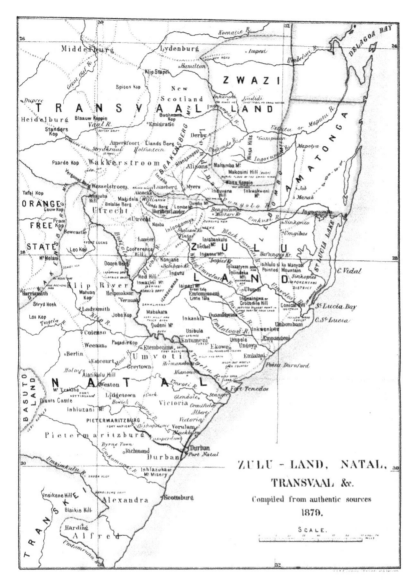

MAP 1: Zulu-land, Natal, Transvaal &c. (Source: William Clifford Holden, *British Rule in South Africa. Illustrated in the Story of Kama and his tribe, and of the war in Zululand*. 1879. British Library HMNTS 9061.b.9, from Wikimedia Commons: https://commons.wikimedia.org/wiki/File:Map_of_Zululand,_Natal,_Transvaal _(1879).jpg

The annexation served Queen-Regent Zambili's strategy for independence from the Zulu, and by agreeing to assist the British in suppression of Zulu authority, she engineered British support for her position. The Anglo-Mabhudu "treaty of friendship" was signed in July 1887. When the British refused to extend her territory south of the Mkhuze River, she switched her allegiance to the Portuguese. In response, the British annexed Zambili's land in 1888 to the new colony of Zululand to prevent the extension of Portuguese claims. Under this claim, the northern shores of Lake St Lucia fell under the minor Mabhudu amakhosi Sibonda and Ncamana. The British asserted that all the people living along the shores of Lake St Lucia were henceforth to be considered "Zulu" subjects of the British Crown. In 1897 Zululand was incorporated into the Natal colony. In 1896, Zululand was struck by severe drought and by an epidemic of rinderpest that devastated cattle herds, killing 85 percent of all cattle in Zululand. The Natal government delivered maize imported from America by steamship to Port Durnford, south of Richards Bay, but because of restrictions on the movement of cattle, had to rely on the railroad being built by the sugar baron J. L. Hulett to connect Durban with Zululand to transport the coal that was discovered at Somkhele.[45] The swampy land around the coastal forests of Dukuduku cramped Hulett's plans for sugar plantations in Zululand because malaria, flooding, locusts, and tsetse flies made for fatal conditions.

Forced Removals during Apartheid

The years after this initial intrusion by rail and sugar led to the initial draining of the swamplands, afforestation for timber, and the consolidation of the colonial order.[46] Of particular note here is the 1936 Native Trust and Land Act, one of the most significant pieces of legislation in the history of twentieth-century South Africa, the effect of which was to sharpen the division between freehold property within reserve areas and that outside of reserves. Although most freehold land was incorporated into the reserves through the 1936 act, a significant amount was excluded. These areas became known as "black spots." The freehold land that was not released in 1936 became increasingly vulnerable because it usually consisted in isolated holdings surrounded by White farmers hostile to their Black neighbors. While the 1936 act defined the category of "black spot," it was in the 1960s and 1970s that its full effects were felt. During this period, when former "native reserves" were being dressed up as homelands and then Black national states, some released areas were earmarked for excision from the areas allocated for African ownership and occupation in order to further "consolidate" homeland areas. Some freehold farms in these areas were again marked as "black spots" and subjected to "consolidation" planning, this time under the term "badly situated area." Officials were inconsistent in their use of these terms, however, and used them indiscriminately. Irrespective of the terms used, Black landowners and tenants were equally threatened with expropriation, dispossession, and removal from their land. In some respects, class differences based on land ownership were eroded in that more people found themselves subject to colonial regulation of customary land ownership in reserve areas. However, powerful families were still able to exert claims through kin-based assertions to customary authority. The net effects of the act on local forms of authority and class stratification continue to drive postapartheid insecurity of tenure and revitalized claims to customary authority.

The period between 1936 and 1960 led to the rise of the National Party (coming into government in 1948) and the transformation of native reserves into quasi-independent political units to house, control, and administer the vast bulk of South Africa's workforce.[47] Crucial in this process was the passage of the Bantu Self-Government Act of 1951 and the Promotion of Bantu Self-Government Act in 1959, which introduced the concept of ethnic Bantustans, to be based on existing reserves. Whereas there was no serious program of removal of black spots before the National Party came to power, there was an explicit statement of intent after 1948 to eradicate all the black spots as quickly as possible, hampered only by the shortage of land on which to relocate people. While the land in northern KwaZulu-Natal was consolidated through diverse legal mechanisms and complex political processes (which continue to shape porous and inconstant boundaries today), all the categories of relocation that were deployed across Natal and KwaZulu were important in shaping the social terrain upon which claims to conservation and plantation land have been and are being made.

From the 1950s to the early 1980s around twelve hundred "isiZulu-speaking households" were removed from what is now the Eastern Shores of the iSimangaliso Wetland Park and absorbed into neighboring polities as part of the broader attempt to consolidate the apartheid vision of a White South Africa with independent, ethnically defined Bantustans that were the "natural homes" of the various tribes of southern Africa "outside" the space of the national state.[48] Many thousands of households across Zululand and Natal, but specifically around the many timber plantations and conservation parks in the north, were subjected to the same forced removals, one of the defining features of apartheid social engineering that sought to distribute sites of Black African habitation and employment: habitation outside South Africa in spaces governed by tradition, and employment within South Africa with restrictions on every aspect of personal conduct and mobility. However, there remains sparse documentation of the exact numbers and experiences of those forced to make way for conservation, timber, and agriculture in KwaZulu-Natal in the service of strategies and spatial logics of racialized and ethnicized difference. The Surplus People Project's 1983 report was the only systematic attempt to document forced removals across South Africa, and it remains a vital document in tracking the history of twentieth-century dislocation in KwaZulu. The report documents the way in which Black Africans, Indians, Coloureds, and anyone that the apartheid government determined to be "non-White" were subject to a vast array of laws and extralegal tactics designed to curtail movement and control labor.

Relocation in Natal from the 1960s to the 1980s was premised on the logic of apartheid that had as its goal "no more Black South Africans." However, the overwhelming majority of Black Africans in the province of Natal made the implementation of a spatial logic of separation impossible to effect in any pure form. The relocations that flowed from the institutions created by the Bantu Authorities Act of 1951 were particularly harsh across South Africa, but the attempt to consolidate land under a KwaZulu homeland was challenged by a number of "special features" in both rural and urban areas.[49] Key among them were the size of the homeland and its demographic features. As the largest and most populous homeland, it occupied 38 percent of the landmass of Natal but contained 55 percent of the total population in the region. The central government's classification of ethnic groups produced the largest single grouping in South Africa in "the Zulu": in the Natal region, including KwaZulu, over 77 percent of the population were African and over 90 percent were Zulu-speaking. Local differences of forms of association, linguistic dialects, and political loyalties were all subjected to the strategic creation of "ethnic identities"; thus, the production of a "Zulu nation" cannot be understood outside of the logic of population control and resistance to it.[50] In addition, the difficulty of implementing the Bantustan plan in Natal was not only because of popular African resistance to removal but also because of resistance from White interest groups opposed to handing agricultural land over to KwaZulu (in particular sugar farmers north of Durban up to and beyond St Lucia).

Thus, the attempt, after 1960, to redistribute territory between White South African and Black KwaZulu homeland into a more contiguous mass was frustrated by the diverse land ownership arrangements that had developed over a century of colonial rule. In 1978 the KwaZulu Bantustan consisted officially of 48 major pieces of land and 157 small pieces of land scattered through the province. It was highly fragmented as a political entity, "a consolidationist's nightmare."[51] The overwhelming African majority in the population meant that the apartheid state found it increasingly difficult to control the territory spatially, despite attempts to redraw the adjoining borders of South Africa, Swaziland, and Mozambique, an area of significant strategic military interest.[52]

In the 1960s, extensive but poorly documented removals took place in the northern coastal regions where large afforestation programs were developed on land once owned by the state. Labor tenancy was abolished at the end of the 1960s, resulting in massive evictions of farmworkers and tenants. Many "closer settlements" were established in this period in northern Natal to soak up the flood of displaced people. The effort to consolidate the homeland of KwaZulu intensified in the 1970s and took on a new political dimension with the establishment of the Zulu Territorial Authority and the Homeland Citizenship Act of 1970. The attempt to consolidate "a more rational and unified geopolitical entity" met with great resistance from organized White-owned agriculture, the sugar industry, and the Natal Chamber of Industries, as well as the KwaZulu government itself.[53] Strategic security considerations became more important for the state during this period, spurred by the fear of the Frelimo victory over Portuguese rule in Mozambique in 1975. This sped up the program of removals in the militarily sensitive areas along the northern coastline and the borders with Mozambique and Swaziland.

Attempts to consolidate the homeland saw constant adjustments to boundaries and numerous additions and subtractions in an attempt to lend political legitimacy to the social-engineering project at large. The logic that drove the consolidation plans was founded on the Tomlinson Commission's notion of "ethnic heartlands" around which ethnic groups could be constructed.[54] Seven blocks were imagined: a Tswana block, a Venda-Tsonga block, a Pedi block, a Swazi block, a Zulu block, a southeastern Nguni block, and a South Sotho block. Group Areas legislation also powerfully shaped the social landscape around the plantations. Proclaimed in 1950, the Group Areas Act enforced a system of ethnic residential segregation in urban areas and supported the rigid race classification system refined by apartheid policy. While nationally the Group Areas Act most severely affected those people classified as Coloured and Indian, since African occupation of land was already controlled by the 1923 Natives (Urban Areas) Act, it shaped the entire field of social relations in cities and small towns, including those around the plantations and wetlands of northern KwaZulu-Natal.[55] The proclamations of Group Areas occurred at different times in different places, producing a highly uneven terrain of relations, residence, ownership, and livelihood. For example, Shakaskraal was proclaimed Indian in 1980; Ifafa Beach, Coloured in 1981; Richards Bay, White, Coloured, and Indian in 1981; Mtubatuba, White, Coloured, and Indian in 1982; Gingindlovu, White, Coloured, and Indian in 1982; and Eshowe as White and Coloured in 1982. The spatial arrangements of towns as well as the economic and social relations between towns and rural reserves was thus imagined and cemented by these laws.[56]

Thirty to fifty years after forced removal by the apartheid state, after several generations of intermarriage and cohabitation, almost everyone living in northern KwaZulu-Natal has kin who were displaced by the state or have been accommodated by neighboring polities. Their movements across the land bump up against layer upon layer of fragments—of homes, histories, solidarities, and livelihoods. As others have found, many land claimants have a strong memory of the day they were forced to move—the callousness of the government workers who tore down their homes, threw their belongings into the notorious "GG" trucks, and dumped them without resources on others' lands.[57] The experiences of those dislocated in this manner suggest that, in many ways, the destruction and dislocation of people's lives in the making and reshaping of sovereign space serviced a vision of "apartness," "separate development," and a need for cheap labor that was at its core a cartographic project constituted as a metropolitan concern with securing and surveilling labor.

Restitution and Repair

During 2008, I conducted interviews with members of land claim trusts and others who had been dislocated from land now under conservation in the iSimangaliso Wetland Park. The aim of the interviews was to help thicken accounts of their experiences in the years since forced removals. The ethnographic record is thin and the activist accounts from the 1980s too focused. Oral histories suggest a proliferation of memories, narrations, and genealogical relations that exceed the narrow terms imagined by juridical efforts at land reform and restitution.[58] The post-1994 land and agricultural reform program of the liberal, newly democratic government sought, in the first place, to redress the historical injustices of land dispossession since the passing of the 1913 Land Act. Such redress would engage both the moral debt accrued to Black citizens and the structural marginalization of rural homeland populations.[59] However, the diversity of each of the fourteen land claims on what is now the iSimangaliso Wetland Park, and the many other smaller claims on the timber plantations around the park, point to the varied milieus that must be articulated in genealogical terms in order for claimants to access the forms of compensation flowing from the land claim settlements.[60] The temporalities indexed by genealogical modes of reckoning and cartographic representations of relations are thus formed by what Elizabeth A. Povinelli calls the "spacing of social tense" within the liberal modes of government in northern KwaZulu-Natal (in which constitutional and customary law are uncomfortably accommodated for the time being, and their points of conflict deferred for final resolution during the course of everyday struggles). By "spacing," Povinelli means the distinction and juxtaposition of political subjectivities imagined to cohere naturally around those who inhabit a mythical past, a "tribal" time of custom, in contradistinction to modern liberal subjects who inhabit the liberated time of the present (and which, not coincidentally, find spatial and cartographic expression in colonial histories of conquest). Such spacing, I suggest, though highly productive of racialized imaginaries of difference, not only retains the ethical horizon of late liberal concerns with inclusion but also transforms the life worlds of those who "relax" into genealogical (and racialized) vocabularies.[61]

The Bhangazi land claim settlement in 1999 was significant for the lengths the then regional land claims commissioner went to create a model resolution.

Since then, progress on resolving land claims on the iSimangaliso Wetland Park and surrounding timber plantations has been slow and disjointed, with suggestions that the office of the regional lands claims commissioner has been in disarray.[62] Some claimants and their committees understood that resolution was obstructed by false claims from others who argued for their own historical connection to the same land. While relatives of those who were forcibly removed and who have since died demand recognition and inclusion, in other cases the designated representatives of extended kin networks named in the claims' legal papers continue to be challenged by others who have since become disappointed in them. The legal agreements of the restitution claims between the state and claimants (settled in terms of the Restitution of Land Rights Act no. 22 of 1994) is formulated on the basis of a picture of "land," "community," "claimant community," and "beneficiary family" in whose interests the trusts and their committees are intended to act.[63] And crucially, it is indexed by a map of the area to which the settlement agreement refers. While all thirteen land claims on the iSimangaliso Wetland Park have been settled to varying degrees, most claimant trusts do not function as legally constituted entities and remain hotly contested sites of struggle between clan members, descendants, newly married newcomers, and opportunists. The idea of the trust and the territory it indexes remains a lively and fluid opening for many new struggles over life and livelihood, increasingly loosely tied to the legal terms of their settlement. Land claimant trusts, as secular legal vehicles of reparation, have increasingly come into tension with new claims to customary authority in the legal vacuum since 1996, when Parliament passed the Interim Protection of Informal Land Rights Act (IPILRA) and has not replaced it with more lasting legislation.[64]

SECOND TOPOLOGY: POPULATION AND PATHOGEN

While the first topology described the history of the colonial cartography and forced displacement of the region with the aim of situating contemporary land claims and efforts to repair the historical injustices of land dispossession, the second topology concerns the HIV surveillance conducted by the Africa Centre for Health Population Studies (hereafter "the Africa Centre" or AC), whose Demographic Surveillance Area (DSA) abuts the timber and sugar plantations and conservation parks near the town of

Mtubatuba.[65] To be sure, the emergence of the uMkhanyakude region can be traced through the production of maps that plot births and deaths, epidemiological risks, population characteristics, or municipal service provision, each of which have a distinct cartographic history. However, recent advances in spatial epidemiology developed by scientists at the Africa Centre draw together geographic information systems and demographic data in new ways.[66] The new topologies of spatial epidemiology articulate well-being and disease in terms of sexual networks, topographical setting, connection to the highway or the city—in short, a topology of nodes, networks, and intensities. The cartographic commitment to the real and to a succession of presents not only makes new categories of disease and ill-being visible but also grounds a particular conception of "society," of "the social," and opens the possibility for novel forms of citizenship to emerge from new techniques of inclusion.[67] It also transforms the lifeworlds of those arranged around and outside the DSA as services, interventions, and knowledge work to redistribute the ill effects of apartheid exclusion and abandonment.

Established in 1998, thirty kilometers inland from the coastal wetlands of iSimangaliso and two hundred kilometers north of Durban, the Africa Centre was a collaboration between the University of KwaZulu-Natal and the South African Medical Research Council, with funding from the Wellcome Trust. In 2016, the Africa Centre merged with the KwaZulu-Natal Research Institute for TB-HIV (K-RITH) to form the Africa Health Research Institute (AHRI).[68] The Africa Centre defined a demographic surveillance area whose arbitrary borders intentionally contain a variability of topography, density of settlement, and infrastructure and encompass both "rural" areas and a "periurban" township. In 2012, there were approximately 11,000 households in the DSA, including 90,000 resident and nonresident individuals. The DSA is situated in one of the poorest districts in KwaZulu-Natal, with a fluid population and high rates of mobility.[69] The designated area includes land under the Zulu tribal authority that was formerly classified as a homeland under the apartheid-era Bantu Authorities Act of 1951 as well as an urban township, formerly designated for "African" residents, under municipal authority. Though the area is often defined as "rural" South Africa, there is a large variation in population densities from twenty to three thousand people per square kilometer with little in the way of a functioning agrarian economy. Similarly, infrastructure development across the area is heterogeneous, ranging from fully serviced "modern" houses to isolated homesteads without water, electricity, or sanitation. Unemployment is extremely high (around 42 percent), most residents rely on government welfare payments, and agrarian livelihoods are marginal.[70]

Information about these subjects, including mortality, fertility, and migration, is stored longitudinally in a single database: the Africa Centre Demographic Information System (ACDIS). Using GIS mapping, households and individuals are located within "bounded structures" with fixed spatial coordinates. Since 2003, a population-based HIV surveillance program has been nested within the demographic surveillance program, which began in 2000.[71] The HIV surveillance program is unique in that all data collected in the HIV survey is spatialized and can be linked anonymously to longitudinal data collected from a number of trials in ACDIS. Each surveillance round has consisted of forty "week blocks" during which eligible participants were visited and asked to consent to provide a dried blood spot (DBS) sample that is tested for HIV as part of an anonymous linked surveillance program. The Africa Centre partnered with the local department of health and international donors to provide expertise and life-saving pharmaceuticals in each of the clinics and hospitals in the region, a good example of what Geissler and Nguyen call the "para-state."[72] Many people refuse to give blood samples to the surveillance; for those who consent, their blood is sent to laboratories in Durban three hours away to be analyzed and transformed into data. The data is returned to the DSA and uploaded onto handheld computers that (almost) anonymously deliver to the donor their status—positive or negative—and a social verdict: life or death.[73] Not only was the Africa Centre materially implicated in the state's local provisioning of ART in the district's health system, but the scientific claims emerging from its data inform national and global policy on treatment and prevention of HIV.

Local and Spatial

The topology of this new spatial epidemiology is captured well in two articles published by Africa Centre scientists in *Science* magazine in 2013—one by Frank Tanser et al. and one by Jacob Bor et al.[74] They are significant for the ways in which they fold together several cartographic possibilities and produce space within a distinctly "fluid" topology. The first of the two papers, by Tanser et al., describes the use of spatial analytical techniques to demonstrate with empirical observation that high coverage of ART in one locality with extremely high rates of HIV significantly reduces the risk of acquiring HIV and produces radical gains in life expectancy in a population. In the second paper, Bor et al. show how cost effective those gains in life expectancy have been in the context of a nurse-driven, community-based, public-sector scale-up of ART in sub-Saharan Africa. Their findings were significant because they provided evidence to support global health policy and fed directly into national treatment planning and programming. These two publications found that in 2003, the year before ART become available in the public-sector health system, adult life expectancy in the DSA in northern KwaZulu-Natal at age fifteen had fallen to 49.2 years (compared to the WHO estimation of 61.4 years for South Africa as a whole), and had begun to rise immediately after the introduction of ART in 2004, reaching 60.5 years in 2011—an 11.3-year gain. The second significant finding was that an HIV-uninfected individual living in a community with high ART coverage was 38 percent less likely to acquire HIV than someone living in a community where ART coverage was low. High coverage was defined as 30 to 40 percent of all HIV-infected individuals on ART, and low coverage as less than 10 percent. While predictive mathematical models had suggested that under certain conditions, high coverage of ART could lead to a substantial decrease in the rate of new HIV infections, the findings of Tanser et al. were the first empirical demonstration of the effects of ART scale-up on transmission rates and life expectancy. Their findings built on the results from the HPTN 052 study, which showed that if an HIV-infected person adhered to an effective antiretroviral therapy regimen, the risk of transmitting the virus to an uninfected sexual partner could be reduced by 96 percent.[75] The methods of both papers relied on a set of spatial techniques making use of population data that encoded several layers of history: colonial and postcolonial; industrial and agricultural labor and postwork welfare and treatment regimes; constitutional and customary legal entanglements; and "corporate social responsibility" and environmental conservation concerns.

Tanser, Bor, and their respective coauthors used a cohort of 17,000 individuals who in 2003 were HIV-negative, tracking the number of sero-conversions from 2004 to 2011, regressing the time-to-HIV sero-conversion on the extent of ART coverage in the "local community" surrounding each HIV uninfected "individual." The key methodological innovation that draws together individual and community in the analysis of Tanser et al. is the use of a moving two-dimensional Gaussian kernel to derive the strength of the effect of community treatment on individual risk. To do that, they individually geolocated 16,667 repeat testers who were HIV-uninfected at first test to their "homesteads" using the GIS. HIV prevalence and ART coverage for each individual's "surrounding community" were then determined for every year of observation. Previous work by Tanser et al. (2009) had revealed significant geographical variation in local HIV prevalence within what they saw as a "relatively homogenous population" and provided clear empirical evidence for the localized clustering of HIV infections—that is, the existence of "several localized HIV epidemics of varying intensity that are partly contained within *geographically defined communities.*"[76] Their method was apparently well suited to this setting because it did not "impose any static geographical boundaries on the data but uses the precise location of each individual to derive a sensitive community level measure that is both responsive to local variations and robust to the effects of random noise."[77]

What is significant here is the use of a statistical technique of smoothing (i.e., Gaussian blurring) to make sense of a "noisy" distribution of a pathogen in a social landscape in which physical residence is not sharply clustered by a concept like "village" (to wit, "homesteads are not concentrated into villages or compounds as in many parts of Africa") and yet is shaped by diverse concepts of locality—on the one hand, a Euclidian distance of three kilometers from each data point; on the other, a sociopolitical unit called in isiZulu "isigodi."[78] The word has come to designate a district, division, or territory and in postcolonial South Africa operates as a point of articulation between municipal and customary authorities. An isigodi according to Tanser et al. is "a traditional Zulu area (plural: izigodi)"; there are a total of twenty-three izigodi in this surveillance area. The Gaussian kernel method does not rely on this minimal geopolitical unit but rather systematically moves across two-dimensional cartographic space to sample the uneven distribution of HIV prevalence relative to each individual. Nonetheless, when the customary space of the isigodi is used as a unit of analysis, the results prove similar, "confirming a strong ART coverage effect."[79] The science here is in fact remarkably well informed by the available ethnographic work, reflecting a sophisticated demographic information system sensitively responsive to the empirical fluidity of persons, households, and built form.

The distribution of HIV in this landscape is evidently powerfully shaped by a complex set of social relations that, when observed in this fashion, cast those sexual networks in a spatial idiom that can stretch and twist as the relations themselves morph and move. This topology has a distinct topographical quality. The Euclidian distance between individuals, households, communities, and any number of other institutions clearly matters—that is, it shapes and reflects the organization of concerns as they come to matter in the material distribution of care and injury, and the way in which matters-of-concern distribute bodies in social and political life.[80] However, the measurement and representation of a thick set of social relations and practices in a spatial idiom does not produce space ex nihilo, nor does it simply reflect or reveal a preexisting "spatial fix," nor does it simply render "the social" or its obverse, "the para-state," as biosocial givens.[81] If "the social" here is in question, what does this technology of global health produce?

The topology of global health operates here by means of extending life, in epidemiological terms, and putting the terms on which they rely, such as individual, household, and community, into circulation with various material substances such as blood, timber, and calories, and thus helps (re)distribute the laboratory in whose image the world must be recreated for the pharmaceuticalized felicity conditions of Treatment as Prevention (TasP) to be satisfied.[82] In examining the topology of HIV research and state provision of antiretroviral therapy, two conceptions of the social come into focus. The first I take from James Ferguson's *Give a Man a Fish,* in which he thinks through the genealogies of social welfare payments in contemporary South Africa in order to make an argument for cash transfers in a postwork, postcolonial age.[83] Without a state premised on a labor regime that underwrites social protection, there is no "social" in the classical sociological, that is, Euro-American sense. His question is thus, What comes after the southern African social? The second debate comes from Vinh-Kim Nguyen's suggestion that Treatment as Prevention randomized controlled trials for the treatment of whole populations for HIV has inaugurated what he calls an "experimental society" living in the shadows of the "para-state." Along with P. Wenzell Geissler and others, he also argues that because there is no "social" premised on full employment, state welfare, and the like, population trials cannot be said to be "medicalizing" or "remedicalizing" social problems, for example in Africa, because there have not been the same bureaucratic forms that undergird the history of state welfare.[84] On the one hand, Ferguson claims that there has indeed been a "social" in South Africa and that its complex, racialized genealogy constitutes the conditions of possibility for the current South African welfare apparatus that is shifting toward direct cash transfers, and from September 2016, ART for all without a CD4 count eligibility criterion. On the other hand, Nguyen suggests that in the afterlife of clinical and population trials, "a kind of para-state, in the form of the MRC, CDC, or Harvard University, tills the soil left fallow by existing states," generating novel social forms, unstable forms of exchange, and new forms of subjectivity.[85] The space of the para-state, it turns out, is not devoid of, or destructive of, "the social," in the strict sociological sense critiqued by Ferguson and Nguyen, but rather is a cypher of sorts, as will become clear.

The AC's technology of surveillance not only produces a milieu as a field of planning and intervention; it also transforms local milieus by realigning inside and outside in what Kaushik Sunder Rajan calls *pharmocratic* terms— that is, the ways in which the Euro-American, research and development (R&D)-driven pharmaceutical industry operates to institute forms of governance across the world that are beneficial to its own interests.[86] Although the surveillance area was constructed to be representative of the variety of social milieus common to the region at large, the fact of inclusion for those residents within the DSA in various forms of research over the past decade has shifted and altered the wider social landscape in profound and subtle ways. The "hot spots" of high HIV prevalence in the Demographic Surveillance Area revealed by GIS mapping gives the virus a geographic home that links two forms of life, virus and host, through the representation of their spatial distribution, and places them in relation to state infrastructure, customary authority, and research and philanthropic concern.[87] When variation in the spatial distribution of the virus is revealed by such mapping techniques, the causes of such variation fall to various interrelated milieus: the physical environment (roads, hills, water), the political environment (the competent management of municipal services by competing parties), the human environment (nutrition, sanitation, housing), or even the physiological context of the human body (the gut, the immune system, wounds, other microbiota).

What Social, Which Topology?

If the innovative techniques developed by Tanser et al. and Bor et al. establish the grounds for describing characteristics of the epidemic—for example,

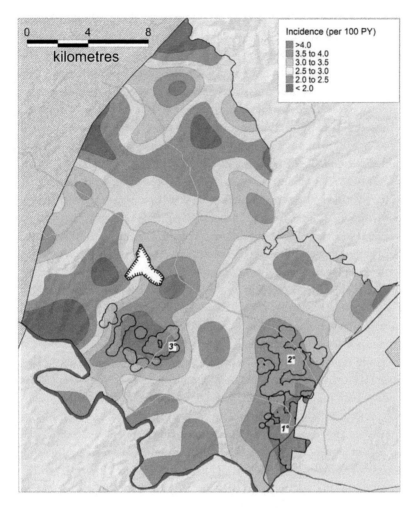

MAP 2: Hot spots, from Frank Tanser et al., "Identifying 'Corridors of HIV Transmission' in a Severely Affected Rural South African Population," *International Journal of Epidemiology* 47, no. 2 (2017): "Geographical variations in population-level HIV incidence (ages 15–54) as measured by a standard Gaussian kernel (3.0 km radius). Superimposed on the map are the high-risk clusters identified by the Tango's flexibly shaped spatial scan statistic."

the transmissibility of the virus in a population, or its uneven distribution among men and women, old and young; or its correlation with socioeconomic variables such as income or asset ownership—and thus show the usefulness of concepts of hot spot and topology, and of milieu and "social" context, it is because the spatial forms are enlivened by more than just the grammar of the "postsocial" para-state. If indeed there are local lifeworlds, emergent subjectivities, unstable categories, that move through and across these techniques and operations, then what kinds of social and political life do these intersecting distributional regimes produce?

Over twenty-five years of explicitly reparative postapartheid welfare policy, the South African state has expanded provision of cash transfers to the poor without any attachment to normative family arrangements of care or labor, and widened access to life-saving antiretroviral drugs to all, irrespective of any virological threshold.[88] Nonetheless, it has been unable to stem the loss of jobs, as the increasing mechanization of timber in KZN shows. Clearly some kind of "postsocial" social is at stake here, even with all the elements of what appears to be the "para-state."[89] If "the laboratory" is not a literal space with actual machines, but a set of procedures, as Nguyen suggests, then the postsocial "experimental society" is one in which the laboratory-as-procedure remakes the world in order to generalize the conditions under which HIV treatment as prevention might be successful. Politics remade as the distribution of the clinical is potentially both a fragmented and totalizing project, animated by pharmaceutical desire and hope, and identitarian projects old and new. However, if the spatializing techniques encode partial histories of personhood and territory and rely on failed social engineering projects of Bantustans as well as *pharmocratic* subject-citizens, then the laboratory-as-analytic must account for those incomplete and emergent social forms in which drugs and cash, custom and constitution, ex-labor and consumption, are stitched together. Already in 2015, scientists were whispering their anxieties that the Treatment as Prevention trials would not produce the necessary evidence, and indeed its results proved less important than anticipated: the South African state moved quickly to align with new WHO guidelines for full test-and-treat programs, even while doubts remained about the long-term efficacy of available combination therapies and population treatment.[90]

A key feature of the fight against HIV has been the involvement of social scientists seeking to explicate the social and structural conditions that sustain the virus, as well as ways in which research itself shapes knowledge and intervention. A substantial literature attests to this history of involvement and critique, as well as its ambivalences and ambiguities, advocating both a normative ethical case for intervention as well as a reflexive posture of critique. An appeal to a "critical global health praxis" suggests a stronger formulation of critique *and* commitment to a progressive politics.[91] "Critical" suggests absorbing the irony of trials continuing in the knowledge they will fail even while national policy preempts the findings. "Praxis" suggests attending to the efforts that make life possible in the midst of shifting regimes of value, of postcolonial pharmaceuticals both new and old, of jobless profit in old sites of labor; it suggests seeking out the new forms of life that might make for desirable social forms or attractive politics. Perhaps the laboratory will not wholly remake the world, and the social will not be entirely unrecognizable. In postsocial, postwork, and potentially postpharma South Africa, state-provided ART and welfare payments, corporate calories, and global medical research data are not simply constitutive of social relations, or a "postsocial" experimental society in the ruins or shadows of a biopolitical state, but indeed are an extension of much older forms of governance and authority that recombine in new conditions, just as the postcolonial state has always governed—the recombinant customary, if you will.

What emerges from the complex distributional regimes that undergird life in northern KwaZulu-Natal is less a full-blown postsocial, experimental society than a form of life in which the localized grammars of personhood, citizenship, and biology are circulated through a global syntax of pharma, profit, flexibility, and even professional theories of the social. In one sense, the state and its publics have always been "para," as Hellen Tilley has shown.[92] But the rearrangements of value and values, technique and topos, person and population, that Ferguson and Nguyen point to are about a reconfiguration of care and concern as public values around a different kind of person; one that is both more than ever a "citizen" and someone or something else. It is this uncertainty, openness, or inventiveness, in the midst of enduring forms of social life, that is critical to understanding the postpharma futures that lie in the shadows of these debates. How, then, to locate the agential action of persons whose capacities to bring into being a form of flourishing are so powerfully constrained not merely by the material entailments of these long histories of violent cartography, but equally by the imaginative terms on offer for conceiving of institutions, persons, and possibility?

THIRD TOPOLOGY:
DISPLACED DOMESTICITIES, PROJECTING WORLDS

While the first two topologies concern the production of space for empire, capital, and global health, the third topology in this triptych is more elusive, its fugitive traces etched in a school notebook and in the dust. In early 2010, Dumo and I were visiting Nobuhle and learning about her family's homestead—its spatial layout, who planted the mango trees, the rationale for the arrangement of rooms around the yard, the flat-roofed squares and the thatched rounds. In the midst of this, her daughter Ntombi called for our attention to show us the map she had drawn in her school exercise book. Too shy to explain the map, all Ntombi would say as she proudly opened her exercise book was that she had drawn it for her teacher at school. In blue ballpoint pen, across two pages, the world was charted (see fig. 7). In the center lies the village of Gazilini, its rural character marked by trees, round huts, and igqukwane, the small woven shelters dedicated to the shades. There is no obvious point from which to start one's journey, but snaking roads lead from the skyscrapers and beach resorts of Durban's North Beach, through white and wealthy Umhlanga Rocks, north to the market towns of Zululand, and then to the "rural area" amid the trees. Another branch of roads leads through the former homelands, through rows of matchbox houses to the towering apartment blocks of Johannesburg. At each junction sits a taxi rank or a bus stop; each locale has distinct housing types; the roads are either tarred and painted or empty and unpaved. Hospitals, schools, clinics, hostels, hotels, even erosion, are carefully marked. The sprawling township of Umlazi, the urban periphery of Durban famous for its migrant laborers' hostels, cosmopolitan mixing, and sheer size, is dislocated here. In this map it lies beyond the city, tucked into the "rural area" of the upper left corner. In fact, the map rearranges rural and urban into alternative proximities, each indexed by housing type and environmental feature (such as trees or "erosion"). In the photograph, Ntombi's fingers are also captured on the edges of the map, holding it up.

In this twelve-year-old's neat drawing, a network of intensities emerges that hints at what Gilles Deleuze in "What Children Say" calls a "dynamic

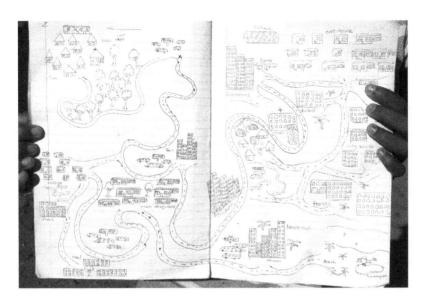

FIGURE 7: Ntombi's map

trajectory."[93] The routes and worlds captured in this drawing dislodge the panoptic and synoptic conventions of cartography and make uncertain the location of the drawer, the reader, the traveler, or the production of the map itself. Although these are not quite Kurt Lewin's hodological spaces "with their routes, their detours, their barriers, their agents," the figurations of desire are clear: the revolving restaurant on the John Ross House in Durban, or the township near "Johannesburg" which she has labeled "empilenhle."[94] (Could she mean "good health"? "The good life"? "Toward or at the place of the good life"?) I take this map to indicate the presence of alternative geographies, and of the imaginative possibilities of being otherwise, what Veena Das calls "a possibility of exile, of there being an 'elsewhere'" that makes "worldmaking" possible.[95] When Deleuze says, "It is the libido's business to haunt history and geography, to organize formations of worlds and constellations of universes, to make continents drift and to populate them with races, tribes, and nations," I take him to be pointing to the ways in which desire, anticipation, and possibility upend disciplines and conventions of knowledge, and forge new trajectories for being otherwise. The drawing stretches out as a form of what Jean Hunleth calls "imaginal caring," extending Cindy Dell Clark's notion of "imaginal coping" to enfold the work of fantasy and imagination that T. O. Beidelman suggests: how people envision and critique their worlds and also try on their "what ifs" and "construct other versions of existence besides those actually experienced."[96]

The underneath of this map, its double, was right there on the ground beneath it (see fig. 8). Ntombi and her sister had been avoiding their younger brother Sizwe and his friend who were playing under the mango tree in the corner of the yard. The two boys had been making their own world out of mud and at our excitement at the girls' map, they drew us to their own creation. Not written on paper produced by the sweat of their mothers' labor, this was the ground itself. A road had been scraped in the earth from the center of the yard to the private space behind the mango tree, and in the corner, made out of the detritus of rural life, was a detailed scene of domesticity. The boys had constructed cars, bedrooms, kitchens, stoves, lounges, and all the fine accoutrements of everyday life from repurposed batteries, staplers, medicine boxes, cell phones, circuit boards, and sponges. It was an exploded view from above that allowed an intimate look at the microdetails of domestic space. Tiny pieces of chopped guava cooking on a two-plate electric stove made from bottle tops; a toy car parked in its garage with a trailer cut from the bottom of a box of sour milk.[97] Thin insulated telephone wires connected the bottle-top stoves in the kitchen, where the top of a lotion dispenser provided a water tap, to the bedroom, where a sponge made for a foam mattress. The bed was accompanied by a carpet and a table fashioned from an old light fitting with one tiny candelabra still intact. The remains of a car tape player gave the room a hi-fi system, and an empty box of Vicks cough syrup provided a cupboard. The pinched mud walls, cleared roads, and upright sticks for a gateway that marked out the cleared space of the miniature yard-within-a-yard expressed a disconcerting accuracy of observation. The creative repurposing of discarded and broken objects into the material for a complete scene of domestic construction was uncanny in its approximations and correspondences.[98]

These two maps, on paper and on the ground, suggest a different emplotment of Zikhali domesticity and genealogical relations that exceed the cartographic, statistical, and epidemiological techniques brought to bear on them. Thus, the bonds that tie together spatialized notions of the yard (Zikhali), the local area (Mfekayi), the plantation (Nyalazi), the municipality (uMkhanyakude), the district (Hlabisa), and the province (KwaZulu-Natal)—and the names attached to those concepts—are loosened by these

FIGURE 8: The boys' map

creative gestures. The girls drew the open highway and big city in an exercise book from school. The boys built from earth and discarded microobjects. Making use of available materials and gestures—lined paper, schooled habits of drawing, discarded objects, and the earth itself—the children's maps show how the lifeworlds of timber plantation laborers and their families both absorb the presuppositions of cartography and break them open to forge creative alternatives.

The differences between the children's worldly renderings; Nobuhle's utterances regarding clan, lineage, language, and custom; and how the plantation labor regime, land-claims settlements, and population surveillance organize the spatial referents of social life produce a dissonance that is revealing of the "continuities of effort" required to sustain life and limb in the plantations and that opens up new creative possibilities.[99] However, the difference between spatial forms and their meaning in the everyday lives of the laborers must be "braced," as Povinelli puts it, by acts of interpretive framing that coordinate such efforts.[100] At stake in my descriptions here are the struts that brace the interpretative possibilities and constraints of plantation laborers' lives and their milieus.

The plantation, the wetlands, the DSA, and the children's maps each relied on distinct topologies of life. They are topological in that the signs, actors, and relations between people, things, and values are each subjected to distinct and yet overlapping regimes of cartography and calculability. At stake are the forms of action proper to each topology, and thus the scope for ethical and political life. How action and its "contexture" are composed matters—that is, they take material form, whether conceived in colonial terms of tribes and territories or conservation's terms of species diversity and ecologies, or epidemiological hot spots and intensities. In returning to the oral accounts of dislocation that I collected in 2008, I was struck not by any sense of growing amnesia, as Andrew Spiegel describes for the ways in which constraints on walking made for a "loss" of memory of landscape, but rather the struggle to recognize oneself and one's relations after the brutal disruptions of the forced removals of the twentieth century.[101] The various negotiations of territory and space in the everyday rounds of timber plantation labor, HIV surveillance, and domestic relations speak to those efforts to recognize oneself and one's milieus. In one sense, the apartheid state's efforts to rearrange the landscape constituted a racialized biopolitical concern with the proper coordination of labor and population—that is, the state sought to establish the territorial grounds for a racialized sovereignty and to assert the "hierarchical and functional distribution of elements" proper to a disciplinary mode of governance that could "capitalize" the territory.[102]

This capitalization of space, in which a milieu is transformed into a series of possible events to be regulated within a flexible mode of liberal government, was effective because of its power to exclude the majority of Black Africans from an ethical horizon of concern, and moreover to radically qualify the terms of their inclusion within the economy and polity of South Africa. The lack of census data or welfare services did not produce zones of radical abandonment, as some of the scholarship of apartheid has argued; rather, the lack of these things created an interdigitation of domestic and industrial economies and of regimes of custom and modernity that condition postapartheid possibilities for constituting life and livelihoods.[103] As forestry and conservation land claims are resolved in favor of securing the territory for the foreseeable future, the fragments and layers of diverse milieus are naturalized through new cartographic techniques brought to bear on the landscape and its population by remote-sensing geographic information systems (GIS) and population surveillance research conducted in the uMkhanyakude Municipality. Through the powerful combination of demography, epidemiology, and remote sensing, the fragments of the milieus of those living around the plantations and conservation parks are transformed into a space of population "events" whose meaning and governance must be secured.

Central to the account here is the concept of vicinity as it appears in anthropological accounts of social process in southeastern Africa, spatial analysis in health surveillance, and Science and Technologies Studies scholarship on global health. "The vicinity" is a key term in the anthropology of indigenous life in southeastern Africa; it drives the logic of labor recruitment for the plantations; and it is also an analytical technique in the calculation of HIV risk and antiretroviral cost-effectiveness. Those who lived in and around the plantations must navigate, negotiate, and (playfully, partially) slip between topologies as a key modality through which living and dying are held in tension. Alberto Corsin Jimenez's reformulation of space in terms of capacity, bringing together phenomenological, embodied concerns with social action and emplaced history, is a crucial step in deconstructing Euro-American assumptions about cartography and the places in which social life is understood to unfold.[104] The history of the state, the generational accumulation of violence, and the embodied reflection on labor bring together and locate the concern with amandla and the work of repair. Conceiving of space *as* capacity is one powerful possibility, while "vicinality" indexes the particular shape of personhood in southern Africa. However, it is not one topology or another that is in question here; rather it is the uptake and deployment of several topologies at once, and their looping effects, that configure or qualify amandla.[105] In asking "What does this or that topology capacitate?" I seek to draw out a dialectic between histories of spatialization and imaginative efforts to forge a possible politics of life.

João de Pina-Cabral argues that "the vicinity" is the key modality through which persons, houses, and relations are composed in southeastern Africa; a strong African social logic of incomplete becoming.[106] On Pina-Cabral's reading, "vicinage" is a word that emerged in southern African ethnography in the 1960s to describe how, within a neighborhood, "some houses are more constitutionally linked with each other due to the residential and kinship history of the people who inhabit them (that is, due to the *continued identities* that the residents transport)."[107] Pina-Cabral suggests that vicinage does much the same job by relation to "relatedness" as the word "kindred" once did to filiation and descent: "it allows us to describe familial sociality as a process of fuzzy constitution, rather than having to start from defined groups with well determined boundaries."[108] The word's history as an anthropological concept dates back to the sources of the anglophone tradition of southern African ethnography and, most directly, to W. David Hammond-Tooke's description of beer drinking among the Xhosa Mpondomise of the Eastern Cape in South Africa.[109] The image of houses-in-ontogeny through loose cohabitation certainly captures the topographical grammar of the landscape around the plantations, and comes to play a key role in the HIV surveillance I described above. On this reading, it is houses that are dividual, much as Marilyn Strathern argued for persons in Melanesia, in that "their singularity comes about through an act of alliance, but they remain ever enmeshed within a set of co-presences that mean they are also *partible*, for their existence is ever dependent on the existence of other households in the vicinage."[110] *Vicinage*, as an organizing logic, means that the classical anthropological figures of "persons" and "houses" can shed something of their structural functionalist baggage and allow the southern African empirics to enter into conversation with classic Melanesian materials. Reworking the insides and outsides of persons, houses, and relations, as a specifically anthropological conception of "the relation," is topological thinking at its clearest, as da Col argues.[111]

While a "topological turn" in social theory might have peaked in the mid-2010s, the "social life" of topology continues, both as an increasingly vernacular term and as a useful tool for thinking about continuities, ruptures, and the twists and torsions of meaning and material relations.[112] Attempts to think the form of the social by cannibalizing concepts from other sciences has been anthropology's trick since at least Émile Durkheim, as Bruno Latour suggests.[113] Nonetheless, the sociological tendency to "comprehend the social as a mutating field of forces that can nonetheless be both set in motion and calculated through an instrumental rationality" is useful for generating a critique of the social and for asking after politics.[114] The various forms of calculability demand attention: price per tonne of timber, workers' pay, cost-effectiveness of ART, ecosystem services. Where John W. P. Phillips locates a hollowness in topology's success beyond mathematics, we can detect the beginnings of a dispute: "This nonetheless calculable field can appear compromised because the quasi-topological treatments often want to celebrate the incalculable and (that most suggestive aspect of topological processes) the transformation, as if in antagonism towards topology, which commands its privileged role in mathematics because topological invariants are those that remain unaffected by extreme transformation: they are the fixed points in the flux of otherwise unending change."[115]

Adjacent to anthropology, critical studies of global health have also usefully developed topological approaches, revealing how very different sets of practices and equipment, involving human and nonhuman actants and their ecologies, give rise to very different concepts of space and programs of action. Famously, Annemarie Mol and John Law argue that topology "articulates different *rules for localizing in a variety of coordinate systems*" and establish a triad of topologies in their analysis of anemia as an object of global health concern: regions, networks, and fluid spatialities.[116] Ann Kelly and Javier Lezaun brilliantly take up these terms in their analysis of research and interventions on mosquito breeding grounds in Tanzania, to which my argument here is indebted. What they show is how the topological "infralogics" of research programs construct different spatializations that sustain alternative visions of "doability" and scalability in public health interventions—namely, "territorial" and "bionomic" imaginaries of the malaria breeding ground.[117] Crucially, they show how scaling up, or escalating, global health interventions is not merely a technical exercise but a political process, involving decisions over what constitutes impact and for whom, and, ultimately, which actors and institutions will be empowered and held accountable: "'Scaling up' an intervention, or escalating a particular research program, is never simply a matter of enlarging or extending a particular geographical area. If only because shifts in scale imply changes in the number and type of actors involved, and in the quality of their relations, an intervention is hardly ever kept constant as it is transposed across different contextures of action; each reconfiguration of the intervention area must contend with, and be shaped by, a different ecology of actors and practices."[118]

Kelly et al. build on this topological thinking when they show how domestic spaces perform heavy conceptual work for global health malaria interventions: while the modern household is often understood as a site of separation, vector-borne diseases brutally undercut the prophylactic capacities of the household and blur the boundaries between public and private spaces.[119] They argue instead for "vicinities"—the yard, the lawn, the threshold, back-alley plots, and pathways—that constitute malaria's contemporary spaces of concern. Such "vicinal" thinking is thus powerfully topological and poses serious questions for how political projects build on particular visions of the social across distinct forms of topological thinking. Adjacent to the plantations, the HIV surveillance also depends on an ethnological translation of vicinage, viz the local area or isigodi, in order to operationalize a demonstration of the efficacy of population treatment with antiretrovirals.

In asking what each topology capacitates (or incapacitates), I have sought to show in this chapter how the virus, the vicinity, the body, and the population are stitched together through the slippages and intersections between distinct topologies. "Mapping," "sketching," or "tracing" the historical and institutional forces that condition the production of life and labor is itself obligated to a cartographic imagination that underpins social analysis. The problem of which "postsocial" imaginary is at work in postapartheid South Africa suggests distinct horizons of ethical and political life. However, by thinking with vicinality as an unstable and impure analytic, a more complex picture of the work of repair emerges, between the logics of historical redress, population welfare and health, and the political economy of plantation labor and productivity.

CONCLUSION

The Work of Repair

Taking the figure of the laborer as a particular object of concern within the postapartheid distribution of care and discipline, this book has offered an account of the thick set of relations that sustain bodies and nurture moral projects around the timber plantations of northern KwaZulu-Natal, South Africa. An initial impetus to study the corporate nutrition intervention introduced in the timber plantations grew into a larger exploration of a set of questions that circle around citizenship, welfare, violence, hunger, and ethics. The nutrition intervention, as it was conceived and implemented, was not simply about augmenting laborers' capacity to be more productive; to the extent that the logic of "corporate social responsibility" can be understood to mount a claim to a certain kind of ethical conduct, that is, we might say that it was also an ethical response by a large employer to a humanitarian crisis of poverty and disease. While the corporation certainly articulated the nutrition intervention in these terms, we might remain skeptical of the criteria by means of which such a claim was mounted.

"Capacity" itself was the central concern for both employer and worker: on the one hand, the capacity to labor, namely labor power; on the other, the capacity to act, and to forge a livable world. The laborers' ingestion of substances, both nutritional and curative, as another means of forging capacity, points to an array of ethical projects and temporalities. For the workers, one's capacity to endure was a matter not only of dietary and bodily regimes of well-being, but also of social and governmental orders of life. These efforts to maintain life and limb are at the center of amandla—figurations of power, strength, or capacity which I understand to be the "ethical substance" out of which laborers sought to fashion a habitable world.

Amandla is both a diagnostic tool and a technique in the effort to endure a labor regime profoundly entangled with the colonial, then apartheid, and now the postapartheid state. The lives and worlds in which this group of women endured show us something of how techniques of repair are consti-tuted when labor is increasingly made surplus to new systems of produc-tion, on the threshold of disposability of "the human-as-waste."[1] By placing alongside one another several different kinds of investment in these women's capacities to labor, I have mapped out a set of questions about how life, labor, and value emerge from these scenes of extraction and excretion.

I have described efforts to augment amandla, or the capacity of laborers, in and around the timber plantations through various social projects and practices, and I have called these efforts *the work of repair*. I have attended to the everyday domains of food, nutrition, digestion, marriage, kinship, and domesticity. One form this took is of ngoma, which John Janzen terms a widespread "cult of affliction," and Robert Thornton frames in terms of "healing the exposed being" (by augmentation).[2] Louise Meintjies locates ngoma as a competitive form of male dance; emerging out of legacies of co-lonialism and apartheid, its political and ethical significance lies in the embodiment of South African history.[3] The commodified liquid tonics circulating under the sign of ngoma described in chapter 4 are no less concerned with aesthetics and expression, but they figure the force of ngoma in a different register than that of masculine dance, in the intimate folds of flesh and the ordinary actions of eating and expelling. Whether as rhythm, cult, dance, or liquid tonic, ngoma in these forms resists the claims of tra-dition or custom and instead points to contingent histories of labor and commodities, persons and citizens, fragility and capacity, action and struc-tural determination.[4]

The concern with amandla thus offers a perspective on the relationship of capital to ordinary life—that is, of life in the midst of capital, subtending capital, making capital something other than it is, making fugitive moves beyond determination and capture by capital's operations.

A clearer picture of repair has, I hope, emerged, together with the ques-tion of work. The classic tension between Hannah Arendt's and Karl Marx's approaches to work has formed the ground on which to consider repair. On the one hand is Arendt's distinction between labor and work—that is, her distinction between the demands of animality, biology, and nature which stand opposed to work that violates the realm of nature by shaping and transforming it according to the plans and needs of humans. This makes work a distinctly human—that is, nonanimal—activity, according to Arendt.[5] On the other hand is a Marxian approach to the labor theory of value in terms of a political economy that is constitutively racial, and racializing.[6] Without insisting on a definitive distinction between work and labor, I have understood the effort entailed in repair to be a matter of responding to this tension, and thus a mattering forth of creative action in the midst of capital's excruciating demands. This tension, and thus this reading of repair, has a particular charge for scholars and activists in South Africa.

The analytical terms of Marxian historical materialism provided for several decades the necessary critical purchase in South African historiographies of both colonial and apartheid capitalism and its postapartheid afterlife. For example, Marx's sense of the fate of the human as waste, as excreta in the process of production, provided a vital critique for many scholars and activists of the particular means by which apartheid was able to transform labor into surplus value and profit. As Marx writes in the third volume of *Capital*, "If we consider capitalist production in the narrow sense and ignore the process of circulation and the excesses of competition, it [capitalist production] is extremely sparing with the realized labor that is objectified in commodities. Yet it squanders human beings, living labor, more readily than does any other mode of production, squandering not only flesh and blood, but nerves and brain as well."[7] Thus Steven Feierman, in writing about the social effects of the South African mines, "where the migrant system is carried to a level of cynical perfection," described how the "foreign enterprises which have been most disastrous for the survival of Africans on their own continent have been those which are capitalist in ethos, motivation, and organization, but which do not (or cannot) invest sufficient capital and which therefore intensify exploitation in order to survive."[8] Harold Wolpe's "neo-Marxist" argument that the supply of African migrant labor power at a wage below its cost of reproduction was a function of the existence of a precapitalist mode of production, and whose dissolution by capital threatened the conditions of reproduction of cheap migrant labor power, was one such demonstration of this critique.[9] Martin Legassick, Michael Williams, and Simon Clarke each debated the continuing existence of a "precapitalist mode of production," the differentiation of the interests of "capital," the questionable stability of a "liberal" project, and the rural areas as immiserate holding pens for the reserve army of labor.[10] They all saw apartheid and segregation as responses to challenges posed by "labor" itself—its unruliness or resistance. Commentary and scholarship on the nature of the transition to postapartheid economies of abandonment have identified a range of factors contributing to the new modes of accumulation and dispossession: conflicting economic visions; ideological attachment to the figure of the worker; corruption or deskilling; political compromise; and the rise of a bureaucratic machinery of poverty.[11] In particular, Andries du Toit and others have attempted to repoliticize the "management" of poverty by highlighting the active forms of impoverishment within liberal democratic systems—not abandonment, they suggest, but "adverse incorporation."[12] Despite the extremely high rates of death by HIV and apparently complete proletarianization (in Wolpe's sense) of rural KwaZulu-Natal, the regime of life and death around the plantations is not unambiguously "necropolitical";[13] neither is it straightforwardly a "politics of the belly" in Jean-François Bayart's sense, nor a "race to consume."[14] Rather than abandonment, the particular mode of inclusion around the plantations, of a highly qualified and circumscribed "contribution" of human effort, is saturated with liberal concerns with working conditions, human and democratic rights, and cultural self-determination.[15] The capacity to stretch the productivity of human bodies, whether in explicitly violent forms of slavery or in camouflaged forms of structural violence, depends on the ability to reach into the material and social relations that sustain life and organize their rhythms and potentials.[16]

By cleaving close to a descriptive sensibility that seeks out the rhythms of life and labor in its local instantiations, I have sought to characterize those qualities of work and food, curatives and marriage events, and in particular the distribution of relations and materials within and beyond the plantations, that produce particular forms of subjectivation. By taking *amandla* in its most material and embodied aspects, I suggest that it is possible to ask methodological and operational questions of these rhythms by tracing the transformations of work and labor as they articulate domestic and industrial economies within the modes of reproduction historically observed in "Zululand." As an ethnographic description of the timber plantations of KwaZulu-Natal, it does not, however, resolve a tension that Archie Mafeje saw between "nomothetic inquiry" and "idiographic insights"—that is, the analytical and typologizing work of generalization and abstraction versus the contingent, historical specificity of the ethnographic in recognizing the mediation of African thought and experience.[17] Bernard Dubbeld's claim that appeals to "context" have been a means by which to deny the mediation of social life by capitalism in histories of southern Africa is relevant here, and in particular his turn to Moishe Postone's point that appeals to freedom and political potential "can serve as an ideology of legitimation for the new configuration of capitalism."[18] Rather than take capitalism for granted, the ethnographic account here has sought to elucidate the constraints that capitalism imposes on social life. As one crucially mediating context, capitalism mediates social life and yet also produces particular forms of life that do not follow the neat class categorizations once considered intrinsic to Marx's analysis, as Dubbeld suggests.

ENDURANCE AND REPAIR

In understanding amandla as ethical substance, there is something of what Hayder Al-Mohammad and Daniela Peluso call an "intercorporeal ethics," shaped by the "rough ground" of the everyday traversed by the laborers on their daily beat: new names for entanglements, friendships, relationships, modes of compositing care, attentional recognition and love, and mundane affairs and encounters.[19] In thinking with Elizabeth Povinelli's terms for the "organization and disorganization, the channeling and blockage, of immanent social life," my sense has been that the viruses, calories, liquid substances, bodies, plant life, the plantation itself—that is, the materiality of these things and their forms of "mattering"—sit at an oblique angle to the concerns that shape their forms and effects. In this sense, it is helpful to follow the distinction between the corporeal and carnal that Povinelli develops in order to trace the shape of the "forms of the otherwise" pointed to by immanent concerns such as amandla.[20] The difference between flesh as a discursive and juridical "maneuver" and flesh as a "physical mattering forth" of these maneuvers is crucial to developing (and maintaining) a critique of the metaphysics of substance that has allowed for a de-essentializing of sex, gender, race, and the chronotopes of tradition and modernity. It is this interest in exploding "substances in their pre-discursive authenticity" that allows Povinelli to show how "flesh" is not merely an effect of liberal biopolitics or the disciplining of discourses and knowledge of the body, but also "an independent, unruly vector" at play within these biopolitics.[21]

Where discourse organizes categories and divisions between categories (say, of the body, sex, or gut), carnality is the material manifestations of that discourse which are neither discursive nor prediscursive.[22] This is one point of departure for seeing how techniques focused on the gut or marriage games or children's drawings point toward "the otherwise."

Writing the social from the point of view of "social projects," specifically the project of fashioning a world in and through the space of the plantation, puts into question poor sociological assumptions about culture, society, and individuals. It attends to the projects themselves, the effort to make the world otherwise, the compositional efforts of people whose capacity to endure is critically in question. Two pictures of endurance have informed the "sociographic" effort here. The first is anchored in what Povinelli calls a "critical theory that is oriented to progressive life and yet refuses to be lulled by the promises of miraculous endurance or sacrificial love."[23] For Povinelli, endurance is a mode of life conditioned by "tense" and "eventfulness." "Internal to the concept of endurance (and exhaustion) is the problem of substance: its strength, hardiness, callousness; its continuity through space; its ability to suffer and yet persist."[24] The grammatical tense that structures "late liberalism" adjudicates which subjects enjoy recognition and inclusion—namely, the tense of the future anterior that constructs the formulation that this present suffering will have been worth it from the point of view of an anticipated future in which liberal subjects are fully self-possessed agents with access to the state's recognition and care—and which are trapped by an obligation to genealogical ties and the time of custom. While the continuities and disjunctures between Australian settler colonialism and southern African histories of slavery and liberation place limits on the translocation of such an analytics, it is useful for reflecting more carefully on the critical events, and eventfulness, of South African liberation, including the 1994 elections, and the chronic forms of immiseration that loop through and around the political projects of the early twenty-first century.[25] If "postapartheid" is conceived less in terms of an event marking before and after, and more as a chronotope in which eventfulness recedes as a dominant form of historical consciousness, then stubbornness as a modality for refusing the terms on which liberal "rainbow" politics operates can be understood to capacitate a very different horizon of possibility.[26]

The second picture of endurance that informs this project comes from Veena Das's long dialogue with Povinelli, but takes on the question of voice in the context of trauma, namely the unspeakability of pain. Das offers a notion of healing carried by two ideas: the idea of endurance, and the capacity to establish a particular relationship to death. Pain, she says, "writes itself enduringly in people's lives. It was not about a thunderous voice of pain, but about the manner in which pain was woven into the patterns of life. . . . Being attentive to acknowledgement in relationship to pain is not a question of locating broken lives and healed ones. It is about learning to recognize both the pain and the way that pain enduringly writes a person's relationships, and yet, remains open to the possibility of an adjacent self, if you will, of a self coming into being."[27] I make no claim regarding the failure of voice or the work of remembering but rather have sought to show how ordinary social projects in and around the timber plantations refract the concern with capacity in ways that do not break along conventional lines of psyche and soma. One implication of Das's argument for the way in which the social is understood is that "agreement within the social is not a cognitive, rationally chosen agreement in opinions, but rather that one's allegiance to society is secured through the experience of pain and its memory that is inscribed on the body."[28] I have sought to show how agreement in and around the plantations is less about inscription on surfaces than it is about the mutual absorption of psyche and soma, personal and political, ethics and materials, in the dense folds of language, performance, and the gut. Precisely what picture of the social emerges in South Africa from such processes of absorption (not to mention metabolism) is critically in question. It is in this space between two pictures of endurance that the work of repair emerges—partial, fragmentary, incomplete.

The continuities and disjunctures of this particular form of plantation labor—namely, timber plantations in postapartheid South Africa—are revealed in the grammars that attach themselves to the various "plantation-analytics" that emerge from, say, North American critiques of race and ecology, South Asian historiographies of colonial plantations, Central African experiences of terror and the erotics of rainforest capitalism, or accounts of South American extractivism.[29] Sugar and slavery in the Americas were organized by a flattening, surficial topology whose coordinates were arranged by a racialized distinction between life "on" the plantation (those who are owned) and life "off" the plantation (those who own, and are free to move). I found myself writing in terms of life "in" and "around" the timber plantations, suggesting a somewhat different topological form, possibly caught in the historical moment of the shift, during the 1990s and 2000s, toward the outsourcing of labor now recruited from within a five-kilometer radius. Where laborers used to live "in" the plantations in company "forest villages," they now must house and feed themselves "on" land under customary authority (what used to be called "communal areas") and are transported into and out of the plantations daily. Rather than imply that the difference is one of surface versus depth, I suggest that the grammar of plantation labor, of "in" and "on" the plantation, expresses something of the ordering of life, labor, and value across distinct historical contexts. Within and across these temporal and spatial connections and differences in plantation systems, a double articulation emerges: on the one hand, "the plantation," premised on folded forms of unfree and free labor, and "the human," as a universal figure awaiting full emancipation or realization; on the other, the specificity of the Nyalazi and Dukuduku timber stands, and the concern with amandla and the difficult work of cultivating a vulnerability through which repair becomes possible, as I showed in chapter 4.

STRENGTH, LABOR, AND VALUE

The situations in which capacity has emerged in these chapters as both a challenge and a response, in the complex relationship between labor power and amandla, inter-involve the provision of calories; the ingesting of substances; the enacting of rituals of eating and purging; the gifting and dancing of umshado wokudlala; and the plotting and navigating of territory and topology. One crucial site in which amandla routes through the body, and which is central to the work of repair, is (what I am calling) the gut. The notion that eating and relating are interminably linked is not new, but it is newly invigorated by recent transformations in scientific ideas about food and eating that promise to undo assumptions about the relationships between eaters and what is eaten.[30] This transformation, characterized as a shift from a "machinic" model to what Hannah Landecker calls a "hallucinogenic" model of food and its incorporation, endows foodstuffs with much more agency and potency than they had in the standard "fuel + building blocks" model. In Landecker's words, "Food speaks, cues and signals. . . . Eating as interlocution is a conceptual development that carries with it potentially disorienting new representations of human interiority and autonomy."[31] The scenes in the timber plantation prefigure a shift from a modernist vision that sees the eating body as a factory, a human motor, to an understanding of the gut as mediating social worlds.[32] However, to appeal to science to authorize such a claim is, potentially, to affirm the division between truth and belief, making a turn to the ethnographic archive a fraught exercise.

The ethnographic record is, indeed, filled with descriptions of "the gut" and the vital force of this or that cosmology, such that anthropology is rife with claims to have discovered a possible universal. Stephen Gudeman suggests a "complex" of ideas about "strength" that stretches between older European ideas of vis vitae—life force or the energy of life—and Spanish-speaking agriculturalists in Latin America.[33] He claims that "vital energy" is a central idea in the economies of Panama and Colombia. "La fuerza," which Gudeman translates as "strength" or "force," is assembled from the environment; it is a current that connects all activities in the local economies and establishes relationships, from kin to strangers. In Gudeman's hands, this economy contrasts a "social current" with a "market currency" and provides a critique of standard economics ("sharing rather than reciprocity or rational choice is the 'fundamental' economic practice").[34] The comparativist appeal to a cultural universal is as dangerous as it is affirmative because anthropology's power derives partly from its epistemological capacity to drive nomothetic synthesis and partly from its aesthetic or political effects, namely, affirming a universal set of human qualities or preoccupations. I have sought rather to decompose the apparent "cultural" continuities in figurations of hunger, vitality, gut thinking, or curative technique and turned toward the political and ethical questions that have organized the material substrate of everyday life here in stronger historiographical terms.

I have avoided casting the struggles over labor, life, and health as questions of luck and fortune, fate and destiny, because appeals to a "foundational trope of an economic cosmology" seem to do no justice to the terms in which plantation laborers speak of their lives.[35] The comparative effect so privileged by anthropology seems to allow the sharpness of political aspects of the ordinary to leach out of summative analyses. In short, there can be no easy appeal to a general technique of dealing with "uncontrolled relatedness" without a historical and empirical method for tracing those convergences.[36] Thus, for example, Hylton White's rendering of the question of contingent authority as a critique of cosmology and political power is far

more helpful than da Col's and others' comparative analyses for its historical materialism and ethnographic attentiveness to the lives of ancestors and
spirits around these same plantations.[37]

In the intervening years since the fieldwork on which this book is based
was completed, much has changed. The scenes described in this book take
on a different hue in light of the financial crash of 2008; the Marikana massacre in 2012 in which thirty-four mine workers were shot and killed by police; the COVID-19 pandemic since 2020; and the so-called insurrection
and violence of July 2021. These "critical events" are not self-evident mark-
ers of state violence or structural decay, but rather cyphers or knots in the
worn fabric of late liberal governmentality. Since 2010, the forestry industry has been increasingly mechanized. Just before the COVID-19 pandemic
arrived, the major ratings agencies had downgraded South Africa to junk
status. The devastation of COVID-19 on health, health systems, and regional
economies has rendered the possibility of full employment a distant and im-
probable dream.[38] The structural conditions have become much more
acute, and new forms of living and dying are emerging in response to the
demands of the day.[39]

At the time of writing—February 2022—KwaZulu-Natal is a complex
location from which to think. Rates of HIV infection among young people
have increased nationally, although a decline has been observed in the
northern KwaZulu-Natal surveillance area.[40] The virological capacity developed at the Africa Centre in Somkhele has relocated to Durban, where
scientists established the KwaZulu-Natal Research Innovation and Sequencing Platform (KRISP). It was this capacity that enabled the SARS-CoV-2
Beta variant to be identified (also known as lineage B.1.351, or 20H/501Y.V2
[formerly 20C/501Y.V2], or the 501Y.V2 variant, or even "the South African
COVID-19 variant") in October 2020. By February 2022, the number of con-
firmed deaths in South Africa due to COVID-19 were 99,412, with excess
mortality estimated at 299,233 (503 per 100,000 population).[41] South Africa
has thus been one of the hardest-hit countries in the world, although much
remains to be understood about the relationships between SARS-CoV-2,
HIV, TB, and the structural conditions in which immunity is compromised.
Two years after the global shock of March 2020, new rhythms and habits are
emerging in South Africa, as elsewhere. Building on a strong pharmaceutical sector developed in part by the history of the HIV/AIDS pandemic, the
manufacture of COVID-19 vaccines in South Africa began in January 2022.[42]

While no one has been left untouched, the afflictions caused by the pandemic and responses to it have been, and remain, very unevenly distributed, as with HIV and TB. Who has died from the disease, whose immune system remains compromised, who has access to vaccines or treatment, and whose livelihood has been destroyed are not merely a matter of the distribution of things, bodies, viruses, and resources; they are a signal of the emergence of new biopolitical trajectories in which such terms as health, well-being, rights and citizenship no longer index the familiar institutions and constitutions of liberal governance. The biopolitical state, itself in question in the face of new forms of authoritarian populism, might no longer have a monopoly over debilitation and capacitation as anchors of a right to maim, as Jasbir Puar claims.[43]

The Quarterly Labour Force Survey of June 2021 showed that KwaZulu-Natal had an official unemployment rate of 30.5 percent, and an "expanded" rate of 46.4 percent. Nationally, the official unemployment rate among youth (15–34 years) was 46.3 percent.[44] The NIDS-CRAM Survey (National Income Dynamics Study—Coronavirus Rapid Mobile Survey) of mid-2021 revealed that the COVID-19 pandemic has triggered a rise in hunger in South Africa.[45] Extreme poverty was one of the reasons offered by commentators to explain the explosion of violence and looting in July 2021, which was focused in KwaZulu-Natal and Gauteng provinces. For others, it was mobilized partly around Zulu ethnonationalist identifications and was closely connected to the corruption trial of former president Jacob Zuma and associated political and criminal networks. The unexamined role of the ANC Youth League in the far north of KwaZulu-Natal in mobilizing support for Zuma and his provincial counterpart, Premier Sihle Zikalala, has been central, since 2010, to the complex contestations over territory, authority, and profit in the area in which lie the Tendele Coal Mine in Somkhele, the iSimangaliso Wetland Park, the timber plantations, and the demographic surveillance of the Africa Centre. The former Zulu king, Goodwill Zwelethini, died in March 2021, reportedly from COVID-19. Months later, in June 2021, the High Court in Pietermaritzburg found that the Ingonyama Trust had been illegally collecting rent from people living on customary land that had been placed in trust in the 1994 transition to ensure the participation of the Inkatha Freedom Party and its Zulu nationalist supporters.[46] As a residue of two hundred years of nationalist contestation, colonial dislocation, and Bantustan governance, Ingonyama Trust land now constitutes 32 percent of the area of KwaZulu-Natal province. The coal mine that abuts the plantations and sits in the center of the demographic surveillance area continues to blast rock and alienate rural residents from their ancestral lands, with the blessing of the newly installed Zulu king, Misuzulu Zulu. Access to waged employment remains an acute crisis for many.

What kinds of repair will be required, or will be elicited, in this context? The devastating effects of COVID-19 on the organization of labor in the plantations and beyond remain to be seen, but the outlook is dire. Certainly, the appeal to dignified work as the salve to the wounded history of racialized capital seems dead, and in its place is a contested outline of the "post-social" social of the distributional state that circulates welfare and pharmaceuticals.[47] Other processes and forces that direct the distribution of hope and harm, living and dying, food and pharma, grant and graft, will continue to shape the political question of repair in South Africa. The legitimacy and authority of the negotiated compromise is increasingly in question as the failures of the postapartheid developmental state project become clear. Reinvigorated institutions of customary authority are staking a claim to radically novel understandings of tradition, law, and power by reinventing patriarchal authority within the remains of ex-Bantustans.[48] How parliamentary and constitutional authority will respond to and absorb these struggles is an urgent question. The growing availability of HIV testing and treatment has undoubtedly shifted the ways in which curative substances are policed and consumed. How notions of substance and relatedness might articulate with the new technologies of HIV and COVID-19 treatment and emerging infectious disease surveillance remains to be seen. The new forms of hunger produced by HIV drugs raise their own political challenges, even apart from the phenomenological and experiential aspects of their consumption.[49] Homophobic and gender-based violence also continues to pose a challenge to those who proclaim the realization of liberal rights of protection and inclusion codified in the Constitution. Each of these material and political questions demands further attention and analysis.

Two significant themes that animate the possibility of repair in contemporary public discourse in South Africa (and beyond) are, first, Universal Basic Income (UBI) and, second, what in South Africa is referred to as "the land question."[50] They are both symptomatic of the perceived limits of the nation-state as the frame within which claims to the social might be made or collective life might be reimagined. Concerning UBI, James Ferguson suggests reconceiving social support and obligation in terms of "presence" so that nonnationals are included in the terms of recognition: those who are here, however "here" is defined.[51] Adjacent to this, in relation to land, Andries du Toit suggests that the hidden and implicit question animating the land debate is the question of political belonging; namely, that land stands for a demand both for recognition of a history of traumatic dislocation and for a claim to be recognized as legitimate members of the political community.[52] Thus, for du Toit, the question of what we owe and can expect of one another as members of a shared political community, caring for "all who live in it," is something that must be continually kept alive and renegotiated.

The experiments of value being worked out in one part of South Africa, with the intercalation of postwork cash transfers, pharmaceuticalization of entire populations, and corporate social concern, are relevant not just for southern Africa but for many parts of the world undergoing similar experimentation. To say that questions of value—for example, of calorific or nutrient value to the body, or wages or the cost of bread, or aspirations to family relations or personal flourishing—are now subject to vast engines of equivalence is merely a restatement of Marx's analysis of capital. What is at stake here is an understanding of the particular workings of those engines of equivalence in the early twenty-first century in and through techniques of the body that rely not only on supposedly tired concepts of fatigue and biological life, as Anson Rabinbach suggests in his claim that the "human motor" has given way to a more digital metaphor of life, but more importantly, on the specific arrangements of land, labor, and diet in this corner of postapartheid South Africa.[53] However, a technology of the self with the gut at its fleshy center, as both corporeal and carnal concern, is not a cultural exception particular to South Africa. It is a vital node through which global circuits of capital are mediated; it reveals the ways in which obstinacies and resistance throw up cultural difference, personal failure, or historical idiosyncrasy as artifacts.[54] Far from being a *thing*, stabilized as an object of reflection or a tool that extends thought, the work of repair is thus a situated, embodied, ordinary question posed to the problem of what worlds will accommodate our very human concerns—and the more-than-human ecologies so urgently in need of reparation.[55]

The argument I have offered concerning amandla and the work of repair has centered a constitutive and historically contingent vulnerability that must be modulated, mediated, and augmented. The dangers attendant on such an ethic of vulnerability require further careful elaboration, not least because of the analytical pitfalls of fetishizing the words and worlds of those on the sharp end of the violence of abstraction. Through each of the ethnographic scenes in the text, I have sought to show something of the difficult relation between word and world. The argument thus makes five critical interventions.

First has been a refusal to accede to the standard "West" / "indigenous other" binary that all too often implicitly pervades scholarship of southern Africa. Second, the text's ethnographic descriptions are put to work not to describe others' ways of being but, at least in part, to ask about anthropology's own certainty about its concepts. What, for instance, is "family," in the long shadow of labor migration, HIV, and changing patterns of marriage? How might we understand a "game" "played" with deep seriousness, in which women marry women in ceremonies attended by the trappings of customary marriage, generating deeply meaningful relations that are not fully socially sanctioned and are always almost-deniable? What definitions of gender, sexual identity, relation, power, playfulness, meaning result from such "games"? What does that tell us about our anthropological concepts of affinity, or social reproduction, or about standard categories of gendered identity? Third, tracing the layering of concatenating topologies enables a description of flows of power, life, disease, medicines, and relationships that distribute health unevenly across people and landscapes. Fourth, I have asked about the formation of the social itself, and the possibilities this may afford for an "otherwise." Departing from some romantic treatments of such an appeal to the otherwise, I am less certain about such possibilities. Finally, these arguments turn back to the question of the relation of concept to world, showing how language is generated from the world. What I have offered here is a reflection both on the specifics of a southern African context and on how we might think about it and, by extension, about thinking; in particular, on the relation of concepts to world.[56] Alongside a description of a place and time configured by distressing histories of violence,what has emerged is a troubled reflection on anthropological certitudes, thereby opening, among other things, a conversation about what terms are conducive to a fuller understanding of forms of life and of the living, as well as forms of death and dying. Between living and dying remains the challenge posed by repair.

Finally, in speaking about "the repair," Kader Attia grounds the notion in a genealogy of the term "reappropriation," or rather, the "re-situation" of things as well as of words—of both material and immaterial signs.[57] More specifically, he locates reappropriation in the thought of Pierre-Joseph Proudhon ("property is theft"); Oswald de Andrade ("Tupi or not Tupi: that is the question"); and Frantz Fanon (reparation and restitution of what people have been dispossessed of). While the term arose within European anarchism during the Industrial Revolution and developed within different colonial contexts, Attia suggests that reappropriation "governs all relations between modernity and tradition. It sheds light on the parallel relationship between power and modernity and, more precisely, colonization and modernity." Reappropriation, recirculation, repair. The question that emerges from this account of life in-and-around the timber plantations is how, then, to *work with* amandla, not only as imminent critique, but also as a modality of action that orients, and is oriented by, repair: an augmenting capacity, a pedagogy of healing, and a reparative politics.

In the words of Antjie Krog, the South African poet, "To be vulnerable is to be fully human. It is the only way you can bleed into other people"—to which Denis Hirson responds, "But vulnerability is also a state in which one might be tempted to retract into oneself, in response to the raw emotion of loss, the feeling of uneasiness in the face of the unknown."[58] The ways we stretch toward one another, in "mutuomorphic" vulnerability, thus depend on an embrace of the scar, the mark of the sutured wound.[59]

ACKNOWLEDGMENTS

Many people have supported this project along the way, and their kindness, support, and critical accompaniment were crucial to its completion. In the first place, the generosity and patience extended by my interlocutors and hosts in Shikishela and Mfekayi, KwaZulu-Natal, cannot be repaid, and I am most grateful for their warm embrace, although I cannot identify them by name here. Ntombizodumo Mkhwanazi has been far more than an assistant, and I value her friendship profoundly. This book would not have been possible without her.

I have been fortunate to have had excellent and generous mentors in several contexts. I offer profound thanks to my teachers, Pamela Reynolds, Aaron Goodfellow, Jane Guyer, Vinh-Kim Nguyen, Todd Meyers, and Fiona Ross. I have benefited also from the mentorship of Kaushik Sunder Rajan, Andries du Toit, and Hylton White, all of whose input shaped the project in important ways. I would never have been able to enter the plantations were it not for the help of Jeanette Clarke, whose friendship has been foundational.

While a student at Johns Hopkins University, I had generous teachers in Veena Das, Naveeda Khan, Deborah Poole, Niloofar Haeri, Randy Packard, Lori Leonard, Siba Grovogui, Sara Berry, and Clara Han. I had supportive and inspiring peers in Sylvain Perdigon, Bhrigupati Singh, Sidharthan Maunaguru, Sameena Mulla, Isaias Rojas-Perez, Abigail Baim-Lance, Valeria Procupez, Richard Baxstrom, Ross Parsons, Andrew Bush, Neena Mahadev, Hester Betlem, Bican Polat, Amrita Ibrahim, Maya Ratnam, Citlalli Reyes-Kipp, Lindsey Reynolds, Chitra Venkataramani, Vaibhav Saria, Aditi Saraf, Brian Tilley, Fouad Halbouni, Caroline Block, Andrew Brandel, David

Platzer, Victor Kumar, Gregoire Hervouet-Zeiber, Sruti Chaganti, Amy Krauss, and Pooja Satyogi.

Fieldwork for this project was funded by a grant from the National Science Foundation (Doctoral Dissertation Improvement Grant, Science and Society), and the Program for the Study of Women, Gender, and Sexuality (Summer Research Grant 2006), the Institute for Global Studies (Summer Research Grant 2006), and the Center for Africana Studies (Summer Research Grant 2007), all at the Johns Hopkins University. The writing was supported by two teaching fellowships from the Dean's Teaching Fellowship program at the Johns Hopkins University. I gratefully acknowledge the support of these institutions.

At the Africa Centre for Health and Population Studies, I was warmly welcomed by John Imrie, Richard Lessells, Tulio D'Oliveira, Tinofa and Portia Mutevedzi, Till Barnighausen, Ruth Bland, Natsayi Chimbindi, Kobus and Corina Herbst, Graeme Hoddinott, Victoria Hosegood, Tshepiso Mafojane, Abraham Malaza, Nuala McGrath, Kevindra Naidu, James Ndirangu, Makandwe Nyirenda, Tamsen Rochat, Frank Tanser, Mpume Mkwanazi, and Marie-Louise and Colin Newell. I thank them and all the fieldworkers who helped me during 2009. Staff at Mondi were gracious in their help, for which I thank Melanie Dass, Linda Lang-Gordon, and Sipho Zulu. I owe a particular debt of thanks to Bronwyn James and her colleagues at the iSimangaliso Wetland Authority, including Nerosha Govender, Sizo Sibiya, Thembisile Buthelezi, Mininhle Zikhali, and Andrew Zaloumis, and in Durban to Matt and Lauren Young. The friendship of Mark and Hannah Mattson, Roland Vorwerk, and Ida, Dewald, and Eduard Scheepers was vital to my time in Mtubatuba.

While teaching at Stellenbosch University, I enjoyed the stimulating and warm environment provided by colleagues and students, and I thank them for their engagement and support, in particular Bernard Dubbeld, Steven Robins, C. S. "Kees" van der Waal, Cherryl Walker, Jan Vorster, Lindy Heinecken, Rob Pattman, Graeme Hoddinott, Antonio Tomas, Mandisa Mbali, Shaheed Tayob, Rene Raad, and the Indexing the Human team. I am also indebted to friends and colleagues at the University of Cape Town, including Fiona Ross, Shannon Morreira, Patti Henderson, Francis Nyamnjoh, Lesley Green, Deborah Posel, and Susan Levine.

In Oxford, I am fortunate to have many wonderful colleagues who have engaged with this project generously: Stanley Ulijaszek, David Gellner, David Pratten, Ramon Sarro, Peter McDonald, Javier Lezaun, Ann Kelly, Jamie Lorimer, Max Bolt, Jocelyn Alexander, William Beinart, Maan Barua, and Jonny Steinberg. I appreciate the warm support of many others, in particular Elizabeth Ewart, Elish Angiolini, Nayanika Mathur, Deborah James, and Lomin Saayman. I am grateful to my students who have provided excellent feedback on earlier drafts: Elie Danziger, Sydney Vennin, Luke Stalley, Michael Pierson, Femke Vulto, and Tanuj Luthra.

Over the years, many people have contributed to this book, as commentators on paper presentations or readers of draft chapters and articles. I was fortunate to receive feedback when presenting this material to several groups, in particular the Johns Hopkins Department of Anthropology; Perig Petrou and the Anthropology of Life group at the CNRS in Paris; graduate students at the University of Cape Town; and the South Africa Discussion Group at Oxford. Special thanks to the organizers of the Johannesburg Workshop in Theory and Criticism, including Kelly Gillespie, Leigh-Ann Naidoo, Julia Hornberger, and Achille Mbembe. I benefited immensely from conversations with Elizabeth Povinelli, Ann Allison, Nancy Rose Hunt, Anthony Stavrianakis, Marilyn Strathern, João de Pina-Cabral, Robert Thornton, Kris Peterson, and Emilia Sanabria. In helping this book to completion, I am deeply grateful for the encouragement and support from Clara Han and Bhrigupati Singh as editors of the series Thinking from Elsewhere, the excellent editorial input from Trevor Perri, and the stewardship of Thomas Lay at Fordham University Press. The generous comments and suggestions of two anonymous reviewers have greatly improved the text.

In particular, I owe much to the friendship and mentorship of Aaron Goodfellow, who has sustained me and pushed me beyond what I thought possible. His immense generosity and intelligence have been a true inspiration; I cannot thank him enough.

There are many others I am unable to name here, friends, family (both given and chosen), colleagues, and students, whose stimulating engagement and contributions have been vital to this book—I thank them all. I owe special thanks to Colleen Crawford-Cousins, Ben Cousins, Kezia Crawford-Cousins, and Maud Scheydeker, and to Brian and Trish Pentecost, for their fierce love and support.

I gratefully acknowledge William Kentridge and the Kentridge Studio for permission to use his artwork *Universal Archive (Ref. 47)*, 2012, as the cover image.

And most of all, an unending debt of gratitude to my partner, Michelle, whose generous love and brilliance never ceases to inspire.

NOTES

INTRODUCTION: REPAIR AND THE QUESTION OF CAPACITY

1. "Forest" in isiZulu is "ihlati," a generic term that includes indigenous forests and plantations. "Imithi" (sing. muthi) in English is "trees," but it carries the extra meaning of "indigenous species that can be used for medicinal purposes" as well as for a range of socially meaningful activities—often glossed in popular usage as "traditional medicine."

2. I have chosen to italicize non-English words only where emphasis is intended. On the politics of typeface, see Thu-Huong Ha, "Bilingual Authors Are Challenging the Practice of Italicizing Non-English Words," *Quartz*, June 24, 2018, https://qz .com/quartzy/1310228/bilingual-authors-are-challenging-the-practice-of -italicizing-non-english-words/; Peter McDonald, *Artefacts of Writing: Ideas of the State and Communities of Letters from Matthew Arnold to Xu Bing* (Oxford: Oxford University Press, 2017); and Jumoke Verissimo, "On the Politics of Italics," *Literary Hub*, August 28, 2019, https://lithub.com/on-the-politics-of-italics/.

3. See Gregor Dobler, "'Work and Rhythm' Revisited: Rhythm and Experience in Northern Namibian Peasant Work," *Journal of the Royal Anthropological Institute* 22, no. 4 (2016): 864–83, https://doi.org/10.1111/1467-9655.12490. The dance of men appears in the available literature as radically opposed to that of women (e.g., Louise Meintjies, *Dust of the Zulu: Ngoma Aesthetics after Apartheid* [Durham, NC: Duke University Press, 2017]; Deborah James, *Songs of the Women Migrants: Performance and Identity in South Africa* [Edinburgh: Edinburgh University Press for the International African Institute, 1999]). The dance and song that wove through the plantations, the ritual performance on the side of the road, and at home, often blurred these distinctions, as I discuss in chapter 3. In a more mundane register, Dianne Stewart collected songs from women working in the timber and sugar plantations on the KwaZulu-Natal North Coast in 1993–94 ("Izisho Zokusebenza—Work Songs," in *Women Writing Africa: The Southern Region*, ed. Margaret J. Daymond,

Dorothy Driver, and Sheila Meintjies [New York: Feminist Press at the City University of New York, 2003]), pointing to the ways in which they provided ethical commentary and exhortation on the daily rounds:

> Their singing helped the women carry out their manual labor. It was often heavy: stripping bark off felled gum trees ("Separate These People" and "My Child Is Crying"); removing refuse; hoeing and fertilizing the ground ready for planting ("I've Been Abandoned," "My Brother-in-Law," and "It Is This Man"); hoeing between the rows of cane to remove weeds ("Mother Is Not Here" and "What Can You Do?"); and cutting the cane—the latter usually men's work.
>
> A strong rhythmic repetition provides the melody and shapes the interactions between lead singer and chorus—all of which serve to sustain the women in their arduous, monotonous work. . . .
>
> While these songs accompany work in modern farming conditions, several of them draw on much older communal work songs, such as corn-threshing songs. . . .
>
> A blend of gender and politics suggested by "It Is This Man" appears also in "My Brother-in-Law" and "Separate These People." Although rural Zulu women have customarily been confined to a domestic sphere, their songs allow them a spirited interaction with the larger world. (Stewart, 464)

4. Ideas about digestion, energy, metabolism, and the body's capacities are central to the labor regime itself, which I turn to in chapter 1.

5. All those people not classified as "European" or "White" by the apartheid state were profoundly affected by forced removals. Thus, in this instance, the category "Black" includes all those excluded from the category "White." While the political category of Blackness was developed by the Black Consciousness Movement as a way of building solidarity among those marked by apartheid's exclusions, its capacity to mobilize antiracist sentiments in postapartheid South Africa has been contested (see Steve Biko, *I Write What I Like: Selected Writings* (Chicago: University of Chicago Press, 2002); Xolela Mangcu et al., *The Colour of Our Future* (Johannesburg: Wits University Press, 2015); and Andile Mngxitama, Amanda Suzanne Alexander, and Nigel C. Gibson, *Biko Lives! Contesting the Legacies of Steve Biko* (New York: Palgrave Macmillan, 2008). The use of racial categories in this book is informed by a critical historiography of the invention and deployment of a logic of racial difference in South Africa, in dialogue with a critique of race in other parts of Africa and the diaspora. While a recent debate in the US has turned on the virtues of capitalizing either or both the terms "Black" and "White," I draw on a South African critique of the racial logic of apartheid and the bureaucratic violence performed by the social life of these classifications within and beyond the law (see Kwame Anthony Appiah, "The Case for Capitalizing the B in Black," *The Atlantic*,

June 18, 2020; and the German Historical Institute, "Words Matter: Our Thoughts on Language, Pseudo-science, and 'Race,'" *German Historical Institute London Bulletin* 42, no. 2 [2020]: 3–8). Hence, the racial categories used here are strictly those inventions of apartheid law, on which the postapartheid effort at redress is based. For a discussion of historical and contemporary politics of apartheid's racial categories, see Saul Dubow, *Apartheid, 1948–1994* (Oxford: Oxford University Press, 2014); Zimitri Erasmus, "Race," in *New South African Keywords*, ed. Nick Shepherd and Steven Robins (Johannesburg: Jacana, 2008); Joel Modiri, "The Colour of Law, Power and Knowledge: Introducing Critical Race Theory in (Post-)Apartheid South Africa," *South African Journal on Human Rights* 28, no. 3 (2012): 405–36; and Deborah Posel, "Race as Common Sense: Racial Classification in Twentieth-Century South Africa," *African Studies Review* 44, no. 2 (2001): 87–114. No simple historicism resolves the difficult question at the center of these debates, as Achille Mbembe brilliantly shows in *Critique of Black Reason* (Durham, NC: Duke University Press, 2017). Central to Mbembe's problematization is the possibility that "blackness" is the "idea that black, or blackness, is not so much a matter of ontology as it is a matter of historicity or even contingency" (David Theo Goldberg, "In Conversation: Achille Mbembe and David Theo Goldberg on 'Critique of Black Reason,'" *Theory, Culture and Society*, July 3, 2018, lowercase in the original).

6. "1994: The Bloody Miracle" is the title of a powerful documentary about the negotiated transition between 1991 and 1994. Meg Rickards and Bert Haitsma, *1994: The Bloody Miracle* (South Africa: Boondogle Films, 2014). https://www.nelsonmandela.org/news/entry/1994-the-bloody-miracle.

7. While the relationship between formal politics nationally and local political processes in northern KwaZulu-Natal is crucial to understanding the fate of the African National Congress (ANC) between 2005 and 2021, I am unable to address that question here.

8. See Foucault's discussion of the Greek term, *parastēma*, ethical substance, as the material or aspect of self that is morally problematic, taken as the object of one's ethical reflection, and transformed in one's ethical work. Michel Foucault, *The Use of Pleasure*, vol. 2 of *The History of Sexuality*, trans. Robert Hurley (New York: Vintage, 1990), 26. See also Elizabeth A. Povinelli, *Economies of Abandonment: Social Belonging and Endurance in Late Liberalism* (Durham, NC: Duke University Press, 2011), 106; Paul Rabinow and Anthony Stavrianakis, *From Chaos to Solace: Topological Meditations* (Berkeley, CA: Anthropology of the Contemporary Research Collaboratory, 2021); Bob Robinson, "Michel Foucault: Ethics," in *The Internet Encyclopedia of Philosophy*, https://iep.utm.edu/, last accessed January 28, 2022.

9. Jasbir K. Puar, *The Right to Maim: Debility, Capacity, Disability* (Durham, NC: Duke University Press, 2017).

10. Julie Livingston, *Debility and the Moral Imagination in Botswana* (Bloomington: Indiana University Press, 2005).

11. Puar, *Right to Maim*, xviii.

12. Franco Barchiesi, "Wage Labor, Precarious Employment, and Social Inclusion in the Making of South Africa's Postapartheid Transition," *African Studies Review* 51, no. 2 (2008): 119–42.

13. Karl Marx and Friedrich Engels, *The Marx-Engels Reader*, ed. Robert C. Tucker, 2nd ed. (New York: Norton, 1978), 205.

14. Hannah Arendt, *The Human Condition* (1958; repr., Chicago: University of Chicago Press, 1998).

15. Paul Bohannan, "On Anthropologists' Use of Language," *American Anthropologist* 60, no. 1 (1958): 161–63.

16. William F. Hanks and Carlo Severi, "Translating Worlds: The Epistemological Space of Translation," *HAU: Journal of Ethnographic Theory* 4, no. 2 (2014).

17. On nontranslatability, see John Leavitt, "Words and Worlds: Ethnography and Theories of Translation," *HAU: Journal of Ethnographic Theory* 4, no. 2 (2014). On "invaginated," see Elizabeth A. Povinelli, "Routes/Worlds," *E-Flux Journal*, no. 27 (September 2011). On "mutuomorphomutation," see Peter McDonald, *Artefacts of Writing: Ideas of the State and Communities of Letters from Matthew Arnold to Xu Bing* (Oxford: Oxford University Press, 2017). McDonald's project places James Joyce's *Finnegans Wake* in conversation with a wide range of thinkers, writers, and artists such as Es'kia Mphahlele, Rabindranath Tagore, J. M. Coetzee, Antjie Krog, and Xu Bing. See the website that accompanies the book: https://artefactsofwriting .com (last accessed July 20, 2021). There, McDonald writes of Joyce's sense that "cultures are fragile, all-too-human works in progress caught in the crosscurrents of world history, evolving, like writing systems and languages, in an endlessly 'expro-gressive process' of 'decomposition' and 'recombination' with other cultures— 'miscegenations on miscegenations' (*FW* 18 and 614–15). The word he coined for this unpredictable, reciprocally transformative process was 'MUTUOMORPHO-MUTATION,' an appropriately interlingual neologism combining the Latin root for 'mutual,' the Greek for 'form,' and the Latin for 'mutate'—it is a term Tagore would probably have appreciated (*FW* 281)."

18. Dipesh Chakrabarty, *Provincializing Europe: Postcolonial Thought and Historical Difference* (Princeton, NJ: Princeton University Press, 2000), 17–18.

19. Chakrabarty, 18.

20. Chakrabarty, 50.

21. I am not suggesting that amandla is simply an instance of one such History 2, but rather that this relationship of internal, disruptive difference is at stake in the figure of amandla. As Chakrabarty writes:

> History 2s are thus not pasts separate from capital; they inhere in capital and yet interrupt and punctuate the run of capital's own logic....
> ... In other words, History 1 and History 2, considered together, destroy the usual topological distinction of the outside and the inside that marks

debates about whether or not the whole world can be properly said to have fallen under the sway of capital. . . .

. . . That is, History 2s do not constitute a dialectical Other of the necessary logic of History 1. To think thus would be to subsume History 2 to History 1. History 2 is better thought of as a category charged with the function of constantly interrupting the totalizing thrusts of History 1. . . .

. . . But the idea of History 2 suggests that even in the very abstract and abstracting space of the factory that capital creates, ways of being human will be acted out in manners that do not lend themselves to the reproduction of the logic of capital.

It would be wrong to think of History 2 (or History 2s) as necessarily pre-capitalist or feudal, or even inherently incompatible with capital. If that were the case, there would be no way humans could be at home—dwell—in the rule of capital, no room for enjoyment, no play of desires, no seduction of the commodity. Capital, in that case, would truly be a case of unrelieved and absolute unfreedom. The idea of History 2 allows us to make room, in Marx's own analytic of capital, for the politics of human belonging and diversity. (Chakrabarty, 64–67)

Thanks to Bernard Dubbeld and Maan Barua for alerting me to this possibility.

22. Martha Nussbaum and Amartya Sen, eds., *The Quality of Life* (Oxford: Oxford University Press, 1993).

23. Jean Comaroff and John L. Comaroff, "Alien-Nation: Zombies, Immigrants, and Millennial Capitalism," *South Atlantic Quarterly* 101, no. 4 (2002): 779–805; and Elizabeth A. Povinelli, "The Will to Be Otherwise / The Effort of Endurance," *South Atlantic Quarterly* 111, no. 3 (2012): 453–75.

24. Povinelli, "Will to Be Otherwise," 454.

25. Andries du Toit, "'Social Exclusion' Discourse and Chronic Poverty: A South African Case Study," *Development and Change* 35, no. 5 (2004): 987–1010.

26. Povinelli, "Will to Be Otherwise," 454.

27. Goolam Vahed and Ashwin Desai, "After Mandela Met Gandhi: The Past and Future of India–South Africa Relations," in *Africa and India in the 21st Century: Contexts, Comparisons and Cooperation* (University of KwaZulu-Natal, South Africa, and Delhi University, Delhi, India, 2014), 9–18.

28. See Ivor Chipkin, *Do South Africans Exist? Nationalism, Democracy and the Identity of 'the People'* (Johannesburg: Wits University Press, 2007); and James G. Ferguson, *Presence and Social Obligation: An Essay on the Share* (Chicago: Prickly Paradigm, 2021).

29. For a recent review of these debates, see the special issue of *Social Dynamics* 46, no. 1 (2020) titled "Thinking with Capital Today" (edited by Bernard Dubbeld), including essays by Bongani Nyoka, Ulrike Kistner, and Hylton White.

30. See Jock McCulloch, *South Africa's Gold Mines and the Politics of Silicosis* (Johannesburg: James Currey, 2012), and his "Medicine, Politics and Disease on South Africa's Gold Mines," *Journal of Southern African Studies* 39, no. 3 (2013): 543–56; and Randall Packard, *White Plague, Black Labour: Tuberculosis and the Political Economy of Health and Disease in South Africa* (Berkeley: University of California Press, 1989).

31. Howard Phillips, *Plague, Pox and Pandemics: A Jacana Pocket History of Epidemics in South Africa* (Johannesburg: Jacana, 2012), counts five major epidemics in the history of South Africa: smallpox (1713–1893); plague (1901–7); Spanish flu (1918–19); poliomyelitis (1918–63); and HIV/AIDS (1982–). It remains to be seen how devastating COVID-19 will be. See in particular Emily Mendenhall, "Beyond Comorbidity: A Critical Perspective of Syndemic Depression and Diabetes in Cross-Cultural Contexts," *Medical Anthropology Quarterly* 30, no. 4 (2016): 462–78; Emily Mendenhall and Shane A. Norris, "When HIV Is Ordinary and Diabetes New: Remaking Suffering in a South African Township," *Global Public Health* 10, no. 4 (2015): 449–62; and Diana Wylie, "The Changing Face of Hunger in Southern African History 1880–1980," *Past and Present*, no. 122 (April 1989): 159–99.

32. See Raymond Suttner and Jeremy Cronin, *30 Years of the Freedom Charter* (Johannesburg: Ravan, 1985).

33. The phrase remains a vital and potent rhetorical device in contemporary South Africa, popular in ordinary political life, but also folded into a nostalgic manipulation of antiapartheid historiography by the ANC. See in particular the musical documentary *Amandla! A Revolution in Four-Part Harmony*, directed by Lee Hirsch et al. (Nu Metro Home Entertainment, 2002).

34. See N. P. Simelela and W. D. F. Venter, "A Brief History of South Africa's Response to AIDS," *South African Medical Journal* 104, no. 3, suppl. 1 (2014): 249–51, for an excellent summary of the history of South Africa's response to HIV/AIDS up to 2014.

35. Official figures count how many people in South Africa's labor force are out of a job but looking for work. The expanded unemployment figure includes those people as well as anybody who is out of a job and wants a job, and is not looking for work.

36. Statistics South Africa, "Quarterly Labour Force Survey: Quarter 2: 2022," statistical report, Stats SA website, March 29, 2022, https://www.statssa.gov.za/?p=15685.

37. According to the 2019 Household Survey, 45.2 percent of households depend on social grants and 64.8 percent of households receive salaries from various forms of employment, including remittances, income from businesses, and pensions (Statistics South Africa, "General Household Survey, 2019," Pretoria, 2021). The attempted "insurrection" of July 2021 has likely increased this number significantly.

38. For a sense of the long-running critique of work-based policy in South Africa, see Franco Barchiesi, *Precarious Liberation: Workers, the State, and Contested*

Social Citizenship in Postapartheid South Africa (Albany, NY: SUNY Press, 2011); Hannah Dawson and Elizabeth Fouksman, "Labour, Laziness and Distribution: Work Imaginaries among the South African Unemployed," *Africa* 90, no. 2 (2020): 229–51; James G. Ferguson, *Give a Man a Fish: Reflections on the New Politics of Distribution* (Durham, NC: Duke University Press, 2015); and Fiona C. Ross, *Raw Life, New Hope: Decency, Housing and Everyday Life in a Post-apartheid Community* (Cape Town: UCT Press, 2010).

39. See Jean Comaroff and John Comaroff, *Theory from the South: Or, How Euro-America Is Evolving toward Africa* (London: Routledge, 2012).

40. By 2018, this number had risen to 17.666 million people (Statistics South Africa, "Government Spending Climbs to R1,71 Trillion," Stats SA website, November 26, 2019).

41. With 60 percent of state expenditure dedicated to "social spending," the treasury department reported in February 2012 that the average value of the social wage for a family of four was about R3940 (USD 520) a month; Donwald Pressly, "Social Grants Bill to Hit R122bn," *Independent Online*, February 23, 2012, https://www.pressreader.com/south-africa/cape-times/20120223/page/25/textview.

42. Homi Bhabha, *The Location of Culture* (London: Routledge, 1994); Comaroff and Comaroff, *Theory from the South*; and Ferguson, *Give a Man a Fish*.

43. Gemma Wright et al., "Social Assistance and Dignity: South African Women's Experiences of the Child Support Grant," *Development Southern Africa* 32, no. 4 (2015): 443–57.

44. Extending social support to all South Africans irrespective of race after 1994 was a major victory of the democratic project, and has been extended to new categories, with incremental increases, through civil society action. Starting in 2016, the delivery of social grants came into question when civil society activists discovered abuses relating to the way that Net1, the contracted service provider, was enrolling citizens and disbursing payments. That dispute resolved in 2018 with payments being shifted to the Post Office and banks. When the COVID-19 pandemic hit South Africa, the state began a temporary Special COVID-19 Social Relief of Distress grant of R350 (USD 19) per month from May 2020, which was discontinued in April 2021, and was likely one of the factors that sparked the destructive looting of July 2021. The debate about the conditional qualification of social welfare or Universal Basic Income brings into question the social and political compact that underwrites the logic of the grant—namely, a reparative effort premised on recognition of a historical injustice that is nonetheless circumscribed by a biopolitical governance of a working population. An alternative argument by James G. Ferguson in *Presence and Social Obligation* is premised on "co-presence" as the only requirement for establishing a "rightful share" in the nation's resources.

45. CD4 cell count is a laboratory test that measures the number of CD4 T lymphocytes (CD4 cells) in a sample of blood. In people with HIV, the CD4 count is

the most important laboratory indicator of immune function and the strongest predictor of HIV progression. The CD4 count is also used to monitor a person's response to antiretroviral therapy (ART). Marcus Low, "Government Plans Massive PrEP Rollout," *Daily Maverick*, February 5, 2020; Ferguson, *Give a Man a Fish*; Erin Torkelson, "Collateral Damages: Cash Transfer and Debt Transfer in South Africa," *World Development* 126 (2020): 104711.

46. Torkelson, "Collateral Damages"; Deborah James, *Money from Nothing: Indebtedness and Aspiration in South Africa* (Stanford, CA: Stanford University Press, 2014).

47. Channing Arndt et al., "Covid-19 Lockdowns, Income Distribution, and Food Security: An Analysis for South Africa," *Global Food Security* 26 (2020): 100410 2020; Marc C. A. Wegerif, "'Informal' Food Traders and Food Security: Experiences from the Covid-19 Response in South Africa," *Food Security* 12, no. 4 (2020): 797–800.

48. The turn of phrase is Marx's, in his 1847 essay "Wage Labor and Capital." "The exchange value of a commodity estimated in money is called its price. Wages therefore are only a special name for the price of labor-power, and are usually called the price of labor; it is the special name for the price of this peculiar commodity, which has no other repository than human flesh and blood."

49. James Mayers, Jeremy Evans, and Tim Foy, *Raising the Stakes: Impacts of Privatisation, Certification and Partnerships in South African Forestry* (London: Institute for Environment and Development, 2001).

50. W. J. A. Louw, "General History of the South African Forest Industry: 1991 to 2002," *Southern African Forestry Journal* 201, no. 1 (2004): 65–76.

51. Nicolas Pons-Vignon and Ward Anseeuw, "Great Expectations: Working Conditions in South Africa since the End of Apartheid," *Journal of Southern African Studies* 35, no. 4 (2009): 883–99.

52. Doubell Chamberlain et al., *Genesis Report Part I: The Contribution, Costs, and Development Opportunities of the Forestry, Timber, Pulp and Paper Industries in South Africa* (Johannesburg: Genesis Analytics, 2005).

53. Pons-Vignon and Anseeuw, "Great Expectations."

54. Jeanette Clarke, "Investigation of Working Conditions of Forestry Workers in South Africa" (Department of Agriculture, Forestry and Fisheries, Government of South Africa, 2012).

55. Jeanette Clarke, "FSC-Certified Plantations and Local Communities: Challenges, Activities, Standards, and Solutions. Case Study: Changing Labour Practices at Mondi Forests South Africa" (unpublished report, 2011).

56. See Canguilhem's essay "Health as a Crude Concept," and in particular its uptake in anthropology and history by Todd Meyers in *The Clinic and Elsewhere: Addiction, Adolescents, and the Afterlife of Therapy* (Seattle: University of Washington Press, 2013); and Nancy Rose Hunt, *A Nervous State: Violence, Remedies, and Reverie in Colonial Congo* (Durham, NC: Duke University Press, 2015).

57. Nathan Geffen, *Debunking Delusions: The Inside Story of the Treatment Action Campaign* (Johannesburg: Jacana, 2010); Kerry Cullinan and Anso Thom, *The Virus, Vitamins, and Vegetables: The South African HIV/AIDS Mystery* (Johannesburg: Jacana, 2009).

58. Not dissimilar to Foucault's notion of an "incitement to discourse," one can trace the development of an intensifying controversy over the distinction between legitimate biomedicine and quackery throughout the natural history of HIV in South Africa. I do not locate myself outside this interpellation into discursive arrangements of race, class, and expertise as a function of who speaks, who is spoken about, and who is vulnerable to infection.

59. Amanda Atwood, "Harare in Four Pharmacies," *Public Books*, April 2, 2016, https://www.publicbooks.org/harare-in-four-pharmacies.

60. Veena Das and Ranendra K. Das, "Pharmaceuticals in Urban Ecologies: The Register of the Local," in *Global Pharmaceuticals: Ethics, Markets, Practices*, ed. Adriana Petryna, Andrew Lakoff, and Arthur Kleinman (Durham, NC: Duke University Press, 2006).

61. See Timothy Burke, *Lifebuoy Men, Lux Women: Commodification, Consumption, and Cleanliness in Modern Zimbabwe* (Durham, NC: Duke University Press, 1996); Deborah A. Thomas, *Political Life in the Wake of the Plantation: Sovereignty, Witnessing, Repair* (Durham, NC: Duke University Press, 2019).

62. Karen E. Flint, *Healing Traditions: African Medicine, Cultural Exchange, and Competition in South Africa, 1820–1948* (Athens: Ohio University Press, 2008). See also Julie Parle, Rebecca Hodes, and Thembisa Waetjen, "Pharmaceuticals and Modern Statecraft in South Africa: The Cases of Opium, Thalidomide and Contraception," *Medical Humanities* 44, no. 4 (2018): 253–62.

63. John Janzen, *Ngoma: Discourses of Healing in Central and Southern Africa* (Berkeley: University of California Press, 1992).

64. Flint, *Healing Traditions*, 127–57.

65. Susan Reynolds Whyte, Sjaak van der Geest, and Anita Hardon, *Social Lives of Medicines* (Cambridge: Cambridge University Press, 2002).

66. Povinelli, *Economies of Abandonment*. See also Tracey Lee McCormick, "A Critical Engagement? Analysing Same-Sex Marriage Discourses in *To Have and to Hold: The Making of Same-Sex Marriage in South Africa* (2008)—A Queer Perspective," *Stellenbosch Papers in Linguistics Plus* 46 (2015): 105; and Tom Boellstorff and Naisargi N. Dave, "Introduction: The Production and Reproduction of Queer Anthropology," Theorizing the Contemporary, *Fieldsights*, July 21, 2015, https://culanth.org/fieldsights/introduction-the-production-and-reproduction-of-queer-anthropology.

67. See Hylton White, "What Is Anthropology That Decolonising Scholarship Should Be Mindful of It?," *Anthropology Southern Africa* 42, no. 2 (2019): 149–60.

68. For a discussion of how contemporary meanings of kinship and care are framed in relation to "damages," see Mark Hunter, "Fathers without Amandla?

Gender and Fatherhood among IsiZulu Speakers," *Journal of Natal and Zulu History* 22, no. 1 (2004): 149–60, and Nolwazi Mkhwanazi, "Understanding Teenage Pregnancy in a Post-apartheid South African Township," *Culture, Health and Sexuality* 12, no. 4 (2010): 347–58.

69. Repair and reparation have been developed in slightly different directions by, among others, Melanie Klein, *Love, Guilt and Reparation, and Other Works 1921–1945* (New York: Free Press, 1975); Donald W. Winnicott, "The Use of an Object," *International Journal of Psychoanalysis* 50, no. 4 (1969): 711–16; Ta-Nehisi Coates, "The Case for Reparations," *The Atlantic*, June 2014; and Steven J. Jackson, "Rethinking Repair," in *Media Technologies: Essays on Communication, Materiality, and Society* (Boston: MIT Press, 2014). Jackson understands repair as "the subtle acts of care by which order and meaning in complex sociotechnical systems are maintained and transformed, human value is preserved and extended, and the complicated work of fitting to the varied circumstances of organizations, systems, and lives is accomplished." On the sociology of repair, see also Joeri Bruyninckx, "Synchronicity: Time, Technicians, Instruments, and Invisible Repair," *Science, Technology, and Human Values* 42, no. 5 (2017): 822–47; and Christopher Henke, "Negotiating Repair: The Infrastructural Contexts of Practice and Power: Revisiting Breakdown, Relocating Materiality," in *Repair Work Ethnographies*, ed. Ignaz Strebel, Alain Bovet, and Philippe Sormani (London: Palgrave Macmillan, 2019), 255–82. While Jackson's notion of "complex sociotechnical systems" might be useful to understand the tangle of bodies, machines, calories, and markets that make the timber plantations possible, a slightly different sense of repair emerges from the workers' efforts and imaginations that I describe here.

70. On attempts at restitution through the Truth and Reconciliation Commissions, see Penelope E. Andrews, "Reparations for Apartheid's Victims: The Path to Reconciliation," *DePaul Law Review* 53 (2004): 1155–80; Mahmood Mamdani, "Beyond Nuremberg: The Historical Significance of the Post-apartheid Transition in South Africa," *Politics and Society* 43, no. 1 (2014): 61–88; and Fiona C. Ross, "Using Rights to Measure Wrongs," in *Human Rights in Global Perspective: Anthropological Studies of Rights, Claims and Entitlements*, ed. Richard A. Wilson and Jon P. Mitchell (London: Routledge, 2003), 163–82.

71. I am indebted to Todd Meyers for alerting me to Attia's work. See Kader Attia, *The Repair: From Occident to Extra-Occidental Cultures* (Berlin: Green Box, 2014). Two excellent dialogues with Attia's work are Manthia Diawara, "Kader Attia: A Poetics of Re-appropriation," in Attia, *The Repair*; and Françoise Vergès, "Fire, Anger and Humiliation in the Museum," in *Kader Attia: The Museum of Emotion*, exhibition catalog (London: Hayward Gallery, 2019), 86–87.

72. Susanne Gaensheimer, foreword to *Kader Attia: Sacrifice and Harmony*, exhibition catalog, Museum für Moderne Kunst, ed. Susanne Gaensheimer and Klaus Görner (Bielefeld: Kerber, 2016), 4.

73. Diawara, *Poetics of Re-appropriation,* 13. *Lieu-commun* translates as "common ground" and "common place," and further, as truism or topos. I take up the concept of topology in chapter 5, but Diawara's reading of Edouard Glissant's "lieux-communs" is helpful here: "those sites where ideas emerge, illuminate and influence other ideas from other places of the world. In this sense, a common site is different from a commonplace, which is made out of naked truths and obvious statements. By contrast, a common ground . . . is a source of creativity and opacity, a fertile ground of inexhaustible energies, where relationships are continually generated between the ideas and poetics of one place and those of another" (5).

74. Ana Teixeira Pinto, "In No Man's Land," in *Kader Attia: Signes de réappropriation* (Dijon: BlackJack, 2013).

75. Klaus Görner, "Sacrifice and Harmony," in *Kader Attia: Sacrifice and Harmony,* exhibition catalog, Museum für Moderne Kunst, ed. Susanne Gaensheimer and Klaus Görner (Bielefeld: Kerber, 2016), 18.

76. Diawara, *Poetics of Re-appropriation,* 13.

77. Arendt, *Human Condition,* 236.

78. Achille Mbembe, *Necropolitics* (Durham, NC: Duke University Press, 2019), 5.

79. Mbembe, *Critique of Black Reason,* 79.

80. Thomas, *Political Life in the Wake of the Plantation.* For Thomas, the history of the plantation as a certain kind of field necessarily demands placing anthropology within and alongside those histories of violence.

81. Mbembe, *Necropolitics,* 107.

82. Mbembe, 5.

83. Mbembe argues that Fanon regarded the gesture of care as "a practice of re-symbolization, the stake of which is the possibility of reciprocity and mutuality (an authentic encounter with others)" (*Necropolitics,* 5).

84. I am inspired here by Veena Das's writing on Cavell's discussion of "availability" in the late Wittgenstein, in "Wittgenstein and Anthropology," *Annual Review of Anthropology* 27, no. 1 (1998): 171–95; Stanley Cavell, *The Claim of Reason: Wittgenstein, Skepticism, Morality, and Tragedy* (New York: Oxford University Press, 1979). See especially Sandra Laugier, "Politics of Vulnerability and Responsibility for Ordinary Others," *Critical Horizons* 17, no. 2 (2016): 207–23.

85. There is a substantial literature on plantations and their entailments, a selection of which includes Henry Bernstein, Tom Brass, and E. Valentine Daniel, *Plantations, Proletarians, and Peasants in Colonial Asia* (London: Cass, 1992); E. Valentine Daniel, "The Coolie," *Cultural Anthropology* 23, no. 2 (2012): 254–78; Sidney W. Mintz, *Worker in the Cane: A Puerto Rican Life History* (New York: W. W. Norton, 1974); Elias C. Mandala, *Work and Control in a Peasant Economy: A History of the Lower Tshiri Valley in Malawi 1859–1960* (Madison: University of Wisconsin Press, 1990); and Michael T. Taussig, *The Devil and Commodity Fetishism in South America* (Chapel Hill: University of North Carolina Press, 1980).

86. "But it is exactly in this ontotheoretical spacing that political questions begin to emerge: How do new forms of social life maintain the force of existing in specific social spacings of life? How do they endure the effort it takes to strive to persevere?" (Povinelli, "Will to Be Otherwise," 462).

87. I am grateful to Fiona Ross for alerting me to this argument, which she presented to the Anthropology Southern Africa conference at North West University in Potchefstroom in 2015. Note the adjacent sense of "amandla ukubekezela," the capacity to endure.

88. For a sense of different points of departure, see Achille Mbembe, "Passages to Freedom: The Politics of Racial Reconciliation in South Africa," *Public Culture* 20, no. 1 (2008): 5–18; and Kelly Gillespie, "Reclaiming Nonracialism: Reading *The Threat of Race* from South Africa," *Patterns of Prejudice* 44, no. 1 (2010): 61–75.

89. For example, see John Beattie, "Representations of the Self in Traditional Africa," *Africa: Journal of the International African Institute* 50, no. 3 (1980): 313–20; John L. Comaroff and Jean Comaroff, "On Personhood: An Anthropological Perspective from Africa," *Social Identities* 7, no. 2 (2001).

90. Francis B. Nyamnjoh, "A Post-Covid-19 Fantasy on Incompleteness and Conviviality," in *"Post-Covid Fantasies,"* ed. Catherine Besteman, Heath Cabot, and Barak Kalir, *American Ethnologist* website, July 27, 2020, https://americanethnologist .org/features/pandemic-diaries/post-covid-fantasies/a-post-covid-19-fantasy-on -incompleteness-and-conviviality.

91. I am particularly interested in the possibilities for converting one specific object into something else and the potential to capture the force inherent in all matter and beings, which Mbembe suggests constituted the ultimate form of power and agency in precolonial Africa. "The world itself was a transactional world" (Mbembe, *Necropolitics*, 107).

92. On the (im)possibility of mourning, see Sakiru Adebayo, "Unmournable Bodies, Embodied Monuments and Bodily Truths: Rethinking Reconciliation in Zulu Love Letter," *Safundi* 22, no. 1 (2021): 7–10; Teju Cole, "Unmournable Bodies," *New Yorker*, January 9, 2015; Kylie Thomas, *Impossible Mourning: HIV/AIDS and Visuality after Apartheid* (Johannesburg: Wits University Press, 2013). This list of dates refers to events, before 1994, in which antiapartheid protest was met with violent repression by the apartheid state—and after 1994, two key moments of violent rupture, amongst many others; on which, see Karl von Holdt et al., *The Smoke That Calls: Insurgent Citizenship, Collective Violence and the Struggle for a Place in the New South Africa. Eight Case Studies of Community Protest and Xenophobic Violence* (Johannesburg: Centre for the Study of Violence and Reconciliation, Society, Work and Development, 2011). Povinelli, *Economies of Abandonment*, offers a critique of late liberal thought that depends on a form of sacrificial suffering of those not yet included in liberal society as "ordinary, chronic, and cruddy rather

than catastrophic, crisis-laden, and sublime" (132). For an indirect response to Scarry's claim that work as a subject is difficult to represent, see Pamela Reynolds, *The Uncaring, Intricate World: A Field Diary, Zambezi Valley, 1984–1985* (Durham, NC: Duke University Press, 2019), 23.

93. The relationship between justice and memory is a central theme in Jacob Dlamini, *The Terrorist Album: Apartheid's Insurgents, Collaborators, and the Security Police* (Boston: Harvard University Press, 2020), and is complicated by Johnny Steinberg's account of instability of memory in *One Day in Bethlehem* (Johannesburg: Jonathan Ball, 2019). The question of memory and mourning is central to Kylie Thomas's analysis of HIV deaths in South Africa (*Impossible Mourning*). The "secret pact of forgetting" that underpins the postapartheid political order remains a festering wound; David Forbes, "The Secret 'Pact of Forgetting' and the Suppression of Post-TRC Prosecutions," *Daily Maverick*, July 24, 2021, https://www.dailymaverick.co.za/article/2021-07-24-the-secret-pact-of-forgetting-and-the-suppression-of-post-trc-prosecutions.

94. The phrase is Mbembe's, reported by Roger Friedman, "The New Barbarism," *Daily Maverick*, December 14, 2018, https://www.dailymaverick.co.za/article/2018-12-14-the-new-barbarism.

95. Mbembe (*Necropolitics*, 108) claims that "how we assemble [various spare or animate parts] and for what purpose is the question that late modern identity politics raises so unequivocally." See Georges Canguilhem's essay on machine and organism in *Knowledge of Life*, ed. Paola Marrati and Todd Meyers (New York: Fordham University Press, 2008).

96. Todd Meyers, *The Clinic and Elsewhere: Addiction, Adolescents and the Afterlife of Therapy* (Seattle: University of Washington Press, 2013), 14.

97. Meyers, 14.

98. See Thomas Lemke, "'A Zone of Indistinction'—A Critique of Giorgio Agamben's Con-cept of Biopolitics," *Outlines. Critical Practice Studies* 7, no. 1 (2005): 3–13; and Veena Das and Deborah Poole, *Anthropology in the Margins of the State* (Santa Fe, NM: School of American Research Press, 2004).

99. On folded topologies of life, see Michelle Pentecost and Thomas Cousins, "Strata of the Political: Epigenetic and Microbial Imaginaries in Post-apartheid Cape Town," *Antipode* 49 (2017): 1368–84.

100. Hunt, *Nervous State*.

101. While images of vulnerability can be found across the philosophical landscape from Hobbes to Hegel, Levinas to Foucault, often indicating a sense of bodily susceptibility to injury, or of being threatened or wounded, I am less interested here in a Euro-American genealogy than the possibilities for a "Southern" reading of vulnerability. See Faisal Devji, "The Return of Nonviolence," *Critical Times* 4, no. 1 (2021): 93–101, for a critique of Judith Butler, *The Force of Nonviolence: An Ethico-political Bind* (New York: Verso, 2020); see also Danielle Petherbridge, "What's Critical

about Vulnerability? Rethinking Interdependence, Recognition, and Power," *Hypatia* 31, no. 3 (2016): 589–604.

102. See the landmark essays in Arthur Kleinman, Veena Das, and Margaret M. Lock, *Social Suffering* (Berkeley: University of California Press, 1997); Veena Das et al., eds., *Violence and Subjectivity* (Oakland: University of California Press, 2000); and Veena Das and Clara Han, *Living and Dying in the Contemporary World* (Berkeley: University of California Press, 2016).

103. David Lan, *Guns and Rain: Guerrillas and Spirit Mediums in Zimbabwe* (Berkeley: University of California Press, 1985); Pamela Reynolds, *Traditional Healers and Childhood in Zimbabwe* (Athens: Ohio University Press, 1996); and Donald S. Moore, *Suffering for Territory: Race, Place and Power in Zimbabwe* (Durham, NC: Duke University Press, 2005).

104. Robert Thornton, *Healing the Exposed Being: A South African Ngoma Tradition* (Johannesburg: Wits University Press, 2017).

105. Anette Wickström, "'Lungisa'—Weaving Relationships and Social Space to Restore Health in Rural KwaZulu Natal," *Medical Anthropology Quarterly* 28, no. 2 (2014): 203–20.

106. James Fernandez, *Bwiti: An Ethnography of the Religious Imagination in Africa* (Princeton, NJ: Princeton University Press, 1982).

107. Hylton White, "Tempora et Mores: Family Values and the Possessions of a Post-apartheid Countryside," *Journal of Religion in Africa* 31, no. 4 (2001): 457–79.

108. On the transformation of ideas of the concept of man as machine to the late twentieth-century notion of digital organisms, see Anson Rabinbach, *The Eclipse of the Utopias of Labor* (New York: Fordham University Press, 2018).

109. Analogously, on the relationship between capital and nature, see Jason W. Moore, *Capitalism in the Web of Life Ecology and the Accumulation of Capital* (London: Verso, 2015).

110. "Transformation" in the post-1994 era indexes a range of efforts directed at "transforming" the racialized nature of South Africa, and takes many different institutional forms, from affirmative action policies very broadly conceived to hiring quotas, Black Economic Empowerment legislation, and many smaller, more focused efforts to change social relations and institutional cultures across all domains of South African public life. For a critique of South African policy after 1994, see Zine Magubane, "Globalization and the South African Transformation: The Impact on Social Policy," *Africa Today* 49, no. 4 (2002): 89–110, and for a broader review of "transformation" in a more regional perspective, see Marlea Clarke and Carolyn Bassett, "The Struggle for Transformation in South Africa: Unrealised Dreams, Persistent Hopes," *Journal of Contemporary African Studies* 34, no. 2 (2016): 183–89. In this case, the Transformation Office was concerned with hiring Black managers, shifting ownership of the company to Black shareholders, and effecting a range of

labor and land reforms aimed at redressing the historical harms at the core of Mondi's operations and profits.

111. Frank Tanser et al., "Localized Spatial Clustering of HIV Infections in a Widely Disseminated Rural South African Epidemic," *International Journal of Epidemiology* 38 (2009): 1008–16.

112. See Colin Murray, "Displaced Urbanisation: South Africa's Rural Slums," *African Affairs* 86, no. 344 (1987): 311–29; and Premesh Lalu, "Leaving the City: Gender, Pastoral Power and the Discourse of Development in the Eastern Cape," in *Desire Lines: Space, Memory and Identity in the Post-apartheid City*, ed. Nick Shepherd, Noëleen Murray, and Martin Hall (London: Routledge, 2003).

113. See Daryl Collins et al., *Portfolios of the Poor* (Princeton, NJ: Princeton University Press, 2009).

114. For a discussion of the history of hostels and migrant labor in South Africa, see Andries Bezuidenhout and Sakhela Buhlungu, "From Compounded to Fragmented Labour: Mineworkers and the Demise of Compounds in South Africa," *Antipode* 43, no. 2 (2011): 237–63; Glen S. Elder, "Malevolent Traditions: Hostel Violence and the Procreational Geography of Apartheid," *Journal of Southern African Studies* 29, no. 4 (2003): 921–35; Jason Hickel, *Democracy as Death: The Moral Order of Anti-liberal Politics in South Africa* (Berkeley: University of California Press, 2015); Mamphela Ramphele, *A Bed Called Home: Life in the Migrant Labour Hostels of Cape Town* (Athens: Ohio University Press, 1993); and Christo Vosloo, "Extreme Apartheid: The South African System of Migrant Labour and Its Hostels," *Image and Text* 34 (2020): 1–33.

115. On the importance of remittances and cattle, see James G. Ferguson, *The Anti-politics Machine: "Development," Depoliticization, and Bureaucratic Power in Lesotho* (Minneapolis: University of Minnesota Press, 1994).

116. Ritual events are often referred to in English as "functions" and in isiZulu as "umsebenzi," a term whose polysemic range includes, and indexes, a job, work, an event.

117. Thomas Cousins and Lindsey Reynolds, "Blood Relations: HIV Surveillance and Fieldworker Intimacy in KwaZulu-Natal, South Africa," in *Medical Anthropology in Global Africa*, ed. Kathryn Rhine et al. (Lawrence: University of Kansas, Department of Anthropology, 2014), 79–88.

118. Renamed the South African Communist Party in 1953, after its banning in 1950.

119. Shannon Morreira, "Working with Our Grandparents' Illusions on Colonial Lineage and Inheritance in Southern African Anthropology," *HAU: Journal of Ethnographic Theory* 6, no. 2 (2016): 279–95.

120. For accounts of the complex and ambivalent histories of social anthropology in South Africa, see Andrew Bank, *Pioneers of the Field: South Africa's Women Anthropologists. The International African Library* (Cambridge: Cambridge University

Press, 2016); Kelly Gillespie and Bernard Dubbeld, "The Possibility of a Critical Anthropology after Apartheid: Relevance, Intervention, Politics," *Anthropology Southern Africa* 30, nos. 3–4 (2007): 129–34; R. J. Gordon and A. D. Spiegel, "Southern Africa Revisited," *Annual Review of Anthropology* 22 (1993): 83–105; Andrew D. Spiegel and Heike Becker, "South Africa: Anthropology or Anthropologies?," *American Anthropologist* 117, no. 4 (2015): 754–60; Isak Niehaus, "Anthropology and Whites in South Africa: Response to an Unreasonable Critique," *Africa Spectrum* 48, no. 1 (2013): 117–27; and C. S. van der Waal, "Long Walk from Volkekunde to Anthropology: Reflections on Representing the Human in South Africa," *Anthropology Southern Africa* 38, nos. 3–4 (2015): 216–34. See also the sharp critique by Nancy Scheper-Hughes, "The Primacy of the Ethical," *Current Anthropology* 36, no. 3 (1995): 409–40, and reply by Steven Robins, "On the Call for a Militant Anthropology: The Complexity of 'Doing the Right Thing,'" *Current Anthropology* 37, no. 2 (1996): 341–46.

121. Jacob A. Tropp, *Natures of Colonial Change: Environmental Relations in the Making of the Transkei* (Athens: Ohio University Press, 2006).

122. Pamela Reynolds, "Gleanings and Leavings: Encounters in Hindsight," in *Inside African Anthropology: Monica Wilson and Her Interpreters*, ed. Andrew Bank and Leslie J. Bank (Cambridge: Cambridge University Press, 2013).

123. On the limits of critique in relation to a disciplinary unconscious, see Frances E. Mascia-Lees, "The Anthropological Unconscious," *American Anthropologist* 96, no. 3 (1994): 649–60.

124. Elizabeth A. Povinelli, *The Cunning of Recognition: Indigenous Alterities and the Making of Australian Multiculturalism* (Durham, NC: Duke University Press, 2002).

125. For a genealogy of shame, see Ruth Leys, *From Guilt to Shame* (Princeton, NJ: Princeton University Press, 2007).

126. "When an unexpected result is more advantageous than the result we had anticipated, it subjugates us to the task of finding ways to put it to use. The abrupt replacement of the anticipated object with one that is useless or ruinous forces us to recalculate our situation. But at the moment of collapse, our outcries can switch into an outburst of laughter." Alphonso Lingis, *Dangerous Emotions* (Berkeley: University of California Press, 2000), 166.

127. Lingis's perspective on laughter is helpful because it places laughter within a relational structure of becoming with another, or with the situation itself: "Is there something in us that understands the laughter of heroes? In the moment of shared laughter, or weeping, there is a transparency among individuals, as if the emotional outburst gave rise to a single torrent surging within them. If we, who have not yet faced our death with laughter or with whimpering and cowardice, can venture to speak of those who laugh in the face of firing squads or with bodies swimming with deadly viruses, it is because language came into existence to speak of what we laugh

and weep over together" (Lingis, 164). "He who finds himself in laughter delivered from anticipation and from subordination to anticipated results also finds himself delivered from his individual identity. . . . Nonsensical urges break up ruminations and explanations of people who identify themselves as rational individuals" (Lingis, 167).

128. Certainly by the end of my time with this group, I came to regard the women who labor in the plantations as heroes—uncomfortable though such a powerful trope is in White liberal accounts of racialized structural violence.

129. Elaine Scarry, *Resisting Representation* (New York: Oxford University Press, 1994), 57.

130. Scarry, 65.

131. In *The Body Multiple: Ontology in Medical Practice* (Durham, NC: Duke University Press, 2002), Annemarie Mol calls a focus on practice that she has developed through her ethnographic and philosophical work "praxiography." For Mol, reality itself is not prior to practices but rather a consequence of them; in Mol's "practical ontology," actors do not act on pregiven objects but rather bring them into being—a process she calls "enactment." See Christopher Gad, Casper Bruun Jensen, and Brit Ross Winthereik, "Practical Ontology: Worlds in STS and Anthropology," *NatureCulture* 3 (2015): 67–86.

1. LABOR POWER AND AMANDLA

1. "Toolbox talks" are short, mandatory training sessions on such topics as hydration, nutrition, equipment maintenance, or safety around wild animals. The material was devised by the company's Health and Safety team and disseminated through Health and Safety Officers who were employed to deliver training and oversee adherence by contractors to safety standards drawn up in the Forestry Sector Charter, and in accordance with the Occupational Health and Safety Act of 1993. See Hloni Nkomo, Ivan Niranjan, and Poovendhree Reddy, "Effectiveness of Health and Safety Training in Reducing Occupational Injuries among Harvesting Forestry Contractors in KwaZulu-Natal," *Workplace Health and Safety* 66, no. 10 (2018): 499–507.

2. While much of the policy literature and many of the people involved in the forestry sector refer to "forestry workers," I have tended to use the term "timber [plantation] laborer" to refer to people employed in the timber plantations of northern KwaZulu-Natal, as the older sociological literature in South Africa on the "workforce" has a somewhat complicated relationship to the politics of critique—see E. C. Webster, "Race, Labour Process and Transition: The Sociology of Work in South Africa," *Society in Transition* 30, no. 1 (1999): 28–42. This does have the inadvertent effect of distinguishing this category of employment from other activities in the sector not directly concerned with the production of timber.

3. On the relationship between work and rhythm and the division of labor, see Gregor Dobler, "'Work and Rhythm' Revisited: Rhythm and Experience in Northern Namibian Peasant Work," *Journal of the Royal Anthropological Institute* 22, no. 4 (2016): 864–83.

4. Daniela Casale and Dorrit Posel, "The Feminisation of the Labour Force in South Africa: An Analysis of Recent Data and Trends," *South African Journal of Economics* 70, no. 1 (2002): 156–84.

5. See Roger Southall, "Ten Propositions about Black Economic Empowerment in South Africa," *Review of African Political Economy* 34, no. 111 (2007): 67–84; Roger Tangri and Roger Southall, "The Politics of Black Economic Empowerment in South Africa," *Journal of Southern African Studies* 34, no. 3 (2008): 699–716; and Jeanette Clarke and Moenieba Isaacs, *Forestry Contractors in South Africa: What Role in Reducing Poverty?* (London: Programme for Land and Agrarian Studies, University of the Western Cape, South Africa, and International Institute for Environment and Development, 2005), to situate the politics of Black Economic Empowerment in postapartheid South Africa, and the forestry sector, respectively.

6. In this case, SiyaQhubeka, which is a subsidiary of Mondi that operates the plantations of northern KwaZulu-Natal. SiyaQhubeka website, http://www .siyaqhubeka.co.za/, accessed November 13, 2020.

7. Izinduna: traditional leaders; izinyanga: traditional healers; intombi: young woman or girl; insizwa: young man or boy. The categories of intombi and insizwa are taken up directly in chapter 3.

8. There is a rich literature on emergent class striations in rural southern Africa. See Martin Legassick and Harold Wolpe, "The Bantustans and Capital Accumulation in South Africa," *Review of African Political Economy* 3, no. 7 (1976): 87–107; Timothy Keegan, "The Dynamics of Rural Accumulation in South Africa: Comparative and Historical Perspectives," *Comparative Studies in Society and History* 28, no. 4 (1986): 628–50; Michael Neocosmos, *The Agrarian Question in Southern Africa and "Accumulation from Below": Economics and Politics in the Struggle for Democracy,* Research Report 93 (Uppsala: Nordiska Afrikainstitutet, 1993); Ben Cousins, "Smallholder Irrigation Schemes, Agrarian Reform and 'Accumulation from Above and from Below' in South Africa," *Journal of Agrarian Change* 13, no. 1 (2013): 116–39; Ben Cousins et al., "Social Reproduction of 'Classes of Labour' in the Rural Areas of South Africa: Contradictions and Contestations," *Journal of Peasant Studies* 45, no. 5–6 (2018): 1060–85.

9. Summer temperatures are frequently above 35°C (95°F), with humidity above 80 percent, which makes for an approximate Wet Bulb Globe Temperature (WBGT) of 32°C. The WBGT is a composite temperature used to estimate the effect of temperature, humidity, wind speed (wind chill), and solar radiation on humans. Industrial hygienists, athletes, and the military use it to determine appropriate exposure levels to high temperatures. While discomfort is obviously felt very differently,

Chara Biggs, in "The Prevalence and Degree of Dehydration in Rural South African Forestry Workers" (master's thesis, University of KwaZulu-Natal, 2008), shows how forestry workers are vulnerable to dehydration and heat stroke. Discomfort and heat illness are a function of maintaining the body's core temperature, around 37°C (±0.5°C). Workers gain heat from the environment and from the metabolic heat produced during hard physical labor. Core temperature rises if the heat gained is greater than the heat lost. Heat exhaustion occurs at core temperatures of ≤ 40°C. Symptoms include fatigue, headaches, dizziness, nausea, feeling hot or cold, muscle and stomach cramps, headaches, palpitations, and/or heat syncope. The incidence of heat illness amongst forestry workers is unknown as the industry does not require a record to be kept of these symptoms. The greatest threat to core temperature is physical activity in a hot environment; the risk of heat illness increases with duration of the activity, increasing ambient air temperatures, and high humidity levels. According to R. J. Maughan, J. B. Leiper, and S. M. Shirreffs, "Factors Influencing the Restoration of Fluid and Electrolyte Balance after Exercise in the Heat," *British Journal of Sports Medicine* 31, no. 3 (1997): 175–82, high environmental temperatures in combination with high humidity levels inevitably result in a rise in core temperature, compromising work capacity and endangering health.

10. In 2019, the minimum wage for the forestry sector was R18 per hour (USD 1.20 per hour), with monthly wages calculated as 4.33 times a weekly wage. See https://mywage.co.za/salary/minimum-wages/6247-farming-and-forestry, last accessed November 13, 2020.

11. In July 2009, USD 1 = ZAR 7.7; www.xe.com.

12. Clarke and Isaacs, *Forestry Contractors in South Africa.*

13. Lost-time injury frequency rate (LTIFR) (per 200,000 hours worked) for employees and contractors declined by 18 percent compared with the previous year, and by 53 percent over the five-year commitment period (Mondi plc, "Mondi Sustainability Report," Durban, 2010).

14. I bracket this description of timber plantation laborers in terms of "rural black South African forestry workers" as constructions of the research teams from the University of KwaZulu-Natal and the Institute of Commercial Forestry Research because it reveals the racialized figure of the worker whose supposed "rurality" underpins a diet and set of social relations.

15. See Biggs, "Prevalence and Degree of Dehydration." The comparison of coerced energies extracted and expended for the purpose of sustenance with energies expended in a type of play is bizarre and reveals a picture of bodily performance stripped of context and meaning.

16. J. W. C. Hsu et al., "Macronutrients and HIV/AIDS: A Review of Current Evidence" (World Health Organization, Durban, April 10–13, 2005), 10–13; cited in Biggs.

17. N. P. Steyn et al., "Weight and Health Status of Black Female Students," *South African Medical Journal* 90, no. 2 (2000): 146–52; cited in Biggs.

18. Biggs, 1.

19. Biggs, 5. Initially it was thought that only severe dehydration had deleterious health effects, but more recent evidence has shown that chronic exposure to repeated episodes of mild dehydration also compromises health. A study done during the South African summer of January 2004 found that forestry workers in the Kwambonambi area lost 2.9 percent to 3.7 percent of their body mass across a shift indicating significant underhydration (P. A. Scott et al., "Ergonomics Report: Forest Harvesting," in *Ergonomics Report for FESA* [Pietermaritzburg: Institute for Commercial Forestry Research, 2004]). A body mass loss of 2 to 7 percent when exercising in temperatures above 30°C results in decreased exercise performance as well as decreased concentration and coordination. A smaller loss of 1 to 2 percent when exercising for over ninety minutes at temperatures similar to those experienced in South African winters results in a drop-off in physical performance. It increases the risk of bladder cancer, renal failure, urinary stones, urinary tract infections, fatal coronary artery disease, strokes, and probably dental diseases due to the reduced production of saliva. Dehydration therefore has serious implications for both the health of the workers and the health of the forestry industry, although there is little information about the prevalence of dehydration in South African forestry workers.

20. For context on the violence of the region in the 1980s, see Injobo Nebandla, *Freedom from Strife? An Assessment of Efforts to Build Peace in KwaZulu-Natal* (Braamfontein: Centre for the Study of Violence and Reconciliation, 2005); and Marlea Clarke, "Supporting the 'Elite' Transition in South Africa: Policing in a Violent, Neoliberal Democracy," in *Police Abuse in Contemporary Democracies*, ed. Michelle D. Bonner et al. (London: Springer International, 2018).

21. Such a finding is surprising, given the profound importance of purgatives and emetics as part of popular and ordinary techniques of healing—see Michelle Cocks and Valerie Møller, "Use of Indigenous and Indigenised Medicines to Enhance Personal Well-Being: A South African Case Study," *Social Science and Medicine* 54 (2002): 387–97.

In my own 2009 survey in the Mtubatuba region, about 60 percent of workers reported using a variety of emetic and purgative substances for improved well-being.

22. Biggs, "Prevalence and Degree of Dehydration," 7.

23. Richard Parker, Liz Ashby, and Graham Bates, "Dehydration in Loggers: Effects of Season and Time of Day," *COHFE Report* 3, no. 1 (2002): 1174–234.

24. The use of BMI as an indicator of health in the context of HIV and especially in very different national contexts around the world is strongly contested; see T. Matoti-Mvalo and T. B. Puoane, "Perceptions of Body Size and Its Association with HIV/AIDS," *South African Journal of Clinical Nutrition* 24, no. 1 (2011): 40–45; and Kufre Joseph Okop et al., "Perceptions of Body Size, Obesity Threat and the Willingness to Lose Weight among Black South African Adults: A Qualitative Study," *BMC Public Health* 16, no. 1 (2016): 365.

25. What constitutes a household and who might be counted as kin are two key questions that have animated a voluminous literature in South Africa over the past forty years as the effects of colonialism, apartheid, and postapartheid social policy have powerfully shaped ordinary life for many people in and across and southern Africa. See Fiona C. Ross, "Model Communities and Respectable Residents? Home and Housing in a Low-Income Residential Estate in the Western Cape, South Africa," *Journal of Southern African Studies* 31, no. 3 (2005): 631–48; Andrew D. Spiegel, "Changing Patterns of Migrant Labour and Rural Differentiation in Lesotho," *Social Dynamics* 6, no. 2 (1980): 1–13; and Vicky Hosegood and Ian M. Timaeus, "Household Composition and Dynamics in KwaZulu Natal, South Africa: Mirroring Social Reality in Longitudinal Data Collection," in *African Households: An Exploration of Census Data*, ed. Etienne van de Walle (London: Routledge, 2005), 58–77.

26. For a discussion of income and its measurement, see Daryl Collins et al., *Portfolios of the Poor* (Princeton, NJ: Princeton University Press, 2009); and Andries du Toit, "Poverty Measurement Blues: Beyond 'Q-squared' Approaches to Understanding Chronic Poverty in South Africa," in *Poverty Dynamics: Interdisciplinary Perspectives*, ed. Tony Addison, David Hulme, and Ravi Kanbur (Oxford: Oxford University Press, 2009), 225–46.

27. On the gendered significance of livestock, see James G. Ferguson, "The Bovine Mystique," *Man*, n.s., 20 (1985): 647–74; Colin Murray, *Families Divided: The Impact of Migrant Labour in Lesotho* (Cambridge: Cambridge University Press, 1981); and Hylton White, "Ritual Haunts: The Timing of Estrangement in a Post-apartheid Countryside," in *Producing African Futures: Ritual and Reproduction in a Neoliberal Age*, ed. Brad Weiss (Leiden: Koninklijke Brill, 2004).

28. Including sweet potato, onion, lettuce, cabbage, beetroot, beans, pumpkin, and squash.

29. See Alexander Dubb, "Social Reproduction, Accumulation and Class Differentiation: Small-Scale Sugarcane Growers in Mtubatuba, KwaZulu-Natal, South Africa" (PLAAS Working Paper 25, University of the Western Cape, 2012); and John Sender, "Women's Struggle to Escape Rural Poverty in South Africa," *Journal of Agrarian Change* 2, no. 1 (2002): 1–49.

30. Computed using the benchmark of R143 per person per month in 2008, or USD 2 per person per day. William Muhwava et al., *Operational and Methodological Procedures of the Africa Centre Demographic Information System* (Somkhele, South Africa: Africa Centre for Health and Population Studies, 2007); William Muhwava, *Trends in Economic Status of Households in the ACDIS*, Monograph Series no. 3 (Somkhele, South Africa: Africa Centre for Health and Population Studies, 2008).

31. The finding is consonant with Sender, "Women's Struggle"; Andries du Toit and David Neves, "Informal Social Protection in Post-apartheid Migrant Networks:

Vulnerability, Social Networks and Reciprocal Exchange in the Eastern and West-ern Cape, South Africa" (Brooks World Poverty Institute, University of Manches-ter, 2009); and David Neves and Andries du Toit, "Money and Sociality in South Africa's Informal Economy," *Africa* 82, no. 1 (2012): 131–49.

32. Abraham Malaza et al., "Population-Based CD4 Counts in a Rural Area in South Africa with High HIV Prevalence and High Antiretroviral Treatment Coverage," *PLOS ONE* 8, no. 7 (July 23, 2013): e70126.

33. The inference is reasonable, as the Demographic Surveillance Area is pre-mised on its representativeness within the region, and timber plantation laborers around uMkhanyakude, some of whom live in the DSA, could be said to share gen-erally many characteristics with those within the DSA. Besides being immediately adjacent, they are of similar socioeconomic status, have a similar population den-sity, and share similar social values. The estimation might be low relative to others living in the area given that other data suggest that HIV prevalence is higher among those who are mobile, have higher incomes, or have employment. Alternatively, it is possible that prevalence among this group may in fact be lower than this esti-mate suggests because women with timber employment may have less time, are too tired, or are more responsible as wage earners.

34. Meeting minutes, June 19, 2009, Food4Forests training workshop.

35. Scott et al., "Ergonomics Report."

36. Not all answers were numerical and not all were significant. For example, to whether caterers were friendly, all answered affirmatively, as they did to "was the food enough or too much," a fine example of "ask a silly question, get a silly answer."

37. Georges Canguilhem, Stephanos Geroulanos, and Daniela Ginsburg, *Knowl-edge of Life*, ed. Paola Marrati and Todd Meyers (New York: Fordham University Press, 2008); Anson Rabinbach, *The Human Motor: Energy, Fatigue, and the Ori-gins of Modernity* (Berkeley: University of California Press, 1992).

38. Rabinbach, *Human Motor*; see in particular Randall Packard, *White Plague, Black Labour: Tuberculosis and the Political Economy of Health and Disease in South Africa* (Berkeley: University of California Press, 1989), 147–55.

39. Michel Foucault, *The History of Sexuality*, vol. 1, *An Introduction*, trans. Rob-ert Hurley (New York: Vintage Books, 1990), 139.

40. Foucault, 139.

41. Georgio Agamben, *Homo Sacer: Sovereign Power and Bare Life* (Stanford, CA: Stanford University Press, 1998).

42. C. M. Doke et al., *English–Zulu, Zulu–English Dictionary* (Johannesburg: Witwatersrand University Press, 2006), 9.

43. See Mark Hunter, "Fathers without Amandla? Gender and Fatherhood among IsiZulu Speakers," *Journal of Natal and Zulu History* 22, no. 1 (2004): 149–60, in which he describes how Zulu-speaking men struggle with their capacity to be fathers

"without amandla." Here, when Bashingile's partner Gazu had approached her father's family for her hand, the question was how many cattle would be required. "The man of the house would say, it will be this much money. For instance he would say, I want this many cattle. If [Gazu] does not have the strength, or his strength is limited, he would say, Biyela's, please wait for me a bit, I'll do it bit by bit. [It goes like that] until you finish. [Gazu] only finished last year."

44. For descriptions of Shembe's power, see Elizabeth Gunner, *The Man of Heaven and the Beautiful Ones of God* (Leiden: Brill, 2004).

45. Foucault, *History of Sexuality*, 1:26.

46. Drawing on Nigerian writer and activist Wole Soyinka, Harry Garuba, "On Animism, Modernity/Colonialism, and the African Order of Knowledge: Provisional Reflections," *E-Flux Journal* 36 (2012): 1–9, names the logic of animist thought as the "animist unconscious," an unconscious that operates on a refusal of the boundaries, binaries, demarcations, and linearity of modernity. Amandla is thus firmly located within a recognition of the "complex embeddedness of different temporalities, different, discordant discursive formations, and different epistemological perspectives within the same historical moment" (Garuba, 7). Achille Mbembe, Francis Nyamnjoh, and Garuba all draw on a rich archive of debate on the question of the fetish as a nonlocalizable and unstable concern, as I suggested in the introduction and return to in the conclusion. For further analysis of African ideas of things and persons, see William Pietz, "The Problem of the Fetish, I," *Res: Anthropology and Aesthetics* 9 (1985): 5–17, and Wyatt MacGaffey, "African Objects and the Idea of Fetish," *Res: Anthropology and Aesthetics* 25, no. 25 (1994): 123–31.

47. Michel Foucault, *The Birth of Biopolitics: Lectures at the Collège de France, 1978–1979,* ed. Michel Senellart, trans. Graham Burchell (New York: Macmillan, 2010), 226.

48. Foucault, 226.

49. By "social project" I mean the sense of making social worlds otherwise, well described by Elizabeth A. Povinelli, *Economies of Abandonment: Social Belonging and Endurance in Late Liberalism* (Durham, NC: Duke University Press, 2011). See also Tracey Lee McCormick, "A Critical Engagement? Analysing Same-Sex Marriage Discourses in *To Have and to Hold: The Making of Same-Sex Marriage in South Africa* (2008)—A Queer Perspective," *Stellenbosch Papers in Linguistics Plus* 46 (2015): 105; Tom Boellstorff and Naisargi N. Dave, "Introduction: The Production and Reproduction of Queer Anthropology," Theorizing the Contemporary, *Fieldsights,* July 21, 2015, https://culanth.org/fieldsights/introduction-the-production-and-reproduction-of-queer-anthropology; and Hylton White, "Custom, Normativity and Authority in South Africa," *Journal of Southern African Studies* 41, no. 5 (2015): 1005–17.

50. Povinelli, *Economies of Abandonment,* 25.

51. Jane I. Guyer, "The Multiplication of Labor: Historical Methods in the Study of Gender and Agricultural Change in Modern Africa," *Current Anthropology* 29, no. 2 (1988): 247–72.

52. For phenomenological readings of language and body, see Elizabeth A. Grosz, *Volatile Bodies: Toward a Corporeal Feminism* (Bloomington: Indiana University Press, 1994); Maurice Merleau-Ponty, *Phenomenology of Perception*, trans. Colin Smith (London: Routledge, 2005); and David Morris, "The Fold and the Body Schema in Merleau-Ponty and Dynamic Systems Theory," *Chiasmi International: Trilingual Studies concerning Merleau-Ponty's Thought* 1 (1999): 275–86.

53. Ukuchata: cleanse by way of enema. See chapter 4.

54. While Didier Fassin, *When Bodies Remember: Experiences and Politics of AIDS in South Africa* (Berkeley: University of California Press, 2007), suggests that "bodies remember" by means of an embodied, phenomenological relationship to histories of violence, via Merleau-Ponty and an appeal to transcendental significa-tion, I draw on Canguilhem's more materialist, vitalist reading of the history of bi-ology and the construction of milieu as the grounds for a different kind of historicity that is the object of concrete forms of reasoning and action in the work of ritual, in the ways that Hylton White suggests. See also Michael Lambek, "The Value of (Performative) Acts," *HAU: Journal of Ethnographic Theory* 3, no. 2 (2013): 141–60, on the value of performative acts.

2. THE PLANTATION AND THE MAKING OF A LABOR REGIME

1. Pamela Reynolds, "The Ground of All Making: State Violence, the Family and Political Activists," in *Violence and Subjectivity* (Berkeley: University of California Press, 2000), 141–70, draws on Scarry's analysis of pain in her examination of the apartheid state's use of violence in breaking up families and the torture of young political activists: "The unmaking of civilisation inevitably requires a return to and mutilation of the domestic, the ground of all making"; Elaine Scarry, *The Body in Pain: The Making and Un-making of the World* (Oxford: Oxford University Press, 1985), 45.

2. See Stéphane Gros, Kamala Russell, and William F. Stafford, "Introduction: Topology as Method," Theorizing the Contemporary, *Fieldsights,* September 30, 2019, https://culanth.org/fieldsights/introduction-topology-as-method, who show how anthropologists have drawn on the concept of topology to address method-ological issues concerning comparison and generalization to both render and re-fine structure—searching for patterns and a system of internal relations—and to dynamize structuralist concerns of relation, continuity, and change. They cite, for example, Edmund Leach's use of topology as an analogy to describe the flexibility of networks of relations, advocating for the analysis of societies as "assemblages of variables"; Leach, *Rethinking Anthropology* (London: Athlone, 1961), 7. Marilyn

Strathern's topological thinking is discussed by Alfred Gell and Eric Hirsch in *The Art of Anthropology: Essays and Diagrams* (London: Athlone, 1999) and by Giovanni da Col in "Strathern Bottle: On Topology, Ethnographic Theory, and the Method of Wonder," introduction to Strathern's *Learning to See in Melanesia: Four Lectures Given in the Department of Social Anthropology, Cambridge University, 1993–2008* (Chicago: HAU Books, 2013). I am particularly interested in the figure of the bag or container as a topological form suited to thinking with and through the gut and the plantations, which is inspired by Marilyn Strathern's lecture on bags and masks, in *Learning to See in Melanesia*, and Elizabeth A. Povinelli's riff on Lévi-Strauss's totemic operator, in "Routes/Worlds," *E-Flux Journal*, no. 27 (September 2011). I take up three distinct topologies in chapter 5, to show how amandla entails a capacity to navigate topologies.

3. See Margaret Lock, "Recovering the Body," *Annual Review of Anthropology* 46 (2017): 1–14. The definitive historian of vitalism is Georges Canguilhem; see in particular his classic essay on milieu, in *Knowledge of Life* (New York: Fordham University Press, 2008), and Jakob von Uexküll's early essay on the umwelt, *A Foray into the Worlds of Animals and Humans: With A Theory of Meaning*, trans. Joseph D. O'Neill (Minneapolis: University of Minnesota Press, 2010), both of which are foundational.

4. On "multisituated," see Kaushik Sunder Rajan, *Multisituated: Ethnography as Diasporic Praxis* (Durham, NC: Duke University Press, 2021).

5. The layering and concatenating processes that shape biographies are explicated in Michelle Pentecost and Thomas Cousins, "Strata of the Political: Epigenetic and Microbial Imaginaries in Post-apartheid Cape Town," *Antipode* 49 (2017): 1368–84.

6. David M. Schneider, *American Kinship: A Cultural Account* (Chicago: University of Chicago Press, 1968).

7. Although it was not yet legally constituted as such; the colonial frontier was at war with the Xhosa king. The area was established as a Bantustan homeland by the South African government in 1963 with nominal autonomy, and became a nominally independent state in 1976. The territory was reincorporated into South Africa on April 27, 1994, and the area became part of the Eastern Cape province.

8. The small town of Stutterheim in the Eastern Cape province of South Africa is named after Baron Richard Carl Gustav Ludwig Wilhelm Julius von Stutterheim. See J. H. French, "Baron Richard von Stutterheim," *Military History Journal* 3, no. 4 (1975).

9. The classic account is that of Jeffrey B. Peires, *The Dead Will Arise: Nongqawuse and the Great Xhosa Cattle-Killing Movement of 1856–7* (Bloomington: Indiana University Press, 1989), but later accounts complicate the story; see Adam Ashforth, "The Xhosa Cattle Killing and the Politics of Memory," *Sociological Forum* 6, no. 3 (1991): 581–92, and Sheila Boniface Davies, "Raising the Dead: The Xhosa Cattle-Killing and the Mhlakaza-Goliat Delusion," *Journal of Southern African Studies* 33, no. 1 (2007): 19–41.

10. William Beinart and Colin Bundy discuss this map at the start of their 1987 book, *Hidden Struggles in Rural South Africa: Politics and Popular Movements in the Transkei and Eastern Cape, 1890–1930* (London: James Currey, 1987).

11. For an in-depth critique of Henkel's techniques, see Jacob A. Tropp, *Natures of Colonial Change: Environmental Relations in the Making of the Transkei* (Athens: Ohio University Press, 2006).

12. He was born in Fulda, in Hesse, Germany, but it is unlikely he received any training in forestry there as he had left for South Africa at a young age, and so any inheritance of the Prussian scientific forestry program so important to the development of techniques of statecraft would be indirect; see James C. Scott, *Seeing Like a State: How Certain Schemes to Improve the Human Condition Have Failed* (New Haven, CT: Yale University Press, 1998).

13. See S2A3 Biographical Database of Southern African Science, Henkel, Mr Johannes Elias Spurgeon: http://www.s2a3.org.za/bio/Biograph_final.php?serial=1263, last accessed July 30, 2021.

14. C. W. Marwick, *Kwamahlati, the Story of Forestry in Zululand*, Bulletin 49 (Pretoria: Department of Forestry, 1973).

15. Or 1914, according to his obituary, Editor, "Dr JS Henkel, Obituary," *South African Forestry Journal* 42, no. 1 (1962): 30.

16. John S. Henkel, S. Ballenden, and A. W. Bayer, "An Account of the Plant Ecology of the Dukuduku Forest Reserve and Adjoining Areas of the Zululand Coast Belt," in *Annals of the Natal Museum*, ed. R. F. Lawrence (London: Natal Museum, 1937).

17. See Brett Bennett and Fred Kruger, *Forestry and Water Conservation in South Africa: History, Science and Policy* (Acton: ANU Press, 2015); and Gert van den Berg et al., "Genetic Parameters and Genotype by Environment Interaction of *Eucalyptus grandis* Populations Used in Intraspecific Hybrid Production in South Africa," *Southern Forests: A Journal of Forest Science* 79, no. 4 (2016): 287–95.

18. Hylton White, "Tempora et Mores: Family Values and the Possessions of a Post-apartheid Countryside," *Journal of Religion in Africa* 31, no. 4 (2001): 457–79.

19. The process through which local environments in the Transkei were regulated and transformed is well described by Tropp, *Natures of Colonial Change.*

20. See Tropp's summary (*Natures of Colonial Change,* 16) of Richard Grove's work, including *Conservation in Africa: Peoples, Policies and Practice* (Cambridge: Cambridge University Press, 1989) and "Scottish Missionaries, Evangelical Discourses and the Origins of Conservation Thinking in Southern Africa 1820–1900," *Journal of Southern African Studies* 15 (1989): 163–87.

21. Tropp, *Natures of Colonial Change,* 44.

22. After several decades of minor exploitation of the indigenous forests by small numbers of sawyers and traders—see Marwick, *Kwamahlati.*

23. Marwick.

24. The "timber industry" includes forestry and primary transformation industries (sawmills, pulp and paper, etc.). The term "forestry" covers the production cycle of timber, from growing trees (silviculture) to felling and debarking (harvesting), and transport.

25. See Jeff Guy, "Battling with Banality," *Journal of Natal and Zulu History* 18, no. 1 (1998): 156–93; Carolyn Hamilton, *Terrific Majesty: The Powers of Shaka Zulu and the Limits of Historical Invention* (Cape Town: David Philip, 1998); and Carolyn Hamilton and Nessa Leibhammer, *Tribing and Untribing the Archive: Identity and the Material Record in Southern KwaZulu-Natal in the Late Independent and Colonial Periods*, 2 vols. (Durban: University of KwaZulu-Natal Press, 2016).

26. The revitalization of pre-Shakan political formations and reexamination of those histories in the twenty-first century have recently begun to receive renewed attention, for example by Hamilton and Leibhammer's *Tribing and Untribing the Archive* (2016) and Buthelezi's (2012) critical historiography of revitalized clan names emerging from the shadow of Zulu ethnonationalism.

27. Aninka Claassens, *Mining Magnates and Traditional Leaders: The Role of Law in Elevating Elite Interests and Deepening Exclusion, 2002–2018* (Mapungubwe: Mapungubwe Institute for Strategic Reflection, 2019); and John L. Comaroff and Jean Comaroff, *Ethnicity, Inc.* (Chicago: University of Chicago Press, 2008).

28. On the historiography of the Transkei and Natal, and their interconnections, see William Beinart, *The Political Economy of Pondoland 1860 to 1930* (Johannesburg: Cambridge University Press, 1982); and Jeff Guy, *The Destruction of the Zulu Kingdom: Civil War in Zululand 1879–84* (Johannesburg: Ravan, 1982).

29. See John Laband, "Colonial Flotsam: The Zululand Squatters and the Zululand Lands Delimitation Commission 1902–1904," *South African Historical Journal* 49, no. 1 (2003): 53–70.

30. Patrick Harries, "Plantations, Passes and Proletarians: Labour and the Colonial State in Nineteenth Century Natal," *Journal of Southern African Studies* 13, no. 3 (1987): 372–99; Umfolozi Co-operative Sugar Planters Company Limited, "Brochure Issued to Commemorate Fifty Years of Cooperation in the Umfolozi Delta Area," 1973.

31. On the use of Indian labor to overcome labor shortages in Natal and Zululand, see Surendra Bhana, ed., *Essays on Indentured Indians in Natal* (Leeds: Peepal Tree, 1990); and Goolam Vahed and Ashwin Desai, "Identity and Belonging in Post-apartheid South Africa: The Case of Indian South Africans," *Journal of Social Science* 25, no. 1–3 (2010): 1–12.

32. J. W. Turnbull, "Tree Domestication and the History of Plantations," in *The Role of Food, Agriculture, Forestry and Fisheries and the Use of Natural Resources*, ed. V. R. Squires, *Encyclopedia of Life Support Systems Developed under Auspices of UNESCO* (Oxford: EOLSS, 2002).

33. Henkel, Ballenden, and Bayer, "Account of the Plant Ecology of the Dukuduku Forest Reserve."

34. Marwick, *Kwamahlati*.

35. Ben Fine and Zavareh Rustomjee, *The Political Economy of South Africa: From Minerals–Energy Complex to Industrialisation* (London: Westview, 1996).

36. World Health Organization (WHO), "Apartheid and Health," in *International Conference on Apartheid and Health, 1981, in Brazzaville, People's Republic of the Congo* (Geneva: World Health Organization, 1983), 188.

37. WHO, 188.

38. These large corporations were concerned by the severe shortage of semiskilled and skilled labor.

39. South African Timber Growers Association papers, 19/6/1972, National Archives.

40. J. R. Sime, "Review: Investigation of the Forest and Timber Industry of South Africa," *South African Forestry Journal* 52, no. 1 (1965): 34.

41. Minutes of SATGA meeting. Their aims were to standardize conditions of employment and welfare amongst Bantu workers; to make contact with the Transkeian Authority at a high level; to pool recruiting resources; to pool transportation resources; to establish a depot at Port Shepstone where all recruits would be screened and tested; to improve the image of forestry as a source of employment among "the Bantu."

42. Pay in Zululand for plantation labor increased in 1971–72 by 79 cents per day for men, and by 49 cents per day for women in 1972.

43. The report is worth quoting at length, to capture the concern with labor and its correct disposition.

1. The forest and timber industry is highly labor intensive, requiring full time employment throughout the year for Bantu male workers and either full-time or casual employment to a very large number of Bantu female workers. 2. There is a very real need, if the essential growth of the industry is not to be retarded, for the establishment and development of a stable, contented and efficient "permanent" labour force. 3. It is considered necessary that a very substantial proportion of the total labour force employed in forestry should be Bantu male workers employed on a "permanent" basis. 4. Married workers are considered to be far more stable and reliable, particularly when allowed to live a decent family life, domiciled on the property with adequate facilities and amenities. The wives and older children provide the casual labour force required to take up seasonal demand. Such a situation creates a greater sense of security contentment and responsibility as well as providing extra income for the family unit. 5. Workers employed on a "permanent" basis must be trained acquire certain skills and to develop a measure of specialization which will have the effect of raising productivity, giving the worker a sense of usefulness and to some extent eliminating the growing sense of discontent amongst Bantu workers. 6. The remuneration of

Bantu workers in the industry should be adequate to maintain a decent standard of living. Similarly where rations form a part of remuneration, these should conform to definite nutritional standards. 7. There is a clear indication, from the general comments made by person interviewed, that the major problems experienced in the industry in so far as Bantu labor is concerned, are: A. An inability to procure in sufficient numbers, laborers suitable for the work involved, through the normal recognized channels, e.g. Labor bureau; B. Absenteeism and a high labor turnover rate due to family disorganisation arising from the restrictive labor policy concerning the employment and accommodation on the arms of married workers with their families; C. These and other restrictive measures also result in an unstable labor force due to a feeling of insecurity; D. The impermanent nature of the labor force, with the resultant attitude of detachment from the property, and a lesser degree of loyalty to the employer, leaves the employer in constant fear of irreparable losses due to fires, which might occur during non-working periods when labourers are away from the properties. Therefore, for a reliable, responsible, happy and more efficient labour force, it is recommended that serious and immediate consideration be given to the formulation of a Forest and Forest Products Industry Bantu Labor Policy.

44. Michel Foucault, *The Birth of Biopolitics: Lectures at the Collège de France, 1978–1979*, ed. Michel Senellart, trans. Graham Burchell (New York: Macmillan, 2010), 225.

45. For a discussion of concepts of self in southern Africa, see John L. Comaroff and Jean Comaroff, "On Personhood: An Anthropological Perspective from Africa," *Social Identities* 7, no. 2 (2001).

46. Franco Barchiesi, "Wage Labor, Precarious Employment, and Social Inclusion in the Making of South Africa's Postapartheid Transition," *African Studies Review* 51, no. 2 (2008): 119–42.

47. For a brilliant analysis of the photographic albums of "terrorists" circulated by state security forces to police stations around the country, see Jacob Dlamini, *The Terrorist Album: Apartheid's Insurgents, Collaborators, and the Security Police* (Boston: Harvard University Press, 2020).

48. Dlamini, xii.

49. For a discussion of the great transformations to African life in South Africa that established the pattern of migrant labor, see John L. Comaroff and Jean Comaroff, *Of Revelation and Revolution*, vol. 2, *The Dialectics of Modernity on a South African Frontier* (Chicago: University of Chicago Press, 1997); and Hylton White, "Tempora et Mores."

50. Ben Cousins, *At the Crossroads: Land and Agrarian Reform in South Africa into the 21st Century* (Cape Town: Programme for Land and Agrarian Studies, University of the Western Cape/National Land Committee, 2000).

51. Quoted in Surplus People Project, *Forced Removals in South Africa: The SPP Reports,* vol. 4 (Natal: Surplus People Project, 1983), 31.

52. See T. R. H. Davenport and K. S. Hunt, *The Right to the Land: Documents on South African History* (Cape Town: David Philip, 1974).

53. See Chief Moses Zikhali's comments in Surplus People Project, *Forced Removals in South Africa,* 247.

54. While the plantations extend south and north into other Traditional Authorities, the focus of my analysis is on the Dukuduku and Nyalazi plantations in the Mpukunyoni Traditional Authority.

55. Another example, relevant because it impinges on territory under plantations and conservation further north in KwaZulu-Natal, includes the Tsonga-Shangaan kingship. In the late 2000s, dispute over its governance also drew on colonial archives to undermine received ideas about the stability or homogeneity of Zulu identities and polities that existed between St Lucia and Maputo up to the nineteenth century. See http://vatsonga.wordpress.com/about/ (last accessed January 21, 2020) for a fascinating polemic regarding the kingship debate. In the Tsonga-Shangaan example, "Tsonga" historians today draw on the writings of Perestrello (Santa Bento, 1554), Diogo de Couto (Santa Thome, 1589), and Lavanha (Santa Alberto, 1593), whose records show the presence of Ronga chiefdoms between Saint Lucia Bay and the Maputo region in the sixteenth century, recording the names of such chiefdoms as Ngomane, Nyaka, Mpfumo, Lebombo (Livombo), Manyisa, and Tembe; see Mandla Mathebula et al., "Tsonga History Discourse," n.d., accessed August 19, 2021, https://vatsonga.wordpress.com/about/.

56. This description is Mondi's, but fails to include the precariously employed, contracted labor that is the direct concern of this book.

57. See www.fsc.org. For a critique of consumer-based systems of regulation in the South African wine industry, see Andries du Toit, "Globalizing Ethics: Social Technologies of Private Regulation and the South African Wine Industry," *Journal of Agrarian Change* 2, no. 3 (2002): 356–80.

58. KwaMsane is the historically Black township located on the opposite side of the N2 highway to the White town of Mtubatuba, twenty kilometers south of Shikishela.

59. For a discussion of Dukuduku's complex history, see Association for Rural Advancement, *Dukuduku: The Forest of Our Discontent* (Durban: Special Report, 2003); and Knut Nustad, "Property, Rights and Community in a South African Land-Claim Case," *Anthropology Today* 27, no. 1 (2011): 20–24.

60. Foucault, *Birth of Biopolitics,* 226.

61. For a sketch of the contours of the crisis of agricultural labor in South Africa, see Andries du Toit, "Hunger in the Valley of Fruitfulness: Globalization, 'Social Exclusion' and Chronic Poverty in Ceres, South Africa" (paper presented at the conference "Staying Poor: Chronic Poverty and Development Policy," University of

Manchester, April 2003); Nicolas Pons-Vignon and Ward Anseeuw, "Great Expectations: Working Conditions in South Africa since the End of Apartheid," *Journal of Southern African Studies* 35, no. 4 (2009): 883–99; and Barchiesi, "Wage Labor."

62. Franco Barchiesi, "Commodification, Economic Restructuring, and the Changing Urban Geography of Labour in Post-apartheid South Africa: The Case of Gauteng Province, 199Q2001," *Urban Forum* 17 (2006): 93–124.

63. Pons-Vignon and Anseeuw, "Great Expectations."

64. W. J. A. Louw, "General History of the South African Forest Industry: 1975 to 1990," *Southern African Forestry Journal* 200, no. 1 (2004): 77–86.

65. Jeanette Clarke and Moenieba Isaacs, *Forestry Contractors in South Africa: What Role in Reducing Poverty?* (London: Programme for Land and Agrarian Studies, University of the Western Cape, South Africa, and International Institute for Environment and Development, 2005). Various reasons are advanced for this major shift in labor policy in the forest industry in South Africa in the late 1990s. Outsourcing came about soon after the 1994 elections and the promulgation of legislative reforms governing labor relations and basic conditions of employment. The trend also coincided with South Africa's reentry into the global economy at a time when, internationally, labor outsourcing was a dominant trend across many sectors. In Mondi forests, some key events were instrumental in the decision to outsource labor. In 1996–97, the number of wage earners doubled after the acquisition of HL&H and several other medium-sized forestry companies. There were disparate salaries and working conditions among labor as a result of the acquisitions, and financial implications to bringing these on par. Soon after, Mondi's parent company at the time, Anglo American, listed on the London Stock exchange. These and other factors led to fears about the risks associated with direct employment of a large unskilled work force and thereby to the decision to outsource virtually all wage labor.

66. D. Chamberlain et al., "Genesis Report Part I: The Contribution, Costs, and Development Opportunities of the Forestry, Timber," in *Pulp and Paper Industries in South Africa* (Johannesburg: Genesis Analytics, 2005).

67. Nicolas Pons-Vignon, "Forestry Workers Buckle under Outsourcing Pipedream," *South African Labour Bulletin* 30, no. 2 (2006): 27–30; R. Morkel, "The Real Reasons for Outsourcing," *SA Forestry*, March–April 2000.

68. Black Economic Empowerment (BEE) is a program launched by the South African government to redress the inequalities of apartheid by giving previously disadvantaged groups of South African citizens (Black Africans, Coloureds, Indians, and some Chinese) economic opportunities previously not available to them. It includes measures such as employment equity, skills development, ownership, management, socioeconomic development, and preferential procurement. See Roger Southall, "Ten Propositions about Black Economic Empowerment in South Africa," *Review of African Political Economy* 34, no. 111 (2007): 67–84.

69. W. J. A. Louw, "General History of the South African Forest Industry: 1991 to 2002," *Southern African Forestry Journal* 201, no. 1 (2004): 65–76; Pons-Vignon and Anseeuw, "Great Expectations."

70. Pons-Vignon and Anseeuw, "Great Expectations"; Clarke and Isaacs, *Forestry Contractors in South Africa.*

71. Jeanette Clarke, "Investigation of Working Conditions of Forestry Workers in South Africa" (Department of Agriculture, Forestry and Fisheries, Government of South Africa, 2012). I do not address transformations in the forestry sector in the period after 2012, although this would be an important project.

72. Clarke and Isaacs, *Forestry Contractors in South Africa;* L. Bethlehem, *National Forestry Action Programme. Key Issue Paper: Labour Relations* (Pretoria: DWAF, 1997).

73. The Medicines and Related Substances Amendment Act of 2002. Previously the company could hold a single license for all their clinics.

74. Clarke, "Investigation"; Morkel, "Real Reasons for Outsourcing"; and Fakisandla Consulting, "Scope of the Impact: Proposed Changes to Harvesting Operations in the Mkhondo District," *Report to Mondi BP,* 2005.

75. Clarke, "Investigation." Sectoral Determinations provide a "floor of rights" for workers in sectors without union protection or collective bargaining.

76. Jeanette Clarke, "A Job of Choice or a Job of Last Resort?," *SA Forestry Magazine,* October 2011.

77. R. I. Cairns, "Outgrower Timber Schemes in KwaZulu-Natal—Do They Build Sustainable Rural Livelihoods and What Interventions Should Be Made?" (IIED and CSIR, 2000).

78. Marking entails measuring out the spacing for the trees to be planted in straight rows. A row of twenty workers follows a rope across the compartment, "marking" with a small hole the spot where each seedling will be placed shortly thereafter.

79. "Bayaqomana kakhulu!" Ukuqoma is to accept, in the sense that women accept men's proposals or advances. "Courting" is an inadequate gloss of the complex social forms at stake, as Mark Hunter, in *Love in the Time of AIDS: Inequality, Gender, and Rights in South Africa* (Bloomington: Indiana University Press, 2010), has shown so well. Chapter 3 explores this at length.

80. For a small selection of a substantial archive, see Jeremy Seekings and Nicoli Nattrass, *Class, Race, and Inequality in South Africa* (New Haven, CT: Yale University Press, 2005); Gillian Hart, *Reworking Apartheid Legacies: Global Competition, Gender and Social Wages in South Africa, 1980–2000* (Geneva: United Nations Research Institute for Social Development, 2002); and Haroon Bhorat and Safia Khan, "Structural Change and Patterns of Inequality in the South African Labour Market" (Working Papers 201801, University of Cape Town, Development Policy Research Unit, 2018).

81. However, tracking the meanings of those transformations over a broader horizon lend themselves to a range of analytical and methodological questions; see in particular Jean Comaroff and John L. Comaroff, "Alien-Nation: Zombies, Immigrants, and Millennial Capitalism," *South Atlantic Quarterly* 101, no. 4 (2002): 779–805; Zolani Ngwane, "'Christmas Time' and the Struggles for the Household in the Countryside: Rethinking the Cultural Geography of Migrant Labour in South Africa," *Journal of Southern African Studies* 29, no. 3 (2003): 681–99; and Fiona C. Ross, *Raw Life, New Hope: Decency, Housing and Everyday Life in a Post-apartheid Community* (Cape Town: UCT Press, 2010).

82. Jeff Guy, "The Destruction and Reconstruction of Zulu Society," in *Industrialisation and Social Change in South Africa: African Class, Culture, and Consciousness, 1870–1930*, ed. Shula Marks and Richard Rathbone (New York: Longman, 1982), 168.

83. Guy, 168, 173.

84. A moment inaugurated by the civil war of the 1880s and its settlement that saw the invention of "British Zululand" in 1887. It was incorporated into the colony of Natal in 1889.

85. Guy, "Destruction and Reconstruction," 173.

86. Elizabeth A. Povinelli, *Economies of Abandonment: Social Belonging and Endurance in Late Liberalism* (Durham, NC: Duke University Press, 2011), 133.

87. Guy, "Destruction and Reconstruction."

88. Cherryl Walker, "Land of Dreams: Land Restitution on the Eastern Shores of Lake St Lucia," *Transformation: Critical Perspectives on Southern Africa* 59 (2005): 1–25. The series of forced removals from conservation and plantation land from the 1950s until the 1980s meant that many of those removed had to live as interlopers and unwelcome guests of communities that fell within the apartheid-designated tribal areas of KwaZulu.

89. In 2009, pensions were R1010 per month; CSGs were R240 per month per child.

90. For a gendered and generational analysis of bridewealth in the context of migrant labor under apartheid, see James G. Ferguson, "Mobile Workers, Modernist Narratives: A Critique of the Historiography of Transition on the Zambian Copperbelt," *Journal of Southern African Studies* 16, no. 3 (1990): 385–412; and Hylton White, "Ritual Haunts: The Timing of Estrangement in a Post-apartheid Countryside," in *Producing African Futures: Ritual and Reproduction in a Neoliberal Age*, ed. Brad Weiss (Leiden: Koninklijke Brill, 2004).

91. Mark Hunter captures men's expressions concerning amandla, gender, and sex in "Fathers without Amandla? Gender and Fatherhood among IsiZulu Speakers," *Journal of Natal and Zulu History* 22, no. 1 (2004): 149–60. I will return to Foucault's notion of ethical substance and Elizabeth Povinelli's uptake of it in chapter 4 below.

92. Achille Mbembe, *Critique of Black Reason* (Durham, NC: Duke University Press, 2017). In anthropology, Sidney W. Mintz made a major contribution to the study of plantations across many publications, including "Plantations and the Rise of a World Food Economy: Some Preliminary Ideas," *Review (Fernand Braudel Center)* 34, no. 1/2 (2011): 3–14; Sidney W. Mintz, "The Plantation as a Socio-cultural Type," in *Plantation Systems of the New World*, ed. Vera Rubin (Washington, DC: Pan American Union, 1959), 42–53; Sidney W. Mintz, "Was the Plantation Slave a Proletarian?," *Review (Fernand Braudel Center)* 2, no. 1 (1978): 81–98.

93. E. Valentine Daniel, "The Coolie," *Cultural Anthropology* 23, no. 2 (2008): 254–78.

94. Chris Taylor and Adom Getachew, "55603 The Global Plantation" (online course description, 2019, https://english.uchicago.edu/courses/global-plantation; Christopher Taylor and Adom Getachew, "The Global Plantation: An Exchange between Adom Getachew and Christopher Taylor," *b2o: an online journal*, June 23, 2020. In particular, see Deborah A. Thomas, *Political Life in the Wake of the Plantation: Sovereignty, Witnessing, Repair* (Durham, NC: Duke University Press, 2019).

95. See in particular Donna Haraway, "Anthropocene, Capitalocene, Plantationocene, Chthulucene: Making Kin," *Environmental Humanities* 6, no. 1 (2015): 159–65; Anna Lowenhaupt Tsing, *The Mushroom at the End of the World: On the Possibility of Life in Capitalist Ruins* (Princeton, NJ: Princeton University Press, 2015); and Jason W. Moore, *Capitalism in the Web of Life: Ecology and the Accumulation of Capital* (London: Verso, 2015). Raj Patel and Jason W. Moore, in *A History of the World in Seven Cheap Things: A Guide to Capitalism, Nature, and the Future of the Planet* (Berkeley: University of California Press, 2017), suggest that "the 'plantation' is at the heart of the socioecological crisis of our economic system; a system that from the very onset five hundred years ago has built on cheap labor, energy, nature, food exploited elsewhere." Robin Blackburn, *The Making of New World Slavery: From the Baroque to the Modern 1492–1800* (London: Verso, 1997), 260, calls the plantation a "total environment" in which labor was capital and thus could be fully controlled and treated as an object. Stefan Ouma, "From the Plantation to the Fourth Industrial Revolution: Other Economic Geographies" (unpublished conference paper, WISER, 2020), suggests the plantation is a node through which the history of capitalism passes en route to the Fourth Industrial Revolution.

96. Thomas, *Political Life*, 3.

97. Ryan Cecil Jobson, "The Case for Letting Anthropology Burn: Sociocultural Anthropology in 2019," *American Anthropologist* 122, no. 2 (2020): 3.

98. Savannah Shange, *Progressive Dystopia: Abolition, Antiblackness, and Schooling in San Francisco* (Durham, NC: Duke University Press, 2019), 10.

99. In suggesting that the plantations elicit from laborers the particular effort of repair (working, eating, purging, and marrying, described below), I am also

implying that another kind of effort is at stake, sketched between worker and ethnographer, namely the problematization of the plantation and its labor regime, and the diverse forms of life (or rather, pictures of life) entailed in the production of timber, and in the production of the ethnographic account.

3. THE GAME OF MARRIAGE

1. I am indebted to Thomas Hendriks for his inspired reading of "queer power beyond anti-normativity," which informs my argument here, and for his permission to draw on his text prepublication: "'Making Men Fall': Queer Power beyond Anti-normativity," *Africa* 91, no. 3 (2021): 398–417.

2. Here I am informed by the work of Michael Silverstein, "Metapragmatic Discourse and Metapragmatic Function," in *Reflexive Language: Reported Speech and Metapragmatics*, ed. John A. Lucy (Cambridge: Cambridge University Press, 1993); Michael Silverstein, "The Improvisational Performance of Culture in Realtime Discursive Practice," in *Creativity in Performance*, ed. R. Keith Sawyer (London: Ablex, 1997); and Greg Urban, *Metaculture: How Culture Moves through the World* (Minneapolis: University of Minnesota Press, 2001).

3. See A. Agha, *Language and Social Relations: Studies in the Social and Cultural Foundations of Language* (Cambridge: Cambridge University Press, 2007), and Michael Silverstein, "Indexical Order and the Dialectics of Sociolinguistic Life," *Language and Communication* 23, no. 3 (2003): 193–229.

4. While most conversations and interviews were conducted in isiZulu with some translation into English by Dumo Mkwanazi to help when I lost the thread, I give only the English here to aid in readability.

5. See Thomas V. McClendon, *White Chief, Black Lords: Shepstone and the Colonial State in Natal, South Africa, 1845–1878* (Rochester: University of Rochester Press, 2010). iLobolo was a scandal for colonial administrators and missionaries because it appeared to reduce women to currency or payment in a market transaction. David Hammond-Tooke's master's thesis, "The Nature and Significance of Bride Wealth among the South African Bantu" (University of Cape Town, 1948), was framed by this sense of scandal and appealed for "some scientific investigation [to] be made to ascertain, as accurately as possible, the exact nature of this institution and its significance in Bantu society." Bridewealth in South Africa continues to attract anthropological attention: see Adam Kuper, *Wives for Cattle: Bridewealth and Marriage in Southern Africa* (Boston: Routledge and Kegan Paul, 1982); Adam Kuper, "Traditions of Kinship, Marriage and Bridewealth in Southern Africa," *Anthropology Southern Africa* 39, no. 4 (2016): 267–80; Stephanie Rudwick and Dorrit Posel, "Contemporary Functions of *Ilobolo* (Bridewealth) in Urban South African Zulu Society," *Journal of Contemporary African Studies* 32, no. 1 (2014): 118–36; and Christie Sennott, Sangeetha Madhavan, and Youngeun Nam, "Modernizing Marriage:

Balancing the Benefits and Liabilities of Bridewealth in Rural South Africa," *Qualitative Sociology* 44, no. 1 (2021): 55–75.

6. For example, the Recognition of Customary Marriages Act of 1998; see M. Herbst and W. du Plessis, "Customary Law v Common Law Marriages: A Hybrid Approach in South Africa," *Electronic Journal of Comparative Law* 12 (2008): 121–28; and Tom W. Bennett, "Re-introducing African Customary Law to the South African Legal System," *American Journal of Comparative Law* 57, no. 1 (2009): 1–32.

7. For example, Isaac Schapera, *A Handbook of Tswana Law and Custom* (London: International Africa Institute, 1938); and Julius Lewin, *Studies in African Native Law* (Cape Town: African Bookman, 1947). Lewin was an intriguing figure in early twentieth-century South Africa. As a secular Jewish lawyer and ethnologist, he contributed significantly to the development of native administrative law. See John Blacking and Noam J. Pines, "Professor Julius Lewin," *African Studies* 27, no. 1 (January 1, 1968): 45–46. For his collected papers at the University of the Witwatersrand, see http://www.historicalpapers.wits.ac.za/?inventory/U/collections&c =A2357/R/6246.

8. Lewin, *Studies in African Native Law*, 32.

9. Lewin, 34.

10. See chapter 1 and my discussion of the notion of the spacing of autological and genealogical as liberal concerns in Elizabeth A. Povinelli's *Economies of Abandonment: Social Belonging and Endurance in Late Liberalism* (Durham, NC: Duke University Press, 2011).

11. Lewin, *Studies in African Native Law*, 35.

12. E.g., the Recognition of Customary Marriages Act of 1998; see Herbst and Du Plessis, "Customary Law"; Bennett, "Re-introducing African Customary Law."

13. Tracey Lee McCormick, "A Critical Engagement? Analysing Same-Sex Marriage Discourses in To Have and to Hold: The Making of Same-Sex Marriage in South Africa (2008)—A Queer Perspective," *Stellenbosch Papers in Linguistics Plus* 46 (2015): 105; Michael W. Yarbrough, "Something Old, Something New: Historicizing Same-Sex Marriage within Ongoing Struggles over African Marriage in South Africa," *Sexualities* 21, no. 7 (2017): 1092–108; Tommaso M. Milani, "Language, Gender and Sexuality in South Africa," *Stellenbosch Papers in Linguistics Plus* 46 (2015): i–v; Thabo Msibi and Stephanie Rudwick, "Intersections of Two IsiZulu Genderlects and the Construction of 'skesana' Identities," *Stellenbosch Papers in Linguistics Plus* 46 (2015): 51–66.

14. Kirk Fiereck, Neville Hoad, and Danai S. Mupotsa, "A Queering-to-Come," *GLQ: A Journal of Lesbian and Gay Studies* 26, no. 3 (2020): 363–76.

15. See Alfred Reginald Radcliffe-Brown and Darryl Forde, *African Systems of Kinship and Marriage* (London: Oxford University Press, 1950).

16. See J. L. Dohne, *Zulu-Kafir Dictionary: Etymologically Explained* (Pike, 1857); A. T. Bryant, *The Zulu People* (Pietermaritzburg: Shuter and Shooter, 1949); Eileen

Jensen Krige, *The Social System of the Zulus* (London: Longmans, Green, 1936); Isaac Schapera, *Married Life in an African Tribe* (Evanston, IL: Northwestern University Press, 1966); Max Gluckman, "Kinship and Marriage among the Lozi of Northern Rhodesia and the Zulu of Natal," in *African Systems of Kinship and Marriage*, ed. A. R. Radcliffe-Brown and Daryll Forde (London: Oxford University Press, 1950), 166–206; C. Maclean, *A Compendium of Kafir Laws and Customs* (Cape Town: Solomon, 1866); Mark Hunter, *Love in the Time of AIDS: Inequality, Gender, and Rights in South Africa* (Bloomington: Indiana University Press, 2010).

17. Kuper, *Wives for Cattle;* Jeff Guy, "The Destruction and Reconstruction of Zulu Society," in *Industrialisation and Social Change in South Africa: African Class, Culture, and Consciousness, 1870–1930,* ed. Shula Marks and Richard Rathbone (New York: Longman, 1982); Patrick Harries, *Work, Culture, and Identity: Migrant Laborers in Mozambique and South Africa, c. 1860–1910* (Portsmouth, NH: Heinemann, 1994).

18. Gluckman, "Kinship and Marriage," 182.

19. Thus: "I observed no important differences in the psychological relationships of husbands and wives [between Lozi and Zulu], though their social relationships differ widely. Zulu and Lozi marriages do not generally spring from romantic attachments, and their concept of love between the sexes is on the whole restrained, though sexual attraction between men and women may make them brave severe sanctions" (Gluckman, "Kinship and Marriage," 179). Hunter's *Love in the Time of AIDS* rereads romantic love in KwaZulu-Natal to suggest a different understanding of emotions and sanctions surrounding sexuality, marriage, and reproduction.

20. Gluckman, "Kinship and Marriage," 182: "The Zulu in Natal have the same types of marriage-forming families as are reported by Evans-Pritchard from the Nuer in the far distant Sudan."

21. "Finally, the first wife married (who may be called *mama,* my mother) becomes mother of the *uyise wabantwana* (father of the children), a son who ritually replaces the father on his death. These are indigenous gradings. The Natal Code of Native Law hoped to reduce litigation by ruling that the first wife married is the great wife" (Gluckman, 183).

22. Until the reign of King Mpande (1840–72), a woman's person was also permanently transferred to her husband's agnatic lineage.

23. There are two forms: the first, if a man dies, his fiancé marries his kinsman and produces children in the dead man's name; the second, a man wakens a dead kinsman by marrying a wife to his name to raise children for him (Gluckman, "Kinship and Marriage," 184).

24. Gluckman, "Kinship and Marriage," 184. "As among the Nuer a rich and important Zulu woman can marry another woman by giving marriage-cattle for her, and she is the pater of her wife's children begotten by some male kinsman of the female husband. They belong to the latter's agnatic lineage as if she were a man.

If a man dies leaving only daughters and no son, the eldest daughter should take his cattle and marry wives for her father to produce sons for him. This and the preceding forms of marriage are weighty customs enforced by ancestral wrath, and they arise from the importance of continuing the agnatic line."

25. It is important to note that "law" here is taken as an aspect of indigenous institutional social life, and not as a construction of colonial codification.

26. Gluckman, "Kinship and Marriage," 184.

27. Gluckman, 184: "Therefore men who are dead or impotent, and women, all physically incapable of begetting, can be paters of children who have been begotten by other men, and a whole group can be pater to children whose mother's marriage-cattle it has contributed."

28. Gluckman, 185: "If they do the latter [return cattle for a barren woman], a good Zulu does not necessarily send his barren wife home; he may use the returned marriage-cattle to obtain a wife whom he puts 'into the house' of his barren wife to bear children for her. Thus even maternity can be fictitious."

29. The identification and delimitation of something called "custom" is an aspect of the question of naming that I am interested in here. A fuller discussion of the codification of customary law and its impact on marriage can be found in Tom W. Bennett, "Re-introducing African Customary Law to the South African Legal System," *American Journal of Comparative Law* 57, no. 1 (2009): 1–32.

30. See also Hunter, *Love in the Time of AIDS*, and Paul S. Landau, *Popular Politics in the History of South Africa, 1400–1948* (Cambridge: Cambridge University Press, 2010), who interrogate histories of sexuality and the invention of tribalism, respectively, and reflect on the ways in which the people governed by these English terms navigated the violent translations of custom and practice.

31. I have in mind here J. L. Austin's performative speech acts and Michael Silverstein's critique of Austin, putting into question whether certain utterances take on particular force because of their "ritual context" or whether all utterances are conditioned in just the same way; Silverstein, "Metasemiotic Hypertrophy and Dynamic Figuration: Why Ritual Works (When It Does)" (unpublished paper presented at the seminar "The Language of Ritual," EFSSS, Sozopol, Bulgaria, September 9, 2011).

32. Joseph M. Carrier and Steven O. Murray, "Women-Women Marriage in Africa," in *Boy-Wives and Female Husbands: Studies of African Homosexualities*, ed. Stephen O. Murray and Will Roscoe (New York: St Martin's, 1998), 255–66; Denise O'Brien, "Female Husbands in Southern Bantu Societies," in *Sexual Stratification: A Cross-Cultural View*, ed. Alice Schlegel (New York: Columbia University Press, 1977), 109–26; R. S. Oboler, "Is the Female Husband a Man? Woman/Woman Marriage among the Nandi of Kenya," *Ethnology* 19, no. 1 (1980): 69–88.

33. John Blacking, "Fictitious Kinship amongst Girls of the Venda of the Northern Transvaal," *Man* 59, no. 8 (1959): 155–58, and "Uses of the Kinship Idiom in

Friendships at Some Venda and Zulu Schools," in *Social System and Tradition in Southern Africa*, ed. John Argyle and Eleanor Preston-Whyte (Oxford: Oxford University Press, 1978), 101–17; and Judith Gay, "'Mummies and Babies' and Friends and Lovers in Lesotho," *Journal of Homosexuality* 11, no. 3–4 (1986): 97–116.

34. Nicolas Pons-Vignon and Ward Anseeuw, "Great Expectations: Working Conditions in South Africa since the End of Apartheid," *Journal of Southern African Studies* 35, no. 4 (2009): 883–99. The shift away from migrancy to encouraging laborers to live next to the mines or plantations has come into question again after the Marikana tragedy of August 2012. Keith Breckenridge, "Revenge of the Commons: The Crisis in the South African Mining Industry" (History Workshop: Histories of the Present, November 5, 2012), has suggested that this dubious shift in housing policy was premised on Monica Wilson's criticism of the apartheid state's policy of enforced labor migration that exhausted a fund of social capital "of a very strong African family system," prompting mines to offer subsidized local housing (Wilson, quoted in Breckenridge).

35. To accept or to choose. Ukuqoma forms one crucial stage of the long process of customary marriage, the timing of which I discuss in detail below. In describing the event, people used the infinitive form ("noun class 15"), as compared to the grammatical structure of wayemgaxa, "he/she covers her/his shoulders," discussed in the following section.

36. Women should cover their head and not wear trousers to conform to the image of a respectful woman.

37. For a powerful description of male dance, see Louise Meintjies, *Dust of the Zulu: Ngoma Aesthetics after Apartheid* (Durham, NC: Duke University Press, 2017).

38. What happens when the gendered and sexed norms of referentiality are displaced or inverted, such that it is bio-men who must carry the mark of qualification, contra "man" as human?

39. Here biologically sexed males, but the difficulty of maintaining referential consistency in ethnographic description is precisely the point—see Elizabeth A. Povinelli, "Sexuality at Risk: Psychoanalysis Metapragmatically," in *Homosexuality and Psychoanalysis*, ed. Tim Dean and Christopher Lane (Chicago: University of Chicago Press, 2001), 387–411, for a brilliant exposition.

40. Into which she peered while she went through the motions. This is a semiotically complex moment in which she was no longer simply insizwa, but also a woman, miming the gestures of feminine beautification.

41. For "cattle-without-legs," see John L. Comaroff and Jean Comaroff, "Goodly Beasts, Beastly Goods: Cattle and Commodities in a South African Context," *American Ethnologist* 17, no. 2 (1990): 195–216.

42. Hunter, *Love in the Time of AIDS*, translates ukuqoma as "to choose" for when a woman responded favorably to a proposal from a man (139). The different kinds of action at stake (to choose versus to accept) were not apparent to me at the time,

but the encoding of relative positions of action and passivity would need to be explored in relation to the specific histories of practice concerning marriage and custom between the localities and circumstances in which these terms were used. Thus, an older grammar in which young women do the choosing and young men are chosen is caught in the expression. In the game in the plantations, a similar grammar is evident: the young men do the courting (bayashela, they burn with desire for the young women, who in turn choose). Ukuqoma is in the active voice, while the passive voice is ukuqonywa.

43. C. M. Doke et al., *English–Zulu, Zulu–English Dictionary* (Johannesburg: Witwatersrand University Press, 2006), 233: "gaxa. V. Place across, let hang over, put astride, hook on, tie around." Cloth, blankets, clothes, were all vital elements of various gifts exchanges during heterosexual, customary marriage processes, along with other bedroom and kitchen utensils and accoutrements, including a chest in which to store the fabric. Cf. discussions of trousseau in Emilie A. Olson's comments on S. J. Tambiah et al., "Bridewealth and Dowry Revisited: The Position of Women in Sub-Saharan Africa and North India [and Comments and Reply]," *Current Anthropology* 30, no. 4 (1989): 413–35; also J. F. Laubscher, *Sex, Custom and Psychopathology* (London: Routledge, 1937), 169.

44. Abantu abaphansi and amadlozi respectively. The drift in meaning of terms for "ancestor" is entangled in the history of the encounter of Christianity with African concepts of spirit, and the contours of the politics of translation. See James L. Brain, M. T. Ruel, and Igor Kopytoff, "The Authority of Ancestors," *Man*, n.s., 17, no. 3 (1982): 546–48, for a history of the debate on ancestors in Africa, and for more recent argumentation, see Paul S. Landau, *Popular Politics in the History of South Africa, 1400–1948* (Cambridge: Cambridge University Press, 2010) and Hylton White, "Tempora et Mores: Family Values and the Possessions of a Post-apartheid Countryside," *Journal of Religion in Africa* 31, no. 4 (2001): 457–79.

45. An umam'omncane is the junior wife of the pater, younger mother, little mother.

46. According to the dictates of respect (ukuhlonipha), the visiting young man should not sit on the girl's bed, but rather sit and sleep on this mat. Nomvula had no issue with this herself, though. It is merely the form borrowed from the real wedding process.

47. The plural forms operate in the same manner as the T/V form of etiquette, except that the possessives operate by explicitly, i.e., normatively or ideologically, locating the individual within groups—"our" and "their"—see Asif Agha, *Language and Social Relations* (Cambridge: Cambridge University Press, 2007), 38. It is worth repeating that pronouns are not gendered and require agreement with their nouns in context.

48. See Thomas Cousins, "Knowledge of Life: Health, Strength and Labour in KwaZulu-Natal, South Africa," *Anthropology Southern Africa* 37, no. 1–2 (2014): 30–41.

49. For a brilliant exposition of this, see Hylton White, "Ritual Haunts: The Timing of Estrangement in a Post-apartheid Countryside," in *Producing African Futures: Ritual and Reproduction in a Neoliberal Age*, ed. Brad Weiss (Leiden: Koninklijke Brill, 2004).

50. On the production of ritual space, see James Fernandez, *Bwiti: An Ethnography of the Religious Imagination in Africa* (Princeton, NJ: Princeton University Press, 1982), and Hylton White, "Outside the Dwelling of Culture: Estrangement and Difference in Postcolonial Zululand," *Anthropological Quarterly* 83, no. 3 (2010): 497–518.

51. See Bryant, *Zulu People*, 542.

52. See Timothy Burke, *Lifebuoy Men, Lux Women: Commodification, Consumption, and Cleanliness in Modern Zimbabwe* (Durham, NC: Duke University Press, 1996).

53. Doke et al., *English–Zulu, Zulu–English Dictionary*, 80: "Article claimed as part of *ilobolo* or as compensation. *Imvulamlomo isibizo sesilisa* (something given to open up negotiations is what is demanded by the males)."

54. Impahla yasendlini—Doke et al., 509, give "good" (as in a tradable object) for impahla, but in isiXhosa izimpahla are clothes—hence the close association that seems apparent between goods, clothes, and the notion of "trousseau."

55. Ukwembesa abantu balayikhaya. Sometimes, the two families ask for each other's lists to assess the equivalence of gifts to be exchanged. In her case, her brother's illness has delayed the preparations, as he would be the one to buy the gifts for her wedding as the oldest man in the family.

56. Umbongo, from the infinitive ukubonga, to thank. The ordering of gift exchanges is explained in the text that follows.

57. The concatenations of meaning are vital here: umsebenzi as ritual event or ceremony, "function" in the ordinary language of many South Africans, but equally the performance itself, pointing directly to the work of ritual.

58. The verbal noun is ukwembesa: Doke et al., 185, give: to clothe or cover with a blanket, cloak, etc. That part of the ceremony in which gifts of blankets and clothes are distributed to appropriate family members.

59. Iqhikiza lentombi: The girl's older female family member—it is she who distributes the gifts. In the game, this is another laborer who plays the role of iqhikiza.

60. On the transformative splendor at stake in the gift, see Alphonso Lingis, *Dangerous Emotions* (Berkeley: University of California Press, 2000), 174.

61. "This is a game. It is like a stokvel game. If you are my intombi I will make you happy by buying you stuff, and give it to you. And you also do the same and say "I am buying for my man."" Stokvels are clubs or syndicates serving as rotating credit unions in South Africa where members contribute fixed sums of money to a central fund on a weekly, fortnightly, or monthly basis. See Daryl Collins et al., *Portfolios of the Poor* (Princeton, NJ: Princeton University Press, 2009); Deborah James,

"'Women Use Their Strength in the House': Savings Clubs in an Mpumalanga Village," *Journal of Southern African Studies* 41, no. 5 (2015): 1035–52; and G. Verhoef, "Informal Financial Service Institutions for Survival: African Women and Stokvels in Urban South Africa, 1930–1998," *Enterprise and Society* 2, no. 2 (2001): 259–96.

62. The slippage between "clan" name and "surname" is driven by the history of the state's identification systems, specifically the apartheid dompas (pass book) and postapartheid Identity Book, which is crucial for accessing welfare.

63. Doke et al., *English–Zulu, Zulu–English Dictionary*, 386: -Zala. 1. Verb: ukuzala. Bear, give birth, beget, generate. 2. N. Suffix, indicating relation by marriage. Umamezala (my mother-in-law).

64. Doke et al., 506: -mna- formative indicating intimate friendship or relationship, used in compound: umna kwethu my brother/sister-in-law [the plural form -ethu operating as T/V marker of respect].

65. See Aaron Goodfellow, *Gay Fathers, Their Children, and the Making of Kinship* (New York: Fordham University Press, 2015).

66. John L. Comaroff and Jean Comaroff, *Of Revelation and Revolution*, vol. 2, *The Dialectics of Modernity on a South African Frontier* (Chicago: University of Chicago Press, 1997).

67. The slippage between a Euro-American sense of "tomboy" should not be confused with the particular inflections of "i-tomboy / ama-tomboys" as a term that circulates through particular African scenes of uptake and reimagination. See Michelle Ann Abate, *Tomboys: A Literary and Cultural History* (Philadelphia: Temple University Press, 2008), for a history of the term tomboy, and Kristen R. Yount, "Ladies, Flirts, and Tomboys: Strategies for Managing Sexual Harassment in an Underground Coal Mine," *Journal of Contemporary Ethnography* 19, no. 4 (1991): 396–422, for an analysis of tomboys in American coal mining sexual economies. For the particular inflections in South Africa, see Thamar Klein, "Who Decides Whose Gender? Medico-Legal Classifications of Sex and Gender and Their Impact on Transgendered South Africans' Family Rights," *Ethnoscripts* 14, no. 2 (2012): 12–34; and B. Camminga, "The Politics and Limits of Transgender in South Africa," in *Transgender Refugees and the Imagined South Africa: Bodies over Borders and Borders over Bodies* (London: Palgrave Macmillan, 2019), 85–128. The figure of the tomboy moves across diverse African literatures, including for example, Sylvia Tamale, ed., *African Sexualities: A Reader* (Cape Town: Pambazuka, 2011); Sokari Ekine and Hakima Abbas, eds., *Queer African Reader* (Cape Town: Pambazuka, 2011); and Zethu Matebeni, *Reclaiming Afrikan: Queer Perspectives on Sexual and Gender Identities* (Cape Town: Modjadji Books, 2014).

68. Literally, wildebeest. Mmina ngiyinkonkoni what what. "That I am a wildebeest and so on."

69. Both my interlocutors in the plantations and the Doke et al. dictionary give "female" as the gloss for owesifazane (and for feminine the dictionary gives

ubufazane, in the abstract noun class), but the operation of a sex/gender binary across linguistic, historical, and geographical domains deserves its own careful analysis.

70. In ordinary language in 2008, isitabane was a derogatory term for lesbians. Doke et al., 775, from an older time, give: -tabane (umtabane, imitabane): vaginal belt of soft grass worn during menstruation.

71. On African homosexualities, see Marc Epprecht, *Heterosexual Africa? The History of an Idea from the Age of Exploration to the Age of AIDS* (Athens: Ohio University Press, 2008); Graeme Charles Reid, *How to Be a Real Gay: Gay Identities in Small-Town South Africa* (Scottsville: University of KwaZulu-Natal Press, 2013); and Rachel Spronk and Thomas Hendriks, eds., *Readings in Sexualities from Africa* (Bloomington: Indiana University Press, 2020).

72. Note the entanglement of debt and savings in stokvel and the figure of the parent. Equally resonant here is the work of time in the making of kin, on the one side, and on the other, anthropology's use of a genealogical imagination in the making of time in giving accounts of social difference; on which, see Johannes Fabian, *Time and the Other: How Anthropology Makes Its Object* (New York: Columbia University Press, 1983).

73. Here I am inspired by the work of Stanley Cavell, *The Claim of Reason: Wittgenstein, Skepticism, Morality, and Tragedy* (New York: Oxford University Press, 1979), 180.

74. I draw here on Elizabeth A. Povinelli's sense of "the otherwise" as discussed in *The Empire of Love: Toward a Theory of Intimacy, Genealogy, and Carnality* (Durham, NC: Duke University Press, 2006).

75. Guy, *Destruction and Reconstruction*.

76. Rachael Gilmour, *Grammars of Colonialism: Representing Languages in Colonial South Africa* (London: Palgrave Macmillan, 2006), 19. "The collection of lists of words and phrases had been, for centuries, a common ingredient in Western ethnographic writing" (Gilmour, 19). See also Sarah Nuttall, "Flatness and Fantasy: Representations of the Land in Two Recent South African Novels," in *Text, Theory, Space: Post-colonial Representations and Identity*, ed. Kate Darian Smith, Liz Gunner, and Sarah Nuttall (London: Routledge, 1996), 215.

77. Michael Silverstein, "The Improvisational Performance of Culture in Real-time Discursive Practice," in *Creativity in Performance*, ed. R. Keith Sawyer (London: Ablex, 1997).

78. Claude Lévi-Strauss, *Structural Anthropology* (1963; New York: Basic Books, 1990).

79. See Michael Silverstein and Greg Urban, *Natural Histories of Discourse* (Chicago: University of Chicago Press, 1996). I am inspired in particular by Cavell, *Claim of Reason*, 170.

80. See Émile Benveniste, *Problems in General Linguistics* (Miami, FL: University of Miami Press, 1971).

81. Lévi-Strauss, *Structural Anthropology*.

82. On play, see Robert Hamayon, *Why We Play: An Anthropological Study* (Chicago: HAU Books, 2016), 107.

83. Gayle Rubin, "The Traffic in Women: Notes on the 'Political Economy' of Sex," in *Toward an Anthropology of Women*, ed. Rayna R. Reiter (New York: Monthly Review Press, 1975).

84. Sylvia Yanagisako and Jane Collier, "Toward a Unified Analysis of Gender and Kinship," in *Gender and Kinship: Essays toward a Unified Analysis*, ed. Jane Collier and Sylvia Yanagisako (Stanford, CA: Stanford University Press, 1987); and David M. Schneider, *American Kinship: A Cultural Account* (Chicago: University of Chicago Press, 1968).

85. See Danai S. Mupotsa, "Conjugality," *GLQ: A Journal of Lesbian and Gay Studies* 26, no. 3 (2020): 377–403, for a brilliant reading of the "sexuated" body in relation to the situated and situating performance of marriage in contemporary Zimbabwe.

86. On "relaxing" into the struts and braces of sexuality, see Elizabeth A. Povinelli, "Sexuality at Risk: Psychoanalysis Metapragmatically," in *Homosexuality and Psychoanalysis*, ed. Tim Dean and Christopher Lane (Chicago: University of Chicago Press, 2001), 387–411.

87. Henriette Gunkel, "Some Reflections on Postcolonial Homophobia, Local Interventions, and LGBTI Solidarity Online: The Politics of Global Petitions," *African Studies Review* 56, no. 2 (2013): 67–81.

88. Hendriks, "'Making Men Fall,'" 404.

89. Kirk Fiereck, "After Performativity, beyond Custom: The Queerness of Biofinancial Personhood, Citational Sexualities, and Derivative Subjectivity in South Africa," *GLQ: A Journal of Lesbian and Gay Studies* 26, no. 3 (2020): 503–27.

90. Claude Lévi-Strauss, *The Savage Mind* (Chicago: University of Chicago Press, 1966).

91. Hendriks, "'Making Men Fall,'" 399, 413.

92. On the stakes of reimagining relations in the context of HIV and its effects in South Africa, see Patricia C. Henderson, *AIDS, Intimacy and Care in Rural KwaZulu-Natal: A Kinship of Bones* (Amsterdam: Amsterdam University Press, 2011); Hylton White, "Outside the Dwelling of Culture: Estrangement and Difference in Postcolonial Zululand," *Anthropological Quarterly* 83, no. 3 (2010): 497–518; and Hunter, *Love in the Time of AIDS*.

93. See Hylton White, "The Materiality of Marriage Payments," *Anthropology Southern Africa* 39, no. 4 (2016): 297–308, where, in the context of a decline of marriage rates in South Africa, partial or incomplete transactions are what give sensuous figuration to both kinship and affinity.

94. See Gananath Obeyesekere, *The Work of Culture: Symbolic Transformation in Psychoanalysis and Anthropology* (Chicago: University of Chicago Press, 1990),

and Marilyn Strathern, "Opening Up Relations," in *A World of Many Worlds*, ed. Marisol de la Cadena and Mario Blaser (Durham, NC: Duke University Press, 2018).

95. Paul Ricoeur's analysis of Marx, Freud, and Nietzsche sets up the ground for a relationship between explanation and understanding. Here I am inspired by Thomas Hendriks's turn toward Eve Kosofsky Sedgwick's response, in *Touching Feeling: Affect, Pedagogy, Performativity* (Durham, NC: Duke University Press, 2003), to such a hermeneutics of suspicion in her elaboration of reparative reading.

96. Deborah Posel, "Sex, Death and the Fate of the Nation: Reflections on the Politicization of Sexuality in Post-apartheid South Africa," *Africa: Journal of the International African Institute* 75, no. 2 (2005): 125–53; Neville Hoad, "Thabo Mbeki's AIDS Blues: The Intellectual, the Archive, and the Pandemic," *Public Culture* 17, no. 1 (2005): 101–27; and Hunter, *Love in the Time of AIDS*, have all usefully sketched out a set of coordinates for mapping the historiography of this set of anxieties and their implications for both scholarly and ordinary hermeneutics, paranoid and otherwise.

97. Amid the failures of postapartheid employment and scenes of plantation labor, the sense that "work" is required, necessarily multiple in the meanings of the term that resonate here, to apprehend the game, to be drawn into it, and to respond appropriately in communicative, ethical, and political terms, is what disrupts the distributions of work and labor, creative action and alienating repetition, scholar and wage-laborer. It is these openings, slippages, torsions, between signs and their "situations"—that is, between scenes of instruction and the uptake of meaning— that give the work of repair its moral, ethical, or political force and destabilizing effect.

98. An Africanist debate on frontiers is productive for considering the internality of the frontier as a productive and playful edge. See Igor Kopytoff, ed., *The African Frontier: The Reproduction of Traditional African Societies* (Bloomington: Indiana University Press, 1987); Francis B. Nyamnjoh, "Incompleteness: Frontier Africa and the Currency of Conviviality," *Journal of Asian and African Studies* 52, no. 3 (2017): 253–70. See also Elizabeth A. Povinelli, "Horizons and Frontiers, Late Liberal Territoriality, and Toxic Habitats," *E-Flux Journal*, no. 90 (April 2018).

4. REPAIR AND THE SUBSTANCE OF OTHERS

1. Georges Canguilhem, "Health: Crude Concept and Philosophical Question," *Public Culture* 20, no. 3 (2008): 467–77.

2. "Umuthi" is the common term in isiZulu for therapeutic substances used by healers. It is an unstable word, most commonly implying an herbal concoction but specifically invoking an African, in distinction from a biomedical, pharmakon. In this instance it was used to denote the fat of a python and thus a more general use than the strict definition of "herb" or "tree bark." On the commercialization

of African curatives, see Karen E. Flint, *Healing Traditions: African Medicine, Cultural Exchange, and Competition in South Africa, 1820–1948* (Athens: Ohio University Press, 2008).

3. Axel-Ivar Berglund, *Zulu Thought-Patterns and Symbolism* (Cape Town: David Philip, 1976); Harold Scheub, *The Uncoiling Python: South African Storytellers and Resistance* (Athens: Ohio University Press, 2010); Edward C. Green, Annemarie Jurg, and Armando Djedje, "The Snake in the Stomach: Child Diarrhea in Central Mozambique," *Medical Anthropology Quarterly* 8, no. 1 (1994): 4–24.

4. T: What do you think makes you sick and affects your eyes? Ucabanga ukuthi yini ekudale ukuthi ugule bese kukubulala namehlo?

S: Witches tried to kill me by placing medicine in my path so that this thing [the snake] rose up and entered through my legs. Kusho ukuthi abathakathi bebegqaba ngendlela yabo yakhuphuka lento yakhuphuka ukugqaba—to try to kill someone, to put muthi into that person so that they get sick.

5. "Umoya" could also be glossed here as spirit, although its etymology lies in the missionary encounter well described by Paul S. Landau, *Popular Politics in the History of South Africa, 1400–1948* (Cambridge: Cambridge University Press, 2010), and whose exhortation to resist these kinds of missionary-inflected glosses I support.

6. Most conversations were in a jagged mix of isiZulu and English, with copious hesitations and midflow translations. For ease of reading, I have chosen to give the English translation, and where possible, the isiZulu in endnotes in order to hint at the resonant images and slippages that fall out of translation.

> TC: Bathini uma besho bathi le nyoka ingene kanjani ingene kanjani esiswini.
> S: Yafakwa ngephupho ngomoya ukuthi umuntu engabiza igama lakho bese eyayi futha leyonto bese ingena lapha ulele wena.

7. TC: Ucabanga u kuthi umuntu okhona eduze noma owasekhaya? (Do you think it's somebody far away or near your home?)
J: Akekho eduze wuye owasekhaya. (It's someone not around here but near my home).

8. On the relationship between skepticism and witchcraft in anthropology, see Jeanne Favret-Saada, *Deadly Words: Witchcraft in the Bocage* (Cambridge: Cambridge University Press, 1980); Peter Geschiere, *The Modernity of Witchcraft: Politics and the Occult in Postcolonial Africa* (Charlottesville: University Press of Virginia, 1997); and James T. Siegel, *Naming the Witch* (Stanford, CA: Stanford University Press, 2006).

9. See in particular Tanser's brilliant analysis of spatial epidemiology of schistosomiasis in the Demographic Surveillance Area of the Africa Center. Compare

with the claims of Green, Jurg, and Djedje, "Snake in the Stomach," that the discourse of izinyoka is simply an ethnobiology of diarrhea.

10. For a description of Inkosi yaManzi, King of the Waters, a giant snake in urban Soweto, see Adam Ashforth, "Reflections on Spiritual Insecurity in a Modern African City (Soweto)," *African Studies Review* 41, no. 3 (1998): 39–67; for a brilliant analysis of affliction and spiritual insecurity in postapartheid South Africa, see Adam Ashforth, *Witchcraft, Violence, and Democracy in South Africa* (Chicago: University of Chicago Press, 2004).

11. The range of associated meanings is important and would require more space than I have available here to explicate the glosses provided in the colonial moment of its translation. C. M. Doke et al., *English–Zulu, Zulu–English Dictionary* (Johannesburg: Witwatersrand University Press, 2006), 337: "1. Medicinal herb; herbal decoction used for medicinal purposes as household remedies; as opposed to amakhubalo, professional medicines. 2. The so-called intestinal beetle, believed by Natives to be parasitic in the intestines. 3. Large edible tree-caterpillar. 4. Nervous disorder, mental derangement. Lomuntu unekhambi (This person is mentally unsound)."

12. See in particular Flint, *Healing Traditions,* and Michelle Cocks and Anthony Dold, "The Role of 'African Chemists' in the Health Care System of the Eastern Cape Province of South Africa," *Social Science and Medicine* 51, no. 10 (2000): 1505–15.

13. I am informed here by Audrey I. Richards, *Hunger and Work in a Savage Tribe: A Functional Study of Nutrition among the Southern Bantu* (Glencoe, IL: Free Press, 1948), and J. M. Garrido, *On Time, Being, and Hunger: Challenging the Traditional Way of Thinking Life* (New York: Fordham University Press, 2012).

14. Elizabeth A. Povinelli, *The Empire of Love: Toward a Theory of Intimacy, Genealogy, and Carnality* (Durham, NC: Duke University Press, 2006), distinguishes between carnality and corporeality as modes of enfleshment in late liberalism. This distinction informs my thinking here and will be explicated below.

15. For an excellent history of state regulation of medicine and African healing from the late nineteenth century in South Africa, see Flint, *Healing Traditions*; and for older European histories of the making of medicine, see Alison Klairmont Lingo, "Empirics and Charlatans in Early Modern France: The Genesis of the Classification of the 'Other' in Medical Practice," *Journal of Social History* 19, no. 4 (1986): 583–603, and David Gentilcore, "'Charlatans, Mountebanks and Other Similar People': The Regulation and Role of Itinerant Practitioners in Early Modern Italy," *Social History* 20, no. 3 (1995): 297–314.

16. For a definitive account of the drama of that period, see Nathan Geffen, *Debunking Delusions: The Inside Story of the Treatment Action Campaign* (Johannesburg: Jacana, 2010).

17. For an account of the biopolitics of nutrition and HIV, see Thomas Cousins, "Antiretroviral Therapy and Nutrition in Southern Africa: Citizenship and the

Grammar of Hunger," *Medical Anthropology: Cross-Cultural Studies in Health and Illness* 35, no. 5 (2016): 433–46.

18. Academy of Science of South Africa (ASSAf), *HIV/AIDS, TB and Nutrition: Scientific Enquiry into the Nutritional Influences on Human Immunity with Special Reference to HIV Infection and Active TB in South Africa* (Pretoria: Academy of Science of South Africa, 2007); Donald P. Kotler, "HIV Infection and the Gastrointestinal Tract," *AIDS* 19 (2005): 107–17.

19. ASSAf, *HIV/AIDS, TB and Nutrition*.

20. Peter Bai James et al., "Traditional, Complementary and Alternative Medicine Use in Sub-Saharan Africa: A Systematic Review," *BMJ Global Health* 3, no. 5 (2018).

21. Gyorgy Scrinis, *Nutritionism: The Science and Politics of Dietary Advice* (New York: Columbia University Press, 2015).

22. That these questions should be articulated around labeling and the medicinal claims attached to particular substances is partly a result of the way pharmaceuticals have been marketed and regulated—the South African legal understanding of such issues having been directly influenced by the American history of drug labeling and drug regulation. See Harry Marks, "Law, Markets and Regulatory Cultures: A Historian's Vain Pursuit of Social Theory," *Drugs*, 96–118 (unpublished).

23. See Ashforth, *Witchcraft, Violence, and Democracy*; Deborah Posel, "Sex, Death and the Fate of the Nation: Reflections on the Politicization of Sexuality in Post-apartheid South Africa," *Africa: Journal of the International African Institute* 75, no. 2 (2005): 125–53; Robert Thornton, "The Market for Healing and the Elasticity of Belief: Medical Pluralism in Mpumalanga, South Africa," in *Markets of Well-Being: Navigating Health and Healing in Africa*, ed. Marleen Dekker and Rijk van Dijk (Leiden: Koninklijke Brill, 2010); and Claire Laurier Decoteau, *Ancestors and Antiretrovirals: The Biopolitics of HIV/AIDS in Post-apartheid South Africa* (Chicago: University of Chicago Press, 2013), for wide-ranging discussions of the "market for healing" at the height of the AIDS crisis.

24. Their opinion that HIV did not cause AIDS justified the state's refusal to make widely available free antiretroviral treatment. See Nicoli Nattrass, "AIDS and the Scientific Governance of Medicine in Post-apartheid South Africa," *African Affairs* 107, no. 427 (2008): 157–76; Nathan Geffen, "Echoes of Lysenko: State-Sponsored Pseudo-science in South Africa," *Social Dynamics* 31, no. 2 (2005): 183–210; and Steven Robins, "'Long Live Zackie, Long Live': AIDS Activism, Science and Citizenship after Apartheid," *Journal of Southern African Studies* 30, no. 3 (2004): 651–72.

25. Between 2009 and 2012, the words, images, and claims shifted subtly. In October 2009 most labels stated clearly that the substance does not cure HIV but "boosts the immune system." Of the 146 products I surveyed in the four pharmacies of Mtubatuba, 34 percent could be classified as "izifo zonke," 10 percent are "immune

boosters," and the rest had specific illness profiles. The typology I have imposed on this range of products does not stand up to scrutiny; its borders are too porous and the degree of overlap between them is too large to maintain these distinctions. The range of products known as "izifo zonke" is wide. Each product was distinguished by a subtle reference in its packaging to its efficacy, contents, sources, and the persona of its creator. While there were not as many distinct "immune booster" brands, they far outnumbered the other substances in their total quantity.

26. See http://www.quackdown.info/article/mcc-and-decade-deliberate -deception/, accessed August 4, 2020.

27. Veena Das and Ranendra K. Das, "Pharmaceuticals in Urban Ecologies: The Register of the Local," in *Global Pharmaceuticals: Ethics, Markets, Practices*, ed. Adriana Petryna, Andrew Lakoff, and Arthur Kleinman (Durham, NC: Duke University Press, 2006).

28. The isiZulu-speaking staff working in allopathic pharmacies are the key figures who mediate the reputation of the various brands. As my informants told me, they receive requests from customers who have heard or seen advertisements or recommendations by word of mouth, and transmit the requests to the (White) pharmacists who place the order for the popular curative with Alpha-Pharm. In one store in Mtubatuba, two hours north of Durban, I counted 146 medicinal substances in March 2009.

29. See Keith Hart, Jean-Louis Laville, and Antonio David Cattani, "Building the Human Economy Together," in *The Human Economy: A Citizen's Guide*, ed. Hart, Laville, and Cattani (Cambridge: Polity Press, 2010), 1–20. Richard Dobson and Caroline Skinner, *Working in Warwick: Including Street Traders in Urban Plans* (Durban: University of KwaZulu-Natal Press, 2009), and Keith Hart, "Africa's Urban Revolution and the Informal Economy," in *The Political Economy of Africa*, ed. Vishnu Padayachee (London: Routledge, 2010), document the vibrant histories of the market and downtown melee of Durban.

30. Colleen E. Archer et al., "Endo-parasites of Public-Health Importance Recovered from Rodents in the Durban Metropolitan Area, South Africa," *Southern African Journal of Infectious Diseases* 32, no. 2 (2017): 57–66, describe endoparasites in rodents in Durban, while Alison Swartz et al., "Toxic Layering through Three Disciplinary Lenses: Childhood Poisoning and Street Pesticide Use in Cape Town, South Africa," *Medical Humanities* 44, no. 4 (2018): 247–52, discuss the "toxic layering" of street pesticides in domestic economies of Cape Town.

31. Ugazi can mean blood; a relative, most often a familiar term for cousin; personality; and attractiveness, among many other inflections. Uqedizikinga roughly translates as "it finishes your problems."

32. See the Ugazi website, http://www.ugazi.co.za/ugproducts.asp, last visited August 4, 2020. Wittgenstein's notion of "family resemblance" is useful for learning to recognize which criteria serve to link these concerns.

33. A substantial anthropological literature has taken up the "social life of things," materia medica, and pharmaceuticals in particular; Arjun Appadurai, ed., *The Social Life of Things: Commodities in Cultural Perspective* (Cambridge: Cambridge University Press, 1986); Susan Reynolds Whyte, Sjaak van der Geest, and Anita Hardon, *Social Lives of Medicines* (Cambridge: Cambridge University Press, 2002); Sjaak van der Geest, Susan Reynolds Whyte, and Anita Hardon, "The Anthropology of Pharmaceuticals: A Biographical Approach," *Annual Review of Anthropology* 25 (1996): 153–78; Anita Hardon and Emilia Sanabria, "Fluid Drugs: Revisiting the Anthropology of Pharmaceuticals," *Annual Review of Anthropology* 46, no. 1 (2017): 117–32; Kaushik Sunder Rajan, *Pharmocracy: Value, Politics, and Knowledge in Global Biomedicine* (Durham, NC: Duke University Press, 2017).

34. Flint, *Healing Traditions*, 135. I give the anglicized version of the plural of inyanga ("inyangas" rather than "izinyanga") to highlight the unstable naming practices of the colonial authorities unable to recognize the indigenous forms before them. On colonialism and grammar, see Rachael Gilmour, *Grammars of Colonialism: Representing Languages in Colonial South Africa* (London: Palgrave Macmillan, 2006).

35. A claim that all the major brands of izifo zonke and immune boosters made.

36. Used also for close friends, as in "Heita! Ugazi lam!" "Hey, my cousin!"

37. Vomit. "Spew" being Pretty's translation of the word "ukuhlanza," meaning to cleanse by vomiting. Pretty explained that one also cleanses the body (ukuhlanza umzimba) and cleanses the blood (ukuhlanza igazi) by purging.

38. The "immune system" in isiZulu is described as amashosa omzimba—literally, the soldiers of the body—and is now used equally to describe CD4 cells.

39. Ordinary conversations would slide between English and isiZulu, and both "witchcraft" and "ubuthakathi" would be used, indexically locating participants in these conversations within recognizable matrixes of race, class, and language.

40. Flint, *Healing Traditions*.

41. All details have been changed to protect the identity of businesses and individuals.

42. See Michelle Cocks and Anthony Dold, "The Trade in Medicinal Plants in the Eastern Cape Province, South Africa," *South African Journal of Science* 98 (November/December 2002), and Flint, *Healing Traditions*, for a history of therapeutic hybridity and exchange in southern Africa.

43. His product of choice during 2009 was Ngoma, which is produced by a wealthy, White chemist-turned-businessman in Pietermaritzburg who assured me that his product contained only natural ingredients with biomedically recognized benefits to immune system functioning, such as vitamins and essential oils. "Ngoma" is also a healing and dance cult widespread across Africa—see John M. Janzen, "Self-Presentation and Common Cultural Structures in Ngoma Rituals of Southern Africa," *Journal of Religion in Africa* 25, no. 2 (1995): 141–62;

Rijk van Dijk, Ria Reis, and Marja Spierenburg, eds., *The Quest for Fruition through Ngoma: Political Aspects of Healing in Southern Africa* (Athens: Ohio University Press, 2000); Hugh Tracey, "A Case for the Name Mbira," *African Music* 2, no. 4 (1961): 17–25; and Rebecca Gearhart, "Ngoma Memories: A History of Competitive Music and Dance Performance on the Kenya Coast" (PhD diss., University of Florida, 1998).

44. "Positive" here refers to testing positive for HIV, although key to its ordinary usage is the careful avoidance of directly naming the disease.

45. See Rosalind C. Morris, "Deconstruction's Doubt," *HAU: Journal of Ethnographic Theory* 6, no. 1 (2016): 511–18:

> Following the lethal violence at Marikana, South Africa, in August 2012, when confrontations between striking miners, state police, mining corporations, and unions led to the deaths of forty-four people, analyses of the events were riven by the question of whether and how to discuss the presence of *sangomas* and the practice of *muti* magic in the events. Many black South African analysts insisted that *muti* be taken seriously and they chastised timid white commentators who, wanting to explain the violence in materialist terms, effaced the force of magic in the lives of the migrant laborers. For them, the magic was a not matter of resurgent tradition. Nor was it a phantom projection of anxious modernists. It was a matter of power: visceral, strategically instrumentalizable, and absolutely lethal power. The kind that enables people to go to war, the kind that operates at the point where language fails. (512)

46. For historiographical accounts, see Drucilla Cornell, *Ubuntu and the Law: African Ideals and Postapartheid Jurisprudence* (New York: Fordham University Press, 2011); Flint, *Healing Traditions*; Jeff Guy, "The Destruction and Reconstruction of Zulu Society," in *Industrialisation and Social Change in South Africa: African Class, Culture, and Consciousness, 1870–1930*, ed. Shula Marks and Richard Rathbone (New York: Longman, 1982); Landau, *Popular Politics in the History of South Africa*; and in particular Carolyn Hamilton and Nessa Leibhammer, *Tribing and Untribing the Archive: Identity and the Material Record in Southern KwaZulu-Natal in the Late Independent and Colonial Periods*, 2 vols. (Durban: University of KwaZulu-Natal Press, 2016).

47. Barbara Oomen, *Chiefs in South Africa: Law, Power and Culture in the Postapartheid Era* (New York: Palgrave Macmillan, 2005).

48. Paul K. Bjerk, "They Poured Themselves into the Milk: Zulu Political Philosophy Under Shaka," *Journal of African History* 47 (2006): 1–19. James Stuart was a colonial historian and administrator who spent twenty-five years collecting Zulu oral history from over two hundred sources, now compiled in *The James Stuart Archive of Recorded Oral Evidence Relating to the History of the Zulu and Neighbouring*

Peoples, ed. Colin Webb and John B. Wright (Pietermaritzburg: University of Natal Press, 2014).

49. Landau, *Popular Politics in the History of South Africa*; Paul S. Landau, *The Realm of the Word: Language, Gender, and Christianity in a Southern African Kingdom* (Johannesburg: Heinemann, 1995); David Maxwell, *African Gifts of the Spirit: Pentecostalism and the Rise of a Zimbabwean Transnational Religious Movement* (Oxford: James Currey, 2007).

50. A. T. Bryant, *Zulu Medicine and Medicine Men* (Cape Town: Struik, 1966 [1909]), 23.

51. For structuralist accounts, see Berglund, *Zulu Thought-Patterns and Symbolism*, and Harriet Ngubane, *Body and Mind in Zulu Medicine* (Madison, WI: Academic, 1977), who both follow closely Mary Douglas's approach in *Purity and Danger: An Analysis of Concept of Pollution and Taboo* (London: Routledge, 1984 [1966]). Alternatively, Edward C. Green, Annemarie Jurg, and Armando Djedje, "The Snake in the Stomach: Child Diarrhea in Central Mozambique," *Medical Anthropology Quarterly* 8, no. 1 (1994): 4–24, and Edward C. Green, "Purity, Pollution and the Invisible Snake in Southern Africa," *Medical Anthropology* 17, no. 1 (1996): 83–100, see these as straightforward analogues of biomedical categories.

52. Harriet Ngubane, "Some Notions of 'Purity' and 'Impurity' among the Zulu," *Africa: Journal of the International African Institute* 46, no. 3 (1976): 274–84.

53. Ngubane, 275.

54. Ngubane, 282–83.

55. Douglas, *Purity and Danger.*

56. In chapter 3 I describe "playful marriage" (umshado wokudlala) between women laborers in the plantations who talk about ukushisa as a preliminary stage of courting crucial to the marriage process (as in to burn, to burn for, to desire, to flirt with).

57. Berglund, *Zulu Thought-Patterns and Symbolism*, 253.

58. Berglund, 253.

59. Jason Hickel, "Democracy and Sabotage" (PhD diss., University of Virginia, 2011), 201.

60. Jason Hickel, *Democracy as Death: The Moral Order of Anti-liberal Politics in South Africa* (Berkeley: University of California Press, 2015), 162.

61. Hickel, 159.

62. Hickel, 159. I thank Jason Hickel for bringing this aspect of his work to my attention. For a fuller exposition of the "beastly work" of animals in the production of social differentiation, see Hylton White, "Beastly Whiteness: Animal Kinds and the Social Imagination in South Africa," *Anthropology Southern Africa* 34, no. 3 (2011): 104–13; and John L. Comaroff and Jean Comaroff, "Goodly Beasts, Beastly Goods: Cattle and Commodities in a South African Context," *American Ethnologist* 17, no. 2 (1990): 195–216.

63. Hickel, *Democracy as Death*, 160–61.

64. Hickel, 159.

65. Joost Fontein and John Harries, "The Vitality and Efficacy of Human Substances," *Critical African Studies* 5, no. 3 (2013): 119. On "torque," see Christopher Pinney, "Things Happen: Or, From Which Moment Does That Object Come?," in *Materiality*, ed. Daniel Miller (Durham, NC: Duke University Press, 2005), 256–72.

66. Fontein and Harries, 119.

67. Harris Solomon, *Metabolic Living: Food, Fat, and the Absorption of Illness in India* (Durham, NC: Duke University Press, 2016), 22.

68. Doke et al., *English–Zulu, Zulu–English Dictionary*, 321; Berglund, *Zulu Thought-Patterns and Symbolism*, 328.

69. Berglund, 322.

70. See Hylton White, "Tempora et Mores: Family Values and the Possessions of a Post-apartheid Countryside," *Journal of Religion in Africa* 31, no. 4 (2001): 457–79, on the question of the efficacy of ritual action in postapartheid South Africa. See Berglund, *Zulu Thought-Patterns and Symbolism*, 348.

71. Georges Canguilhem, *The Normal and the Pathological* (New York: Zone Books, 1994).

72. I have discussed the biopolitical aspects of nutrition, hunger, and the gut in three related essays: "Antiretroviral Therapy and Nutrition in Southern Africa: Citizenship and the Grammar of Hunger," *Medical Anthropology: Cross Cultural Studies in Health and Illness* 35, no. 5 (2016): 433–46; "HIV and the Remaking of Hunger and Nutrition in South Africa: Biopolitical Specification after Apartheid," *BioSocieties* 10, no. 2 (2015): 143–61; and "A Mediating Capacity toward an Anthropology of the Gut," *Medicine Anthropology Theory* 2, no. 2 (2015): 1–27.

73. Elizabeth A. Wilson, *Psychosomatic: Feminism and the Neurological Body* (Durham, NC: Duke University Press, 2004).

74. Wilson, 8.

75. Wilson, 22.

76. Wilson, 41.

77. Wilson, 42.

78. David B. Coplan, "History Is Eaten Whole: Consuming Tropes in Sesotho Auriture," *History and Theory* 32, no. 4 (1993): 80–104, and *In the Time of Cannibals: The Word Music of South Africa's Basotho Migrants* (Chicago: University of Chicago Press, 1994); Sidney W. Mintz and Christine M. du Bois, "The Anthropology of Food and Eating," *Annual Review of Anthropology* 31 (2002): 99–119; and *The Intestines of the State: Youth, Violence, and Belated Histories in the Cameroon Grassfields* (Chicago: University of Chicago Press, 2007).

79. Wilson, *Psychosomatic*, 45.

80. See Elizabeth A. Povinelli, *Economies of Abandonment: Social Belonging and Endurance in Late Liberalism* (Durham, NC: Duke University Press, 2011).

81. D. J. H. Niehaus et al., "A Culture-Bound Syndrome 'Amafufunyana' and a Culture-Specific Event 'Ukuthwasa,'" *Psychopathology* 37, no. 2 (2004): 59–63.

82. Karin Ensink and Brian Robertson, "Indigenous Categories of Distress and Dysfunction in South African Xhosa Children and Adolescents as Described by Indigenous Healers," *Transcultural Psychiatry* 33, no. 2 (1996): 137–72; and Karin Ensink and Brian Robertson, "Patient and Family Experiences of Psychiatric Services and African Indigenous Healers," *Transcultural Psychiatry* 36, no. 1 (1999): 23–43. See also Leslie Swartz, "Transcultural Psychiatry in South Africa," *Transcultural Psychiatry* 23, no. 4 (1986): 273–303, for an excellent historiography and critique of transcultural psychiatry in South Africa.

83. Janet Carsten, *After Kinship* (Cambridge: Cambridge University Press, 2004).

84. Marshall Sahlins, *What Kinship Is—And Is Not* (Chicago: University of Chicago Press, 2013).

85. Elizabeth A. Wilson, *Gut Feminism* (Durham, NC: Duke University Press, 2015); James M. Wilce Jr., *Social and Cultural Lives of Immune Systems* (London: Taylor and Francis, 2003).

86. Robert Thornton, *Healing the Exposed Being: A South African Ngoma Tradition* (Johannesburg: Wits University Press, 2017).

87. Michael Silverstein, "Metapragmatic Discourse and Metapragmatic Function." In *Reflexive Language: Reported Speech and Metapragmatics*, ed. John A. Lucy (Cambridge: Cambridge University Press, 1993), 33. See Elizabeth A. Povinelli, "Sexuality at Risk: Psychoanalysis Metapragmatically," in *Homosexuality and Psychoanalysis*, ed. Tim Dean and Christopher Lane (Chicago: University of Chicago Press, 2001), 387–411, for the uptake of Silverstein and her projection of metapragmatic action in corporeal terms.

88. See Hylton White, "Ritual Haunts: The Timing of Estrangement in a Post-apartheid Countryside," in *Producing African Futures: Ritual and Reproduction in a Neoliberal Age*, ed. Brad Weiss (Leiden: Koninklijke Brill, 2004), and "Custom, Normativity and Authority in South Africa," *Journal of Southern African Studies* 41, no. 5 (2015): 1005–17.

89. Francis B. Nyamnjoh, ed., *Eating and Being Eaten: Cannibalism as Food for Thought* (Bamenda, Cameroon: Langaa RPCIG, 2018). See also Marilyn Strathern, "Eating (and Feeding)," *Cambridge Journal of Anthropology* 30, no. 2 (2012): 1–14; and Carlos Fausto and Luiz Costa, "Feeding (and Eating): Reflections on Strathern's 'Eating (and Feeding),'" *Cambridge Journal of Anthropology* 31, no. 1 (2013): 156–62.

90. Thornton, *Healing the Exposed Being*.

91. Catherine Malabou, *What Should We Do with Our Brain?* (New York: Fordham University Press, 2008).

92. Wilson, *Psychosomatic*.

93. Solomon, *Metabolic Living*.

94. Tobias Rees, Thomas Bosch, and Angela E. Douglas, "How the Microbiome Challenges Our Concept of Self," *PLOS Biology* 16, no. 2 (February 9, 2018): e2005358.

95. Stephen Mulhall, *The Wounded Animal: J. M. Coetzee and the Difficulty of Reality in Literature and Philosophy* (Princeton, NJ: Princeton University Press, 2009).

5. IN THE VICINITY OF THE SOCIAL

1. They were her father's father's son's by his second wife, and thus named baba, or "father."

2. On the house in anthropology see Janet Carsten and Stephen Hugh-Jones, *About the House: Lévi-Strauss and Beyond* (Cambridge: Cambridge University Press, 1995). For an African and South African debate on this concept, see in particular Jane I. Guyer, "Household and Community in African Studies," *African Studies Review* 24, no. 2/3 (1981): 87–137; Adam Kuper, "The 'House' and Zulu Political Structure in the Nineteenth Century," *Journal of African History* 34, no. 3 (1993): 469–87; Hylton White, "Outside the Dwelling of Culture: Estrangement and Difference in Postcolonial Zululand," *Anthropological Quarterly* 83, no. 3 (2010): 497–518; Mark Hunter, "Is It Enough to Talk of Marriage as a Process? Legitimate Co-habitation in Umlazi, South Africa," *Anthropology Southern Africa* 39, no. 4 (2016): 281–96; Chris J. de Wet and Eric A. Mgujulwa, "Innovative Reworkings of Ancestor Ritual as a Response to Forced Villagisation: An Eastern Cape Example," *Anthropology Southern Africa* 43, no. 4 (2020): 246–58. Embedded in the English gloss, "house," is the anthropological interest in those social structures and offices that constitute "house societies" beyond their physical expression in "built structures," a distinction that informed the demographic surveillance system discussed below.

3. See Cherryl Walker, *Landmarked: Land Claims and Land Restitution in South Africa* (Cape Town: Jacana, 2008) for a fuller explication of this history. Walker was integral to the Surplus People Project's report for Natal and KwaZulu in 1983 and later served as the Land Claims Commissioner for KwaZulu-Natal from 1995 to 2000. See in particular Surplus People Project, *Forced Removals in South Africa: The SPP Reports,* vol. 4, *Natal* (Cape Town: Surplus People Project, 1983), 261–67.

4. "Gogo" refers to patrilineal or matrilineal grandmother, but in general usage the term refers to any older woman deserving the respect accorded a grandmother. In this instance, she is Nobuhle's father's father's brother's second wife.

5. KwaMsane was originally the "location" for Blacks servicing the then Whites-only town of Mtubatuba. "Township," in ordinary and policy South African discourse, refers to those areas once formally designated for Black residence by the apartheid state, and still characterized by extremely poor services and low-income households. See Michelle Pentecost and Thomas Cousins, "Strata of the Political: Epigenetic and Microbial Imaginaries in Post-apartheid Cape Town," *Antipode* 49 (2017): 1368–84, https://doi.org/10.1111/anti.12315.

6. "Rondawel" is a word of Dutch origin meaning "round hut" and is used in common parlance to indicate the traditional architecture of the region. As White, "Outside the Dwelling of Culture," 512, notes of housing types in KwaZulu-Natal, "Architecture is one of several domains governed by a complex metacultural discourse concerning issues of difference, authenticity, and tradition."

7. R. I. Cairns, "Outgrower Timber Schemes in KwaZulu-Natal—Do They Build Sustainable Rural Livelihoods and What Interventions Should Be Made?" (IIED and CSIR, 2000).

8. See Ara Wilson, "Visual Kinship," *History of Anthropology Newsletter* 42 (2018).

9. Isabel Hofmeyr, *"We Spend Our Years as a Tale That Is Told: Oral Historical Narrative in a South African Chiefdom* (London: James Currey, 1994), and Elizabeth A. Povinelli, "Routes/Worlds," *E-Flux Journal*, no. 27 (September 2011), http://www.e-flux.com/journal/routesworlds/, each offer images of the knotting of narrative and relatedness. On knots and genealogical lines, see Stefania Pandolfo, *Knot of the Soul* (Chicago: University of Chicago Press, 2018). On the texture of the ordinary, see Veena Das, *Textures of the Ordinary* (New York: Fordham University Press, 2020).

10. Annemarie Mol and John Law, "Regions, Networks and Fluids: Anaemia and Social Topology," *Social Studies of Science* 24, no. 4 (1994): 641–71.

11. Half a square kilometer, 0.5 km^2 is 50 hectares, equivalent to 123.5 acres. These inexact equivalents carry histories of state power, surveillance, and the development of standards, as James C. Scott's *Seeing Like a State: How Certain Schemes to Improve the Human Condition Have Failed* (New Haven, CT: Yale University Press, 1998) shows.

12. "Muthi" (singular) and "imithi" (plural) are literally the bark and leaves of trees or bushes and generally understood to indicate traditional African medicine.

13. See Andrew D. Spiegel, "Walking Memories and Growing Amnesia in the Land Claims Process: Lake St Lucia, South Africa," *Anthropology Southern Africa* 27, no. 1/2 (2004): 3–10.

14. See in particular Paul S. Landau, *Popular Politics in the History of South Africa, 1400–1948* (Cambridge: Cambridge University Press, 2010), for a rereading of a "Highveld" political logic, alongside James G. Ferguson, "Declarations of Dependence: Labour, Personhood, and Welfare in Southern Africa," *Journal of the Royal Anthropological Institute* 19 (2013): 223–42.

15. For a recent critique of the concept of life in anthropology, see Didier Fassin, *Life: A Critical User's Manual* (New York: John Wiley and Sons, 2018).

16. See John W. P. Phillips, "On Topology," *Theory, Culture and Society* 30, no. 5 (2013): 122–52, and Stephen J. Collier, "Topologies of Power: Foucault's Analysis of Political Government beyond 'Governmentality,'" *Theory, Culture and Society* 26, no. 6 (2009): 78–108, for how topology has entered social theory from mathematics.

The Wikipedia page for topology gives a surprisingly good lay introduction to the field of topology, including its origins and travels into an array of disciplines, from mathematics and logic to biology and social theory; https://en.wikipedia.org/wiki/Topology.

17. Georges Canguilhem, *Knowledge of Life*, ed. Paola Marrati and Todd Meyers, trans. Stephanos Geroulanos and Daniela Ginsburg (New York: Fordham University Press, 2008.

18. On the relation between "life" and "topology" see Fassin, *Life*; Mol and Law, "Regions, Networks and Fluids"; and Ann H. Kelly and Javier Lezaun, "Walking or Waiting? Topologies of the Breeding Ground in Malaria Control," *Science as Culture* 22, no. 1 (2013): 86–107.

19. The genealogy of milieu that I have found useful derives from Georges Canguilhem's famous essay in *Knowledge of Life*, ed. Marrati and Meyers, and its uptake in more political terms by Michel Foucault, *Security, Territory, Population. Lectures at the Collège de France, 1977–1978*, ed. Michel Senellart, trans. Graham Burchell (London: Palgrave Macmillan, 2007). See Stuart Elden, *Canguilhem* (New York: John Wiley and Sons, 2019).

20. I am grateful to João de Pina-Cabral for bringing his writing on vicinality to my attention.

21. Carolyn Hamilton and Nessa Leibhammer, *Tribing and Untribing the Archive: Identity and the Material Record in Southern KwaZulu-Natal in the Late Independent and Colonial Periods*, 2 vols. (Durban: University of KwaZulu-Natal Press, 2016).

22. Mbongiseni Buthelezi, "We Need New Names Too," in Hamilton and Leibhammer, *Tribing and Untribing*, 2:587, riffs off the title of Zimbabwean novelist NoViolet Bulawayo's 2013 novel, *We Need New Names*. On the relationship between naming and pointing, see Veena Das, "Naming beyond Pointing: Singularity, Relatedness and the Foreshadowing of Death," *South Asia Multidisciplinary Academic Journal*, no. 12 (2015). A subterranean thread to this chapter concerns the possibility that naming the otherwise (as opposed to cartography as colonial violence) is concerned with "opening the person to the world as it also makes her vulnerable to the world" (Das, 18).

23. Dirk J. Potgieter, ed., *Standard Encyclopaedia of Southern Africa* (Pretoria: NASOU, 1973), 14. P. E. Raper, *Dictionary of Southern African Place Names* (Johannesburg: Jonathan Ball, 1987), 478. The latter was written by the head of the Onomastic Research Centre at the Human Sciences Research Council in the service of an apartheid project that sought to stabilize places and their names according to a vision of White supremacy and privilege. "Since 1967 the United Nations Group of Experts on Geographical Names (UNGEGN) has provided for co-ordination and liaison between countries to further the standardization of geographical names. . . . In most countries of the world there are institutes and centres for onomastic research,

official bodies for the national standardization of place names, and names societies. South Africa has not been lagging behind in this regard. Since 1939 a Place Names Committee (now the National Place Names Committee or NPNC) has seen to the standardization of official place names, while since 1970 the Onomastic Research Centre of the Human Sciences Research Council has undertaken, stimulated and helped to co-ordinate research into names" (Raper, i).

24. Graham A. Dominy, "History of Lake St. Lucia Eastern Shores," *Environmental Impact Assessment, Eastern Shores of Lake St. Lucia, Kingsa/Tojan Lease Area, Reports on the Key Issues* 2 (1992); and Armando Cortesão, "Note on the Castiglioni Planisphere," *Imago Mundi* 11, no. 1 (1954): 55, https://doi.org/10.1080/0308569540 8592058.

25. Dominy, "History of Lake St. Lucia," 195.

26. Ian Duncan Colvin, *The Cape of Adventure, Being Strange and Notable Discoveries, Perils, Shipwrecks, Battles, Upon Sea and Land, with Pleasant and Interesting Observations Upon the Country and the Natives of the Cape of Good Hope* (Cape Town: Maskew Miller, 1916).

27. Sihawukele Ngubani, "Language, Identity and Place Names," unpublished, (Wetlands 101s. St Lucia, 2006), suggests that before its naming by Europeans, St Lucia was known as eChwebeni "at the place of the lagoon."

28. See http://www.archive.org/details/capeofadventureboocolv for a complete ebook of the original 1912 version that includes a full translation of Manuel de Mesquita Perestrello's account of the 1554 wreck. Perestrello's 1564 account of the Sao Bento, published in Portugal, is the oldest book dealing exclusively with events on South African soil. See Hamilton and Leibhammer, *Tribing and Untribing*, for a discussion of the work of excavating an unstable, and destabilizing, precolonial history.

29. David Webster, "Tembe-Thonga Kinship: The Marriage of Anthropology and History," *Cahiers d'études africaines* 26, no. 104 (1986): 611–32.

30. David William Hedges, "Trade and Politics in Southern Mozambique and Zululand in the Eighteenth and Early Nineteenth Centuries" (PhD diss., School of Oriental and African Studies [University of London], 1978), cited in David Webster, "Abafazi Bathonga Bafihlakala: Ethnicity and Gender in a KwaZulu Border Community," *African Studies* 50, no. 1 (1991): 243–71. I place the term "Tembe chief" in quotation marks for two reasons. First, the terms in which such a polity might have been understood by Tembe people themselves at the time is a question subject to ongoing debate about the colonial imposition of terms such as "tribe" and "chief" and how such terms were codified during the nineteenth and twentieth centuries (and continue to be fought over in the twenty-first century). Second, the history of the emergence of this polity in relation to others over the thousand years before this moment of colonial encounter remains to be explicated—as Mbongiseni Buthelezi, "Sifuna Umlando Wethu (We Are Searching for Our History): Oral Literature and the

Meanings of the Past in Post-apartheid South Africa" (PhD diss., Columbia University, 2012), and Hamilton and Leibhammer, *Tribing and Untribing*, cogently argue.

31. Hedges, "Trade and Politics," shows that the *amabutho* age regiments, which Shaka made famous in his military successes after 1790, were developed by Mabudu in an earlier period than is commonly understood.

32. Historiographical debate on the nature, development, and destruction of southern African political systems, with a particular focus on Zulu political history, has turned on the correct interpretation of events, social structure, political formations, economic forces, and religious contributions to nineteenth- and twentieth-century social history—much of it made possible by the rich archives of missionaries, explorers, administrators, traders, and their maps, and only latterly a turn toward indigenous voices. For a small selection of a voluminous literature, see, in chronological order by date of publication: Henri Junod, "The Life of a South African Tribe" (Neuchatel, Switzerland: Attinger Frères, 1912); R. R. R. Dhlomo, *UShaka* (Pietermaritzburg: Shuter and Shooter, 1935); Eileen Jensen Krige, *The Social System of the Zulus* (London: Longmans, Green, 1936); Max Gluckman, *Analysis of a Social Situation in Modern Zululand* (Manchester: Manchester University Press [Rhodes Livingstone Institute], 1958 [1940]); Jeff Guy, *The Destruction of the Zulu Kingdom: The Civil War in Zululand, 1879–84* (Johannesburg: Ravan, 1982); Jeffrey B. Peires, *The Dead Will Arise: Nongqawuse and the Great Xhosa Cattle-Killing Movement of 1856–7* (Bloomington: Indiana University Press, 1989); Jean Comaroff and John L. Comaroff, *Of Revelation and Revolution*, vol. 1, *Christianity, Colonialism, and Consciousness in South Africa* (Chicago: University of Chicago Press, 1991); Carolyn Hamilton, *Terrific Majesty: The Powers of Shaka Zulu and the Limits of Historical Invention* (Cape Town: David Philip, 1998); Benedict Carton, John Laband, and Jabulani Sithole, *Zulu Identities: Being Zulu, Past and Present* (Pietermaritzburg: University of KwaZulu-Natal Press, 2008); Julian Cobbing, "The Mfecane as Alibi: Thoughts on Dithakong and Mbolompo," *Journal of African History* 29, no. 3 (2009): 487–519; Landau, *Popular Politics* (2010); Hamilton and Leibhammer, *Tribing and Untribing* (2016); Shadreck Chirikure, *Great Zimbabwe: Reclaiming a 'Confiscated' Past* (London: Routledge, 2021).

33. KwaZulu-Natal is the current name for the province, which betrays a view from the early twenty-first century; this is not meant to imply any form of presentism or claims to authenticity.

34. Dingiswayo kaJobe was the son of the Mthethwa chief Jobe, later to be designated a "clan" name and given as a place name of the Jobe people. The prefix ka- indicates a possessive formative used before proper nouns of people. For a full treatment of the historiography of Shaka, see Carolyn Hamilton's *Terrific Majesty*. Particularly striking for the Euro-mythologizing of Shaka were his punishing training regimens, forbidding his soldiers to marry before the age of forty, and ordering them to go barefoot into battle.

35. *Inkosi*, pl. *amakhosi*. C. M. Doke et al., *English–Zulu, Zulu–English Diction-ary* (Johannesburg: Witwatersrand University Press, 2006) give: 1. King, paramount chief, chief; 2. term of respect for royalty or for a person in high governmental au-thority; lord, sir; 3. Magistrate; 4. (pl. only) Spirits of the departed; 5. Lord (New Testament usage). For a recent historiographical critique of the translation of the concepts of political authority embedded in *inkosi*, see Landau, *Popular Politics*.

36. For a critical rereading of the historiography of "the Tsonga," see Patrick Har-ries, "Exclusion, Classification and Internal Colonialism: The Emergence of Eth-nicity among the Tsonga-Speakers of South Africa," in *The Growth of Tribalism in Southern Africa*, ed. Leroy Vail (Berkeley: University of California Press, 1989), 82–117. Harries argues that Tsonga identity emerged as the product of a variety of forces, chief among them class interests engendered by the historical regional division of labor or center-periphery form of internal capitalism that has emerged in southern Africa. He points to the European obsession with social classifications; a govern-ment policy that attempted to divide Africans along ethnic lines; and an awareness expressed by many Africans of the numerous benefits that accrued from the mobi-lization of people along ethnic lines (Harries, 83). See Landau, *Popular Politics*, on the question of consciousness in the new historiographies of southern Africa.

37. The Natalia Republic was a short-lived Boer republic, established in 1839 by local Afrikaans-speaking Voortrekkers shortly after the Battle of Blood River. The republic was located on the coast of the Indian Ocean beyond the Eastern Cape, and was previously named Natalia by Portuguese sailors. After the Natalia Repub-lic was conquered and annexed by Britain in 1843, most local Voortrekker Boers trekked north into Transorangia, later known as the Orange Free State, and the Transvaal. For a strongly critical review of Zulu social history, see Jeff Guy, "The Destruction and Reconstruction of Zulu Society," in *Industrialisation and Social Change in South Africa: African Class, Culture, and Consciousness, 1870–1930*, ed. Shula Marks and Richard Rathbone (New York: Longman, 1982).

38. Edgar H. Brookes and Colin Webb, *A History of Natal* (Pietermaritzburg: University of Natal Press, 1965), 49.

39. On the "great cattle-killing movement," see Peires, *The Dead Will Arise*, and Noel Mostert, *Frontiers: The Epic of South Africa's Creation and the Tragedy of the Xhosa People* (New York: Knopf, 1992).

40. Nozingile's loyalty was secured when Mpande presented him with a wife from his kraal.

41. Although coal was first mined, unsuccessfully, in 1903, the open pit coal mine was commissioned in 2007 and has had a major impact on local employment, so-cial investment, and environmental change. See https://saveourwilderness.org for ongoing resistance to the devastation caused by the mine.

42. Sonia Clarke, *Zululand at War, 1879: The Conduct of the Anglo-Zulu War* (Houghton, South Africa: Brenthurst, 1984); Graham A. Dominy, "Lake St. Lucia,

the Eastern Shores: Cultural Resources in an Historical Perspective," *Southern African Humanities* 6, no. 10 (1994): 195–214; and Walker, *Landmarked*.

43. After the ex-empress of the French, Eugénie, who had visited Zululand in 1880 on a pilgrimage to the spot where her son, the prince imperial, was killed during the Anglo-Zulu War; see Graham A. Dominy, "The New Republicans: A Centennial Reappraisal of the Nieuwe Republiek, 1884–1888," *Natalia* 14 (1984): 87–97.

44. The British claim on St Lucia excluded substantial western tracts taken by Boer farmers. Threatening European interests included in particular German expansionary threats to their ocean trade routes and the newly discovered Transvaal goldfields. See Graham A. Dominy, "History of Lake St. Lucia Eastern Shores," *Environmental Impact Assessment, Eastern Shores of Lake St. Lucia, Kingsa/Tojan Lease Area, Reports on the Key Issues* 2, 1992.

45. Dominy, "History of Lake St. Lucia." The railroad arrived at Somhkele in 1903, but the mine venture fizzled out. Coal mining began again in 2007.

46. See Jeff Guy, "Destruction and Reconstruction of Zulu Society," for a fuller account of this period.

47. Surplus People Project (SPP), *Forced Removals in South Africa*, 4:37.

48. SPP, 4:37.

49. SPP, 4:30.

50. Carton, Laband, and Sithole, *Zulu Identities*, xi.

51. SPP, *Forced Removals in South Africa*, 4:2.

52. The Surplus People Project (SPP) identified ten categories of relocation that the apartheid state developed, some of which had a more direct impact on people living around the timber plantations and conservation land, but all of which affected livelihoods for all nonwhite people in Natal. The major categories they identified were eviction of farmworkers and tenants from farms in the white countryside; removal of black spots, both African freehold and missionary properties; removals for consolidation of reserve areas; urban relocations; influx control and repatriation; destruction of informal settlements; Group Areas removals; removals relating to infrastructural, other development, and conservation schemes; removals for strategic reasons (including the missile range, the northern boundaries, and the coast); and removals caused by the implementation of "betterment" planning within KwaZulu. The massive population removals effected through these means were integral to the overall strategy adopted by the white ruling class to retain and enhance its political domination and economic survival. The SPP estimated that in Natal between 1948 and 1982 (the publication date of their report), 745,500 people had been removed from their land through these techniques. A further 606,000, probably more, faced the threat of removal in the 1980s.

53. SPP, *Forced Removals in South Africa*, 4:56.

54. Headed by Frederick R. Tomlinson, professor of agricultural economics at the University of Pretoria, the Commission for the Socioeconomic Development of

the Bantu Areas (known as the Tomlinson Commission) was established by the South African government in 1950 to study the economic viability of the "native reserves" (later formed into the bantustans), which were intended to serve as the homelands for the black population. The Tomlinson Report was released in 1954.

55. The terms of racial classifications under the legal system of apartheid (1948–94) were not stable, as shown by Saul Dubow, *Apartheid, 1948–1994* (Oxford: Oxford University Press, 2014); Zimitri Erasmus, "Race," in *New South African Keywords*, ed. Nick Shepherd and Steven Robins (Johannesburg: Jacana, 2008); and Deborah Posel, "What's in a Name? Racial Categorisations under Apartheid and Their Afterlife," *Transformation: Critical Perspectives on Southern Africa* 47 (2001): 50–74. The Population Registration Act (Act 30 of 1950) defined South Africans as belonging to one of three races: White, Black, or Coloured. People of Indian ancestry were considered Coloured under this act. See introduction, note 5.

56. As the system of apartheid became firmly entrenched, and while many other African nations were asserting their claims to independence from colonial oppression, South Africa became more isolated politically, making the remote coastal area from St Lucia to the border with Mozambique more strategically important. Thus, in 1968 the South African Defence Force established a missile testing range extending from the tip of the Ndlozi Peninsula, over the northern reaches of Lake St Lucia, to Sodwana Bay. The military installation led to the forced relocation of about 3,400 Mbila people, the northern neighbors of the Bhangazi people, between 1972 and 1979; see SPP, *Forced Removals in South Africa*, 4:261–67; and Cherryl Walker, "Land of Dreams: Land Restitution on the Eastern Shores of Lake St Lucia," *Transformation: Critical Perspectives on Southern Africa* 59 (2005): 8. The missile range also affected Bhangazi homesteads north of Lake Bhangazi, who were forced to shift southward before being moved from the area altogether. Many of my interlocutors working and living in the timber plantations were forced to move during this period, and I discuss their experiences of dislocation more concretely in the pages that follow.

57. The trucks that visited such terror on those forcibly removed had government-issued vehicle registration plates, "Government Garage," by which they became known. See Spiegel, "Walking Memories," and Walker, "Land of Dreams."

58. When beginning fieldwork in 2008, I conducted contract research for the iSimangaliso Wetland Park on oral histories of forced removals from land now under conservation—see Thomas Cousins, *Land Claims on ISimangaliso: Problems of Kinship, History, and Memory. Preliminary Report to the ISimangaliso Authority on Ethnographic Research with Land Claimants* (St Lucia: iSimangaliso Wetland Authority, 2008). This chapter does not engage directly with the hugely important and vexed politics of the "land question" since 1994, either as a national debate or in terms of the politics of land reform in KwaZulu-Natal, where customary tenure and authority have come acutely into question around communities' rights to refuse

mining and the extortionary reinvention of apartheid tribal law—on this complex debate, see Aninka Claassens, *Mining Magnates and Traditional Leaders: The Role of Law in Elevating Elite Interests and Deepening Exclusion, 2002–2018* (Mapungubwe: Mapungubwe Institute for Strategic Reflection, 2019).

59. The Surplus People Project, *Forced Removals in South Africa*, 4:3, argues that by the early 1980s, the supposedly "independent" homeland of KwaZulu was characterized by "grinding poverty; lack of infrastructural and industrial development; a high rate of male migrant labor; a high degree of landlessness among the supposedly subsistence sector; an overblown local bureaucracy; [and] poor health and welfare services. It [had] no basis for independent economic development but [was] totally dependent on the metropolitan/industrial centers that are located beyond its boundaries."

60. By mid-2012, Mondi had settled nine claims on land it owned, with thirty-three claims still outstanding. In total, approximately 50 percent of Mondi's forestry acreage was subject to land claims.

61. See Elizabeth A. Povinelli, "Sexuality at Risk: Psychoanalysis Metapragmatically," in *Homosexuality and Psychoanalysis*, ed. Tim Dean and Christopher Lane (Chicago: University of Chicago Press, 2001), 389, and in particular Elizabeth A. Povinelli, *The Cunning of Recognition: Indigenous Alterities and the Making of Australian Multiculturalism* (Durham, NC: Duke University Press, 2020).

62. Walker, *Landmarked*, 198.

63. These particular definitions derive from the Mabaso Land Claims Settlement Agreement of 2001: "'Claimed Land' means the land from which rights in land where dispossession was effected and for which the claim was lodged against the State for the restoration of such rights in land, which Claimed Land is more fully described by reference to the map attached hereto, marked Annexure A." "'Community' means the Mabaso households that were directly dispossessed of their rights in land, whether registered or not, and the households in the vicinity of the Claimed Land who are under the same governance structure and share the same area [*sic*] cultural, social and economic needs." "'Claimant Community' means those members of the Mabaso community who were dispossessed of their rights inland in 1970s due to the forced removal of members of the community from the land, as well as their direct descendants, the members of which are more fully described in the list attached hereto, marked annexure B." "'Beneficiary family' means where the original dispossessed is deceased and there is more than one direct descendant ('direct descendant' shall have the same meaning as assigned in Section 1 of the Act, and therefore includes the spouse or customary law spouse/s of an original family head) who is entitled to benefit under this agreement, such family shall be referred to as beneficiary."

64. For a critique of the Interim Protection of Informal Land Rights Act (IPILRA), see Claassens, *Mining Magnates*, and Claassens, "Denying Ownership and Equal

Citizenship: Continuities in the State's Use of Law and 'Custom,' 1913–2013," *Journal of Southern African Studies* 40, no. 4 (2014): 761–79; and Aninka Claassens and Catherine O'Regan, "Editorial Citizenship and Accountability: Customary Law and Traditional Leadership under South Africa's Democratic Constitution," *Journal of Southern African Studies* 47, no. 2 (2021): 155–72. For a fuller analysis of postapartheid land reform, see Ben Cousins, *At the Crossroads: Land and Agrarian Reform in South Africa into the 21st Century* (Cape Town/Johannesburg: Programme for Land and Agrarian Studies, University of the Western Cape/National Land Committee, 2000); Ben Cousins and Cherryl Walker, eds., *Land Divided, Land Restored: Land Reform in South Africa for the 21st Century* (Johannesburg: Jacana, 2015); Donna Hornby et al., eds., *Untitled: Securing Land Tenure in Urban and Rural South Africa* (Pietermaritzburg: UKZN Press, 2017); and Thembela Kepe and Ruth Hall, "Land Redistribution in South Africa: Towards Decolonisation or Recolonisation?," *Politikon* 45, no. 1 (2018): 128–37. In brief, IPILRA was intended to provide temporary protection for all people living on "communal" land in the former Bantustans, people living on trust land, people who previously had Permissions to Occupy (PTOs), and anyone living on land uninterrupted since 1997 "as if they were the owner," i.e., for those who had informal land rights not otherwise adequately protected by law. The people living in the former Bantustans were the most affected by the Land Acts and forced removals. Their structural vulnerability and poverty had been exacerbated by the breakdown in land administration. It was put in place to make sure that vulnerable people's informal land rights were protected and that these people were recognized as important stakeholders in any development or tenure upgrades on their land. IPILRA was therefore aimed at protecting people's rights while Parliament passed another permanent law that would strengthen people's land rights. It originally applied for a period of eighteen months, but also provided that the minister of land affairs could extend its provisions for up to twelve months at a time. The former Land Rights Bill of 1999 would have replaced IPILRA but was never introduced in Parliament. This has meant that IPILRA has been renewed by Parliament every year. The Communal Land Tenure Policy (CLTP) of September 2014, like the Communal Land Rights Act (CLRA) of 2003, proposed to transfer the "outer boundaries" of "tribal" land in the former Bantustans to "traditional councils" (the new name for the tribal authorities created during the Bantustan era). It has been extended each year since then. Its key provision requires that no person may be deprived of an informal land right without their consent.

65. As a collaboration between the Universities of Natal and Durban Westville (now combined in the University of KwaZulu-Natal) and the South African Medical Research Council, with funding from the Wellcome Trust, the Africa Centre has been collecting data since 1999. Information about these subjects, including mortality, fertility, and migration, is stored longitudinally in a single database: the

Africa Centre Demographic Information System (ACDIS). See Till Bärnighausen et al., "High HIV Incidence in a Community with High HIV Prevalence in Rural South Africa: Findings from a Prospective Population-Based Study," *AIDS* 22, no. 1 (2008): 139–44. It is one of only a few rural, long-term surveillance sites in the world with the capacity for such powerful spatial analysis of HIV in a population.

66. See S. D. Walter, "Disease Mapping: A Historical Perspective," in *Spatial Epidemiology: Methods and Applications*, ed. Paul Elliott, Jon Wakefield, and Nicola Best (Oxford: Oxford University Press, 2001), 223–39, and Paul Elliott and Daniel Wartenberg, "Spatial Epidemiology: Current Approaches and Future Challenges," *Environmental Health Perspectives* 112, no. 9 (2004): 998–1006.

67. For a critique of recruitment into clinical trials, see Steven Epstein, *Inclusion: The Politics of Difference in Medical Research* (Chicago: University of Chicago Press, 2007).

68. For the sake of historical accuracy, I refer here to the Africa Centre (AC) rather than AHRI, as the research in question was published under that institutional form.

69. See Anne Case and Cally Ardington, "The Impact of Parental Death on School Outcomes: Longitudinal Evidence from South Africa," *Demography* 43, no. 3 (2006): 401–20; and Anne Case, Alicia Menendez, and Cally Ardington, "Health Seeking Behavior in Northern KwaZulu-Natal," Working Paper no. 504 (Irving B. Harris Graduate School of Public Policy Studies, University of Chicago, 2005).

70. Bärnighausen et al., "High HIV Incidence." For a reappraisal of the crucial contributions of natural resources to marginal, multiple rural livelihood strategies, see Sheona Shackleton, Charlie Shackleton, and Ben Cousins, *Re-valuing the Communal Lands of Southern Africa: New Understandings of Rural Livelihoods* (London: Overseas Development Institute, 2000).

71. For a summary profile of the cohort, see Dickman Gareta et al., "Cohort Profile Update: Africa Centre Demographic Information System (ACDIS) and Population-Based HIV Survey," *International Journal of Epidemiology* 50, no. 1 (2021): 33–34.

72. P. Wenzel Geissler, ed., *Para-states and Medical Science: Making African Global Health* (Durham, NC: Duke University Press, 2015).

73. While HIV has been transformed, seemingly miraculously, from a death sentence to a chronic condition over the course of this research, the lived experience of receiving a diagnosis, in social terms, remains devastatingly lethal. See Lindsey Reynolds et al., "The Social Dynamics of Consent and Refusal in HIV Surveillance in Rural South Africa," *Social Science and Medicine* 77 (2013): 118–25; and Thomas Cousins and Lindsey Reynolds, "Blood Relations: HIV Surveillance and Fieldworker Intimacy in KwaZulu-Natal, South Africa," in *Medical Anthropology in Global Africa*, ed. Kathryn Rhine et al. (Lawrence: University of Kansas, Department of Anthropology, 2014), 79–88.

74. Frank Tanser et al., "High Coverage of ART Associated with Decline in Risk of HIV Acquisition in Rural KwaZulu-Natal, South Africa," *Science* 339, no. 6122 (2013): 966–71; and Jacob Bor et al., "Increases in Adult Life Expectancy in Rural South Africa: Valuing the Scale-Up of HIV Treatment," *Science* 339, no. 6122 (2013): 961–65.

75. For a critique of adherence to antiretroviral drugs, see Jonathan Stadler et al., "Adherence and the Lie in a HIV Prevention Clinical Trial," *Medical Anthropology* 35, no. 6 (2016): 503–16; Rebecca Hodes et al., "Pesky Metrics: The Challenges of Measuring ART Adherence among HIV-Positive Adolescents in South Africa," *Critical Public Health* 30, no. 2 (2020): 179–90; Eric Mykhalovskiy, Liza McCoy, and Michael Bresalier, "Compliance/Adherence, HIV, and the Critique of Medical Power," *Social Theory and Health* 2, no. 4 (2004): 315–40; and Vinh-Kim Nguyen et al., "Adherence as Therapeutic Citizenship: Impact of the History of Access to Antiretroviral Drugs on Adherence to Treatment," *AIDS* 21, no. 5 (2007): S31–35.

76. Frank Tanser et al., "Localized Spatial Clustering of HIV Infections in a Widely Disseminated Rural South African Epidemic," *International Journal of Epidemiology* 38, no. 4 (2009): 1 (emphasis added).

77. Tanser et al., "High Coverage," 966.

78. Tanser et al., 967.

79. Tanser et al., 970.

80. Tanser et al., "Localized Spatial Clustering." See also Robert Thornton, *Unimagined Community: Sex, Networks, and AIDS in Uganda and South Africa* (Berkeley: University of California Press, 2008).

81. David Harvey, *The New Imperialism* (Oxford: Oxford University Press, 2003).

82. For a critique of Treatment as Prevention, see Vinh-Kim Nguyen, "Treating to Prevent HIV: Population Trials and Experimental Societies," in *Para-states and Medical Science: Making African Global Health*, ed. Paul Wenzel Geissler (Durham, NC: Duke University Press, 2015).

83. James G. Ferguson, *Give a Man a Fish: Reflections on the New Politics of Distribution* (Durham, NC: Duke University Press, 2015).

84. Geissler, *Para-states and Medical Science.*

85. Nguyen, "Treating to Prevent HIV," 68.

86. Kaushik Sunder Rajan, *Pharmocracy: Value, Politics, and Knowledge in Global Biomedicine* (Durham, NC: Duke University Press, 2017).

87. So-called HIV hot spots were first revealed by Tanser et al., "Localized Spatial Clustering."

88. On shifting state perspectives on normative arrangements of domesticity, housing, and family, see Fiona C. Ross, *Raw Life, New Hope: Decency, Housing and Everyday Life in a Post-apartheid Community* (Cape Town: UCT Press, 2010).

89. Antiretroviral (ARV) treatment for everyone who tests positive was made fully available from September 2016. In 2020, the new fixed-dose combination ARV

called tenofovir/lamivudine/dolutegravir, simply known as TLD, was approved. See Thabo Molelekwa, "South Africa Rolls Out New Three-in-One HIV Pill," Health-e News, updated November 28, 2019, https://health-e.org.za/2019/11/28/south-africas -new-hiv-treatment-projected-to-roll-out-in-january/.

90. Till Bärnighausen, Nir Eyal, and Daniel Wikler, "HIV Treatment-as-Prevention Research at a Crossroads," *PLOS Medicine* 11, no. 6 (2014): e1001654.

91. On the ambivalent involvement of social scientists in HIV and global health interventions, see Randall Packard and Paul Epstein, "Epidemiologists, Social Scientists, and the Structure of Medical Research on AIDS in Africa," *Social Science and Medicine* 33, no. 7 (1991): 771–94; Didier Fassin, "That Obscure Object of Global Health," in *Medical Anthropology at the Intersections: Histories, Activisms, and Futures*, ed. Marcia C. Inhorn and Emily Wentzell (Durham, NC: Duke University Press, 2012); Didier Fassin, "A Case for Critical Ethnography: Rethinking the Early Years of the AIDS Epidemic in South Africa," *Social Science and Medicine* 99 (2013): 119–26; and João Biehl and Adriana Petryna, *When People Come First: Critical Studies in Global Health* (Princeton, NJ: Princeton University Press, 2013). For an explication of "critical praxis" in medical anthropology, see Merrill Singer, "Beyond the Ivory Tower: Critical Praxis in Medical Anthropology," *Medical Anthropology Quarterly* 9, no. 1 1995): 80–106; Chandra L. Ford and Collins O. Airhihenbuwa, "The Public Health Critical Race Methodology: Praxis for Antiracism Research," *Social Science and Medicine* 71, no. 8 (2010): 1390–98; and Michelle Pentecost et al., "Critical Orientations for Humanising Health Sciences Education in South Africa," *Medical Humanities* 44, no. 4 (2018): 221–29.

92. Helen Tilley, *Africa as a Living Laboratory: Empire, Development, and the Problem of Scientific Knowledge, 1870–1950* (Chicago: University of Chicago Press, 2011).

93. Gilles Deleuze, "What Children Say," in *Essays Critical and Clinical*, trans. Daniel W. Smith and Michael A. Greco (London: Verso, 1998), 61. For a brilliant analysis of children's drawings in another part of KwaZulu-Natal, thinking with Deleuze and a phenomenologically informed understanding of situated experience, see Patricia C. Henderson, "Mapping Journeys through Landscape: Phenomenological Explorations of Environment amongst Rural AIDS Orphans," in *Postcolonial African Anthropologies*, ed. Rosabelle Boswell and Francis B. Nyamnjoh (Cape Town: HSRC Press, 2017).

94. In isiZulu, "mpilo" is translated as "health or life"; "nhle" as "good." Here it is in the locative form used for indicating place or direction. Deleuze, in "What Children Say," 61, draws on the notion of path in an essay by Pierre Kaufmann, *Kurt Lewin: Une théorie du champ dans les sciences de l'homme* (Paris: Vrin, 1968).

95. Veena Das, "Tradition, Pluralism, Identity: Framing the Issues," in *Tradition, Pluralism and Identity: In Honour of T N Madan*, ed. Veena Das, Dipankar Gupta, and Patricia Uberoi (Delhi: SAGE, 1999), 9–21, cited in Mani Shekhar Singh, "What

Should Happen, but Has Not Yet Happened: Painterly Tales of Justice," *Contributions to Indian Sociology* 53, no. 1 (2019): 184–216.

96. Jean Hunleth, "Zambian Children's Imaginal Caring: On Fantasy, Play, and Anticipation in an Epidemic," *Cultural Anthropology* 34, no. 2 (2019): 155–86.

97. While this might look like play, in Jean Piaget's sense (*Play, Dreams and Imitation in Childhood* [London: Routledge, 1962]), even in the sense that Adam B. Seligman et al. (*Ritual and Its Consequences: An Essay on the Limits of Sincerity* [New York: Oxford University Press, 2008]) give it, I argue against this picture of play and developmentalism in the figure of the child.

98. I mean "uncanny" in the sense that Veena Das takes up the notion from Stanley Cavell: the shimmering sense that the ordinary, and the domestic, is constituted through the effort to brace meaning and everyday life against the possibility of its own misconstrual, its own implosion.

99. On the continuity of effort required for youth to go on resisting the state in the face of violent oppression, see Pamela Reynolds, *War in Worcester: Youth and the Apartheid State* (New York: Fordham University Press, 2013).

100. "If spatial forms are metapragmatic principles in another semiotic register, discourses must continually retranscribe these forms"; Povinelli, "Sexuality at Risk," 402.

101. Spiegel, "Walking Memories."

102. Foucault, *Security, Territory, Population*, 20.

103. For analyses of the political economy of migrant labor in the late apartheid period, see Colin Murray, *Black Mountain: Land, Class, and Power in the Eastern Orange Free State, 1880s to 1980s* (Edinburgh: Edinburgh University Press, 1992); Andrew D. Spiegel, "Changing Patterns of Migrant Labour and Rural Differentiation in Lesotho," *Social Dynamics* 6, no. 2 (1980): 1–13; and John Sharp and Andrew D. Spiegel, "Vulnerability to Impoverishment in South African Rural Areas: The Erosion of Kinship and Neighbourhood as Social Resources," *Africa: Journal of the International African Institute* 55, no. 2 (1985): 133–52. For a somewhat different account of domesticity and migrancy that brings "homeland" and "township" family life into a more imaginative relation, see Zolani Ngwane, "'Christmas Time' and the Struggles for the Household in the Countryside: Rethinking the Cultural Geography of Migrant Labour in South Africa," *Journal of Southern African Studies* 29, no. 3 (2003): 681–99.

104. Alberto Corsin Jimenez, "On Space as a Capacity," *Journal of the Royal Anthropological Institute* 9, no. 1 (2003): 137–53.

105. On the looping effects that help to "make up people," see Ian Hacking, "Making Up People," in *Reconstructing Individualism: Autonomy, Individuality, and the Self in Western Thought*, ed. Thomas C. Heller, Morton Sosna, and David E. Wellbery (Stanford, CA: Stanford University Press, 1986).

106. João de Pina-Cabral, "Agnatas, vizinhos e amigos: Variantes da vicinalidade em África, Europa e América," *Revista de antropologia* 57, no. 2 (2014): 23–56; João

de Pina-Cabral, "Partible Houses: Variants of Vicinage in Mozambique, Portugal and Brazil," *Articulo* 20 (2019); João de Pina-Cabral, "My Mother or Father: Person, Metaperson, and Transcendence in Ethnographic Theory," *Journal of the Royal Anthropological Institute* 25, no. 2 (2019): 303–23.

107. Pina-Cabral, "My Mother or Father," 1, original emphasis.

108. Pina-Cabral, 4. On "relatedness" in anthropology, see Janet Carsten, "Introduction: Cultures of Relatedness," in *Cultures of Relatedness: New Approaches to the Study of Kinship*, ed. Janet Carsten (Cambridge: Cambridge University Press, 2000).

109. W. David Hammond-Tooke, "Kinship, Locality, and Association: Hospitality Groups among the Cape Nguni," *Ethnology* 2, no. 3 (1963): 302–19.

110. Pina-Cabral, "Partible Houses," 1.

111. Giovanni da Col, "Strathern Bottle: On Topology, Ethnographic Theory, and the Method of Wonder," introduction to *Learning to See in Melanesia: Four Lectures Given in the Department of Social Anthropology, Cambridge University, 1993–2008*, by Marilyn Strathern (Chicago: HAU Books, 2013).

112. Phillips, "On Topology," 124, provides a brilliant review of the travels of topology from logic to mathematics and social theory, usefully troubling claims to novelty of a "topological turn" and suggesting that these new inventions of topological thinking themselves display topological qualities:

> It is now a matter of thinking through conceptions of the topos from at least Plato (the topos noetos) to contemporary adventures in urban geo-psychology, in which the topos signals a vogue for linking subject, space, place and relation in logicomathematical figures and forms. But beneath the appearance of a fashion perhaps something deeper should be comprehended. If a "turn" involves some kind of transformation, then, in the idiom of topology, we would have to acknowledge that the concern would be for the invariant properties that map it on the previous figures, now distorted by twists and turns into seductive new shapes.

113. Bruno Latour, *Reassembling the Social: An Introduction to Actor-Network-Theory* (Oxford: Oxford University Press, 2005). See also Frédéric Keck, "A Genealogy of Animal Diseases and Social Anthropology (1870–2000)," *Medical Anthropology Quarterly* 33, no. 1 (2019): 24–41.

114. Phillips, "On Topology," 125.

115. Phillips, 125.

116. Mol and Law, "Regions, Networks and Fluids," 643, emphasis in original.

117. Ann H. Kelly and Javier Lezaun, "Walking or Waiting? Topologies of the Breeding Ground in Malaria Control," *Science as Culture* 22, no. 1 (2013): 89.

118. Kelly and Lezaun, 90–91.

119. Ann H. Kelly, Hermione N. Boko Koudakossi, and Sarah J. Moore, "Repellents and New 'Spaces of Concern' in Global Health," *Medical Anthropology* 36, no. 5

(2017): 464–78. For analyses of houses and space, see Mary Douglas, "The Idea of a Home: A Kind of Space," *Social Research* 58, no. 1 (1991): 287–307, and Peter Sloterdijk, "Sphären III (Spheres III): Schäume (Foams)," *Plurale Sphärologie* (Frankfurt: Suhrkamp, 2004).

CONCLUSION: THE WORK OF REPAIR

1. Michelle Yates, "The Human-as-Waste, the Labor Theory of Value and Disposability in Contemporary Capitalism," *Antipode* 43, no. 5 (2011): 1679–95.

2. John M. Janzen, *Ngoma: Discourses of Healing in Central and Southern Africa* (Berkeley: University of California Press, 1992), and Robert Thornton, *Healing the Exposed Being: A South African Ngoma Tradition* (Johannesburg: Wits University Press, 2017).

3. "Ngoma dancers play in the space/time between vulnerability and aspiration, in an enduring relation with the history of violent encounter. In this space/time, ngoma's warrior politics hover between the easy instrumentalization of the arts and their relation to mere expression, between the enactment of violence and the pleasures of artfully rendering form. Ngoma rides the tension, finding its eloquence by pushing at the limits where the question of violence as performance is excited." Louise Meintjies, *Dust of the Zulu: Ngoma Aesthetics after Apartheid* (Durham, NC: Duke University Press, 2017), 2.

4. John M. Janzen, *Health in a Fragile State* (Madison: University of Wisconsin Press, 2019), shows how "health," as a complex object of concern for ordinary people and states alike, is premised on the notion that it is the political and social grounding of people's lives that constructs their well-being. And, crucially, that these political and social conditions are shaped profoundly by multiple histories—from the global and colonial to the microdynamics of contemporary African politics. It is a brilliant ethnographic exposition of health in terms of a "fragile state" in the history of the lower Congo.

5. Hannah Arendt, *The Human Condition* (1958; repr., Chicago: University of Chicago Press, 1998).

6. On the long debate on the relation between class and race, see Ulrike Kistner, "How 'Class' Came to Marx—Taking a Longer View on 'Race'-'Class' Conjunctions and Disjunctions," *Social Dynamics* 46, no. 1 (2020): 36–49.

7. Karl Marx, *Capital*, vol. 3 (London: Electric Book, 2000), 116.

8. Steven Feierman, "Struggles for Control: The Social Roots of Health and Healing in Modern Africa," *African Studies Review* 28, no. 2–3 (1985): 90.

9. Harold Wolpe, "Capitalism and Cheap Labour-Power in South Africa: From Segregation to Apartheid," *Economy and Society* 1, no. 4 (1972): 425–56.

10. Martin Legassick, "South Africa: Capital Accumulation and Violence," *Economy and Society* 3, no. 3 (1974): 253–91; Michael Williams, "An Analysis of South

African Capitalism—Neo-Ricardianism or Marxism?," *Bulletin of the Conference of Socialist Economists* 1, no. 4 (1975); Simon Clarke, "Capital, Fractions of Capital and the State: 'Neo-Marxist' Analysis of the South African State," *Capital and Class* 2, no. 2 (1978): 32–77; Martin Legassick and Harold Wolpe, "The Bantustans and Capital Accumulation in South Africa," *Review of African Political Economy* 3, no. 7 (1976): 87–107. See also Nicoli Nattrass, "Controversies about Capitalism and Apartheid in South Africa: An Economic Perspective," *Journal of Southern African Studies* 17, no. 4 (1991): 654–77.

11. Patrick Bond, *Elite Transition: From Apartheid to Neoliberalism in South Africa* (London: Pluto, 2000); Gillian Hart, *Reworking Apartheid Legacies: Global Competition, Gender and Social Wages in South Africa, 1980–2000* (Geneva: United Nations Research Institute for Social Development, 2002); Haroon Bhorat and Rashad Cassim, "The Challenge of Growth, Employment and Poverty in the South African Economy since Democracy: An Exploratory Review of Selected Issues," *Development Southern Africa* 21, no. 1 (2004): 7–31; Franco Barchiesi, *Precarious Liberation: Workers, the State, and Contested Social Citizenship in Postapartheid South Africa* (Albany, NY: SUNY Press, 2011); Ivor Chipkin et al., *Shadow State* (Johannesburg: Wits University Press, 2018); and Andries du Toit, "Poverty Measurement Blues: Beyond 'Q-squared' Approaches to Understanding Chronic Poverty in South Africa", in *Poverty Dynamics: Interdisciplinary Perspectives*, ed. Tony Addison, David Hulme, and Ravi Kanbur (Oxford: Oxford University Press, 2009, 225–46).

12. Du Toit, "Poverty Measurement Blues"; Andries du Toit, "'Social Exclusion' Discourse and Chronic Poverty: A South African Case Study," *Development and Change* 35, no. 5 (2004): 987–1010; Sam Hickey and Andries du Toit, "Adverse Incorporation, Social Exclusion and Chronic Poverty" (Chronic Poverty Research Centre Working Paper 81, Institute for Development Policy and Management, School of Environment and Development, University of Manchester, 2007).

13. Achille Mbembe, "Necropolitics," *Public Culture* 15, no. 1 (2003): 11–40; see also Jason Hickel, *Democracy as Death: The Moral Order of Anti-liberal Politics in South Africa* (Berkeley: University of California Press, 2015).

14. Jean-François Bayart, *The State in Africa: The Politics of the Belly* (New York: Pantheon Books, 1993); Deborah Posel, "Races to Consume: Revisiting South Africa's History of Race, Consumption and the Struggle for Freedom," *Ethnic and Racial Studies* 33, no. 2 (2010): 157–75.

15. See Stephanie Barrientos, "Contract Labour: The 'Achilles Heel' of Corporate Codes in Commercial Value Chains," *Development and Change* 39, no. 6 (2008): 977–90.

16. On slavery and adverse incorporation, see Nicola Phillips and Leonardo Sakamoto, "The Dynamics of Adverse Incorporation in Global Production Networks: Poverty, Vulnerability and 'Slave Labour' in Brazil" (Chronic Poverty Research Centre Working Paper 175, 2011). On structural violence, see Paul Farmer, "On

Suffering and Structural Violence: A View from Below," in *Social Suffering*, ed. Arthur Kleinman, Veena Das, and Margaret Lock (Berkeley: University of California Press, 1997).

17. Archie Mafeje, "On the Articulation of Modes of Production: Review Article," *Journal of Southern African Studies* 8, no. 1 (1981): 123–38.

18. Moishe Postone, "Theorizing the Contemporary World: Robert Brenner, Giovanni Arrighi, David Harvey," in *Political Economy and Global Capitalism: The 21st Century, Present and Future*, ed. Robert Albritton, Robert Jessop, and Richard Westra (London: Anthem, 2007), 22, quoted in Bernard Dubbeld, "Thinking with Capital Today: A Brief Introduction," *Social Dynamics* 46, no. 1 (2020): 4.

19. Hayder Al-Mohammad and Daniela Peluso, "Ethics and the 'Rough Ground' of the Everyday: The Overlappings of Life in Postinvasion Iraq," *HAU: Journal of Ethnographic Theory* 2, no. 2 (2012): 42–58.

20. "I take for granted that an *otherwise* exists everywhere in the world, but my question is: What are the institutions that make certain forms of *otherwise* invisible and impractical? And one answer takes me to the corporeal and the other to the carnal." Povinelli, in Kim Turcot DiFruscia, "Shapes of Freedom: An Interview with Elizabeth A. Povinelli," *Altérités* 7, no. 1 (2010): 90.

21. Elizabeth A. Povinelli, *Economies of Abandonment: Social Belonging and Endurance in Late Liberalism* (Durham, NC: Duke University Press, 2011), 108.

22. See DiFruscia, "Shapes of Freedom." See also Povinelli, *Economies of Abandonment*, 108: "I have distinguished carnality and corporeality as an order of substance (carnality) that is excreted from the organization of substance (corporeality) but not equivalent to it."

23. Povinelli, *Economies of Abandonment*, 45.

24. Povinelli, 32.

25. "Every scene of endurance, and certainly the scenes that concern this book, is shot through with multiple and incommensurate configurations of tense, eventfulness, and ethical substance and aggregations of life. The alternative social projects that lie within these stretched and striated spaces must survive eventfulness that is below the threshold of the catastrophic and ethical substance as sacrifice" (Povinelli, 32).

26. On the chronotopes of apartheid, see Julia Sonnleitner, "Chronotopes of Apartheid," *Wiener linguistische Gazette* 83 (2018): 27–48.

27. Kim Turcot DiFruscia, "Listening to Voices: An Interview with Veena Das," *Altérités* 7, no. 1 (2010): 140.

28. Roma Chatterji, ed., *Wording the World: Veena Das and Scenes of Inheritance* (New York: Fordham University Press, 2014), 4.

29. For North American critiques of race and ecology, see Deborah A. Thomas, *Political Life in the Wake of the Plantation: Sovereignty, Witnessing, Repair*

(Durham, NC: Duke University Press, 2019); and Donna Haraway, "Anthropocene, Capitalocene, Plantationocene, Chthulucene: Making Kin," *Environmental Humanities* 6, no. 1 (2015): 159–65. For South Asian historiographies of colonial plantations, see Henry Bernstein, Tom Brass, and E. Valentine Daniel, *Plantations, Proletarians, and Peasants in Colonial Asia* (London: Cass, 1992). On Central African experiences of terror, see Adam Hochschild, *King Leopold's Ghost: A Story of Greed, Terror, and Heroism in Colonial Africa* (New York: Houghton Mifflin Harcourt, 1998); and on the erotics of rainforest capitalism, see Thomas Hendriks, *Rainforest Capitalism: Power and Masculinity in a Congolese Timber Concession* (Durham, NC: Duke University Press, 2022). For accounts of South American extractivism, see Marc Edelman, "'Haciendas and Plantations': History and Limitations of a 60-Year-Old Taxonomy," *Critique of Anthropology* 38, no. 4 (2018): 387–406, and Michael T. Taussig, *The Devil and Commodity Fetishism in South America* (Chapel Hill: University of North Carolina Press, 1980).

30. Hannah Landecker, "Eating as Dialogue, Food as Technology," *Noēma*, June 18, 2020, https://www.noemamag.com/eating-as-dialogue-food-as-technology/.

31. Landecker.

32. Anson Rabinbach, *The Human Motor: Energy, Fatigue, and the Origins of Modernity* (Berkeley: University of California Press, 1992).

33. Stephen Gudeman, "Vital Energy," *Social Analysis* 56, no. 1 (2012): 57–73.

34. Gudeman, 57.

35. Giovanni da Col, "Introduction: Natural Philosophies of Fortune—Luck, Vitality, and Uncontrolled Relatedness," *Social Analysis* 56, no. 1 (2012): 9.

36. See da Col, 13–15, for a genealogy of "uncontrolled relatedness" and an anthropological theory of analogic fortune.

37. Hylton White, "Custom, Normativity and Authority in South Africa," *Journal of Southern African Studies* 41, no. 5 (2015): 1005–17.

38. Hannah J. Dawson and Elizabeth Fouksman, "Labour, Laziness and Distribution: Work Imaginaries among the South African Unemployed," *Africa* 90, no. 2 (2020): 229–51.

39. See Paul Rabinow and Anthony Stavrianakis, *From Chaos to Solace: Topological Meditations* (Berkeley, CA: Anthropology of the Contemporary Research Collaboratory, 2021).

40. Isolde Birdthistle et al., "Recent Levels and Trends in HIV Incidence Rates among Adolescent Girls and Young Women in Ten High-Prevalence African Countries: A Systematic Review and Meta-analysis," *Lancet Global Health* 7, no. 11 (2019): e1521–40; and Alain Vandormael et al., "Declines in HIV Incidence among Men and Women in a South African Population-Based Cohort," *Nature Communications* 10, no. 1 2019): 5482.

41. South African Medical Research Council (SAMRC), "Report on Weekly Deaths in South Africa: 29 Dec 2019–19 Feb 2022," SAMRC website, last accessed

February 28, 2022, https://www.samrc.ac.za/reports/report-weekly-deaths-south
-africa.

42. David J. Hunter et al., "Addressing Vaccine Inequity—Covid-19 Vaccines as a Global Public Good," *New England Journal of Medicine*, February 23, 2022; *Nature*, editorial, "Africa Is Bringing Vaccine Manufacturing Home," February 9, 2022, https://www.nature.com/articles/d41586-022-00335-9.

43. Jasbir K. Puar, *The Right to Maim: Debility, Capacity, Disability* (Durham, NC: Duke University Press, 2017).

44. Statistics South Africa, "Quarterly Labour Force Survey: Quarter 2: 2022," statistical report, Stats SA website, March 29, 2022, https://www.statssa.gov.za/?p =15685.

45. Servaas van der Berg and Leila Patel, "COVID-19 Pandemic Has Triggered a Rise in Hunger in South Africa," *The Conversation*, July 21, 2021, https://thecon versation.com/covid-19-pandemic-has-triggered-a-rise-in-hunger-in-south-africa -164581.

46. Ben Cousins, "What Landmark Kwazulu-Natal Court Ruling Means for Land Reform in South Africa," *The Conversation*, June 22, 2021, https://theconversation .com/what-landmark-kwazulu-natal-court-ruling-means-for-land-reform-in -south-africa-162969.

47. On the exhaustion of the logic of work and the emergence of a new politics of distribution, see James G. Ferguson, *Give a Man a Fish: Reflections on the New Politics of Distribution* (Durham, NC: Duke University Press, 2015). For a critique of appeals to work as a political technique, see Barchiesi, *Precarious Liberation,* and Bernard Dubbeld, "Translating E. P. Thompson's Marxian Critique: Contesting 'Context' in South African Studies," *Social Dynamics* 46, no. 1 (2020): 67–85.

48. Aninka Claassens and Catherine O'Regan, "Editorial Citizenship and Account-ability: Customary Law and Traditional Leadership under South Africa's Demo-cratic Constitution," *Journal of Southern African Studies* 47, no. 2. (2021): 155–72.

49. On the relationship between HIV and hunger, see Ippolytos Kalofonos, *All I Eat Is Medicine: Going Hungry in Mozambique's AIDS Economy* (Oakland: Univer-sity of California Press, 2021); and Thomas Cousins, "Antiretroviral Therapy and Nutrition in Southern Africa: Citizenship and the Grammar of Hunger," *Medical Anthropology: Cross-Cultural Studies in Health and Illness* 35, no. 5 (2016): 433–46.

50. Ben Cousins and Cherryl Walker, eds., *Land Divided, Land Restored: Land Reform in South Africa for the 21st Century* (Johannesburg: Jacana, 2015); and Lun-gisile Ntsebeza and Ruth Hall, eds., *The Land Question in South Africa: The Chal-lenge of Transformation and Redistribution* (Johannesburg: HSRC Press, 2007).

51. James G. Ferguson, *Presence and Social Obligation: An Essay on the Share* (Chicago: Prickly Paradigm, 2021).

52. Andries du Toit, "The Land and Its People: The South African 'Land Ques-tion' and the Post-apartheid Political Order" (unpublished manuscript, 2021).

53. See Anson Rabinbach, *The Eclipse of the Utopias of Labor* (New York: Fordham University Press, 2018); and Rabinbach, *Human Motor*.

54. See Alexander Kluge and Oskar Negt, *History and Obstinacy*, ed. Devin Fore (Cambridge, MA: MIT Press, 2014); and Anna Lowenhaupt Tsing, *Friction: An Ethnography of Global Connection* (Princeton, NJ: Princeton University Press, 2005).

55. On the question of ecological reparation, see Dimitris Papadopoulos, Maria Puig de la Bellacasa, and Maddalena Tacchetti, *Ecological Reparation: Repair, Remediation and Resurgence in Social and Environmental Conflict* (Bristol: Bristol University Press, 2022).

56. Michael D. Jackson, "Life and Concept," in *Living and Dying in the Contemporary World: A Compendium*, ed. Veena Das and Clara Han (Oakland: University of California Press, 2016), 449–62.

57. Kader Attia, "In Conversation: Kitty Scott and Kader Attia Discuss the Concept of Repair," in *The Repair: From Occident to Extra-Occidental Cultures* (Berlin: Green Box, 2014).

58. Denis Hirson, *White Scars: On Reading and Rites of Passage* (Johannesburg: Jacana, 2006), 14.

59. "The ways we stretch toward one another"—the felicitous phrase comes from Pamela Reynolds, and is the title of a collection of essays on her work; see Todd Meyers, ed., *The Ways We Stretch toward One Another: Thoughts on Anthropology through the Work of Pamela Reynolds* (Bamenda, Cameroon: Langaa RPCIG, 2017). On the "mutuomorphic" qualities of language, see Peter McDonald, *Artefacts of Writing: Ideas of the State and Communities of Letters from Matthew Arnold to Xu Bing* (Oxford: Oxford University Press, 2017).

BIBLIOGRAPHY

Abate, Michelle Ann. *Tomboys: A Literary and Cultural History*. Philadelphia: Temple University Press, 2008.

Academy of Science of South Africa (ASSAf). *HIV/AIDS, TB and Nutrition: Scientific Enquiry into the Nutritional Influences on Human Immunity with Special Reference to HIV Infection and Active TB in South Africa*. Pretoria: Academy of Science of South Africa, 2007.

Adebayo, Sakiru. "Unmournable Bodies, Embodied Monuments and Bodily Truths: Rethinking Reconciliation in Zulu Love Letter." *Safundi* 22, no. 1 (2021): 7–10. https://doi.org/10.1080/17533171.2020.1823736.

Agamben, Giorgio. *Homo Sacer: Sovereign Power and Bare Life*. Stanford, CA: Stanford University Press, 1998.

Agha, Asif. *Language and Social Relations*. Cambridge: Cambridge University Press, 2007.

Al-Mohammad, Hayder, and Daniela Peluso. "Ethics and the 'Rough Ground' of the Everyday: The Overlappings of Life in Postinvasion Iraq." *HAU: Journal of Ethnographic Theory* 2, no. 2 (2012): 42–58.

Andrews, Penelope E. "Reparations for Apartheid's Victims: The Path to Reconciliation." *DePaul Law Review* 53 (2004): 1155–80.

Appadurai, Arjun, ed. *The Social Life of Things: Commodities in Cultural Perspective*. Cambridge: Cambridge University Press, 1986.

Appiah, Kwame Anthony. "The Case for Capitalizing the B in Black." *The Atlantic*, June 18, 2020.

Archer, Colleen E., Christopher C. Appleton, Samson Mukaratirwa, Jennifer Lamb, and M. Corrie Schoeman. "Endo-parasites of Public-Health Importance Recovered from Rodents in the Durban Metropolitan Area, South Africa." *Southern African Journal of Infectious Diseases* 32, no. 2 (2017): 57–66.

Arendt, Hannah. *The Human Condition*. 1958. Reprint, Chicago: University of Chicago Press, 1998.

Argenti, Nicolas. *The Intestines of the State: Youth, Violence, and Belated Histories in the Cameroon Grassfields.* Chicago: University of Chicago Press, 2007.

Arndt, Channing, Rob Davies, Sherwin Gabriel, Laurence Harris, Konstantin Makrelov, Sherman Robinson, Stephanie Levy, Witness Simbanegavi, Dirk van Seventer, and Lillian Anderson. "Covid-19 Lockdowns, Income Distribution, and Food Security: An Analysis for South Africa." *Global Food Security* 26 (2020): 100410. https://doi.org/https://doi.org/10.1016/j.gfs.2020.100410.

Ashforth, Adam. "Reflections on Spiritual Insecurity in a Modern African City (Soweto)." *African Studies Review* 41, no. 3 (1998): 39–67. https://doi.org/10.2307/525353.

———. *Witchcraft, Violence, and Democracy in South Africa.* Chicago: University of Chicago Press, 2004.

———. "The Xhosa Cattle Killing and the Politics of Memory." *Sociological Forum* 6, no. 3 (1991): 581–92.

Association for Rural Advancement (AFRA). *Dukuduku: The Forest of Our Discontent.* Durban: Special Report, 2003.

Attia, Kader. *Continuum of Repair: The Light of Jacob's Ladder.* London, UK: Whitechapel Gallery, 2013. Exhibition catalog.

———. "In Conversation: Kitty Scott and Kader Attia Discuss the Concept of Repair." In *The Repair: From Occident to Extra-Occidental Cultures.* Berlin: Green Box, 2014.

———. *The Repair: From Occident to Extra-Occidental Cultures.* Berlin: Green Box, 2014.

Atwood, Amanda. "Harare in Four Pharmacies." *Public Books*, April 2, 2016.

Bank, Andrew. *Pioneers of the Field: South Africa's Women Anthropologists. The International African Library.* Cambridge: Cambridge University Press, 2016. https://doi.org/DOI: 10.1017/CBO9781316584187.

Barchiesi, Franco. "Commodification, Economic Restructuring, and the Changing Urban Geography of Labour in Post-apartheid South Africa: The Case of Gauteng Province, 199Q2001." *Urban Forum* 17 (2006): 93–124.

———. "Imagining the Patriotic Worker: The Idea of 'Decent Work' in the ANC's Political Discourse." In *One Hundred Years of the ANC: Debating Liberation Histories Today*, edited by Arianna Lissoni, Jon Soske, Natasha Erlank, Noor Nieftagodien, and Omar Badsha, 111–34. Johannesburg: Wits University Press, 2012.

———. "Precarious Liberation: A Rejoinder." *South African Review of Sociology* 43, no. 1 (2012): 98–105. https://doi.org/10.1080/21528586.2012.678639.

———. *Precarious Liberation: Workers, the State, and Contested Social Citizenship in Postapartheid South Africa.* Albany, NY: SUNY Press, 2011.

———. "Wage Labor, Precarious Employment, and Social Inclusion in the Making of South Africa's Postapartheid Transition." *African Studies Review* 51, no. 2 (2008): 119–42. https://doi.org/10.1353/arw.0.0083.

Bärnighausen, Till, Nir Eyal, and Daniel Wikler. "HIV Treatment-as-Prevention Research at a Crossroads." *PLOS Medicine* 11, no. 6 (2014): e1001654.

Bärnighausen, Till, Frank Tanser, Zanomsa Gqwede, Clifford Mbizana, Kobus Herbst, and Marie-Louise Newell. "High HIV Incidence in a Community with High HIV Prevalence in Rural South Africa: Findings from a Prospective Population-Based Study." *AIDS* 22, no. 1 (2008): 139–44.

Barrientos, Stephanie. "Contract Labour: The 'Achilles Heel' of Corporate Codes in Commercial Value Chains." *Development and Change* 39, no. 6 (2008): 977–90.

Bayart, Jean-François. *The State in Africa: The Politics of the Belly*. New York: Pantheon Books, 1993.

Beattie, John. "Representations of the Self in Traditional Africa." *Africa: Journal of the International African Institute* 50, no. 3 (1980): 313–20.

Beinart, William. *The Political Economy of Pondoland 1860 to 1930*. Johannesburg: Cambridge University Press, 1982.

Beinart, William, and Colin Bundy. *Hidden Struggles in Rural South Africa: Politics and Popular Movements in the Transkei and Eastern Cape, 1890–1930*. London: James Currey, 1987.

Bennett, Brett, and Fred Kruger. *Forestry and Water Conservation in South Africa: History, Science and Policy*. Acton: ANU Press, 2015.

Bennett, Tom W. "Re-introducing African Customary Law to the South African Legal System." *American Journal of Comparative Law* 57, no. 1 (2009): 1–32.

Benveniste, Émile. *Problems in General Linguistics*. Miami, FL: University of Miami Press, 1971.

Berglund, Axel-Ivar. *Zulu Thought-Patterns and Symbolism*. Cape Town: David Philip, 1976.

Berlant, Lauren. "Slow Death (Sovereignty, Obesity, Lateral Agency)." *Critical Enquiry* 33, no. 4 (2007): 754–80.

Bernstein, Henry, Tom Brass, and E. Valentine Daniel. *Plantations, Proletarians, and Peasants in Colonial Asia*. London: Cass, 1992.

Besky, Sarah. "Can a Plantation Be Fair? Paradoxes and Possibilities in Fair Trade Darjeeling Tea Certification." *Anthropology of Work Review* 29, no. 1 (2008): 1–9. https://doi.org/10.1111/j.1548-1417.2008.00006.x.

Bethlehem, L. *National Forestry Action Programme. Key Issue Paper: Labour Relations*. Pretoria: DWAF, 1997.

Bezuidenhout, Andries, and Sakhela Buhlungu. "From Compounded to Fragmented Labour: Mineworkers and the Demise of Compounds in South Africa." *Antipode* 43, no. 2 (2011): 237–63. https://doi.org/https://doi.org/10.1111/j.1467-8330.2010.00758.x.

Bhabha, Homi. *The Location of Culture*. London: Routledge, 1994.

Bhana, Surendra, ed. *Essays on Indentured Indians in Natal*. Leeds: Peepal Tree, 1990.

Bhorat, Haroon, and Rashad Cassim. "The Challenge of Growth, Employment and Poverty in the South African Economy since Democracy: An Exploratory Review of Selected Issues." *Development Southern Africa* 21, no. 1 (2004): 7–31.

Bhorat, Haroon, and Safia Khan. "Structural Change and Patterns of Inequality in the South African Labour Market." Working Papers 201801, University of Cape Town, Development Policy Research Unit, 2018.

Biehl, João, and Adriana Petryna. *When People Come First: Critical Studies in Global Health*. Princeton, NJ: Princeton University Press, 2013.

Biggs, Chara. "The Prevalence and Degree of Dehydration in Rural South African Forestry Workers." Master's thesis, University of KwaZulu-Natal, 2008. https://researchspace.ukzn.ac.za/jspui/handle/10413/3448, last accessed January 28, 2022.

Biko, Steve. *I Write What I Like: Selected Writings*. Edited by Aelred Stubbs. Preface by Desmond Tutu. Introduction by Malusi and Thoko Mpumlwana. New foreword by Lewis R. Gordon. Chicago: University of Chicago Press, 2002. First published 1978.

Birdthistle, Isolde, Clare Tanton, Andrew Tomita, Kristen de Graaf, Susan B. Schaffnit, Frank Tanser, and Emma Slaymaker. "Recent Levels and Trends in HIV Incidence Rates among Adolescent Girls and Young Women in Ten High-Prevalence African Countries: A Systematic Review and Meta-analysis." *Lancet Global Health* 7, no. 11 (2019): e1521–40.

Bjerk, Paul K. "They Poured Themselves into the Milk: Zulu Political Philosophy under Shaka." *Journal of African History* 47 (2006): 1–19.

Blackburn, Robin. *The Making of New World Slavery: From the Baroque to the Modern 1492–1800*. London: Verso, 1997.

Blacking, J. "Fictitious Kinship amongst Girls of the Venda of the Northern Transvaal." *Man* 59, no. 8 (1959): 155–58. http://www.jstor.org/stable/10.2307/2796752.

———. "Uses of the Kinship Idiom in Friendships at Some Venda and Zulu Schools." In *Social System and Tradition in Southern Africa*, edited by John Argyle and Eleanor Preston-Whyte, 101–17. Oxford: Oxford University Press, 1978.

Blacking, John, and Noam J. Pines. "Professor Julius Lewin." *African Studies* 27, no. 1 (January 1, 1968): 45–46. https://doi.org/10.1080/00020186808707275.

Boellstorff, Tom, and Naisargi N. Dave. "Introduction: The Production and Reproduction of Queer Anthropology." Theorizing the Contemporary, *Fieldsights*, July 21, 2015. https://culanth.org/fieldsights/introduction-the-production-and-reproduction-of-queer-anthropology.

Bohannan, Paul. "On Anthropologists' Use of Language." *American Anthropologist* 60, no. 1 (1958): 161–63. http://www.jstor.org/stable/665617.

Bolt, Maxim. "Camaraderie and Its Discontents: Class Consciousness, Ethnicity and Divergent Masculinities among Zimbabwean Migrant Farmworkers in South Africa." *Journal of Southern African Studies* 36, no. 2 (2010): 377–93. https://doi.org/10.1080/03057070.2010.485790.

Bond, Patrick. *Elite Transition: From Apartheid to Neoliberalism in South Africa.* London: Pluto, 2000.

Bor, Jacob, Abraham J. Herbst, Marie-Louise Newell, and Till Bärnighausen. "Increases in Adult Life Expectancy in Rural South Africa: Valuing the Scale-up of HIV Treatment." *Science* 339, no. 6122 (2013): 961–65.

Boswell, Rosabelle, and Francis B. Nyamnjoh. *Postcolonial African Anthropologies.* Cape Town: HSRC Press, 2017.

Bouquet, Mary. "Family Trees and Their Affinities: The Visual Imperative of the Genealogical Diagram." *Journal of the Royal Anthropological Institute* 2, no. 1 (1996): 43–66. https://doi.org/10.2307/3034632.

Brain, James L., M. T. Ruel, and Igor Kopytoff. "The Authority of Ancestors." *Man,* n.s., 17, no. 3 (1982): 546–48.

Breckenridge, Keith. "Revenge of the Commons: The Crisis in the South African Mining Industry." History Workshop: Histories of the Present, November 5, 2012. https://www.historyworkshop.org.uk/revenge-of-the-commons-the -crisis-in-the-south-african-mining-industry/.

Brookes, Edgar H., and Colin Webb. *A History of Natal.* Pietermaritzburg: University of Natal Press, 1965.

Bruyninckx, Joeri. "Synchronicity: Time, Technicians, Instruments, and Invisible Repair." *Science, Technology, and Human Values* 42, no. 5 (2017): 822–47. https://doi.org/10.1177/0162243916689137.

Bryant, A. T. *Zulu Medicine and Medicine Men.* 1909. Cape Town: Struik, 1966.

———. *The Zulu People.* Pietermaritzburg: Shuter and Shooter, 1949.

Burke, Timothy. *Lifebuoy Men, Lux Women: Commodification, Consumption, and Cleanliness in Modern Zimbabwe.* Durham, NC: Duke University Press, 1996.

Buthelezi, Mbongiseni. "Sifuna Umlando Wethu (We Are Searching for Our History): Oral Literature and the Meanings of the Past in Post-apartheid South Africa." PhD diss., Columbia University, 2012.

———. "We Need New Names Too." In *Tribing and Untribing the Archive: Identity and the Material Record in Southern KwaZulu-Natal in the Late Independent and Colonial Periods,* edited by Carolyn Hamilton and Nessa Leibhammer, 2:586–99. 2 vols. Durban: University of KwaZulu-Natal Press, 2016.

Butler, Judith. *The Force of Nonviolence: An Ethico-political Bind.* New York: Verso Books, 2020.

Cairns, R. I. "Outgrower Timber Schemes in KwaZulu-Natal—Do They Build Sustainable Rural Livelihoods and What Interventions Should Be Made?" IIED and CSIR, 2000.

Camminga, B. "The Politics and Limits of Transgender in South Africa." In *Transgender Refugees and the Imagined South Africa: Bodies over Borders and Borders over Bodies,* 85–128. London: Palgrave Macmillan, 2019.

Canguilhem, Georges. "Health: Crude Concept and Philosophical Question." *Public Culture* 20, no. 3 (2008): 467–77.

———. *Knowledge of Life.* Edited by Paola Marrati and Todd Meyers. Translated by Stephanos Geroulanos and Daniela Ginsburg. New York: Fordham University Press, 2008.

———. *The Normal and the Pathological.* New York: Zone Books, 1994.

Carrier, Joseph, and S. O. Murray. "Women-Women Marriage in Africa." In *Boy-Wives and Female Husbands: Studies of African Homosexualities,* edited by Stephen O. Murray and Will Roscoe, 255–66. New York: St Martin's, 1998.

Carsten, Janet. *After Kinship.* Cambridge: Cambridge University Press, 2004.

———. "Introduction: Cultures of Relatedness." In *Cultures of Relatedness: New Approaches to the Study of Kinship,* edited by Janet Carsten. Cambridge: Cambridge University Press, 2000.

Carsten, Janet, and Stephen Hugh-Jones. *About the House: Lévi-Strauss and Beyond.* Cambridge: Cambridge University Press, 1995.

Carton, Benedict, John Laband, and Jabulani Sithole. *Zulu Identities: Being Zulu, Past and Present.* Pietermaritzburg: University of KwaZulu-Natal Press, 2008.

Casale, Daniela, and Dorrit Posel. "The Feminisation of the Labour Force in South Africa: An Analysis of Recent Data and Trends." *South African Journal of Economics* 70, no. 1 (2002): 156–84.

Case, Anne, and Cally Ardington. "The Impact of Parental Death on School Outcomes: Longitudinal Evidence from South Africa." *Demography* 43, no. 3 (2006): 401–20.

Case, Anne, Alicia Menendez, and Cally Ardington. "Health Seeking Behavior in Northern KwaZulu-Natal." Working Paper no. 504, Irving B. Harris Graduate School of Public Policy Studies, University of Chicago, 2005.

Cavell, Stanley. *The Claim of Reason: Wittgenstein, Skepticism, Morality, and Tragedy.* NewYork: Oxford University Press, 1979.

Chakrabarty, Dipesh. *Provincializing Europe: Postcolonial Thought and Historical Difference.* Princeton, NJ: Princeton University Press, 2000.

Chamberlain, Doubell, Hassan Essop, Christine Hougaard, Stephan Malherbe, and Richard Walker. *Genesis Report Part I: The Contribution, Costs, and Development Opportunities of the Forestry, Timber, Pulp and Paper Industries in South Africa.* Johannesburg: Genesis Analytics, 2005.

Chatterji, Roma, ed. *Wording the World: Veena Das and Scenes of Inheritance.* New York: Fordham University Press, 2014.

Chipkin, Ivor. *Do South Africans Exist? Nationalism, Democracy and the Identity of 'the People.'* Johannesburg: Wits University Press, 2007. https://doi.org/10.18772/12007044457.

Chipkin, Ivor, Mark Swilling, Haroon Bhorat, Mbongiseni Buthelezi, Sikhulekile Duma, Hannah Friedenstein, Lumkile Mondi, et al. *Shadow State.* Johannesburg: Wits University Press, 2018.

Chirikure, Shadreck. *Great Zimbabwe: Reclaiming a 'Confiscated' Past*. London: Routledge, 2021.

Claassens, Aninka. "Denying Ownership and Equal Citizenship: Continuities in the State's Use of Law and 'Custom,' 1913–2013." *Journal of Southern African Studies* 40, no. 4 (2014): 761–79.

———. *Mining Magnates and Traditional Leaders: The Role of Law in Elevating Elite Interests and Deepening Exclusion, 2002–2018*. Mapungubwe: Mapungubwe Institute for Strategic Reflection, 2019.

Claassens, Aninka, and Catherine O'Regan. "Editorial Citizenship and Accountability: Customary Law and Traditional Leadership under South Africa's Democratic Constitution." *Journal of Southern African Studies* 47, no. 2 (2021): 155–72.

Clarke, Jeanette. "FSC-Certified Plantations and Local Communities: Challenges, Activities, Standards, and Solutions. Case Study: Changing Labour Practices at Mondi Forests South Africa." Unpublished report, 2011.

———. "Investigation of Working Conditions of Forestry Workers in South Africa." Department of Agriculture, Forestry and Fisheries, Government of South Africa, 2012.

———. "A Job of Choice or a Job of Last Resort?" *SA Forestry Magazine*, October 2011.

Clarke, Jeanette, and Moenieba Isaacs. *Forestry Contractors in South Africa: What Role in Reducing Poverty?* London, UK: Programme for Land and Agrarian Studies, University of the Western Cape, South Africa, and International Institute for Environment and Development, 2005.

Clarke, Marlea. "Supporting the 'Elite' Transition in South Africa: Policing in a Violent, Neoliberal Democracy." In *Police Abuse in Contemporary Democracies*, edited by Michelle D. Bonner, Guillermina Seri, Mary Rose Kubal, and Michael Kempa. London: Springer International, 2018.

Clarke, Marlea, and Carolyn Bassett. "The Struggle for Transformation in South Africa: Unrealised Dreams, Persistent Hopes." *Journal of Contemporary African Studies* 34, no. 2 (2016): 183–89. https://doi.org/10.1080/02589001.2016.1202501.

Clarke, Simon. "Capital, Fractions of Capital and the State: 'Neo-Marxist' Analysis of the South African State." *Capital and Class* 2, no. 2 (1978): 32–77.

Clarke, Sonia. *Zululand at War, 1879: The Conduct of the Anglo-Zulu War*. Houghton, South Africa: Brenthurst, 1984.

Coates, Ta-Nehisi. "The Case for Reparations." *The Atlantic*, June 2014.

Cobbing, Julian. "The Mfecane as Alibi: Thoughts on Dithakong and Mbolompo." *Journal of African History* 29, no. 3 (2009): 487–519.

Cocks, Michelle, and Anthony Dold. "The Role of 'African Chemists' in the Health Care System of the Eastern Cape Province of South Africa." *Social Science and Medicine* 51, no. 10 (2000): 1505–15.

——. "The Trade in Medicinal Plants in the Eastern Cape Province, South Africa." *South African Journal of Science* 98 (November/December 2002).

Cocks, Michelle, and Valerie Møller. "Use of Indigenous and Indigenised Medicines to Enhance Personal Well-Being: A South African Case Study." *Social Science and Medicine* 54 (2002): 387–97.

Cohen, Daniel. *Shaka, King of the Zulus: A Biography*. New York: Doubleday Books, 1973.

Cole, Teju. "Unmournable Bodies." *New Yorker*, January 9, 2015.

Collier, Stephen J. "Topologies of Power: Foucault's Analysis of Political Government beyond 'Governmentality.'" *Theory, Culture and Society* 26, no. 6 (2009): 78–108.

Collins, Daryl, Jonathan Morduch, Stuart Rutherford, and Orlanda Ruthven. *Portfolios of the Poor*. Princeton, NJ: Princeton University Press, 2009.

Colvin, Ian Duncan. *The Cape of Adventure, Being Strange and Notable Discoveries, Perils, Shipwrecks, Battles, Upon Sea and Land, with Pleasant and Interesting Observations Upon the Country and the Natives of the Cape of Good Hope*. Cape Town: Maskew Miller, 1916.

Comaroff, Jean, and John L. Comaroff. "Alien-Nation: Zombies, Immigrants, and Millennial Capitalism." *South Atlantic Quarterly* 101, no. 4 (2002): 779–805. https://doi.org/10.1215/00382876-101-4-779.

——. *Millennial Capitalism and the Culture of Neoliberalism*. Durham, NC: Duke University Press, 2001.

——. *Of Revelation and Revolution*. Vol. 1, *Christianity, Colonialism, and Consciousness in South Africa*. Chicago: University of Chicago Press, 1991.

——. *Theory from the South: Or, How Euro-America Is Evolving toward Africa*. London: Routledge, 2012.

Comaroff, John L., and Jean Comaroff. *Ethnicity, Inc.* Chicago: University of Chicago Press, 2008.

——. "Goodly Beasts, Beastly Goods: Cattle and Commodities in a South African Context." *American Ethnologist* 17, no. 2 (1990): 195–216.

——. *Of Revelation and Revolution*. Vol. 2, *The Dialectics of Modernity on a South African Frontier*. Chicago: University of Chicago Press, 1997.

——. "On Personhood: An Anthropological Perspective from Africa." *Social Identities* 7, no. 2 (2001).

Coplan, David B. "History Is Eaten Whole: Consuming Tropes in Sesotho Auriture." *History and Theory* 32, no. 4 (1993): 80–104.

——. *In the Time of Cannibals: The Word Music of South Africa's Basotho Migrants*. Chicago: University of Chicago Press, 1994.

Cornell, Drucilla. *Ubuntu and the Law: African Ideals and Postapartheid Jurisprudence*. New York: Fordham University Press, 2011.

Cortesão, Armando. "Note on the Castiglioni Planisphere." *Imago Mundi* 11, no. 1 (1954): 55. https://doi.org/10.1080/03085695408592058.

Cousins, Ben. *At the Crossroads: Land and Agrarian Reform in South Africa into the 21st Century*. Cape Town: Programme for Land and Agrarian Studies, University of the Western Cape / National Land Committee, 2000.

———. "Smallholder Irrigation Schemes, Agrarian Reform and 'Accumulation from Above and from Below' in South Africa." *Journal of Agrarian Change* 13, no. 1 (2013): 116–39. https://doi.org/https://doi.org/10.1111/joac.12000.

———. "What Landmark Kwazulu-Natal Court Ruling Means for Land Reform in South Africa." *The Conversation*, June 22, 2021. https://theconversation.com /what-landmark-kwazulu-natal-court-ruling-means-for-land-reform-in-south -africa-162969.

Cousins, Ben, Alex Dubb, Donna Hornby, and Farai Mtero. "Social Reproduction of 'Classes of Labour' in the Rural Areas of South Africa: Contradictions and Contestations." *Journal of Peasant Studies* 45, no. 5–6 (2018): 1060–85. https://doi.org/10.1080/03066150.2018.1482876.

Cousins, Ben, and Cherryl Walker, eds. *Land Divided, Land Restored: Land Reform in South Africa for the 21st Century*. Johannesburg: Jacana, 2015.

Cousins, Thomas. 2016. "Antiretroviral Therapy and Nutrition in Southern Africa: Citizenship and the Grammar of Hunger." *Medical Anthropology: Cross-Cultural Studies in Health and Illness* 35, no. 5 (2016): 433–46.

———. "HIV and the Remaking of Hunger and Nutrition in South Africa: Biopolitical Specification after Apartheid." *BioSocieties* 10, no. 2 (2015): 143–61. https://doi.org/10.1057/biosoc.2015.8.

———. "Knowledge of Life: Health, Strength and Labour in KwaZulu-Natal, South Africa." *Anthropology Southern Africa* 37, no. 1–2 (2014): 30–41.

———. *Land Claims on iSimangaliso: Problems of Kinship, History, and Memory. Preliminary Report to the iSimangaliso Authority on Ethnographic Research with Land Claimants*. St Lucia: iSimangaliso Wetland Authority, 2008.

———. "A Mediating Capacity: Toward an Anthropology of the Gut." *Medicine Anthropology Theory* 2, no. 2 (2015): 1–27.

Cousins, Thomas, and Lindsey Reynolds. "Blood Relations: HIV Surveillance and Fieldworker Intimacy in KwaZulu-Natal, South Africa." In *Medical Anthropology in Global Africa*, edited by Kathryn Rhine, John M. Janzen, Glenn Adams, and Heather Aldersey, 79–88. Lawrence: University of Kansas, Department of Anthropology, 2014.

Crankshaw, Owen. "Squatting, Apartheid and Urbanisation on the Southern Witwatersrand." *African Affairs* 92, no. 366 (1993): 31–51. http://www.jstor.org /stable/723095.

Cullinan, Kerry, and Anso Thom. *The Virus, Vitamins, and Vegetables: The South African HIV/AIDS Mystery*. Johannesburg: Jacana, 2009.

da Col, Giovanni. "Introduction: Natural Philosophies of Fortune—Luck, Vitality, and Uncontrolled Relatedness." *Social Analysis* 56, no. 1 (2012): 1–23.

———. "Strathern Bottle: On Topology, Ethnographic Theory, and the Method of Wonder." Introduction to *Learning to See in Melanesia: Four Lectures Given in the Department of Social Anthropology, Cambridge University, 1993–2008*, by Marilyn Strathern. Chicago: HAU Books, 2013.

Daniel, E. Valentine. "The Coolie." *Cultural Anthropology* 23, no. 2 (2008): 254–78. https://doi.org/10.1525/can.2008.23.2.254.C.

Dankwa, Serena Owusua. "'It's a Silent Trade': Female Same-Sex Intimacies in Post-Colonial Ghana." *NORA—Nordic Journal of Feminist and Gender Research* 17, no. 3 (2009): 192–205. https://doi.org/10.1080/08038740903117208.

Das, Veena. "Naming beyond Pointing: Singularity, Relatedness and the Foreshadowing of Death." *South Asia Multidisciplinary Academic Journal*, no. 12 (2015).

———. "Public Good, Ethics, and Everyday Life: Beyond the Boundaries of Bioethics." *Daedalus* 128, no. 4: Bioethics and Beyond (1999): 99–133.

———. *Textures of the Ordinary*. New York: Fordham University Press, 2020.

———. "Tradition, Pluralism, Identity: Framing the Issues." In *Tradition, Pluralism and Identity: In Honour of T N Madan*, edited by Veena Das, Dipankar Gupta, and Patricia Uberoi, 9–21. Delhi: SAGE, 1999.

———. "Wittgenstein and Anthropology." *Annual Review of Anthropology* 27, no. 1 (1998): 171–95. https://doi.org/10.1146/annurev.anthro.27.1.171.

Das, Veena, and Ranendra K. Das. "Pharmaceuticals in Urban Ecologies: The Register of the Local." In *Global Pharmaceuticals: Ethics, Markets, Practices*, edited by Adriana Petryna, Andrew Lakoff, and Arthur Kleinman. Durham, NC: Duke University Press, 2006.

Das, Veena, and Clara Han, eds. *Living and Dying in the Contemporary World*. University of California Press, 2016 http://www.jstor.org/stable/10.1525/j .ctv1xxwdf.

Das, Veena, Arthur Kleinman, Mamphela Ramphele, and Pamela Reynolds, eds. *Violence and Subjectivity*. Oakland: University of California Press, 2000.

Das, Veena, and Deborah Poole. *Anthropology in the Margins of the State*. Santa Fe, NM: School of American Research Press, 2004.

Davenport, T. R. H., and K. S. Hunt. *The Right to the Land: Documents on South African History*. Cape Town: David Philip, 1974.

Davies, Sheila Boniface. "Raising the Dead: The Xhosa Cattle-Killing and the Mhlakaza-Goliat Delusion." *Journal of Southern African Studies* 33, no. 1 (2007): 19–41.

Dawson, Hannah J., and Elizabeth Fouksman. "Labour, Laziness and Distribution: Work Imaginaries among the South African Unemployed." *Africa* 90, no. 2 (2020): 229–51.

Decoteau, Claire Laurier. *Ancestors and Antiretrovirals: The Biopolitics of HIV/AIDS in Post-apartheid South Africa*. Chicago: University of Chicago Press, 2013.

Deleuze, Gilles. "What Children Say." In *Essays Critical and Clinical*, translated by Daniel W. Smith and Michael A. Greco, 61–67. London: Verso, 1998.

Devji, Faisal. "The Return of Nonviolence." *Critical Times* 4, no. 1 (2021): 93–101. https://doi.org/10.1215/26410478-8855243.

de Wet, Chris J., and Eric A. Mgujulwa. "Innovative Reworkings of Ancestor Ritual as a Response to Forced Villagisation: An Eastern Cape Example." *Anthropology Southern Africa* 43, no. 4 (2020): 246–58. https://doi.org/10.1080/23323256.2020.1860781.

Dhlomo, R. R. R. *UShaka*. Pietermaritzburg: Shuter and Shooter, 1935.

Diawara, Manthia. "Kader Attia: A Poetics of Re-appropriation." In *The Repair: From Occident to Extra-Occidental Cultures*, by Kader Attia et al., 5–13. Berlin: Green Box, 2014.

DiFruscia, Kim Turcot. "Listening to Voices: An Interview with Veena Das." *Altérités* 7, no. 1 (2010): 136–45.

———. "Shapes of Freedom: An Interview with Elizabeth A. Povinelli." *Altérités* 7, no. 1 (2010): 88–98.

Dlamini, Jacob. *The Terrorist Album: Apartheid's Insurgents, Collaborators, and the Security Police*. Boston: Harvard University Press, 2020.

Dobler, Gregor. "'Work and Rhythm' Revisited: Rhythm and Experience in Northern Namibian Peasant Work." *Journal of the Royal Anthropological Institute* 22, no. 4 (2016): 864–83. https://doi.org/10.1111/1467-9655.12490.

Dobson, Richard, and Caroline Skinner. *Working in Warwick: Including Street Traders in Urban Plans*. Durban: University of KwaZulu-Natal Press, 2009.

Dohne, J. L. *Zulu-Kafir Dictionary: Etymologically Explained*. Pike, 1857.

Doke, C. M., D. M. Malcolm, J. M. A. Sikakana, and B. W. Vilakazi. *English–Zulu, Zulu–English Dictionary*. Johannesburg: Witwatersrand University Press, 2006.

Dominy, Graham A. "History of Lake St. Lucia Eastern Shores." *Environmental Impact Assessment, Eastern Shores of Lake St. Lucia, Kingsa/Tojan Lease Area, Reports on the Key Issues* 2, 1992.

———. "Lake St Lucia, the Eastern Shores: Cultural Resources in an Historical Perspective." *Southern African Humanities* 6, no. 10 (1994): 195–214.

———. "The New Republicans: A Centennial Reappraisal of the Nieuwe Republiek, 1884–1888." *Natalia* 14 (1984): 87–97.

Douglas, Mary. "The Idea of a Home: A Kind of Space." *Social Research* 58, no. 1 (1991): 287–307.

———. *Purity and Danger: An Analysis of Concept of Pollution and Taboo*. London: Routledge, 1984. First published 1966 by Routledge and Kegan Paul.

Dubb, Alexander. "Social Reproduction, Accumulation and Class Differentiation: Small-Scale Sugarcane Growers in Mtubatuba, KwaZulu-Natal, South Africa." PLAAS Working Paper 25. University of the Western Cape, 2012.

Dubbeld, Bernard. "Thinking with Capital Today: A Brief Introduction." *Social Dynamics* 46, no. 1 (2020): 1–9.

———. "Translating E. P. Thompson's Marxian Critique: Contesting 'Context' in South African Studies." *Social Dynamics* 46, no. 1 (2020): 67–85.

Dubow, Saul. *Apartheid, 1948–1994.* Oxford: Oxford University Press, 2014.

du Toit, Andries. "Globalizing Ethics: Social Technologies of Private Regulation and the South African Wine Industry." *Journal of Agrarian Change* 2, no. 3 (2002): 356–80. http://onlinelibrary.wiley.com/doi/10.1111/1471-0366.00038/abstract.

———. "Hunger in the Valley of Fruitfulness: Globalization, 'Social Exclusion' and Chronic Poverty in Ceres, South Africa." Paper presented at the conference "Staying Poor: Chronic Poverty and Development Policy," University of Manchester, April 2003.

———. "The Land and Its People: The South African 'Land Question' and the Post-apartheid Political Order." Unpublished manuscript, 2021.

———. "Poverty Measurement Blues: Beyond 'Q-squared' Approaches to Understanding Chronic Poverty in South Africa." In *Poverty Dynamics: Interdisciplinary Perspectives,* edited by Tony Addison, David Hulme, and Ravi Kanbur, 225–46. Oxford: Oxford University Press, 2009.

———. "'Social Exclusion' Discourse and Chronic Poverty: A South African Case Study." *Development and Change* 35, no. 5 (2004): 987–1010.

du Toit, Andries, and David Neves. "Informal Social Protection in Post-apartheid Migrant Networks: Vulnerability, Social Networks and Reciprocal Exchange in the Eastern and Western Cape, South Africa." BWPI, University of Manchester, 2009.

Edelman, Marc. "'Haciendas and Plantations': History and Limitations of a 60-Year-Old Taxonomy." *Critique of Anthropology* 38, no. 4 (2018): 387–406.

Editor. "Dr JS Henkel, Obituary." *South African Forestry Journal* 42, no. 1 (1962): 30. https://doi.org/10.1080/00382167.1962.9629731.

Ekine, Sokari, and Hakima Abbas, eds. *Queer African Reader.* Nairobi: Pambazuka, 2013.

Elden, Stuart. *Canguilhem.* New York: John Wiley and Sons, 2019.

———. "Terrain, Politics, History." *Dialogues in Human Geography* 11, no. 2 (2020): 170–89. https://doi.org/10.1177/2043820620951353.

Elder, Glen S. "Malevolent Traditions: Hostel Violence and the Procreational Geography of Apartheid." *Journal of Southern African Studies* 29, no. (December 2003): 921–35. https://doi.org/10.1080/0305707032000135897.

Elliott, Paul, and Daniel Wartenberg. "Spatial Epidemiology: Current Approaches and Future Challenges." *Environmental Health Perspectives* 112, no. 9 (2004): 998–1006.

Ensink, Karin, and Brian Robertson. "Indigenous Categories of Distress and Dysfunction in South African Xhosa Children and Adolescents as Described by Indigenous Healers." *Transcultural Psychiatry* 33, no. 2 (1996): 137–72.

————. "Patient and Family Experiences of Psychiatric Services and African Indigenous Healers." *Transcultural Psychiatry* 36, no. 1 (1999): 23–43.

Epprecht, Marc. *Heterosexual Africa? The History of an Idea from the Age of Exploration to the Age of AIDS.* Athens: Ohio University Press, 2008.

Epstein, Steven. *Inclusion: The Politics of Difference in Medical Research.* Chicago: University of Chicago Press, 2007.

Erasmus, Zimitri. "Race." In *New South African Keywords*, edited by Nick Shepherd and Steven Robins. Johannesburg: Jacana, 2008.

Fabian, Johannes. *Time and the Other: How Anthropology Makes Its Object.* New York: Columbia University Press, 1983.

Fakisandla Consulting. "Scope of the Impact: Proposed Changes to Harvesting Operations in the Mkhondo District." *Report to Mondi BP*, 2005.

Farmer, P. "On Suffering and Structural Violence: A View from Below." In *Social Suffering*, edited by Arthur Kleinman, Veena Das, and Margaret Lock. Berkeley: University of California Press, 1997.

Fassin, Didier. "A Case for Critical Ethnography: Rethinking the Early Years of the AIDS Epidemic in South Africa." *Social Science and Medicine* 99 (2013): 119–26.

————. *If Truth Be Told: The Politics of Public Ethnography.* Durham, NC: Duke University Press, 2017.

————. *Life: A Critical User's Manual.* New York: John Wiley and Sons, 2018.

————. "That Obscure Object of Global Health." In *Medical Anthropology at the Intersections: Histories, Activisms, and Futures*, edited by Marcia C. Inhorn and Emily Wentzell. Durham, NC: Duke University Press, 2012.

————. *When Bodies Remember: Experiences and Politics of AIDS in South Africa.* California Series in Public Anthropology. Berkeley: University of California Press, 2007.

Fausto, Carlos, and Luiz Costa. "Feeding (and Eating): Reflections on Strathern's 'Eating (and Feeding).'" *Cambridge Journal of Anthropology* 31, no. 1 (2013): 156–62.

Favret-Saada, Jeanne. *Deadly Words: Witchcraft in the Bocage.* Cambridge: Cambridge University Press, 1980.

————. "Witchcraft in the Bocage." Cambridge and Paris: Cambridge University Press and Editions de La Maison des Sciences de l'Homme, 1980.

Feierman, Steven. "Struggles for Control: The Social Roots of Health and Healing in Modern Africa." *African Studies Review* 8, no. 2–3 (1985): 73–147.

Ferguson, James G. *The Anti-politics Machine: "Development," Depoliticization, and Bureaucratic Power in Lesotho.* Minneapolis: University of Minnesota Press, 1994.

————. "The Bovine Mystique." *Man*, n.s., 20 (1985): 647–74.

————. "Declarations of Dependence: Labour, Personhood, and Welfare in Southern Africa." *Journal of the Royal Anthropological Institute* 19 (2013): 223–42.

————. *Give a Man a Fish: Reflections on the New Politics of Distribution.* Durham, NC: Duke University Press, 2015.

———. "Mobile Workers, Modernist Narratives: A Critique of the Historiography of Transition on the Zambian Copperbelt [Part One]." *Journal of Southern African Studies* 16, no. 3 (1990): 385–412.

———. *Presence and Social Obligation: An Essay on the Share.* Chicago: Prickly Paradigm, 2021.

Fernandez, James. *Bwiti: An Ethnography of the Religious Imagination in Africa.* Princeton, NJ: Princeton University Press, 1982.

Fiereck, Kirk. "After Performativity, beyond Custom: The Queerness of Biofinancial Personhood, Citational Sexualities, and Derivative Subjectivity in South Africa." *GLQ: A Journal of Lesbian and Gay Studies* 26, no. 3 (2020): 503–27. https://doi.org/10.1215/10642684-8311829.

Fiereck, Kirk, Neville Hoad, and Danai S. Mupotsa. "A Queering-to-Come." *GLQ: A Journal of Lesbian and Gay Studies* 26, no. 3 (2020): 363–76. https://doi.org/10.1215/10642684-8311743.

Fine, Ben, and Zavareh Rustomjee. *The Political Economy of South Africa: From Minerals–Energy Complex to Industrialisation.* London: Westview, 1996.

Flint, Karen E. *Healing Traditions: African Medicine, Cultural Exchange, and Competition in South Africa, 1820–1948.* Athens: Ohio University Press, 2008.

Fontein, Joost, and John Harries. "The Vitality and Efficacy of Human Substances." *Critical African Studies* 5, no. 3 (2013): 115–26.

Forbes, David. "The Secret 'Pact of Forgetting' and the Suppression of Post-TRC Prosecutions." *Daily Maverick*, July 24, 2021. https://www.dailymaverick.co.za /article/2021-07-24-the-secret-pact-of-forgetting-and-the-suppression-of-post -trc-prosecutions.

Ford, Chandra L., and Collins O. Airhihenbuwa. "The Public Health Critical Race Methodology: Praxis for Antiracism Research." *Social Science and Medicine* 71, no. 8 (2010): 1390–98.

Foucault, Michel. *The Birth of Biopolitics. Lectures at the Collège de France, 1978–1979.* Edited by Michel Senellart. Translated by Graham Burchell. New York: Macmillan, 2010.

———. *The History of Sexuality.* Vol. 1, *An Introduction.* Translated by Robert Hurley. New York: Vintage, 1990.

———. *The History of Sexuality.* Vol. 2, *The Use of Pleasure.* Translated by Robert Hurley. New York: Vintage, 1990.

———. *Security, Territory, Population. Lectures at the Collège de France, 1977–1978.* Edited by Michel Senellart. Translated by Graham Burchell. London: Palgrave Macmillan, 2007.

French, J. H. "Baron Richard von Stutterheim." *Military History Journal* 3, no. 4 (1975).

Friedman, Roger. "The New Barbarism." *Daily Maverick*, December 14, 2018. https://www.dailymaverick.co.za/article/2018-12-14-the-new-barbarism/.

Gad, Christopher, Casper Bruun Jensen, and Brit Ross Winthereik. "Practical Ontology: Worlds in STS and Anthropology." *NatureCulture* 3 (2015): 67–86.

Gaensheimer, Susanne. Foreword to *Kader Attia: Sacrifice and Harmony*, edited by Susanne Gaensheimer and Klaus Görner. Exhibition catalog, Museum für Moderne Kunst, Frankfurt. Bielefeld: Kerber, 2016.

Gareta, Dickman, Kathy Baisley, Thobeka Mngomezulu, Theresa Smit, Thandeka Khoza, Siyabonga Nxumalo, Jaco Dreyer, et al. "Cohort Profile Update: Africa Centre Demographic Information System (ACDIS) and Population-Based HIV Survey." *International Journal of Epidemiology* 50, no. 1 (2021): 33–34.

Garrido, J. M. *On Time, Being, and Hunger: Challenging the Traditional Way of Thinking Life*. New York: Fordham University Press, 2012.

Garuba, Harry. "On Animism, Modernity/Colonialism, and the African Order of Knowledge: Provisional Reflections." *E-Flux Journal*, no. 36 (2012): 1–9.

Gay, Judith. "'Mummies and Babies' and Friends and Lovers in Lesotho." *Journal of Homosexuality* 11, no. 3–4 (1986): 97–116.

Gearhart, Rebecca. "Ngoma Memories: A History of Competitive Music and Dance Performance on the Kenya Coast." PhD diss., University of Florida, 1998. http://works.bepress.com/rebecca_gearhart/4/.

Geffen, Nathan. *Debunking Delusions: The Inside Story of the Treatment Action Campaign*. Johannesburg: Jacana, 2010.

———. 2005. "Echoes of Lysenko: State-Sponsored Pseudo-science in South Africa." *Social Dynamics* 31, no. 2 (2005): 183–210.

Geissler, P. Wenzel, ed. *Para-states and Medical Science: Making African Global Health*. Durham, NC: Duke University Press, 2015.

Gell, Alfred, and Eric Hirsch. "Strathernograms, or the Semiotics of Mixed Metaphors." In *The Art of Anthropology: Essays and Diagrams*, edited by Alfred Gell, 29–75. London: Athlone, 1999.

Gentilcore, David. "'Charlatans, Mountebanks and Other Similar People': The Regulation and Role of Itinerant Practitioners in Early Modern Italy." *Social History* 20, no. 3 (1995): 297–314.

German Historical Institute. Editorial. "Words Matter: Our Thoughts on Language, Pseudo-science, and 'Race.'" *German Historical Institute London Bulletin* 42, no. 2 (2020): 3–8. https://doi.org/10.5040/9781474208024.06519.

Geschiere, Peter. *The Modernity of Witchcraft: Politics and the Occult in Postcolonial Africa*. Charlottesville: University Press of Virginia, 1997.

Gillespie, Kelly. "Reclaiming Nonracialism: Reading *The Threat of Race* from South Africa." *Patterns of Prejudice* 44, no. 1 (2010): 61–75. https://doi.org/10.1080/00313220903507636.

Gillespie, Kelly, and Bernard Dubbeld. "The Possibility of a Critical Anthropology after Apartheid: Relevance, Intervention, Politics." *Anthropology Southern Africa* 30, nos. 3–4 (2007): 129–34.

Gilmour, Rachael. *Grammars of Colonialism: Representing Languages in Colonial South Africa*. London: Palgrave Macmillan, 2006.

Gluckman, Max. *Analysis of a Social Situation in Modern Zululand*. Manchester: Manchester University Press (Rhodes Livingstone Institute), 1958. First published 1940.

———. "Kinship and Marriage among the Lozi of Northern Rhodesia and the Zulu of Natal." In *African Systems of Kinship and Marriage*, edited by A. R. Radcliffe-Brown and Daryll Forde, 166–206. London: Oxford University Press, 1950.

Goldberg, David Theo. "In Conversation: Achille Mbembe and David Theo Goldberg on 'Critique of Black Reason.'" *Theory, Culture and Society*, July 3, 2018.

Goodfellow, Aaron. *Gay Fathers, Their Children, and the Making of Kinship*. New York: Fordham University Press, 2015.

Gordon, R. J., and A. D. Spiegel. "Southern Africa Revisited." *Annual Review of Anthropology* 22 (1993): 83–105.

Görner, Klaus. "Sacrifice and Harmony." In *Kader Attia: Sacrifice and Harmony*, edited by Susanne Gaensheimer and Klaus Görner. Exhibition catalog, Museum für Moderne Kunst, Frankfurt. Bielefeld: Kerber, 2016.

Government of South Africa. "Health and Safety in Forestry." Pretoria, n.d.

Green, Edward C. "Purity, Pollution and the Invisible Snake in Southern Africa." *Medical Anthropology* 17, no. 1 (1996): 83–100.

Green, Edward C., Annemarie Jurg, and Armando Djedje. "The Snake in the Stomach: Child Diarrhea in Central Mozambique." *Medical Anthropology Quarterly* 8, no. 1 (1994): 4–24.

Gros, Stéphane, Kamala Russell, and William F. Stafford. "Introduction: Topology as Method." *Theorizing the Contemporary*. *Fieldsights*, September 30, 2019. https://culanth.org/fieldsights/introduction-topology-as-method.

Grosz, Elizabeth A. *Volatile Bodies: Toward a Corporeal Feminism*. Bloomington: Indiana University Press, 1994.

Grove, Richard. *Conservation in Africa: Peoples, Policies and Practice*. Cambridge: Cambridge University Press, 1989.

———. "Scottish Missionaries, Evangelical Discourses and the Origins of Conservation Thinking in Southern Africa 1820–1900." *Journal of Southern African Studies* 15 (1989): 163–87.

Gudeman, Stephen. "Vital Energy." *Social Analysis* 56, no. 1 (2012): 57–73.

Gunkel, Henriette. "Some Reflections on Postcolonial Homophobia, Local Interventions, and LGBTI Solidarity Online: The Politics of Global Petitions." *African Studies Review* 56, no. 2 (2013): 67–81. https://doi.org/10.1017/asr.2013.42.

Gunner, Elizabeth. *The Man of Heaven and the Beautiful Ones of God*. Leiden: Brill, 2004.

Guy, Jeff. "Battling with Banality." *Journal of Natal and Zulu History* 18, no. 1 (1998): 156–93.

———. "The Destruction and Reconstruction of Zulu Society." In *Industrialisation and Social Change in South Africa: African Class, Culture, and Consciousness, 1870–1930*, edited by Shula Marks and Richard Rathbone. New York: Longman, 1982.

———. *The Destruction of the Zulu Kingdom: The Civil War in Zululand, 1879–84.* Johannesburg: Ravan, 1982.

———. "Ecological Factors in the Rise of Shaka and the Zulu Kingdom." In *Economy and Society in Pre-industrial South Africa.* London: Longman, 1980.

———. "Remembering the Rebellion: The Zulu Uprising of 1906." Scottsville: University of KwaZulu-Natal Press, 2006.

Guyer, Jane I. "Household and Community in African Studies." *African Studies Review* 24, no. 2/3 (1981): 87–137.

———. "The Multiplication of Labor: Historical Methods in the Study of Gender and Agricultural Change in Modern Africa." *Current Anthropology* 29, no. 2 (1988): 247–72.

Ha, Thu-Huong. "Bilingual Authors Are Challenging the Practice of Italicizing Non-English Words." *Quartz*, June 24, 2018.

Hacking, Ian. "Making Up People." In *Reconstructing Individualism: Autonomy, Individuality, and the Self in Western Thought*, edited by Thomas C. Heller, Morton Sosna, and David E. Wellbery. Stanford, CA: Stanford University Press, 1986.

Hamayon, Robert. *Why We Play: An Anthropological Study.* Chicago: HAU Books, 2016.

Hamilton, Carolyn. *Terrific Majesty: The Powers of Shaka Zulu and the Limits of Historical Invention.* Cape Town: David Philip, 1998.

Hamilton, Carolyn, and Nessa Leibhammer, eds. *Tribing and Untribing the Archive: Identity and the Material Record in Southern KwaZulu-Natal in the Late Independent and Colonial Periods.* 2 vols. Durban: University of KwaZulu-Natal Press, 2016.

Hammond-Tooke, W. David. "Kinship, Locality, and Association: Hospitality Groups among the Cape Nguni." *Ethnology* 2, no. 3 (1963): 302–19.

———. "The Nature and Significance of Bride Wealth among the South African Bantu." MA thesis, University of Cape Town, 1948. http://hdl.handle.net/11427/22263.

Hanks, William F., and Carlo Severi. "Translating Worlds: The Epistemological Space of Translation." *HAU: Journal of Ethnographic Theory* 4, no. 2 (2014).

Haraway, Donna. "Anthropocene, Capitalocene, Plantationocene, Chthulucene: Making Kin." *Environmental Humanities* 6, no. 1 (2015): 159–65.

Hardon, Anita, and Emilia Sanabria. "Fluid Drugs: Revisiting the Anthropology of Pharmaceuticals." *Annual Review of Anthropology* 46, no. 1 (2017): 117–32.

Harries, Patrick. "Exclusion, Classification and Internal Colonialism: The Emergence of Ethnicity among the Tsonga-Speakers of South Africa." In *The Growth of*

Tribalism in Southern Africa, edited by Leroy Vail, 82–117. Berkeley: University of California Press, 1989.

———. "Plantations, Passes and Proletarians: Labour and the Colonial State in Nineteenth Century Natal." *Journal of Southern African Studies* 13, no. 3 (1987): 372–99. https://doi.org/10.1080/03057078708708151.

———. *Work, Culture, and Identity: Migrant Laborers in Mozambique and South Africa, c. 1860–1910*. Portsmouth, NH: Heinemann, 1994.

Hart, Gillian. *Reworking Apartheid Legacies: Global Competition, Gender and Social Wages in South Africa, 1980–2000*. Geneva: United Nations Research Institute for Social Development, 2002.

Hart, Keith. "Africa's Urban Revolution and the Informal Economy." In *The Political Economy of Africa*, edited by Vishnu Padayachee. London: Routledge, 2010.

Hart, Keith, Jean-Louis Laville, and Antonio David Cattani. "Building the Human Economy Together." In *The Human Economy: A Citizen's Guide*, ed. Keith Hart, Jean-Louis Laville, and Antonio David Cattani, 1–20. Cambridge: Polity, 2010.

Harvey, David. *The New Imperialism*. Oxford: Oxford University Press, 2003.

Hedges, David William. "Trade and Politics in Southern Mozambique and Zululand in the Eighteenth and Early Nineteenth Centuries." PhD diss., School of Oriental and African Studies (University of London), 1978.

Heehs, Peter. "Myth, History, and Theory." *History and Theory* 33, no. 1 (1994): 1–19.

Henderson, Patricia C. *AIDS, Intimacy and Care in Rural KwaZulu-Natal: A Kinship of Bones*. Amsterdam: Amsterdam University Press, 2011.

———. "Mapping Journeys through Landscape: Phenomenological Explorations of Environment amongst Rural AIDS Orphans." In *Postcolonial African Anthropologies*, edited by Rosabelle Boswell and Francis B. Nyamnjoh. Cape Town: HSRC Press, 2017.

Hendriks, Thomas. "'Making Men Fall': Queer Power beyond Anti-normativity." *Africa* 91, no. 3 (2021): 398–417.

———. *Rainforest Capitalism: Power and Masculinity in a Congolese Timber Concession*. Durham, NC: Duke University Press, 2022.

Henke, Christopher. "Negotiating Repair: The Infrastructural Contexts of Practice and Power: Revisiting Breakdown, Relocating Materiality." In *Repair Work Ethnographies*, edited by Ignaz Strebel, Alain Bovet, and Philippe Sormani, 255–82. London: Palgrave Macmillan, 2019.

Henkel, J. S., S. Ballenden, and A. W. Bayer. "An Account of the Plant Ecology of the Dukuduku Forest Reserve and Adjoining Areas of the Zululand Coast Belt." In *Annals of the Natal Museum*, edited by R. F. Lawrence. London: Natal Museum, 1937.

Herbst, M., and W. du Plessis. "Customary Law v Common Law Marriages: A Hybrid Approach in South Africa." *Electronic Journal of Comparative Law* 12 (2008): 121–28.

Hickel, Jason. "Democracy and Sabotage." PhD diss., University of Virginia, 2011.

———. *Democracy as Death: The Moral Order of Anti-liberal Politics in South Africa*. Berkeley: University of California Press, 2015.

Hickey, Sam, and Andries du Toit. "Adverse Incorporation, Social Exclusion and Chronic Poverty." Chronic Poverty Research Centre Working Paper 81. Institute for Development Policy and Management, School of Environment and Development, University of Manchester, 2007.

Hirsch, Lee, Desireé Markgraaff, Sherry Simpson Dean, Vusi Mahlasela, Jeremy Cronin, Hugh Masekela, Miriam Makeba, Sophie Mgcina, Dolly Rathebe, and Sifiso Ntuli. *Amandla! A Revolution in Four-Part Harmony*. Nu Metro Home Entertainment, 2002.

Hirson, Denis. *White Scars: On Reading and Rites of Passage*. Johannesburg: Jacana, 2006.

Hoad, Neville. "Thabo Mbeki's AIDS Blues: The Intellectual, the Archive, and the Pandemic." *Public Culture* 17, no. 1 (2005): 101–27.

Hochschild, Adam. *King Leopold's Ghost: A Story of Greed, Terror, and Heroism in Colonial Africa*. New York: Houghton Mifflin Harcourt, 1998.

Hodes, Rebecca, Lucie Cluver, Elona Toska, and Beth Vale. "Pesky Metrics: The Challenges of Measuring ART Adherence among HIV-Positive Adolescents in South Africa." *Critical Public Health* 30, no. 2 (2020): 179–90.

Hofmeyr, Isabel. *"We Spend Our Years as a Tale That Is Told": Oral Historical Narrative in a South African Chiefdom*. London: James Currey, 1994.

Hornby, Donna, Rosalie Kingwill, Lauren Royston, and Ben Cousins, eds. *Untitled: Securing Land Tenure in Urban and Rural South Africa*. Pietermaritzburg: UKZN Press, 2017.

Hosegood, Vicky, and Ian M. Timaeus. "Household Composition and Dynamics in KwaZulu Natal, South Africa: Mirroring Social Reality in Longitudinal Data Collection." In *African Households: An Exploration of Census Data*, edited by Etienne van de Walle, 58–77. London: Routledge, 2005.

Hsu, J. W.-C., P. B. Pencharz, D. Macallan, and A. Tomkins. "Macronutrients and HIV/AIDS: A Review of Current Evidence." World Health Organization, Durban, April 10–13, 2005.

Hunleth, Jean. "Zambian Children's Imaginal Caring: On Fantasy, Play, and Anticipation in an Epidemic." *Cultural Anthropology* 34, no. 2 (2019): 155–86.

Hunt, Nancy Rose. *A Nervous State: Violence, Remedies, and Reverie in Colonial Congo*. Durham, NC: Duke University Press, 2015.

Hunter, David J., Salim S. Abdool Karim, Lindsey R. Baden, Jeremy J. Farrar, Mary Beth Hamel, Dan L. Longo, Stephen Morrissey, and Eric J. Rubin. "Addressing Vaccine Inequity—Covid-19 Vaccines as a Global Public Good." *New England Journal of Medicine*, February 23, 2022.

Hunter, Mark. "Fathers without Amandla? Gender and Fatherhood among IsiZulu Speakers." *Journal of Natal and Zulu History* 22, no. 1 (2004): 149–60. https://doi.org/10.1080/02590123.2004.11964128.

———. "Is It Enough to Talk of Marriage as a Process? Legitimate Co-habitation in Umlazi, South Africa." *Anthropology Southern Africa* 39, no. 4 (2016): 281–96. https://doi.org/10.1080/23323256.2016.1238772.

———. *Love in the Time of AIDS: Inequality, Gender, and Rights in South Africa.* Bloomington: Indiana University Press, 2010.

Jackson, Michael D. "Life and Concept." In *Living and Dying in the Contemporary World: A Compendium*, edited by Veena Das and Clara Han, 449–62. Oakland: University of California Press, 2016.

Jackson, Steven J. "Rethinking Repair." In *Media Technologies: Essays on Communication, Materiality, and Society.* Boston: MIT Press, 2014.

James, Deborah. *Money from Nothing: Indebtedness and Aspiration in South Africa.* Stanford, CA: Stanford University Press, 2014.

———. *Songs of the Women Migrants: Performance and Identity in South Africa.* Edinburgh: Edinburgh University Press for the International African Institute, 1999.

———. "'Women Use Their Strength in the House': Savings Clubs in an Mpumalanga Village." *Journal of Southern African Studies* 41, no. 5 (2015): 1035–52.

James, Peter Bai, Jon Wardle, Amie Steel, and Jon Adams. "Traditional, Complementary and Alternative Medicine Use in Sub-Saharan Africa: A Systematic Review." *BMJ Global Health* 3, no. 5 (2018): e000895.

Janzen, John M. *Health in a Fragile State.* Madison: University of Wisconsin Press, 2019.

———. *Ngoma: Discourses of Healing in Central and Southern Africa.* Berkeley: University of California Press, 1992.

———. "Self-Presentation and Common Cultural Structures in Ngoma Rituals of Southern Africa." *Journal of Religion in Africa* 25, no. 2 (1995): 141–62.

Jimenez, Alberto Corsin. "On Space as a Capacity." *Journal of the Royal Anthropological Institute* 9, no. 1 (2003): 137–53.

Jobson, Ryan Cecil. "The Case for Letting Anthropology Burn: Sociocultural Anthropology in 2019." *American Anthropologist* 122, no. 2 (2020): 259–71.

Junod, Henri. *The Life of a South African Tribe.* Neuchatel, Switzerland: Attinger Frères, 1912.

Kalofonos, Ippolytos. *All I Eat Is Medicine: Going Hungry in Mozambique's AIDS Economy.* Oakland: University of California Press, 2021.

Keck, Frédéric. "A Genealogy of Animal Diseases and Social Anthropology (1870–2000)." *Medical Anthropology Quarterly* 33, no. 1 (2019): 24–41.

Keegan, Timothy. "The Dynamics of Rural Accumulation in South Africa: Comparative and Historical Perspectives." *Comparative Studies in Society and History* 28, no. 4 (1986): 628–50.

Kelly, Ann H., Hermione N. Boko Koudakossi, and Sarah J. Moore. "Repellents and New 'Spaces of Concern' in Global Health." *Medical Anthropology* 36, no. 5 (2017): 464–78.

Kelly, Ann H., and Javier Lezaun. "Walking or Waiting? Topologies of the Breeding Ground in Malaria Control." *Science as Culture* 22, no. 1 (2013): 86–107.

———. "The Wild Indoors: Room-Spaces of Scientific Inquiry." *Cultural Anthropology* 32, no. 3 (2017): 367–98. https://doi.org/10.14506/ca32.3.06.

Kepe, Thembela, and Ruth Hall. "Land Redistribution in South Africa: Towards Decolonisation or Recolonisation?" *Politikon* 45, no. 1 (2018): 128–37.

Keyter, Andrea, Shabir Banoo, Sam Salek, and Stuart Walker. "The South African Regulatory System: Past, Present, and Future." *Frontiers in Pharmacology* 9 (December 2018). https://doi.org/10.3389/fphar.2018.01407.

Kistner, Ulrike. "How 'Class' Came to Marx—Taking a Longer View on 'Race'-'Class' Conjunctions and Disjunctions." *Social Dynamics* 46, no. 1 (2020): 36–49.

Klein, Melanie. *Love, Guilt and Reparation, and Other Works 1921–1945*. New York: Free Press, 1975.

Klein, Thamar. "Who Decides Whose Gender? Medico-Legal Classifications of Sex and Gender and Their Impact on Transgendered South Africans' Family Rights." *Ethnoscripts* 14, no. 2 (2012): 12–34.

Kleinman, Arthur, Veena Das, and Margaret M. Lock. *Social Suffering*. Berkeley: University of California Press, 1997.

Kluge, Alexander, and Oskar Negt. *History and Obstinacy*. Edited by Devin Fore. Cambridge, MA: MIT Press, 2014.

Kopytoff, Igor, ed. *The African Frontier: The Reproduction of Traditional African Societies*. Bloomington: Indiana University Press, 1987.

Kotler, Donald P. "HIV Infection and the Gastrointestinal Tract." *AIDS* 19 (2005): 107–17.

Krige, Eileen Jensen. *The Social System of the Zulus*. London: Longmans, Green, 1936.

Kuper, Adam. "The 'House' and Zulu Political Structure in the Nineteenth Century." *Journal of African History* 34, no. 3 (1993): 469–87.

———. "Traditions of Kinship, Marriage and Bridewealth in Southern Africa." *Anthropology Southern Africa* 39, no. 4 (2016): 267–80. https://doi.org/10.1080/23323256.2016.1243447.

———. *Wives for Cattle: Bridewealth and Marriage in Southern Africa*. Boston: Routledge and Kegan Paul, 1982.

Laband, John. "Colonial Flotsam: The Zululand Squatters and the Zululand Lands Delimitation Commission 1902–1904." *South African Historical Journal* 49, no. 1 (2003): 53–70. https://doi.org/10.1080/02582470308671447.

Lalu, Premesh. "Leaving the City: Gender, Pastoral Power and the Discourse of Development in the Eastern Cape." In *Desire Lines: Space, Memory and*

Identity in the Post-apartheid City, edited by Nick Shepherd, Noëleen Murray, and Martin Hall. London: Routledge, 2003.

Lambek, Michael. "The Value of (Performative) Acts." HAU: Journal of Ethnographic Theory 3, no. 2 (2013): 141–60. https://doi.org/10.14318/hau3.2.009.

Lan, David. Guns and Rain: Guerrillas and Spirit Mediums in Zimbabwe. Berkeley: University of California Press, 1985.

Landau, Paul S. Popular Politics in the History of South Africa, 1400–1948. Cambridge: Cambridge University Press, 2010.

——. The Realm of the Word: Language, Gender, and Christianity in a Southern African Kingdom. Johannesburg: Heinemann, 1995.

Landecker, Hannah. "Eating as Dialogue, Food as Technology." Noēma, June 18, 2020. https://www.noemamag.com/eating-as-dialogue-food-as-technology/.

——. "Food as Exposure: Nutritional Epigenetics and the New Metabolism." BioSocieties 6, no. 2 (2011): 167–94.

Latour, Bruno. Reassembling the Social: An Introduction to Actor-Network-Theory. Oxford: Oxford University Press, 2005.

Laubscher, J. F. Sex, Custom and Psychopathology. London: Routledge, 1937.

Laugier, Sandra. "Politics of Vulnerability and Responsibility for Ordinary Others." Critical Horizons 17, no. 2 (2016): 207–23. https://doi.org/10.1080/14409917.2016.1153891.

Leach, Edmund. Rethinking Anthropology. London: Athlone, 1961.

Leavitt, John. "Words and Worlds: Ethnography and Theories of Translation." HAU: Journal of Ethnographic Theory 4, no. 2 (2014).

Legassick, Martin. "Legislation, Ideology and Economy in Post-1948 South Africa." Journal of Southern African Studies 1, no. 1 (1974): 5–35.

——. "South Africa: Capital Accumulation and Violence." Economy and Society 3, no. 3 (1974): 253–91.

Legassick, Martin, and Harold Wolpe. "The Bantustans and Capital Accumulation in South Africa." Review of African Political Economy 3, no. 7 (1976): 87–107.

Lemke, Thomas. "'A Zone of Indistinction'—A Critique of Giorgio Agamben's Con-cept of Biopolitics." Outlines: Critical Practice Studies 7, no. 1 (2005): 3–13.

Levinas, Emmanuel. Time and the Other. Pittsburgh: Duquesne University Press, 1990.

Lévi-Strauss, Claude. The Savage Mind. Chicago: University of Chicago Press, 1966.

——. Structural Anthropology. 1963. New York: Basic Books, 1990.

——. Wild Thought: A New Translation of "La Pensée sauvage." Translated by Jeffrey Mehlman and John Leavitt. Chicago: University of Chicago Press, 2020.

Lewin, Julius. Studies in African Native Law. Cape Town: African Bookman, 1947.

Leys, Ruth. From Guilt to Shame. Princeton, NJ: Princeton University Press, 2007.

Lingis, Alphonso. Dangerous Emotions. Berkeley: University of California Press, 2000.

Lingo, Alison Klairmont. "Empirics and Charlatans in Early Modern France: The Genesis of the Classification of the 'Other' in Medical Practice." *Journal of Social History* 1, no. 4 (1986): 583–603.

Livingston, Julie. *Debility and the Moral Imagination in Botswana*. Bloomington: Indiana University Press, 2005.

Lock, Margaret. "Recovering the Body." *Annual Review of Anthropology* 46 (2017): 1–14. https://doi.org/10.1146/annurev-anthro-102116-041253.

Louw, W. J. A. "General History of the South African Forest Industry: 1991 to 2002." *Southern African Forestry Journal* 201, no. 1 (2004): 65–76.

———. "General History of the South African Forest Industry: 1975 to 1990." *Southern African Forestry Journal* 200, no. 1 (2004): 77–86.

Low, Marcus. "Government Plans Massive PrEP Rollout." *Daily Maverick*, February 5, 2020. https://www.dailymaverick.co.za/article/2020-02-05 -government-plans-massive-prep-rollout/.

MacGaffey, Wyatt. "African Objects and the Idea of Fetish." *Res: Anthropology and Aesthetics* 25, no. 25 (1994): 123–31.

———. *Kongo Political Culture: The Conceptual Challenge of the Particular*. Bloomington: Indiana University Press, 2000.

Maclean, C. *A Compendium of Kafir Laws and Customs*. Cape Town: Solomon, 1866.

Mafeje, Archie. "On the Articulation of Modes of Production: Review Article." *Journal of Southern African Studies* 8, no. 1 (1981): 123–38.

Magubane, Zine. "Globalization and the South African Transformation: The Impact on Social Policy." *Africa Today* 49, no. 4 (2002): 89–110. http://www .jstor.org/stable/4187532.

Malabou, Catherine. *What Should We Do with Our Brain?* New York: Fordham University Press, 2008.

Malaza, Abraham, Joël Mossong, Till Bärnighausen, Johannes Viljoen, and Marie-Louise Newell. "Population-Based CD4 Counts in a Rural Area in South Africa with High HIV Prevalence and High Antiretroviral Treatment Coverage." *PLOS ONE* 8, no. 7 (July 23, 2013): e70126. https://doi.org/10.1371 /journal.pone.0070126.

Mamdani, Mahmood. "Amnesty or Impunity? A Preliminary Critique of the Report of the Truth and Reconciliation Commission of South Africa (TRC)." *Diacritics* 32, no. 3/4 (2002): 33–59. http://www.jstor.org/stable/1566444.

———. "Beyond Nuremberg: The Historical Significance of the Post-apartheid Transition in South Africa." *Politics and Society* 43, no. 1 (2014): 61–88. https://doi.org/10.1177/0032329214554387.

Mandala, Elias C. *Work and Control in a Peasant Economy: A History of the Lower Tshiri Valley in Malawi 1859–1960*. Madison: University of Wisconsin Press, 1990.

Mangcu, Xolela, Nina G. Jablonski, Lawrence Blum, Steven Friedman, Mark Swilling, Vusi Gumede, Joel Netshitenzhe, Suren Pillay, Crain Soudien, and Hlonipha Mokoena. *The Colour of Our Future.* Edited by Xolela Mangcu. Johannesburg: Wits University Press, 2015. https://doi.org/10.18772/22015075690.

Marks, Harry M. "Law, Markets and Regulatory Cultures: A Historian's Vain Pursuit of Social Theory." Unpublished seminar paper presented to the Critical Global Health seminar series, Johns Hopkins University (September 26, 2010): 1–54.

Marwick, C. W. *Kwamahlati, the Story of Forestry in Zululand.* Bulletin 49. Pretoria: Department of Forestry, 1973.

Marx, Karl. *Capital.* Vol. 3. London: Electric Book, 2000.

Marx, Karl, and Friedrich Engels. *The Marx-Engels Reader.* Edited by Robert C. Tucker. 2nd ed. New York: Norton, 1978.

Mascia-Lees, Frances E. "The Anthropological Unconscious." *American Anthropologist* 96, no. 3 (1994): 649–60. http://www.jstor.org/stable/682305.

Matebeni, Zethu. *Reclaiming Afrikan: Queer Perspectives on Sexual and Gender Identities.* Cape Town: Modjadji Books, 2014.

Mathebula, Mandla, Robert Nkuna, Hlengani Mabasa, and Mukhacani Maluleke. "Tsonga History Discourse." N.d. Accessed August 19, 2021. https://vatsonga.wordpress.com/about/.

Matoti-Mvalo, T., and T. B. Puoane. "Perceptions of Body Size and Its Association with HIV/AIDS." *South African Journal of Clinical Nutrition* 24, no. 1 (2011): 40–45. http://www.ajol.info/index.php/sajcn/article/viewFile/65390/53082.

Maughan, R. J., J. B. Leiper, and S. M. Shirreffs. "Factors Influencing the Restoration of Fluid and Electrolyte Balance after Exercise in the Heat." *British Journal of Sports Medicine* 31, no. 3 (1997): 175–82. https://doi.org/10.1136/bjsm.31.3.175.

Maxwell, David. *African Gifts of the Spirit: Pentecostalism and the Rise of a Zimbabwean Transnational Religious Movement.* Oxford: James Currey, 2007.

Mayers, James, Jeremy Evans, and Tim Foy. *Raising the Stakes: Impacts of Privatisation, Certification and Partnerships in South African Forestry.* London: Institute for Environment and Development, 2001.

Mbembe, Achille. *Critique of Black Reason.* Durham, NC: Duke University Press, 2017.

———. "Necropolitics." *Public Culture* 15, no. 1 (2003): 11–40.

———. *Necropolitics.* Durham, NC: Duke University Press, 2019.

———. "Passages to Freedom: The Politics of Racial Reconciliation in South Africa." *Public Culture* 20, no. 1 (2008): 5–18. https://doi.org/10.1215/08992363-2007-012.

McClendon, Thomas V. *White Chief, Black Lords: Shepstone and the Colonial State in Natal, South Africa, 1845–1878.* Rochester: University of Rochester Press, 2010.

McCormick, Tracey Lee. "A Critical Engagement? Analysing Same-Sex Marriage Discourses in *To Have and to Hold: The Making of Same-Sex Marriage in South Africa* (2008)—A Queer Perspective." *Stellenbosch Papers in Linguistics Plus* 46 (2015): 105. https://doi.org/10.5842/46-0-656.

McCulloch, Jock. "Medicine, Politics and Disease on South Africa's Gold Mines." *Journal of Southern African Studies* 39, no. 3 (2013): 543–56. https://doi.org/10.1080/03057070.2013.818850.

———. *South Africa's Gold Mines and the Politics of Silicosis.* Johannesburg: James Currey, 2012.

McDonald, Peter. *Artefacts of Writing: Ideas of the State and Communities of Letters from Matthew Arnold to Xu Bing.* Oxford: Oxford University Press, 2017.

Meintjies, Louise. *Dust of the Zulu: Ngoma Aesthetics after Apartheid.* Durham, NC: Duke University Press, 2017.

Mendenhall, Emily. "Beyond Comorbidity: A Critical Perspective of Syndemic Depression and Diabetes in Cross-Cultural Contexts." *Medical Anthropology Quarterly* 30, no. 4 (2016): 462–78.

Mendenhall, Emily, and Shane A. Norris. "When HIV Is Ordinary and Diabetes New: Remaking Suffering in a South African Township." *Global Public Health* 10, no. 4 (2015): 449–62.

Merleau-Ponty, Maurice. *Phenomenology of Perception.* Translated by Colin Smith. London: Routledge, 2005.

Meyers, Todd. *The Clinic and Elsewhere: Addiction, Adolescents, and the Afterlife of Therapy.* Seattle: University of Washington Press, 2013.

———, ed. *The Ways We Stretch toward One Another: Thoughts on Anthropology through the Work of Pamela Reynolds.* Bamenda, Cameroon: Langaa RPCIG, 2017.

Milani, Tommaso M. "Language, Gender and Sexuality in South Africa." *Stellenbosch Papers in Linguistics Plus* 46 (2015): i–v. https://doi.org/10.5842/46-0-672.

Mintz, Sidney W. "The Plantation as a Socio-cultural Type." In *Plantation Systems of the New World*, edited by Vera Rubin, 42–53. Washington, DC: Pan American Union, 1959.

———. "Plantations and the Rise of a World Food Economy: Some Preliminary Ideas." *Review (Fernand Braudel Center)* 34, no. 1/2 (2011): 3–14.

———. "Was the Plantation Slave a Proletarian?" *Review (Fernand Braudel Center)* 2, no. 1 (1978): 81–98.

———. *Worker in the Cane: A Puerto Rican Life History.* New York: W. W. Norton, 1974.

Mintz, Sidney W., and Christine M. du Bois. "The Anthropology of Food and Eating." *Annual Review of Anthropology* 31 (2002): 99–119.

Mkhwanazi, Nolwazi. "Understanding Teenage Pregnancy in a Post-apartheid South African Township." *Culture, Health and Sexuality* 12, no. 4 (2010): 347–58.

Mngxitama, Andile, Amanda Suzanne Alexander, and Nigel C. Gibson. *Biko Lives! Contesting the Legacies of Steve Biko*. Contemporary Black History. New York: Palgrave Macmillan, 2008.

Modiri, Joel. "The Colour of Law, Power and Knowledge: Introducing Critical Race Theory in (Post-)Apartheid South Africa." *South African Journal on Human Rights* 28, no. 3 (2012): 405–36.

Moguerane, Khumisho. "A Home of One's Own: Women and Home Ownership in the Borderlands of Post-apartheid South Africa and Lesotho." *Canadian Journal of African Studies / Revue canadienne des études africaines* 52, no. 2 (2018): 139–57.

Mol, Annemarie. *The Body Multiple: Ontology in Medical Practice*. Durham, NC: Duke University Press, 2002.

Mol, Annemarie, and John Law. "Regions, Networks and Fluids: Anaemia and Social Topology." *Social Studies of Science* 24, no. 4 (1994): 641–71.

Molelekwa, Thabo. "South Africa Rolls Out New Three-in-One HIV Pill." Health-e News, updated November 28, 2019. https://health-e.org.za/2019/11/28 /south-africas-new-hiv-treatment-projected-to-roll-out-in-january/.

Mondi plc. "Mondi Sustainability Report." Durban, 2010.

Moore, Donald S. *Suffering for Territory: Race, Place, and Power in Zimbabwe*. Durham, NC: Duke University Press, 2005.

Moore, Jason W. *Capitalism in the Web of Life: Ecology and the Accumulation of Capital*. London: Verso, 2015.

Morkel, R. "The Real Reasons for Outsourcing." *SA Forestry*, March–April 2000.

Morreira, Shannon. "Working with Our Grandparents' Illusions: On Colonial Lineage and Inheritance in Southern African Anthropology." *HAU: Journal of Ethnographic Theory* 6, no. 2 (2016): 279–95.

Morris, David. "The Fold and the Body Schema in Merleau-Ponty and Dynamic Systems Theory." *Chiasmi International: Trilingual Studies concerning Merleau-Ponty's Thought* 1 (1999): 275–86.

Morris, Rosalind C. "Deconstruction's Doubt." *HAU: Journal of Ethnographic Theory* 6, no. 1 (2016): 511–18.

Mostert, Noel. *Frontiers: The Epic of South Africa's Creation and the Tragedy of the Xhosa People*. New York: Knopf, 1992.

Msibi, Thabo, and Stephanie Rudwick. "Intersections of Two IsiZulu Genderlects and the Construction of 'skesana' Identities." *Stellenbosch Papers in Linguistics Plus* 46 (2015): 51–66. https://doi.org/10.5842/46-0-616.

Muhwava, William. *Trends in Economic Status of Households in the ACDIS*. Monograph Series no. 3. Somkhele, South Africa: Africa Centre for Health and Population Studies, 2008.

Muhwava, William, M. Nyirenda, T. Mutevedzi, A. J. Herbst, and V. Hosegood. *Operational and Methodological Procedures of the Africa Centre Demographic Information System.* Somkhele, South Africa: Africa Centre for Health and Population Studies, 2007.

Mulhall, Stephen. *The Wounded Animal: J. M. Coetzee and the Difficulty of Reality in Literature and Philosophy.* Princeton, NJ: Princeton University Press, 2009.

Mupotsa, Danai S. "Conjugality." *GLQ: A Journal of Lesbian and Gay Studies* 26, no. 3 (2020): 377–403. https://doi.org/10.1215/10642684-8311758.

Murray, Colin. *Black Mountain: Land, Class, and Power in the Eastern Orange Free State, 1880s to 1980s.* Edinburgh: Edinburgh University Press, 1992.

———. "Displaced Urbanisation: South Africa's Rural Slums." *African Affairs* 86, no. 344 (1987): 311–29.

———. *Families Divided: The Impact of Migrant Labour in Lesotho.* Cambridge: Cambridge University Press, 1981.

Murray, Stephen O., and Will Roscoe, eds. *Boy-Wives and Female Husbands: Studies in African Homosexualities.* New York: Palgrave Macmillan, 2001.

Mykhalovskiy, Eric, Liza McCoy, and Michael Bresalier. "Compliance/Adherence, HIV, and the Critique of Medical Power." *Social Theory and Health* 2, no. 4 (2004): 315–40.

Nattrass, Nicoli. "AIDS and the Scientific Governance of Medicine in Post-apartheid South Africa." *African Affairs* 107, no. 427 (2008): 157–76.

———. "Controversies about Capitalism and Apartheid in South Africa: An Economic Perspective." *Journal of Southern African Studies* 17, no. 4 (1991): 654–77.

Nature. Editorial. "Africa Is Bringing Vaccine Manufacturing Home." February 9, 2022. https://www.nature.com/articles/d41586-022-00335-9.

Nebandla, Injobo. *Freedom from Strife? An Assessment of Efforts to Build Peace in KwaZulu-Natal.* Braamfontein: Centre for the Study of Violence and Reconciliation, 2005.

Needham, Rodney. *Remarks and Inventions: Skeptical Essays about Kinship.* London: Routledge, 2004. First published in 1974.

Neocosmos, Michael. *The Agrarian Question in Southern Africa and "Accumulation from Below": Economics and Politics in the Struggle for Democracy.* Research Report 93. Uppsala: Nordiska Afrikainstitutet, 1993.

Neves, David, and Andries du Toit. "Money and Sociality in South Africa's Informal Economy." *Africa* 82, no. 1 (2012): 131–49.

Ngubane, Harriet. *Body and Mind in Zulu Medicine.* Madison, WI: Academic, 1977.

———. 1976. "Some Notions of 'Purity' and 'Impurity' among the Zulu." *Africa: Journal of the International African Institute* 46, no. 3 (1993): 274–84.

Ngubane, Sihawukele. "Language, Identity and Place Names." Unpublished, Wetlands 101s. St Lucia, 2006.

Nguyen, Vinh-Kim. *The Republic of Therapy: Triage and Sovereignty in West Africa's Time of AIDS*. Durham, NC: Duke University Press, 2010.

———. "Treating to Prevent HIV: Population Trials and Experimental Societies." In *Para-states and Medical Science: Making African Global Health*, ed. Paul Wenzel Geissler. Durham, NC: Duke University Press, 2015.

Nguyen, Vinh-Kim, Cyriaque Yapo Ako, Pascal Niamba, Aliou Sylla, and Issoufou Tiendrébéogo. "Adherence as Therapeutic Citizenship: Impact of the History of Access to Antiretroviral Drugs on Adherence to Treatment." *AIDS* 21, no. 5 (2007): S31–35.

Ngwane, Zolani. "'Christmas Time' and the Struggles for the Household in the Countryside: Rethinking the Cultural Geography of Migrant Labour in South Africa." *Journal of Southern African Studies* 29, no. 3 (2003): 681–99.

Niehaus, D. J. H., P. Oosthuizen, C. Lochner, R. A. Emsley, E. Jordaan, N. I. Mbanga, N. Keyter, C. Laurent, J.-F. Deleuze, and D. J. Stein. "A Culture-Bound Syndrome 'Amafufunyana' and a Culture-Specific Event 'Ukuthwasa': Differentiated by a Family History of Schizophrenia and Other Psychiatric Disorders." *Psychopathology* 37, no. 2 (2004): 59–63.

Niehaus, Isak. "Anthropology and Whites in South Africa: Response to an Unreasonable Critique." *Africa Spectrum* 48, no. 1 (2013): 117–27.

Nkomo, Hloni, Ivan Niranjan, and Poovendhree Reddy. "Effectiveness of Health and Safety Training in Reducing Occupational Injuries among Harvesting Forestry Contractors in KwaZulu-Natal." *Workplace Health and Safety* 66, no. 10 (2018): 499–507.

Ntsebeza, Lungisile, and Ruth Hall, eds. *The Land Question in South Africa: The Challenge of Transformation and Redistribution*. Johannesburg: HSRC Press, 2007.

Nussbaum, Martha, and Amartya Sen, eds. *The Quality of Life*. Oxford: Oxford University Press, 1993.

Nustad, Knut. "Property, Rights and Community in a South African Land-Claim Case." *Anthropology Today* 27, no. 1 (2011): 20–24.

Nuttall, Sarah. "Flatness and Fantasy: Representations of the Land in Two Recent South African Novels." In *Text, Theory, Space: Land, Literature and History in South Africa and Australia*, edited by Kate Darian-Smith, Liz Gunner, and Sarah Nuttall, 219–30. London: Routledge, 1996.

Nyamnjoh, Francis B., ed. *Eating and Being Eaten: Cannibalism as Food for Thought*. Bamenda, Cameroon: Langaa RPCIG, 2018.

———. "Incompleteness: Frontier Africa and the Currency of Conviviality." *Journal of Asian and African Studies* 52, no. 3 (2017): 253–70.

———. "A Post-Covid-19 Fantasy on Incompleteness and Conviviality." In "Post-Covid Fantasies," edited by Catherine Besteman, Heath Cabot, and Barak Kalir. *American Ethnologist* website, July 27, 2020. https://americanethnologist

.org/features/pandemic-diaries/post-covid-fantasies/a-post-covid-19-fantasy
-on-incompleteness-and-conviviality.

Nyoka, Bongani. "Mafeje on Black Struggles in South Africa: History and
Theory." *Social Dynamics* 46, no. 1 (2020): 50–66.

Obeyesekere, Gananath. *The Work of Culture: Symbolic Transformation in
Psychoanalysis and Anthropology.* Chicago: University of Chicago Press, 1990.

Oboler, Regine Smith. "Is the Female Husband a Man? Woman/Woman Marriage
among the Nandi of Kenya." *Ethnology* 19, no. 1 (1980): 69–88. http://www.jstor
.org/stable/10.2307/3773320.

O'Brien, Denise. "Female Husbands in Southern Bantu Societies." In *Sexual
Stratification: A Cross-Cultural View*, edited by Alice Schlegel, 109–26. New
York: Columbia University Press, 1977.

Okop, Kufre Joseph, Ferdinand C. Mukumbang, Thubelihle Mathole, Naomi
Levitt, and Thandi Puoane. "Perceptions of Body Size, Obesity Threat and the
Willingness to Lose Weight among Black South African Adults: A Qualitative
Study." *BMC Public Health* 16, no. 1 (2016): 365. https://doi.org/10.1186/s12889
-016-3028-7.

Oomen, Barbara. *Chiefs in South Africa: Law, Power and Culture in the Post-
apartheid Era.* New York: Palgrave Macmillan, 2005.

Ouma, Stefan. "From the Plantation to the Fourth Industrial Revolution: Other
Economic Geographies." Unpublished conference paper, WISER, 2020.

Packard, Randall. *White Plague, Black Labour: Tuberculosis and the Political
Economy of Health and Disease in South Africa.* Berkeley: University of
California Press, 1989.

Packard, Randall, and Paul Epstein. "Epidemiologists, Social Scientists, and
the Structure of Medical Research on AIDS in Africa." *Social Science and
Medicine* 33, no. 7 (1991): 771–94.

Pandolfo, Stefania. *Knot of the Soul.* Chicago: University of Chicago Press, 2018.

Papadopoulos, Dimitris, Maria Puig de la Bellacasa, and Maddalena Tacchetti.
*Ecological Reparation: Repair, Remediation and Resurgence in Social and
Environmental Conflict.* Dis-Positions: Troubling Methods and Theory in STS
Series. Bristol: Bristol University Press, 2022.

Parker, Richard, Liz Ashby, and Graham Bates. "Dehydration in Loggers: Effects
of Season and Time of Day." *COHFE Report* 3, no. 1 (2002): 1174–234, https://
scion.contentdm.oclc.org/digital/collection/p20044coll14/id/1/.

Parle, Julie, Rebecca Hodes, and Thembisa Waetjen. "Pharmaceuticals and
Modern Statecraft in South Africa: The Cases of Opium, Thalidomide
and Contraception." *Medical Humanities* 44, no. 4 (2018): 253–62. https://doi
.org/10.1136/medhum-2018-011478.

Peires, Jeffrey B. *The Dead Will Arise: Nongqawuse and the Great Xhosa Cattle-
Killing Movement of 1856–7.* Bloomington: Indiana University Press, 1989.

Pentecost, Michelle, and Thomas Cousins. "Strata of the Political: Epigenetic and Microbial Imaginaries in Post-apartheid Cape Town." *Antipode* 49 (2017): 1368–84. https://doi.org/10.1111/anti.12315.

———. "The Temporary as the Future: Ready-to-Use Therapeutic Food and Nutraceuticals in South Africa." *Anthropology Today* 34, no. 4 (2018): 9–13. https://doi.org/10.1111/1467-8322.12447.

Pentecost, Michelle, Berna Gerber, Megan Wainwright, and Thomas Cousins. "Critical Orientations for Humanising Health Sciences Education in South Africa." *Medical Humanities* 44, no. 4 (2018): 221–29.

Petherbridge, Danielle. "What's Critical about Vulnerability? Rethinking Interdependence, Recognition, and Power." *Hypatia* 31, no. 3 (2016): 589–604. https://doi.org/10.1111/hypa.12250.

Phillips, Howard. *Plague, Pox and Pandemics: A Jacana Pocket History of Epidemics in South Africa.* Johannesburg: Jacana, 2012.

Phillips, John W. P. "On Topology." *Theory, Culture and Society* 30, no. 5 (2013): 122–52. https://doi.org/10.1177/0263276413480951.

Phillips, Nicola, and Leonardo Sakamoto. "The Dynamics of Adverse Incorporation in Global Production Networks: Poverty, Vulnerability and 'Slave Labour' in Brazil." Chronic Poverty Research Centre Working Paper 175, 2011.

Piaget, Jean. *Play, Dreams and Imitation in Childhood.* London: Routledge, 1962.

Pietz, William. "The Problem of the Fetish, I." *Res: Anthropology and Aesthetics* 9 (1985): 5–17.

Pina-Cabral, João de. "Agnatas, vizinhos e amigos: Variantes da vicinalidade em África, Europa e América." *Revista de antropologia* 57, no. 2 (2014): 23–56.

———. "My Mother or Father: Person, Metaperson, and Transcendence in Ethnographic Theory." *Journal of the Royal Anthropological Institute* 25, no. 2 (2019): 303–23.

———. "Partible Houses: Variants of Vicinage in Mozambique, Portugal and Brazil." *Articulo* 20 (2019). https://doi.org/10.4000/articulo.4434.

Pinney, Christopher. "Things Happen: Or, From Which Moment Does That Object Come?" In *Materiality,* edited by Daniel Miller, 256–72. Durham, NC: Duke University Press, 2005.

Pinto, Ana Teixeira. "In No Man's Land." In *Kader Attia: Signes de réappropriation.* Dijon: BlackJack, 2013.

Pons-Vignon, Nicolas. "Forestry Workers Buckle under Outsourcing Pipedream." *South African Labour Bulletin* 30, no. 2 (2006): 27–30.

Pons-Vignon, Nicolas, and Ward Anseeuw. "Great Expectations: Working Conditions in South Africa since the End of Apartheid." *Journal of Southern African Studies* 35, no. 4 (2009): 883–99. https://doi.org/10.1080/03057070903313236.

Posel, Deborah. "Race as Common Sense: Racial Classification in Twentieth-Century South Africa." *African Studies Review* 44, no. 2 (2001): 87–114.

———. "Races to Consume: Revisiting South Africa's History of Race, Consumption and the Struggle for Freedom." *Ethnic and Racial Studies* 33, no. 2 (2010): 157–75.

———. "Sex, Death and the Fate of the Nation: Reflections on the Politicization of Sexuality in Post-apartheid South Africa." *Africa: Journal of the International African Institute* 75, no. 2 (2005): 125–53.

———. "What's in a Name? Racial Categorisations under Apartheid and Their Afterlife." *Transformation: Critical Perspectives on Southern Africa* 47 (2001): 50–74.

Postone, Moishe. "Theorizing the Contemporary World: Robert Brenner, Giovanni Arrighi, David Harvey." In *Political Economy and Global Capitalism: The 21st Century, Present and Future*, edited by Robert Albritton, Robert Jessop, and Richard Westra, 7–23. London: Anthem, 2007.

Potgieter, Dirk J., ed. *Standard Encyclopaedia of Southern Africa*. Pretoria: NASOU, 1970.

Povinelli, Elizabeth A. *The Cunning of Recognition: Indigenous Alterities and the Making of Australian Multiculturalism*. Durham, NC: Duke University Press, 2002.

———. *Economies of Abandonment: Social Belonging and Endurance in Late Liberalism*. Durham, NC: Duke University Press, 2011.

———. *The Empire of Love: Toward a Theory of Intimacy, Genealogy, and Carnality*. Durham, NC: Duke University Press, 2006.

———. "The Governance of the Prior." *Interventions* 13, no. 1 (2011): 13–30. https://doi.org/10.1080/1369801X.2011.545575.

———. "Horizons and Frontiers, Late Liberal Territoriality, and Toxic Habitats." *E-Flux Journal*, no. 90 (April 2018). https://www.e-flux.com/journal/90/191186/horizons-and-frontiers-late-liberal-territoriality-and-toxic-habitats/.

———. "Notes on Gridlock: Genealogy, Intimacy, Sexuality." *Public Culture* 14, no. 1 (2002): 215–38. https://doi.org/10.1215/08992363-14-1-215.

———. "Routes/Worlds." *E-Flux Journal*, no. 27 (September 2011). http://www.e-flux.com/journal/routesworlds/.

———. "Sexuality at Risk: Psychoanalysis Metapragmatically." In *Homosexuality and Psychoanalysis*, edited by Tim Dean and Christopher Lane, 387–411. Chicago: University of Chicago Press, 2001.

———. "The Will to Be Otherwise / The Effort of Endurance." *South Atlantic Quarterly* 111, no. 3 (2012): 453–75.

Povinelli, Elizabeth A., and Kim Turcot DiFruscia. "Shapes of Freedom: An Interview with Elizabeth A. Povinelli." *Altérités* 7, no. 1 (2010): 88–98.

Povinelli, Elizabeth A, and Clara Bessijelle Johansson. "Stubborn." *E-Flux Journal*, no. 95 (November 2018). https://www.e-flux.com/journal/95/228045/stubborn/.

Pressly, Donwald. "Social Grants Bill to Hit R122bn." *Independent Online*, February 23, 2012. https://www.pressreader.com/south-africa/cape-times/20120223/page/25/textview.

Puar, Jasbir K. *The Right to Maim: Debility, Capacity, Disability.* Durham, NC: Duke University Press, 2017.

Rabinbach, Anson. *The Eclipse of the Utopias of Labor.* New York: Fordham University Press, 2018.

———. *The Human Motor: Energy, Fatigue, and the Origins of Modernity.* Berkeley: University of California Press, 1992.

Rabinow, Paul, and Anthony Stavrianakis. *From Chaos to Solace: Topological Meditations.* Berkeley, CA: Anthropology of the Contemporary Research Collaboratory, 2021.

Radcliffe-Brown, Alfred Reginald, and Darryl Forde. *African Systems of Kinship and Marriage.* London: Oxford University Press, 1950.

Rajan, Kaushik Sunder. *Multisituated: Ethnography as Diasporic Praxis.* Durham, NC: Duke University Press, 2021.

———. "Pharmaceutical Crises and Questions of Value: Terrains and Logics of Global Therapeutic Politics." *South Atlantic Quarterly* 111, no. 2 (2012): 321–46.

———. *Pharmocracy: Value, Politics, and Knowledge in Global Biomedicine.* Durham, NC: Duke University Press, 2017.

Ramphele, Mamphela. *A Bed Called Home: Life in the Migrant Labour Hostels of Cape Town.* Athens: Ohio University Press, 1993.

Raper, P. E. *Dictionary of Southern African Place Names.* Johannesburg: Jonathan Ball, 1987.

Rees, Tobias, Thomas Bosch, and Angela E. Douglas. "How the Microbiome Challenges Our Concept of Self." *PLOS Biology* 16, no. 2 (February 9, 2018): e2005358.

Reid, Graeme Charles. *How to Be a Real Gay: Gay Identities in Small-Town South Africa.* Scottsville: University of KwaZulu-Natal Press, 2013.

Reynolds, Lindsey, Thomas Cousins, Marie-Louise Newell, and John Imrie. "The Social Dynamics of Consent and Refusal in HIV Surveillance in Rural South Africa." *Social Science and Medicine* 77 (2013): 118–25.

Reynolds, Pamela. "Gleanings and Leavings: Encounters in Hindsight." In *Inside African Anthropology: Monica Wilson and Her Interpreters,* edited by Andrew Bank and Leslie J. Bank. The International African Library. Cambridge: Cambridge University Press, 2013. https://doi.org/DOI: 10.1017/CBO9781139333 634.011.

———. "The Ground of All Making: State Violence, the Family and Political Activists." In *Violence and Subjectivity,* edited by Veena Das, Arthur Kleinman, Mamphela Ramphele, and Pamela Reynolds, 141–70. Berkeley: University of California Press, 2000.

———. *Traditional Healers and Childhood in Zimbabwe.* Athens: Ohio University Press, 1996.

———. *The Uncaring, Intricate World: A Field Diary, Zambezi Valley, 1984–1985.* Durham, NC: Duke University Press, 2019.

———. *War in Worcester: Youth and the Apartheid State*. New York: Fordham University Press, 2013.

Richards, Audrey Isabel. *Hunger and Work in a Savage Tribe: A Functional Study of Nutrition among the Southern Bantu*. Glencoe, IL: Free Press, 1948.

Rickards, Meg, and Bert Haitsma. *1994: The Bloody Miracle*. South Africa: Boondogle Films, 2014. https://www.nelsonmandela.org/news/entry/1994-the-bloody-miracle.

Robins, Steven. "'Long Live Zackie, Long Live': AIDS Activism, Science and Citizenship after Apartheid." *Journal of Southern African Studies* 30, no. 3 (2004): 651–72.

Robins, Steven, and Nancy Scheper-Hughes. "On the Call for a Militant Anthropology: The Complexity of 'Doing the Right Thing.'" *Current Anthropology* 37, no. 2 (1996): 341–46.

Robinson, Bob. "Michel Foucault: Ethics." In *The Internet Encyclopedia of Philosophy*, edited by James Fieser and Bradley Dowden. 2021. https://iep.utm.edu/.

Ross, Fiona C. "Model Communities and Respectable Residents? Home and Housing in a Low-Income Residential Estate in the Western Cape, South Africa." *Journal of Southern African Studies* 31, no. 3 (2005): 631–48.

———. "Nyamezela." Unpublished conference paper, presented at Anthropology Southern Africa Annual Conference, North-West University, August 25, 2015.

———. "Raw Life and Respectability: Poverty and Everyday Life in a Postapartheid Community." *Current Anthropology* 56, no. S11 (2015): S97–107. https://doi.org/10.1086/682078.

———. *Raw Life, New Hope: Decency, Housing and Everyday Life in a Post-apartheid Community*. Cape Town: UCT Press, 2010.

———. "Sense-Scapes: Senses and Emotion in the Making of Place." *Anthropology Southern Africa* 27, nos. 1–2 (2004): 35–42.

———. "Using Rights to Measure Wrongs." In *Human Rights in Global Perspective: Anthropological Studies of Rights, Claims and Entitlements*, edited by Richard A. Wilson and Jon P. Mitchell, 163–82. London: Routledge, 2003.

Rubin, Gayle. "The Traffic in Women: Notes on the 'Political Economy' of Sex." In *Toward an Anthropology of Women*, edited by Rayna R. Reiter. New York: Monthly Review Press, 1975.

Rudwick, Stephanie, and Dorrit Posel. "Contemporary Functions of *Ilobolo* (Bridewealth) in Urban South African Zulu Society." *Journal of Contemporary African Studies* 32, no. 1 (2014): 118–36. https://doi.org/10.1080/02589001.2014.900310.

Sahlins, Marshall. *What Kinship Is—And Is Not*. Chicago: University of Chicago Press, 2013.

Scarry, Elaine. *The Body in Pain: The Making and Un-making of the World*. Oxford: Oxford University Press, 1985.

———. *Resisting Representation*. New York: Oxford University Press, 1994.

Schapera, Isaac. *A Handbook of Tswana Law and Custom*. London: International Africa Institute, 1938.

———. *Married Life in an African Tribe*. Evanston, IL: Northwestern University Press, 1966.

Scheper-Hughes, Nancy. "The Primacy of the Ethical." *Current Anthropology* 36, no. 3 (1995): 409–40. https://doi.org/10.1086/204378.

Scheub, Harold. *The Uncoiling Python: South African Storytellers and Resistance*. Athens: Ohio University Press, 2010.

Schneider, David M. *American Kinship: A Cultural Account*. Chicago: University of Chicago Press, 1968.

Scott, James C. *Seeing Like a State: How Certain Schemes to Improve the Human Condition Have Failed*. New Haven, CT: Yale University Press, 1998.

Scott, P. A., C. J. Christie, G. James, and A. Todd. "Ergonomics Report: Forest Harvesting." In *Ergonomics Report for FESA*. Pietermaritzburg: Institute for Commercial Forestry Research, 2004.

Scrinis, Gyorgy. *Nutritionism: The Science and Politics of Dietary Advice*. New York: Columbia University Press, 2015.

Sedgwick, Eve Kosofsky. *Touching Feeling: Affect, Pedagogy, Performativity*. Durham, NC: Duke University Press, 2003.

Seekings, Jeremy, and Nicoli Nattrass. *Class, Race, and Inequality in South Africa*. New Haven, CT: Yale University Press, 2005.

Seligman, Adam B., Robert P. Weller, Michael J. Puett, and Bennett Simon. *Ritual and Its Consequences: An Essay on the Limits of Sincerity*. New York: Oxford University Press, 2008.

Sender, John. "Women's Struggle to Escape Rural Poverty in South Africa." *Journal of Agrarian Change* 2, no. 1 (2002): 1–49.

Sennott, Christie, Sangeetha Madhavan, and Youngeun Nam. "Modernizing Marriage: Balancing the Benefits and Liabilities of Bridewealth in Rural South Africa." *Qualitative Sociology* 44, no. 1 (2021): 55–75.

Shackleton, Sheona, Charlie Shackleton, and Ben Cousins. *Re-valuing the Communal Lands of Southern Africa: New Understandings of Rural Livelihoods*. London: Overseas Development Institute, 2000.

Shange, Savannah. *Progressive Dystopia: Abolition, Antiblackness, and Schooling in San Francisco*. Durham, NC: Duke University Press, 2019.

Sharp, John, and Andrew D. Spiegel. "Vulnerability to Impoverishment in South African Rural Areas: The Erosion of Kinship and Neighbourhood as Social Resources." *Africa: Journal of the International African Institute* 55, no. 2 (1985): 133–52.

———. "Women and Wages: Gender and the Control of Income in Farm and Bantustan Households." *Journal of Southern African Studies* 16, no. 3 (1990): 527–49.

Siegel, J. T. *Naming the Witch*. Stanford, CA: Stanford University Press, 2006.

Silverstein, Michael. "The Improvisational Performance of Culture in Realtime Discursive Practice." In *Creativity in Performance*, edited by R. Keith Sawyer. London: Ablex, 1997.

———. "Indexical Order and the Dialectics of Sociolinguistic Life." *Language and Communication* 23, no. 3 (2003): 193–229.

———. "Metapragmatic Discourse and Metapragmatic Function." In *Reflexive Language: Reported Speech and Metapragmatics*, edited by John A. Lucy, 33. Cambridge: Cambridge University Press, 1993.

———. "Metasemiotic Hypertrophy and Dynamic Figuration: Why Ritual Works (When It Does)." Unpublished paper presented at the seminar "The Language of Ritual," EFSSS, Sozopol, Bulgaria, September 9, 2011.

Silverstein, Michael, and Greg Urban. *Natural Histories of Discourse*. Chicago: University of Chicago Press, 1996.

Sime, J. R. "Review: Investigation of the Forest and Timber Industry of South Africa." *South African Forestry Journal* 52, no. 1 (1965): 34. https://doi.org/doi:10.1080/00382167.1965.9629929.

Simelela, N. P., and W. D. F. Venter. "A Brief History of South Africa's Response to AIDS." *South African Medical Journal* 104, no. 3 suppl. 1 (2014): 249–51.

Singer, Merrill. "Beyond the Ivory Tower: Critical Praxis in Medical Anthropology." *Medical Anthropology Quarterly* 9, no. 1 (1995): 80–106.

Singh, Mani Shekhar. "What Should Happen, but Has Not Yet Happened: Painterly Tales of Justice." *Contributions to Indian Sociology* 53, no. 1 (2019): 184–216.

SiyaQhubeka Forests. "SEAT Report: Socio-economic Assessment Report 2005." Anglo-American Plc. https://www.mondigroup.com/media/7452/mondi_seat_siyaqhubeka_forests.pdf.

Skinner, Caroline. "Challenging City Imaginaries: Street Traders' Struggles in Warwick Junction." *Agenda: Empowering Women for Gender Equity*, no. 81 (August 2009): 101–9. http://www.jstor.org/stable/27868984.

Sloterdijk, Peter. "Sphären III (Spheres III): Schäume (Foams)." *Plurale Sphärologie*. Frankfurt: Suhrkamp, 2004.

Solomon, Harris. *Metabolic Living: Food, Fat, and the Absorption of Illness in India*. Durham, NC: Duke University Press, 2016.

Sonnleitner, Julia. "Chronotopes of Apartheid." *Wiener linguistische Gazette* 83 (2018): 27–48.

South African Medical Research Council (SAMRC). "Report on Weekly Deaths in South Africa: 29 Dec 2019–19 Feb 2022." SAMRC website, https://www.samrc.ac.za/reports/report-weekly-deaths-south-africa.

Southall, Roger. "Ten Propositions about Black Economic Empowerment in South Africa." *Review of African Political Economy* 34, no. 111 (2007): 67–84. https://doi.org/10.1080/03056240701340365.

Spiegel, Andrew D. "Changing Patterns of Migrant Labour and Rural Differentiation in Lesotho." *Social Dynamics* 6, no. 2 (1980): 1–13.

———. "Walking Memories and Growing Amnesia in the Land Claims Process: Lake St Lucia, South Africa." *Anthropology Southern Africa* 27, no. 1/2 (2004): 3–10.

Spiegel, Andrew D., and Heike Becker. "South Africa: Anthropology or Anthropologies?" *American Anthropologist* 117, no. 4 (2015): 754–60.

Spronk, Rachel, and Thomas Hendriks, eds. *Readings in Sexualities from Africa*. Bloomington: Indiana University Press, 2020.

Stadler, Jonathan, Fiona Scorgie, Ariane van der Straten, and Eirik Saethre. "Adherence and the Lie in a HIV Prevention Clinical Trial." *Medical Anthropology* 35, no. 6 (2016): 503–16.

Statistics South Africa, Republic of South Africa. "General Household Survey, 2019." Available online at Stats SA website, December 17, 2020. https://www.statssa.gov.za/publications/P0318/P03182019.pdf.

———. "Government Spending Climbs to R1,71 Trillion." Stats SA website, November 26, 2019. https://www.statssa.gov.za/?p=12776.

———. "Quarterly Labour Force Survey: Quarter 2: 2022." Statistical Report, Stats SA website, March 29, 2022, https://www.statssa.gov.za/?p=15685.

Steinberg, Jonny. *One Day in Bethlehem*. Johannesburg: Jonathan Ball, 2019.

Stewart, Dianne. "Izisho Zokusebenza—Work Songs." In *Women Writing Africa: The Southern Region*, edited by Margaret J. Daymond, Dorothy Driver, and Sheila Meintjies. New York: Feminist Press at the City University of New York, 2003.

Steyn, N. P., M. Senekal, S. Brits, M. Alberts, T. Mashego, and J. H. Nel. "Weight and Health Status of Black Female Students." *South African Medical Journal* 90, no. 2 (2000): 146–52.

Strathern, Marilyn. "Eating (and Feeding)." *Cambridge Journal of Anthropology* 30, no. 2 (2012): 1–14.

———. "Gender: Division or Comparison?" *Sociological Review* 45, no. 1 suppl. (1997): 42–63. https://doi.org/https://doi.org/10.1111/j.1467-954X.1997.tb03453.x.

———. *Learning to See in Melanesia: Four Lectures Given in the Department of Social Anthropology, Cambridge University, 1993–2008*. Chicago: HAU Books, 2013.

———. "Opening Up Relations." In *A World of Many Worlds*, edited by Marisol de la Cadena and Mario Blaser. Durham, NC: Duke University Press, 2018.

———. *Relations: An Anthropological Account*. Durham, NC: Duke University Press, 2020.

Surplus People Project (SPP). *Forced Removals in South Africa: The SPP Reports*. Vol. 4, *Natal*. Cape Town: Surplus People Project, 1983.

Suttner, Raymond, and Jeremy Cronin. *30 Years of the Freedom Charter*. Johannesburg: Ravan, 1985.

Swartz, Alison, Susan Levine, Hanna-Andrea Rother, and Fritha Langerman. "Toxic Layering through Three Disciplinary Lenses: Childhood Poisoning and

Street Pesticide Use in Cape Town, South Africa." *Medical Humanities* 44, no. 4 (2018): 247 LP–252.

Swartz, Leslie. "Transcultural Psychiatry in South Africa." *Transcultural Psychiatry* 23, no. 4 (1986): 273–303.

Tamale, Sylvia, ed. *African Sexualities: A Reader.* Cape Town: Pambazuka, 2011.

Tambiah, S. J., M. Goheen, A. Gottlieb, J. I. Guyer, E. A. Olson, C. Piot, K. W. van der Veen, and T. Vuyk. "Bridewealth and Dowry Revisited: The Position of Women in Sub-Saharan Africa and North India [and Comments and Reply]." *Current Anthropology* 30, no. 4 (1989): 413–35. https://www.journals.uchicago.edu/doi/abs/10.1086/203761?journalCode=ca.

Tangri, Roger, and Roger Southall. "The Politics of Black Economic Empowerment in South Africa." *Journal of Southern African Studies* 34, no. 3 (2008): 699–716. https://doi.org/10.1080/03057070802295856.

Tanser, Frank, Daniel K. Azongo, Alain Vandormael, Till Bärnighausen, and Christopher Appleton. "Impact of the Scale-Up of Piped Water on Urogenital Schistosomiasis Infection in Rural South Africa." *ELife* 7 (February 2018).

Tanser, Frank, Till Bärnighausen, Graham S. Cooke, and Marie-Louise Newell. "Localized Spatial Clustering of HIV Infections in a Widely Disseminated Rural South African Epidemic." *International Journal of Epidemiology* 38, no. 4 (2009): 1008–16.

Tanser, Frank, Till Bärnighausen, Adrian Dobra, and Benn Sartorius. "Identifying 'Corridors of HIV Transmission' in a Severely Affected Rural South African Population: A Case for a Shift toward Targeted Prevention Strategies." *International Journal of Epidemiology* 47, no. 2 (2017): 1–13.

Tanser, Frank, Till Bärnighausen, Erofili Grapsa, Jaffer Zaidi, and Marie-Louise Newell. "High Coverage of ART Associated with Decline in Risk of HIV Acquisition in Rural KwaZulu-Natal, South Africa." *Science* 339, no. 6122 (2013): 966–71.

Taussig, Michael T. *The Devil and Commodity Fetishism in South America.* Chapel Hill: University of North Carolina Press, 1980.

Taylor, Christopher, and Adom Getachew. "55603 The Global Plantation." Online course description, 2019. https://english.uchicago.edu/courses/global-plantation.

———. "The Global Plantation: An Exchange between Adom Getachew and Christopher Taylor." *b2o: an online journal,* June 23, 2020.

Thomas, Deborah A. *Political Life in the Wake of the Plantation: Sovereignty, Witnessing, Repair.* Durham, NC: Duke University Press, 2019.

Thomas, Kylie. *Impossible Mourning: HIV/AIDS and Visuality after Apartheid.* Johannesburg: Wits University Press, 2013.

Thomas, Lynn M. *Beneath the Surface: A Transnational History of Skin Lighteners.* Durham, NC: Duke University Press, 2020.

Thornton, Robert. *Healing the Exposed Being: A South African Ngoma Tradition.* Johannesburg: Wits University Press, 2017.

——. "The Market for Healing and the Elasticity of Belief: Medical Pluralism in Mpumalanga, South Africa." In *Markets of Well-Being: Navigating Health and Healing in Africa*, edited by Marleen Dekker and Rijk van Dijk. Leiden: Koninklijke Brill, 2010.

——. *Unimagined Community: Sex, Networks, and AIDS in Uganda and South Africa*. Berkeley: University of California Press, 2008.

Tilley, Helen. *Africa as a Living Laboratory: Empire, Development, and the Problem of Scientific Knowledge, 1870–1950*. Chicago: University of Chicago Press, 2011.

Torkelson, Erin. "Collateral Damages: Cash Transfer and Debt Transfer in South Africa." *World Development* 126 (2020): 104711. https://doi.org/10.1016/j .worlddev.2019.104711.

Tracey, Hugh. "A Case for the Name Mbira." *African Music* 2, no. 4 (1961): 17–25. http://www.jstor.org/stable/10.2307/30249527.

Tropp, Jacob A. 2006. *Natures of Colonial Change: Environmental Relations in the Making of the Transkei*. Athens: Ohio University Press, 2006.

Tsing, Anna Lowenhaupt. *Friction: An Ethnography of Global Connection*. Princeton, NJ: Princeton University Press, 2005.

——. *The Mushroom at the End of the World: On the Possibility of Life in Capitalist Ruins*. Princeton, NJ: Princeton University Press, 2015.

Turnbull, J. W. "Tree Domestication and the History of Plantations." In *The Role of Food, Agriculture, Forestry and Fisheries and the Use of Natural Resources*, ed. V. R. Squires. *Encyclopedia of Life Support Systems Developed under Auspices of UNESCO*. Oxford: EOLSS, 2002.

Uexküll, Jakob von. *A Foray into the Worlds of Animals and Humans: With A Theory of Meaning*. Translated by Joseph D. O'Neil. Minneapolis: University of Minnesota Press, 2010.

Umfolozi Co-operative Sugar Planters Company Limited. 1973. "Brochure Issued to Commemorate Fifty Years of Cooperation in the Umfolozi Delta Area," 1973.

Urban, Greg. *Metaculture: How Culture Moves through the World*. Minneapolis: University of Minnesota Press, 2001.

Vahed, Goolam, and Ashwin Desai. "After Mandela Met Gandhi: The Past and Future of India–South Africa Relations." In *Africa and India in the 21st Century: Contexts, Comparisons and Cooperation*, 9–18. University of KwaZulu-Natal, South Africa and Delhi University, Delhi, India, 2014.

——. "Identity and Belonging in Post-apartheid South Africa: The Case of Indian South Africans." *Journal of Social Science* 25, no. 1–3 (2010): 1–12.

van den Berg, Gert, Steven D. Verryn, Paxie W. Chirwa, and François van Deventer. "Genetic Parameters and Genotype by Environment Interaction of *Eucalyptus grandis* Populations Used in Intraspecific Hybrid Production in South Africa." *Southern Forests: A Journal of Forest Science* 79, no. 4 (2017): 287–95.

van der Berg, Servaas, and Leila Patel. "COVID-19 Pandemic Has Triggered a Rise in Hunger in South Africa." *The Conversation*, July 21, 2021. https://theconversation .com/covid-19-pandemic-has-triggered-a-rise-in-hunger-in-south-africa-164581.

van der Geest, Sjaak, Susan Reynolds White, and Anita Hardon. "The Anthropology of Pharmaceuticals: A Biographical Approach." *Annual Review of Anthropology* 25 (1996): 153–78.

van der Waal, C. S. "Long Walk from Volkekunde to Anthropology: Reflections on Representing the Human in South Africa." *Anthropology Southern Africa* 38, nos. 3–4 (2015): 216–34.

van Dijk, Rijk, Ria Reis, and Marja Spierenburg, eds. *The Quest for Fruition through Ngoma: Political Aspects of Healing in Southern Africa*. Athens: Ohio University Press, 2000.

Vandormael, Alain, Adam Akullian, Mark Siedner, Tulio de Oliveira, Till Bärnighausen, and Frank Tanser. "Declines in HIV Incidence among Men and Women in a South African Population-Based Cohort." *Nature Communications* 10, no. 1 (2019): 5482.

Vergès, Françoise. "Fire, Anger and Humiliation in the Museum." In *Kader Attia: The Museum of Emotion*, exhibition catalog, 86–87. London: Hayward Gallery, 2019. http://kaderattia.de/fire-anger-and-humiliation-in-the-museum-by -francoise-verges-2019/.

Verhoef, G. "Informal Financial Service Institutions for Survival: African Women and Stokvels in Urban South Africa, 1930–1998." *Enterprise and Society* 2, no. 2 (2001): 259–96.

Verissimo, Jumoke. "On the Politics of Italics." *Literary Hub*, August 28, 2019. https://lithub.com/on-the-politics-of-italics/.

von Holdt, Karl, Malose Langa, Sepetla Molapo, Nomfundo Mogapi, Kindiza Ngubeni, Jacob Dlamini, and Adele Kirsten. *The Smoke That Calls: Insurgent Citizenship, Collective Violence and the Struggle for a Place in the New South Africa. Eight Case Studies of Community Protest and Xenophobic Violence*. Johannesburg: Centre for the Study of Violence and Reconciliation, Society, Work and Development Institute, 2011.

Vosloo, Christo. 2020. "Extreme Apartheid: The South African System of Migrant Labour and Its Hostels." *Image and Text* 34 (2020): 1–33.

Walker, Cherryl. "Claiming Community: Restitution on the Eastern Shores of Lake St Lucia." In *Zulu Identities: Being Zulu, Past and Present*, edited by Benedict Carton, John Laband, and Jabulani Sithole. Pietermaritzburg: University of KwaZulu-Natal Press, 2008.

———. *Landmarked: Land Claims and Land Restitution in South Africa*. Cape Town: Jacana, 2008.

———. "Land of Dreams: Land Restitution on the Eastern Shores of Lake St Lucia." *Transformation: Critical Perspectives on Southern Africa* 59 (2005): 1–25.

Walter, S. D. "Disease Mapping: A Historical Perspective." In *Spatial Epidemiology: Methods and Applications*, edited by Paul Elliott, Jon Wakefield, and Nicola Best, 223–39. Oxford: Oxford University Press, 2001.

Webb, Colin, and John B. Wright. *The James Stuart Archive of Recorded Oral Evidence Relating to the History of the Zulu and Neighbouring Peoples*. Pietermaritzburg: University of Natal Press, 2014.

Webster, David. "Abafazi Bathonga Bafihlakala: Ethnicity and Gender in a KwaZulu Border Community." *African Studies* 50, no. 1 (1991): 243–71.

———. "The Political Economy of Food Production and Nutrition in Southern Africa in Historical Perspective." *Journal of Modern African Studies* 24, no. 3 (1986): 447–83.

———. "Tembe-Thonga Kinship: The Marriage of Anthropology and History." *Cahiers d'études africaines* 26, no. 104 (1986): 611–32.

Webster, E. C. "Race, Labour Process and Transition: The Sociology of Work in South Africa." *Society in Transition* 30, no. 1 (1999): 28–42. https://doi.org/10.1080/10289852.1999.10520166.

Wegerif, Marc C. A. "'Informal' Food Traders and Food Security: Experiences from the Covid-19 Response in South Africa." *Food Security* 12, no. 4 (2020): 797–800. https://doi.org/10.1007/s12571-020-01078-z.

White, Hylton. "Beastly Whiteness: Animal Kinds and the Social Imagination in South Africa." *Anthropology Southern Africa* 34, no. 3 (2011): 104–13.

———. "Custom, Normativity and Authority in South Africa." *Journal of Southern African Studies* 41, no. 5 (2015): 1005–17.

———. "How Is Capitalism Racial? Fanon, Critical Theory and the Fetish of Antiblackness." *Social Dynamics* 46, no. 1 (2020): 22–35. https://doi.org/10.1080/02533952.2020.1758871.

———. "The Materiality of Marriage Payments." *Anthropology Southern Africa* 39, no. 4 (2016): 297–308. https://doi.org/10.1080/23323256.2016.1243448.

———. "Outside the Dwelling of Culture: Estrangement and Difference in Postcolonial Zululand." *Anthropological Quarterly* 83, no. 3 (2010): 497–518. https://doi.org/10.1353/anq.2010.0000.

———. "Ritual Haunts: The Timing of Estrangement in a Post-apartheid Countryside." In *Producing African Futures: Ritual and Reproduction in a Neoliberal Age*, edited by Brad Weiss. Leiden: Koninklijke Brill, 2004.

———. "Tempora et Mores: Family Values and the Possessions of a Post-apartheid Countryside." *Journal of Religion in Africa* 31, no. 4 (2001): 457–79.

———. "What Is Anthropology That Decolonising Scholarship Should Be Mindful of It?" *Anthropology Southern Africa* 42, no. 2 (2010): 149–60.

Whyte, Susan Reynolds, Sjaak van der Geest, and Anita Hardon. *Social Lives of Medicines*. Cambridge: Cambridge University Press, 2002.

Wickström, Anette. "'Lungisa'—Weaving Relationships and Social Space to Restore Health in Rural KwaZulu Natal." *Medical Anthropology Quarterly* 28, no. 2 (2014): 203–20. https://doi.org/10.1111/maq.12073.

Wilce, James M., Jr. *Social and Cultural Lives of Immune Systems*. London: Routledge, 2003.

Williams, Gavin. "Capitalism, Class, and Underdevelopment." *Journal of Commonwealth and Comparative Politics* 16, no. 2 (1978): 212–21.

Williams, Michael. "An Analysis of South African Capitalism—Neo-Ricardianism or Marxism?" *Bulletin of the Conference of Socialist Economists* 1, no. 4 (1975).

Wilson, Ara. "Visual Kinship." *History of Anthropology Newsletter* 42 (2018).

Wilson, Elizabeth A. *Psychosomatic: Feminism and the Neurological Body*. Durham, NC: Duke University Press, 2004.

———. *Gut Feminism*. Durham, NC: Duke University Press, 2015. https://doi.org/doi:10.1515/9780822375203.

Winnicott, Donald W. "The Use of an Object." *International Journal of Psychoanalysis* 50, no. 4 (1969): 711–16.

Wolpe, Harold. "Capitalism and Cheap Labour-Power in South Africa: From Segregation to Apartheid." *Economy and Society* 1, no. 4 (1972): 425–56.

World Health Organization. "Apartheid and Health." In *International Conference on Apartheid and Health, 1981, in Brazzaville, People's Republic of the Congo*. Geneva: World Health Organization, 1983.

Wright, Gemma, David Neves, Phakama Ntshongwana, and Michael Noble. "Social Assistance and Dignity: South African Women's Experiences of the Child Support Grant." *Development Southern Africa* 32, no. 4 (2015): 443–57.

Wylie, Diana. "The Changing Face of Hunger in Southern African History 1880–1980." *Past and Present*, no. 122 (April 1989): 159–99. http://www.jstor.org/stable/650954.

———. *Starving on a Full Stomach: Hunger and the Triumph of Cultural Racism in Modern South Africa*. Charlottesville: University Press of Virginia, 2001.

Yanagisako, Sylvia, and Jane Collier. "Toward a Unified Analysis of Gender and Kinship." In *Gender and Kinship: Essays toward a Unified Analysis*, edited by Jane Collier and Sylvia Yanagisako. Stanford, CA: Stanford University Press, 1987.

Yarbrough, Michael W. "Something Old, Something New: Historicizing Same-Sex Marriage within Ongoing Struggles over African Marriage in South Africa." *Sexualities* 21, no. 7 (2017): 1092–108. https://doi.org/10.1177/1363460717718507.

Yates, Michelle. "The Human-as-Waste, the Labor Theory of Value and Disposability in Contemporary Capitalism." *Antipode* 43, no. 5 (2011): 1679–95.

Yount, Kristen R. "Ladies, Flirts, and Tomboys: Strategies for Managing Sexual Harassment in an Underground Coal Mine." *Journal of Contemporary Ethnography* 19, no. 4 (1991): 396–422. https://doi.org/10.1177/089124191019004002.

INDEX

Note: Pseudonyms are alphabetized uninverted followed by (pseud) e.g., Baba Njojo (pseud). Page numbers in *italic* denote illustrations, and **bold** denotes tables.

bodily fluids: and anger, 137–38; bile (inyongo), 91, 102, 132–33; diarrhea, 44, 45, 140; and gender, 134; and pollution, 133; reproductive emissions, 133, 138; vomiting, 44, 128, 137–38

body: energy needs, 42–43, 66, 119–20; as human motor, 50–51; physical demands, 49; repair, 19. *See also* nutrition; nutrition intervention program

Boer trekkers, 153

Bor, Jacob et al, 164–67

bridewealth (ilobolo), 52, 81, 84, 91, 92, 93–94, 235n5, 237n24

Bryant, A. T., 132

Canguilhem, Georges, 14, 22, 116, 139, 148–49

Cantina, Alberto, 151

Cantino map, 150–51

capacity: bodily capacity, 4–7, 21, 53–54, 87, 119–20; meanings, 6, 181; to labor for capital, 67–68, 119

Carsten, Janet, 141

cartography: of conquest and dislocation, 147, 153–56, *155*; new names, 150; Portuguese exploration, 150–51; Transkei, 61

cattle: in homesteads, 27, 46, 83; rinderpest, 156; sacrificial rituals, 90–91, 102, 134–35, **136**. *See also* bridewealth (ilobolo)

Cetshwayo kaMpande, King, 153, 154

Chakrabarty, Dipesh, 6–7, 204n21

chieftainship: Mabhudu, 152, 154; Mpukunyoni Traditional Authority, 63, 70; Ronga ("Southern Tonga"), 151; Shikishela, 72; Thonga, 152; Tsonga-Shangaan kingship, 230n55; Zululand, 152

children's maps, 146, 172–75, *173*, *175*

child support grants, 47, 83–84, 105

citizenship, 68

Clarke, Jeanette, 76–78

class, 82, 124, 127

classificatory kinship, 92–94

Cloete, Henry, 153

clothing, timber workers, 25, 38, 41, 95

Coates, Ta-Nehisi, 18

colonial era: administrative consolidation, 62–63; bridewealth concerns, 92, 235n5; curative substances, 16; exploration and cartography, 150–51; forestry conservationism, 62–63; land dispossession, 63, 68–69, 233n88; oppression, 8–9; political rivalries and cartography, 153–56, *155*; resource extraction, 31; Shepstone system, 82, 89; traditional medicine, 17, 126; Xhosa Cattle Killing, 60–61, 153

Coloured population, 160

Congress of South African Trade Unions (COSATU), 74, 76

contractors: reforms and standards, 77–78. *See also* Baba Njojo (pseud); labor outsourcing

corporate social responsibility, 39, 49–50, 119, 181

COSATU (Congress of South African Trade Unions), 74, 76

COVID-19 pandemic, 12, 190–91, 192, 207n44

curative substances: advertisements, 124–26, *125*; class differences, 124, 127; colonial era, 16; conditions treated, 128–29; definition difficulties, 16–17; expansion, 122–23; "family resemblance," 124–26; immune system boosters, 56, 118, 119, 130–31, 248n25; industrial hybrids, 119; izifo zonke (all diseases), 126, 130; labelling, 126, **127**; marketing and sales, 123–28; ngoma tonics, 16, 124, 182, 250n43; purgatives and cleansers, 15–16, 56–57, 119, 130, 220n21; regional pharmacy, 129–31; "social life," 126; to cure HIV/AIDS, 14–15, 118, 120, 121–23, 131, 248n25

customary law, 90

customary marriage, 89–92, 104

dance, ngoma (masculine dance), 16, 182, 270n3

Davies, G. H., 63

death, as pollution (umnyama), 133

debarking, 38, 40

debility, 4–5

dehydration, 43, 218n9, 220n19

Demographic Surveillance Area (DSA), 28, 148, 162–63, 163–64

Diawara, Manthia, 19

Dictionary of South African Place Names, 150, 257n23

digestive system, 134–37. *See also* the gut; nutrition

Dingiswayo kaJobe, Chief, 152, 259n34

dispossession. *See* forced removals

domesticity and everyday life, 83–84, 172–75, *173*, *175*

dowry. *See* bridewealth (ilobolo)

Dukuduku plantation, 25, 30–31, 45–46, 61–62, 65

Durban: children's map, 172; curative substances sales, 123–26, *125*

Employment Equity Act (2003), 80

endurance (ukunyamezela), 21, 54–56, 186–87

enema (clyster), 56, 123–24, 129, 132, 137

epidemics, 22, 206n31. *See also* COVID-19 pandemic; HIV/AIDS

ethical substance, 4, 17, 24, 52–54, 84, 87, 181, 185
eucalyptus, 61, 146–47

Fanon, Franz, 18, 20, 22
fatigue, 50–51
Ferguson, James, 167–68, 171, 192–93
fertility, 134
fieldwork, 25–33; Duomo's assistance, 27–28; earlier forestry work, 30–31; ethical dilemmas, 31–33; laughter, 32, 33, 216n127; questionnaire, 25; and shame, 31–32; suspicion and mistrust, 28–29
Flint, Karen, 16, 17
Fontein, Joost, 135–36
food: brought from home, 1–2, 49; eaten before leaving home, 49; ration packs, 44. *See also* nutrition; nutrition intervention program
forced removals: apartheid, 3, 68–71, 156–61, 202n5, 233n88; black spots, 156–57; categories for removal, 261n52; colonial era, 63, 68–69, 233n88; experiences since removal, 160; from conservation areas, 69–70; from military installation areas, 70, 262n56; Mbila triangle, 69–70; memories of the day, 160; Mpukunyoni people, 63, 70; opposition from Black and White groups, 159; restitution and repair, 150, 161–62; statistics, 261n52. *See also* land claims
forest fires, 72
Forest Owners Association, Bantu labor report, 67, 228n43
forestry sector: colonial conservationism, 62–63; colonial surveying and draining, 61–62; crisis of labor (2002–6), 13–14, 77–78; definition, 227n24; employment precarity, 10–11; eucalyptus hybrids, 61 forestry workers. *See* timber laborers
Forest Stewardship Council (FSC), 71, 76
Foucault, Michel, 4, 5, 51–52, 53, 67, 203n8
Freedom Charter (1955), 9–10
Freud, Sigmund, 140
FSC (Forest Stewardship Council), 71, 76

gallbladder, 91, 102, 132–33, **136**
gender: and cattle products, 135, **136**; Employment Equity Act (2003), 80; fluidity of context, 108–12; lineage shades, 134; preconquest Zulu differences, 81–82; timber workforce responsibilities, 27, 39
geographical names, 150–51, 257n23
ghost marriage, 93
gifts: customary marriage, 104; umshado wokudlala, 96–98, 96, 97, 100, 103, 104–5, 106; Valentine's Day, 99–100

girls: izintombi (umshado wokudlala), 84–85, 95–98, 99, 105; Venda girls' play, 94
Gluckman, Max, 91–92
Group Areas Act (1950), 160
the gut: and bile (inyongo), 91, 102, 132–33; diseases of, 44, 140; enema (clyster), 56, 123–24, 129, 132, 137; and the immune system, 121; psycho-neuroenterology, 138–43; treatments, 118–19; and the work of repair, 115–16, 188–89. *See also* nutrition
Gwala, Zeblon, 120

Harries, John, 135–36
harvesting laborers, 25–26, 27, 38, 39, 40, 42–43, 44
health: diarrhea, 44, 45, 140; endemic diseases, 65, 66; healing versus curing, 22–23; self-perception of workers, 44; Treatment as Prevention (TasP), 167–68, 170; vomiting, 44, 128, 137–38. *See also* curative substances
health and safety: heat and dehydration, 43, 218n9, 220n19; protective clothing, 25, 38, 41; record keeping, 41; safety talks, 38, 41, 271n1; time lost to accidents, 49
Henkel, Carl Caesar, 31, 60–61, 63
Henkel, John Spurgeon (Johannes E. S.), 31, 61–62, 65
herbal substances. *See* curative substances
Hickel, Jason, 134–35, **136**
HIV/AIDS: BMI recommendations, 45; demographic surveillance, 28, 164; distribution variations, 168; effect on productivity, 13; energy requirements, 43; and the gut, 139–40; hot spots, 168, *169*; immunity boosters and curative substances, 2, 14–15, 118, 120, 121–23, 130–31, 248n25; infection prevalence, 10, 47, *48*, 166, 222n33; Mbeki denialism, 2, 25, 120; miracle cures, 120; National Strategic Plan, 11; and nutrition, 121; Pre-Exposure Prophylaxis (PrEP) program, 11; and social scientists, 170–71; statistical analysis, 165–68; test-and-treat programs, 170; Treatment as Prevention (TasP), 167–68, 170; treatment successes, 11
homelands. *See* Bantustans
homesteads: arrangement, 26–27, 145; cattle, 27, 46, 83; and commercial agriculture, 144; domesticity and everyday life, 83–84, 172–75, *173*, *175*; household income, 46, 206n37; livestock (cattle), 27, 46, 83; preconquest Zulu society, 81–82; predominance of women, 27; size, 46; vegetable crops, 27, 46, 83

homosexuality: amatomboys, 27, 106–8; men-men marriage, 100–1; taboo, 107; woman-woman marriage, 93–94, 237n24. *See also* umshado wokudlala (game of marriage)

honey extraction, 72

housing: Bantu labor, 67; replaced by cash benefits, 144; subsidised provision, 94, 239n34; vicinage, 177–78

Hulett, J. L., 156

hunger, 9, 12, 47

ilobolo (bridewealth), 52, 81, 84, 91, 92, 93–94, 235n5, 237n24

immune system, 15, 56, 118, 120, 130–31, 248n25

incompleteness, 21–22, 112, 113, 146

Indian population, 158, 160

Industrial Conciliation Act (1979), 74

infectious diseases, 9, 206n31

Ingonyama Trust, 191–92

Interim Protection of Informal Land Rights Act (1996), 162, 264n64

iSimangaliso Wetland Park, 28, 64, 69–70, 145, 157–58, 161–62

izifo zonke (curative substance), 126, 130

izinhlawulo (reparations), 18. *See also* work of repair

izinyanga (healers), 40, 119, 122

James Stuart Archives, 132

Jansen, John, 16

jealousy, 88, 94, 100, 105, 118

khanda (pound/fix/mend), 18

kinship: among timber laborers, 38–39, 83, 84; classificatory kinship, 92–94; concepts of substance, 141–42; fluidity of context, 108–12; illness and relationships, 140–41; mobility of relationships, 105–6; and nutrition intervention program, 50; relationship problems, 80; reliability of married workers, 228n43; ritual event for marriage completion, 102; terminology, 101, 105–6; types formed by marriage, 92–94; Umzala (cross cousin), 32–33. *See also* homesteads

Klein, Melanie, 18

KwaZulu Bantustan, 157–60, 263n59

KwaZulu-Natal province, 3

KwaZulu-Natal Research Innovation and Sequencing Platform (KRISP), 190

labor outsourcing: Black-owned business opportunities, 39–40, 75, 231n68; contractor bankruptcies, 77; decline in conditions for workers, 75–76, 77; expansion, 3, 13, 74–75; forestry sector, 3, 13, 74–78, 231n65; risks and disadvantages, 75–76; South Africa, 11

labor power, 3, 5, 53–54, 67–68, 85–87, 119

labor regime: colonial era shortages, 65; feminization, 94–95; forestry sector crisis of labor (2002–6), 13–14, 77–78; labor reforms, 77–78; report on Bantu labor (1973), 67, 228n43; transformation, 24; for White farming and industry, 69; work capability data, 66

Labor Relations Act (1995), 74

land: Crown land, 64; long-term leases for former residents, 73; mutual caring, 193–94; ownership claims, 13–14, 64; reserved for Natives, 64; state appropriation, 65; under customary authority, 64, 70–71, 191–92. *See also* forced removals

land claims, 145, 161–62, 192–93, 263n63, 264n64. *See also* forced removals

land reforms, postapartheid era, 68–69

land tenure, Native Trust and Land Act (1936), 69

late liberalism, 21, 54, 82, 161, 186

laughter, 32, 33, 88, 216n127

lesbianism (amatomboys), 27, 106–8

leviratic family, 93

Lewin, Julius, 90–91, 236n7

liberalism, 21

lieux-commun, 19–20, 211n73. *See also* topology

life expectancy, 165

Lindiwe (pseud), 83–85; domesticity, 26–27, 83–84; girlfriends (umshado wokudlala), 84–85; kinship, 83–84; plantation worker, 60; team leader (induna), 86

Luke Mkhwanazi (pseud), 71–73; community benefits for young men, 72–73; honey extraction, 72; induna (local traditional authority), 72; meat platters, 72–73; security guard, 71–72, 86

lungisa (repair), 18, 23. *See also* work of repair

Mabaso Land Claims Settlement Agreement, 263n63

Makasana, 152

Malanda kaVelane, 153–54

malaria, 65, 66, 179–80

marriage: customary marriage types, 89–93; ghost marriage, 93; men-men, 100–101; woman-woman marriage, 93–94, 237n24. *See also* bridewealth (ilobolo); umshado wokudlala (game of marriage)

Marx, Karl, 5, 6–7, 182–83

materialism, and Zulu thought, 135–37
Mbeki, Thabo, 2, 25, 120
Mbembe, Achille, 20, 22
Mbila triangle, 69–70
Mbombela (formerly Nelspruit), 42–45
Mbuyazi clan, 83
mechanization, 3, 13, 24, 49, 170
Medicines Control Council, 15, 17, 122
men: impotence and 'simple' marriage, 93; men-men marriage, 100–1
Mfekayi, 26, 83, 144
migrant labor, 69, 183–84
mining industry: ancestral lands, 192; demand for timber, 12, 66; destructive aspects, 9, 183; Human Sciences Laboratory, 66; labor, 64, 66; Marikana massacre, 190, 251n45
Mkhwanazi, uNdunankulu, 70
Mondi: employees, 71, 74–75; establishment, 66; Forest Stewardship Council (FSC), 71; global reach, 71; labor outsourcing, 3, 13, 74–75; labor reforms, 77–78; Occupational Health Officers, 41; packaging and paper interests, 70–71; plantation security, 71–73; SiyaQhubeka Forests (SQF), 70–71, 72, 73, 79; South African land, 71; state support, 66; Transformation Office, 25, 214n110; worker benefits and amenities losses, 77. *See also* nutrition intervention program
Mpande, King, 152, 153
Mpukunyoni people, forced removal, 63
Mpukunyoni Traditional Authority, 70
Mthethwa people, 152
Mtubatuba, pharmacies, 15
Mzokhulayo Mkhwanazi, Inkosi, 70
Mzondeni Mineus Mkhwanazi, Inkosi, 70

N2 highway, 26
Natalia Republic, 153, 260n37
Natives Land Act (1913), 68–69, 150
Natives (Urban Areas) Act (1923), 160
Native Trust and Land Act (1936), 69, 156–57
ngoma, 23; healing product, 16, 124, 182, 250n43; masculine dance, 16, 182, 270n3
Ngubane, Harriet, 133
Nguyen, Vinh-Kim, 167–68, 170, 171
Nobuhle Zikhali (pseud): children's maps, 146, 172–75, *173*, *175*; homestead, 145, 172; silviculture work, 144
Nozingile, Inkosi, 153, 154
nutrition: AHRI survey, 46–47; BMI recommendations, 44–45; bodily energy needs, 42–43, 66, 119–20; and digestion, 134–37, **136**; Dukuduku/Nyalazi plantations survey, 45–46; and HIV/AIDS, 121; Mbombela/Richmond surveys, 41–45; vitamins, 120, 121

nutrition intervention program: a capital investment, 54; catering contractors, 48; community-based food gardens, 48; effectiveness, 56; food taken home, 49, 50; menus, 47–48; purpose, 2, 13–14, 181; satisfaction survey, 49–50
Nyalazi plantation, 25, 30–31, 45–46, 61, 95

Other/otherwise, 17–18, 21–22, 108, 112, 173, 185
outsourcing. *See* labor outsourcing

pain, 187
Paper, Printing, Wood and Allied Workers Union (PPWAWU), 76
paper and pulp sector, 66, 68, 74, 75. *See also* Mondi
pay, 26, 40, 46, 67–68, 76, 77, 219n10
Perestrello, Manuel de Mesquita, 151, 258n28
personhood: incompleteness, 21–22; values, 53; vicinality, 177; virtues of (ubuntu), 33
pharmaceutical industry, 168, 170
pharmaceuticals: colonial era, 16; Medicines Control Council, 122; and novel curative substances, 14–15; problems of definition, 122. *See also* curative substances; traditional medicine
piecework, 26, 40
Pina-Cabral, João de, 177–78
plantations: colonial racism and black labor, 20; continuities and disjunctures, 187–88; racialist regime of extraction, 85–86; sugar plantations, 65
pollution, and reproductive events, 133
Portugal, colonial exploration, 150–51
poverty, 46–47, 184, 191
Povinelli, Elizabeth, 7, 8, 21, 32, 54, 82, 161, 185, 186
productivity: effect of dehydration, 43, 220n19; energy requirements, 43; HIV effects, 13; mining industry, 66; nutrition intervention program, 2, 13, 54, 56; records, 41; and training, 228n43
Promotion of Bantu Self-Government Act (1959), 157
Puar, Jasbir, 4–5

queerness, 90–91, 93–94, 108–12, 237n24

race classification system, 158, 160, 202n5, 262n55
railway development, 65, 156
Rath, Mattias, 120
reappropriation, 195
repair: concept, 18–19; terminology, 18. *See also* work of repair

reparation and restitution, 18–21, 150, 161–62, 210n69. *See also* work of repair
reproductive emissions, 133, 138
Restitution of Land Rights Act (1994), 162
rhinoceros, miracle cure, 120, 121
Richmond, KwaZulu-Natal, 42–45
rinderpest, 156

sacrifice, Zulu thought, 90–91, 134–35, **136**
Sappi, 12–13, 66, 68, 70, 73, 75, 77–78
schools, Venda girls' 'play', 94
sexual intercourse, reproductive emissions, 133, 138
sexuality, lesbianism (amatomboys), 27, 106–8
Shaka kaSenzangakhona, King, 52, 132, 152, 259n34
shame, in fieldwork, 31–32
Shikishela, Chief, 72
Shikishela (region), 26, 71–73
shipwrecks, 151
silviculture: activities, 38; contract work, 79–81, 144; health and safety, 41, 42; marking, 79–80, 232n78; pay, 26; working day, 39
Sim, T. R., 63
Siyanda (pseud): cure for afflictions, 15, 117–18, 139; illnesses, 117, 137; immune boosters, 118, 131; purified water cure, 15, 117–18; snake fat cure, 117
SiyaQhubeka Forests (SQF), 70–71, 72, 73, 79
slavery, 20, 85–86
snake afflictions, 15, 117–18
snake fat, as cure, 117, 130, 245n2
social forms, 88, 167–68, 171
social projects, 17–18, 21, 149–50, 186
social scientists, and HIV, 170–71
social tense, 161
social welfare: and cash transfers, 167–68, 170; child support grants, 47, 83–84, 105; disputes, 207n44; importance, 10, 11–12, 207nn40–41; state pension, 47; Universal Basic Income (UBI), 192–93; and work of repair, 170, 192–93
Sodwana, 70
Solomon, Harris, 136–37
Somkhele kaMalanda, 153–54
song, work songs (izisho zokusebenza), 2, 201n3
South Africa: liberation struggles, 8–9; National Intelligence Service, 68; post-1994 transition, 68–69, 184, 214n110; racism, 29–30; White South African exiles, 29
South African Agricultural, Plantations and Allied Workers Union, 74
South African Forestry Company (SAFCOL), 70
South African Timber Growers' Association (SATGA), 67

spitting, 138
SQF (SiyaQhubeka Forests), 70–71, 72, 73, 79
The Standard Encyclopedia of Southern Africa, 150, 257n23
stokvels (savings clubs), 105, 241n61
Storr-Lister, J. (conservator), 63
structuralism, and "Zulu thought," 133, 134–35
structural violence, 184, 190, 191
sugar sector, 64–65, 67, 79, 156
Surplus People Project (SPP), 3, 70, 158, 261n52

Tanser, Frank et al, 164–67, *169*
temporality, 57
Thomas, Deborah, 20
timber laborers: absenteeism, 40, 54, 229n43; age, 45; benefits losses, 77; BMI recommendations, 44–45; clothing, 25, 38, 41, 95; daily work quotas, 40–41; fitness criteria, 41; gender differences, 27, 39; happiness, 67; importance of waged work, 54–55; injury reduction, 41, 219n13; kinship ties, 38–39; living conditions, 27; piecework, 26, 40; residency patterns, 27; women, 27, 38, 45. *See also* harvesting laborers; labor outsourcing; silviculture
timber plantations: as fungible asset, 73; indigenous forest (imithi), 1, 147, 201n1; introduced species, 61, 65, 146; outgrower stands (communal customary land), 70–71; overlapping systems, 147–48; ownership, 70–71; security, 71–73; SiyaQhubeka Forests (SQF), 70–71, 72, 73, 79; topology, 59–60, 63
timber sector: corporate social responsibility, 39, 49–50, 119, 181; data collection, 67; definition, 227n24; employees, 75; employment, 13; growth and state support, 12–13, 65, 66; mechanization, 3, 13, 24, 49, 170; for mineral-energy sector, 12, 66
tomboys, 27, 106–8
Tomlinson Commission, 160, 261n54
topology: cartographic, 146; children's maps, 146, 172–75, *173*, *175*; definition, 148; HIV surveillance, 146, 162–72; labor power, 85–87; lieux-commun, 19–20, 211n73; and life, 148–49; of the plantations, 59–60, 63; and vicinity, 150, 176–80
trade unions, 74, 76
traditional medicine: colonial era, 17, 126; generational differences, 56–57; indigenous forest (imithi), 1, 147, 201n1; izinyanga (healers), 40, 119, 122; muthi (traditional medicine), 247n11, 256n12; popular medicine, 119; vitamins, 56, 120, 121. *See also* curative substances

training: and productivity, 228n43; toolbox talks (health and safety), 38, 271n1
Transkeian Territories, 61–62
translation: amandla, 5–7; ancestor, 240n44; bovine parts, 135, **136**; curatives, 137; kinship terms, 32–33, 101, 105–6, 240n47; marriage rites, 100; muthi (traditional medicine), 247n11, 256n12; Siyanda's healing, 117–18, 246nn4–7; ugazi, 127–28, 250n26; umshado wokudlala, 88, 105–6; and use of indigenous terms, 5–6; White person (umlungu), 33; (work of) repair, 18
Treatment Action Campaign, 14–15, 120, 123, 127
Truth and Reconciliation Commission, 68
Tshabalala-Msimang, Manto, 123
Tsonga/Ronga people, 152

Ubhejane miracle cure, 120, 121
Ugazi (curative substance), 124, 126–29
ukuqoma ceremony, 95–101
ukushisa (heat/anger), 134
umshado wokudlala (game of marriage), 88–114; Baba's opinion, 80–81; costs, 99, 100, 104; criticisms, 104; effect on life outside the plantations, 112–14; emotions, 88; fluidity of context, 108–10; gifts, 96–98, 96, 97, 100, 103, 104–5, 106; insizwa (young men), 95–98, 99, 105; izintombi (young girls), 84–85, 95–98, 99, 105; kin terms, 105–6; preparatory permissions, 99; relationships, 84–85; terminology, 88, 105–6; ukugaxa (blanket ceremony), 97, 100; ukuqoma (acceptance), 95–101; umshado (marriage), 100; Valentine's Day gifts, 99–100; wayemgaxa (second ceremony), 96, 98, 102–3
unemployment, 10, 191
Universal Basic Income (UBI), 192–93
Uvukahlale (curative substance), 125

the vicinity, 150, 176–80
violence: apartheid, 22, 29, 212n92; civil war, 43–44; consequence of failure to repair, 22; and magic, 251n45; structural violence, 184, 190, 191

vomiting, 44, 128, 137–38
Voortrekkers, 153
Vuka Hlale (curative substance), 124
Vuka Uphile (curative substance), 126, **127**
vulnerability, 23, 116, 138, 143
vuselela (repair), 18

wages, 26, 40, 46, 67–68, 76, 77, 219n10
wayemgaxa (second ceremony), 96, 98, 102–3
White, Hylton, 23, 57, 134–35, 189–90
Whiteness, 29, 32–33, 147. See also apartheid; race classification system
WHO, Apartheid and Health report, 66
Wilson, Elizabeth, 140
witchcraft, 117, 118, 137
workers, varied and many, 2
working day: cooked food delivery, 38; food deliveries, 38; journey to work, 26, 37–38; morning prayer, 1; repetitive labour ("pitting" digging holes), 2; return home, 39
work of repair: amandla, 4, 7, 55–56; bodily repair, 19; consequences of failure, 22; creativity of umshado wokudlala, 113–14; endurance, 21, 54–56, 186–87; for forced removals, 150, 161–62; future prospects, 192–93; and the gut, 115–16, 188–89; healing and curing, 22–23; incompleteness, 21–22, 112, 113, 146; new geographical names, 150; reappropriation, 195; reparation and restitution, 18–21, 150, 161–62, 210n69; tensions, 182–84; terminology, 18; welfare programs, 170, 191–92

Xhosa Cattle Killing, 60–61, 153

Zambili, Queen-Regent, 154, 156
Zikhali, Moses, 145
Zululand: "chieftainship," 152; colonial administration, 82; drought and rinderpest, 156; forestry, 61–62, 64; homesteads, 81–82; part of Natal colony, 156; political history, 152; political power and spiritual/medical power, 131–32
"Zulu thought," 133–35
Zuma, Jacob, 24, 52

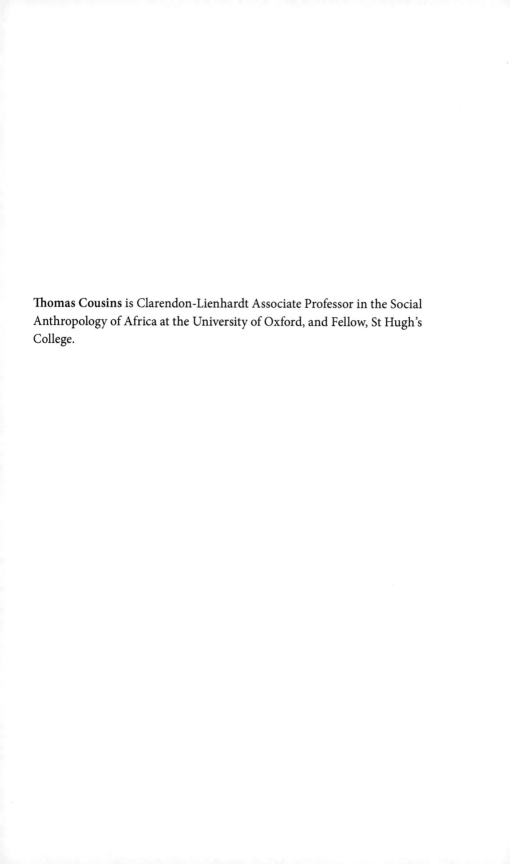

Thomas Cousins is Clarendon-Lienhardt Associate Professor in the Social Anthropology of Africa at the University of Oxford, and Fellow, St Hugh's College.

9 781531 503536